DATE DUE

DEMCO 38-297

The Arch-Conjuror of England

The
Arch-Conjuror
of England

JOHN DEE

GLYN PARRY

YALE UNIVERSITY PRESS
NEW HAVEN AND LONDON

Published with assistance from the foundation established in memory of Oliver Baty Cunningham of the Class of 1917, Yale College

For information about this and other Yale University Press publications, please contact:
U.S. Office: sales.press@yale.edu   www.yalebooks.com
Europe Office: sales@yaleup.co.uk   www.yalebooks.co.uk

Set in Arno by IDSUK (DataConnection) Ltd
Printed in Great Britain by TJ International Ltd, Padstow, Cornwall

Library of Congress Cataloging-in-Publication Data

Parry, G. J. R.
    The arch-conjuror of England: John Dee/Glyn Parry.
        p.cm.
Includes bibliographical references and index.
ISBN 978–0–300–11719–6 (cl:alk. paper)
1. Dee, John, 1527–1608. 2. Great Britain–History—Elizabeth, 1558–1603—Biography.
3. Scientists—Great Britain—Biography. 4. Occultists—Great Britain—Biography.
5. Astrologers—England—Biography. 6. Alchemists—Great Britain—Biography. 7. Elizabeth
I, Queen of England, 1533—1603—Friends and associates. 8. Intellectuals—Great Britain—
Biography. 9. Great Britain—Intellectual life—16th century. I. Title.
    BF1598.D5P37 2012
    130.92—dc23
    [B]
                                                                        2011030702

A catalogue record for this book is available from the British Library.

10 9 8 7 6 5 4 3 2 1

To the memory of Pat Collinson
(10 August 1929–28 September 2011)
A great historian, but a greater human being

Contents

List of Illustrations

10. The Seal of Aemeth. © Clay Holden and The John Dee Publication Project.

11. *Emperor Rudolf II*, from Ludwig Bechstein's *Zweihundert deutsche Manner in Bildnissen und Lebensbeschreibungen*, 1854. © The British Library Board. All rights reserved (10703.i.30).

12. Unknown artist, *Sir Christopher Hatton*, seventeenth century. © National Portrait Gallery, London.

13. Unknown artist, *John Whitgift, Archbishop of Canterbury*, early seventeenth century. © National Portrait Gallery, London.

14. Title page of John Dee's *A Letter, Containing a most briefe Discourse Apologeticall*, 1599. © The British Library Board. All rights reserved (G.2363).

Preface

IN 1642, as civil war broke out between Parliament and Charles I, a large, elegant cedar chest appeared for sale at the corner of a busy London street. Amidst a display of new and second-hand furniture, its refined joinery and high-quality lock and hinges attracted the attention of a newly married couple, Mr and Mrs Jones. The couple bought the chest and for the next twenty years it sat undisturbed in their home. During this period Parliament triumphed in the Civil War and executed Charles I, Oliver Cromwell ruled briefly as Lord Protector, and the monarchy was restored in the person of Charles II. Then in 1662 Mr and Mrs Jones decided to move the chest. As they struggled with it they heard something rattle in one of its corners. Mr Jones inserted a piece of iron into a tiny crevice. There was a click, and a secret compartment slid open. It contained several handwritten books in an incomprehensible language, and a small box. Inside the box lay an olive-wood rosary and crucifix. The chest, it turned out, had once belonged to John Dee, a famous and distinctive Renaissance figure, whether as astrologer, alchemist, polymath intellectual, or sometime adviser to Elizabeth I and her Court.

This book aims to unlock the secret compartments of Dee's life. While there have been many previous books about Dee, this new study will show that he was not an austere magician, remote, shunned and feared. Instead it reveals that he was immersed in Tudor society precisely because of his occult philosophy. Properly understood, the story of Dee's life opens a doorway into a forgotten Tudor landscape, not so much a world that we have lost but more a strange, unfamiliar place that few modern readers can imagine. In that almost alien universe Queen Elizabeth I devotes hours to poring over her alchemical manuscripts and then applies their methods in her laboratory, seeking incessantly for the philosopher's stone that will purify decaying bodies and society alike. In that world the Queen's most influential adviser, Lord Burghley, pleads for a fragment of the stone to help build a navy against the Spanish Armada, and the Queen's favourite, Lord Robert Dudley, believes that Christians can legitimately conjure angels to reveal the political future. It is where experienced politicians wonder what the appearance of comets signals for the future of war in the Netherlands, and where ancient prophecies are applied to Elizabeth as the Last World Empress before Christ's imminent Second Coming.

This new understanding of John Dee demonstrates that his occult philosophy gives him a prominent and legitimate place in histories of a sixteenth-century world saturated by magical thought. In expanding our knowledge of Dee, this book aims to expand our awareness of the sometimes dazzling, often treacherous, Elizabethan Court where he sought advancement. What Dee made, or failed to make, of his opportunities is only part of the story.

In gathering the evidence for this forgotten landscape I have benefited from the assistance of many librarians, archivists and colleagues. I therefore wish to thank the interloan staff of Victoria University of Wellington Library, and the staffs of the National Library of New Zealand, the Alexander Turnbull Library and the Legislative Assembly Library. I owe much to my colleagues Matthew Trundle, Jim Urry and Steve Behrendt, to Linda Gray for her sharp editorial eye on an earlier draft, and to Richard Mason at Yale University Press for his work on the final copy. In San Marino, California, I have been ably helped by the staff of the Henry E. Huntington Library, particularly Mary Robertson of the Manuscripts Department, Christopher Adde, Laura Stalker and Juan Gomez in Reader Services, and, amongst the Readers there, by Barbara Donagan through discussions at afternoon tea and Bruce Moran through discussions at all times. I am much indebted to Peggy Spear for years of hospitality and laughter in Altadena and Claremont, and to Jan Tappan in Pasadena. In London I am grateful to the staff of the British Library, the National Archives, London Metropolitan Archives, the Guildhall Library and Tottenham Borough Archives. I am indebted to my learned friend Dr Ian Adamson and to Vicky Adamson for their friendship and help over the years, and to Helen and Chris Mountfort. Outside London the librarians of the Bodleian Library, Cambridge University Library, Birmingham City Library, Chetham's Library Manchester, Manchester Cathedral Archives and the John Rylands Library of the University of Manchester have been universally helpful, as have the staff of the record offices of Chester and Cheshire, Devon and Exeter, Essex, Kent, Lancashire, Lincoln, Warwickshire and Worcestershire. To Nona I owe much more for years of incisive support, a receptive ear and a lively appreciation for the intricacies of Tudor Court gossip.

To aid the reader obscure spellings and titles in the text have been modernised.

CHAPTER 1

A World Full of Magic

JOHN DEE was born into a world resonating with magical forces, which surrounded him to the end of his life. Within days of his birth on 13 July 1527 he was baptised in the ancient Gothic church of St Dunstan's-in-the-East, just west of the Tower of London, between Tower and Thames streets. His parents, Roland and Jane, like their neighbours, believed that the rituals and prayers of the elaborate ceremony would expel the Devil, save John's soul and rescue him from limbo. The baptismal water, salt and oil had been exorcised by repeated prayers and signs of the cross at a Sunday high Mass. After immersing John in the font three times, the priest, resplendent in a rich cope reflecting the flickering light from dozens of candles burning before images of Christ and the saints, repeated the holy words that gave the hallowed substances power to drive out unclean spirits. He then placed the salt in John's mouth, made the sign of the cross on his head, chest and hands with water, and anointed his forehead with the holy oil, over which he tied a chrisom cloth to be burnt when his mother returned for her purification. Then the holy water was locked away to prevent its use in illicit magic, and John's godparents washed their hands to remove any holy oil.[1]

Fifty years later John would use 'holy oil' in a futile attempt to exorcise demons from one of his servants.[2] To the end of his life he believed implicitly that the sign of the cross, and the formulaic repetition of holy words, had the power to ward off evil. Thus he retained elements of the Catholicism of his childhood and youth, which incorporated the magical beliefs of laypeople into a flexible and familiar ritual marking the seasons of the year. As a child John learnt to pray from a Book of Hours or Primer, designed for laypeople who believed that invisible demonic enemies surrounded them, provoking harm and discord. John would later complain that Satan stirred up backbiters to accuse him of 'conjuring'. Some Primer prayers did not just appeal for God's help, but like spells and charms presumed that incantations of God's magical names and repeated signs of the cross would conjure angelic assistance against human and demonic enemies.[3] Other prayers would win favour before the King, or protect against thieves, fevers, plague, fire and drowning. Young John's contemporaries attributed the results both to God's grace and the inherent power of His magical names, which also featured in spells conjuring spirits for divination, whether into a child's well-polished thumbnail, a sword, a basin of holy water or a crystal.[4]

While John was growing to manhood in the 1540s, and learning to conjure his own spirits, such beliefs remained popular from the King's Court downwards. Only gradually would 'elite' Catholic clergy tacitly accept Protestant criticisms by distancing themselves from 'popular' magical beliefs, leaving John exposed to attacks as a 'conjuror'.[5] John's training in 'magic' therefore began with his experience of the Catholic ritual year during the last decade before Protestants and, in response, Catholic reformers began to undermine its comfortable certainties.

At Candlemas on 2 February every parishioner would carry a blessed candle in procession, before offering it to the priest at Mass to burn before the image of the Virgin. The priest would then bless many more candles, giving them power to make Satan's minions flee. Parishioners took these candles home to protect against demons who filled the air during thunderstorms, for reassurance in times of sickness and to comfort the dying.[6] The ashes distributed on Ash Wednesday, like the 'palms' blessed on Palm Sunday (actually green branches of yew, box or willow) would also protect the house from evil spirits. Handmade crosses assembled during the reading of the Passion story that day were believed to have great protective powers. At Rogationtide in late May or June, parishioners formed processions to drive the Devil and evil spirits from the parish and restore neighbourly unity, singing the litany of the saints and reading the Gospels, carrying banners, handbells and processional crosses. Dee could recall those occasions sixty years later, when he led processions that beat the parish boundaries at Manchester to settle tithe disputes.[7]

Most parishioners received the Blessed Sacrament once a year, at Easter, after confessing and being absolved by a priest, and reconciling quarrels with neighbours, the steps Dee would follow in Prague more than fifty years later. The Easter Mass was the peak of the ritual year and emphasised the special priestly power to recreate the body of Christ, flesh and blood that renewed the bonds of the Christian community. Adoring the Blessed Sacrament at its moment of elevation brought great benefits, not only signifying God's protection over body and soul but also working as a magical charm that protected individuals against sickness, bad weather, robbery, the perils of childbirth and epidemics. Every weekday shorter 'low' versions of the Mass reinforced belief in the priesthood's special status, when priests actually created the Sacrament and distributed other 'sacramentals', holy bread and holy water, which were also imbued with great protective power. Only priests could touch the sacred vessels with bare hands, such was the power that emanated from Christ's body and blood, the 'angel meat' as one contemporary described it.[8] No wonder John Dee became a Catholic priest himself at the age of twenty-six.

In the light of his later occult studies and 'imperial' writings, it is somehow appropriate that Dee grew up in the church of St Dunstan, the much-venerated tenth-century patron saint of goldsmiths, and thus alchemists, renowned for his artistic skill in precious metalwork (hallmarks still change annually on his feast day, 19 May) but excessively prone to visions of angels and evil spirits. According to legend, in one contest he took the Devil by the nose with his red-hot tongs, which became Dunstan's symbol ever afterwards. Sixteenth-century Protestants preferred to retail accusations of witchcraft and necromancy, which had dogged his reputation for five centuries. Dunstan had restored Glastonbury Abbey, the legendary hiding place for mysterious alchemical books and even the philosopher's stone itself, as Dee would discover. As Archbishop of Canterbury, Dunstan had crowned King Edgar, who was later Dee's model as the first 'imperial' monarch of Britain after Arthur.[9]

Merchants and traders congregated in the crowded, noisy parish of St Dunstan's, whose narrow streets ran down to the busy warehouses, quays and cranes near Billingsgate, London's major dock, the Customs House, and the hundreds of ships anchored just below London Bridge. From there brave men set sail on epic voyages of discovery, and to such men the mature John Dee would give important advice. About the time of John's birth, Robert Thorne tried to interest Henry VIII in exploring the North-West Passage to search for the fabled riches of Cathay, and John would later acquire his speculative map of that route. Mercantile wealth accumulated in less ambitious ventures, particularly exporting woollen cloth to the Netherlands, ensured that St Dunstan's large church was well maintained; over fifteen tombs and a small chapel commemorated the local merchant dynasties. When John was a boy the laity controlled much of the church's decoration and services, through the guilds or brother-hoods of the Holy Trinity and 'Our Lady'.

Thanks to generations of devout donors, the wall paintings and windows illustrated the Lord's Prayer, the Hail Mary, the Apostle's Creed, the Ten Commandments, the seven works of mercy, the seven virtues, the seven vices and the seven sacraments. The guilds used their income from properties to ensure that candles burned constantly before the images of the crucified Christ, Mary and Joseph on the Rood screen, and before the many brightly painted images of the saints, those powerful advocates and comforting friends whose shrines filled the church. On festival days, devotees would dress those images in rich velvet coats, with little silver shoes. Even though some precious altar vessels disappeared while John's father, Roland, was churchwarden, in August 1549 St Dunstan's could still count in gold and silver to grace its altar four chalices, two basins, two incense censers, two candlesticks, two cressets (for oil), and several silver sheep, religious symbols but also tokens of the wool trade. Above them rose 'the Great Cross with Beryl', at its centre a huge crystal shining and sparkling in the candlelight. Dee must have seen that cross many times, and whenever in after years he crossed himself he would pause in the middle of his chest in memory of that profound junction, where in his occult philosophy he would place the philosopher's stone.[10]

Dee later claimed descent from Welsh princes, even from Arthur and Cadwallader themselves. In reality the House of Dee clung to its Arthurian legends as threadbare covering for its far more modest Tudor status. On the Radnorshire border with England the extended family, there spelt 'Ddu', the Welsh for 'Black', were accounted mere yeomen cattle farmers, hardly gentlemen at all.[11] When they migrated to London as small-time merchants the Cockneys called them 'Dye'. Roland had followed the example of his first cousin, Hugh Dee, who had risen highest in the world. Hugh had become a Yeoman of the Crown by 1514. Over the next decade Henry VIII rewarded him with important local positions. By 1526 Hugh had become joint mayor of Worcester. He represented the town in the Parliament of 1529, which rejected the Pope's authority and made Henry VIII Supreme Head of the Church of England.[12]

Other branches of the Dee family followed Hugh's example. The Court offered ambitious men of limited means and common blood a path to advancement. Through relatively minor positions close to the King, they could develop strong personal bonds with the monarch, who used trusted men to build up his client network in the localities.[13] Roland Dee tried to emulate his cousin's career. Roland's prospects brightened with his marriage in 1524 to Jane, the fifteen-year-old heiress of William Wilde of Milton-next-Gravesend in Kent. Jane gave birth to a daughter in 1525 and to John in 1527, then to three more sons. The Wilde family had also risen through service in the King's Chamber and through strong connections with the Kentish magnate, Sir Henry Wyatt. By marrying Jane, Roland gained an alliance that offered political insurance.[14] He would need it in the rough and tumble of the Tudor political world he now entered. St Dunstan's lay in Tower Ward, dominated by the looming Norman fortress, where both Roland and John would later find themselves imprisoned for backing the wrong side in deadly infighting at Court. If the instruments of torture in the Tower dungeons, the scaffold and gallows on

Tower Hill, had not warned them, the many fresh traitors' heads displayed on the gatehouse of London Bridge nearby surely would have.

As a Mercer, Roland prospered sufficiently in the cloth trade to enrol John in Chelmsford Grammar School, where as the first in his family to move into the world of learning, John mastered the elements of Latin grammar. Besides funding his son's education, Roland's trade gave young John an appreciation of the power of 'vulgar' numbers, as he later called them, in contrast to those divine 'formal' numbers by which God created the world. To succeed, his father had to calculate speedily and accurately the size and number of cloths, customs dues, exchange rates, and profit-and-loss margins.

Also, merchants looked beyond England's borders. The Mercers dominated the export cloth trade, their customs duties providing much of the Crown's income. Roland Dee's rising status amongst the guild made John appreciate the importance of naval power in the Narrow Seas to protect England's dominant outlet through the great port of Antwerp. Naval power also supported the strategic priorities of King Henry's 'empire'.[15] Both numbers and empire would bulk large in John's life.

Roland followed his kinsmen in becoming a 'gentleman sewer' to Henry VIII. He superintended the table arrangements, seated the guests and served the dishes at the King's lengthy feasts. Roland's title marked his rise into the gentry. His coveted position ensured close personal access to Henry, offering opportunities for influence peddling. It placed Roland alongside useful contacts such as Richard Cecil, and it was to his son William that John Dee would repeatedly turn for patronage.[16] Roland exploited his opportunities, for the 1541 tax assessment rated him as worth £100. This placed him amongst the richest half dozen merchants in St Dunstan's.[17] The Mercers acknowledged his success by taking him into the exclusive Livery of the Company on 19 February 1543.[18] Roland would reach the peak of his fortunes the following year, only to crash disastrously in 1547 (see p. 13).

Roland's position close to the King gave John access to the Court. By now Henry was a bloated caricature of the dazzling young prince on whom many Renaissance humanists had pinned their hopes. Yet his major palaces such as Hampton Court, Greenwich, Windsor and Westminster still provided a backdrop of immense wealth for his swaggering kingship. Stuffed with costly furniture, carpets, tapestries, mirrors, maps of the world, of England, Rome, Jerusalem and other cities, embroidered hangings, statues and clocks, these palaces also offered the young John his first encounter with celestial and terrestrial globes, and perhaps astronomical instruments like astrolabes. He later owned a manuscript by the King's astronomer, Nicholas Kratzer, featuring his famous fixed and portable sundials, which John would also construct. Henry also employed as chaplain and alchemist one Robert Broke, who toiled in the steamy distilling houses at Westminster making the many essential oils and tinctures that the King's decaying body required.[19]

Roland's rise depended on Henry VIII, who liberally rewarded his intimate servants for their services.[20] In return he relied on their personal loyalty in crucial positions. England's kings had always struggled against Customs fraud. Henry's free-spending ways required him to maximise his Customs revenue. By 1534, when the King's break with Rome left England internationally isolated, his need for money had become gargantuan. His chief minister Thomas Cromwell, who was personally familiar with corruption in the cloth trade, in 1534 reminded himself to speak to Henry about 'the packer of London'. Henry later appointed a Privy Chamber servant as King's Packer, to oversee the packing and weighing of merchandise, preventing the City's own Packer from conniving with merchants to defraud the Customs.[21]

By May 1544, needing even greater sums for his French war, Henry intensified Customs oversight by appointing his trusted personal servant Roland Dee as Packer to the Strangers. Roland's experience and loyalty qualified him to oversee the City's Packer, assessing customs on exports by foreigners, and charging fees for packing them.[22] The Packership probably brought Roland £400 a year.[23] (Under Elizabeth I, Customs reformers were to consider Roland's appointment a model for a Queen's Packer whose 'skill and judgement' would enhance Crown revenues.)[24] A year later, in 1545, Flemish merchants officially complained that Roland's charges hindered their trade.[25] Roland's increased income enabled him six months later to join a Mercer syndicate speculating in former monastic lands. Eventually these vast land sales impoverished the Crown and would make John's quest for royal patronage much harder.[26] Yet more immediately, his father's new wealth supported the Cambridge education that would prepare John for royal service.

Dee entered St John's College, Cambridge, in November 1542, when freezing north-easterlies sweeping off the Fens at least moderated the stench from the dung heaps and open sewers befouling the little market town's narrow streets. Barely thirty years old, St John's contained nearly a quarter of the University's student body crammed into its single court, four or five students sleeping on truckle beds in their tutors' spartan rooms. That constellation of intellectual stars, split by regional, factional and religious tensions, had already begun an enduring tradition of backstabbing and skulduggery in Fellowship and Scholarship elections.

St John's Elizabethan reputation for breeding evangelical Protestants has obscured the importance of its Catholic humanists in Dee's time. Several St John's Catholics had already decamped to Louvain in the Habsburg-controlled Netherlands, unable to stomach Henry's schism from Rome. Soon more would choose deprivation, imprisonment and exile rather than accept the Edwardian and Elizabethan Reformations.[27] All the teachers Dee gratefully remembered fifty years later belonged to the conservative humanist Catholic faction in St John's.

At fifteen Dee studied simplified Aristotelian logic with the outspoken Catholic, John Seton. After taking his Bachelor's degree in 1546, he would teach logic and sophistry for two years in the University Schools, before graduating Master of Arts in 1548. In the 1590s he still valued two treatises on logic and sophistry he had written as a young teacher, which mixed medieval scholastic methods with Renaissance humanism in Seton's conservative style. Seton would dispute with the Protestant martyrs Cranmer, Latimer and Ridley in 1554 and die in exile from the Elizabethan Church in 1561.[28] Dee learnt his Aristotelian philosophy from Robert Pember, who became Greek Reader at Trinity College in December 1546, with Dee as his Under-Reader. Pember remained a life-long committed Catholic.[29]

Years after he left Cambridge, Dee complained to Gerard Mercator that the university's deficiencies had forced him abroad to pursue advanced study in mathematics, in which he made his major claims to originality. St John's statutes increasingly emphasised mathematics and Euclidean geometry, supplementing the University's teaching. This emphasis contributed much to England's mathematical apprenticeship.[30] The college statutes also prescribed cosmography and perspective for under-graduates, and perspective for M.A. students. Nonetheless, Dee had some grounds for doubting Cambridge's commitment to mathematical educa-tion. In his advice book *The Schoolmaster*, Roger Ascham, a Fellow of St John's who lectured to the university on mathematics in 1539–40, dismissed excessive devotion to such *manual* studies, which rendered gentlemen 'unapt to serve in the world'. He warned that 'all the geometry' in Euclid, to which Dee was particularly attached, could not teach the judgement and eloquence that gentlemen gained from literary studies.[31]

The university and college curricula did not mention occult philos-ophy, but Dee's occult studies began at Cambridge, where such knowl-edge appeared to be a natural continuation of Aristotelian philosophy. Aristotle's text *On Coming-to-be and Passing Away* gave immense authority to the belief that all matter shared one fundamental substance. Matter differed externally only through varying combinations of the four elements: earth, water, air and fire. Therefore, by alchemically manipu-lating those elements, any kind of matter could be transmuted into another. The conjunction of all elements would produce the philoso-pher's stone.[32] During Dee's time at Cambridge, everyone knew that leading intellectuals such as Thomas Smith, William Cecil and Richard Eden avidly pursued the search for the philosopher's stone.[33] Under Queen Elizabeth, Smith and Cecil would lead the Court's fascination with alchemy.

Dee's alchemical studies at St John's therefore prepared him for later service at Court. In 1570 his 'Mathematical Preface' to Euclid's *Geometry* conventionally described alchemy as 'terrestrial astrology'. It cited Aristotle's *On Coming-to-be*, as well as his *Physics* and *Meteorology*, which discussed the stars, to prove that the rays emanating from heavenly bodies shaped alchemical changes on Earth. Dee's mathematical studies at Cambridge applied perspective and geometry to measure these astrological forces, laying the foundation for his Louvain training in exact astrology, which began in 1547.[34]

Dee's Cambridge studies in perspective also laid the groundwork for his later summoning of angels into crystals through light rays. As an undergraduate Dee befriended John Hatcher, a Fellow of St John's who practised angel magic. Dee's 'Mathematical Preface' defined perspective as an element of natural philosophy that demonstrated how both light rays and unseen, occult rays could be measured and manipulated. Perspective therefore underpinned all natural philosophy, especially astronomy and astrology, and the magical effects of 'Catoptric', or divination using light reflected from polished surfaces.[35] Dee also believed that Christ had supernaturally directed him to the study of perspective.[36]

As a consequence Dee, like many of his fellow students, avidly sought out writings by the thirteenth-century Franciscan friar and natural philosopher Roger Bacon, including magical treatises falsely attributed to him.[37] In Bacon's view, man's intellect required divine aid to understand the world, which was why 'the holy patriarchs and prophets, who first gave sciences to the world, received illumination within and were not dependent on sense alone'. Bacon apparently believed his intuitive insights into Nature were divine revelations, beyond what could be learned from studying ordinary astrology or commonplace alchemy. He asserted that since the time of Christ 'divine inspirations' had illuminated the purest souls, perfecting their understanding of all sciences, but without false magical conjurations.[38] God's inspirations revealed nature's secrets through knowledge of the past, present and future, creating wonderful works.[39] Dee's Cambridge contemporaries understood Bacon to mean that these revelations came through conjuring spirits. Dr John Caius, who returned to Cambridge while Dee studied there, owned a manuscript in which 'Bacon's experimental art' included using a young boy as a 'skryer' of visions in reflective surfaces. It also taught magicians how to command angels into crystals to reveal in an instant the secrets of God's 'marvellous works', and how to conjure a spirit guarding buried treasure.[40]

Yet during Dee's time at Cambridge, magic was losing its grip on the world. In 1536 reformers had changed Church doctrine to remove magical power against demons from the 'sacramentals' – holy water, bread, candles, ashes and palms. They were only reminders of spiritual teachings. Some bishops even attacked the cult of saints and their wonder-working images as 'superstition'. After disturbances between reformers and traditionalists amongst the laity, Henry VIII imposed a messy compromise in May 1543, reaffirming the role of 'sacramentals' in traditional ceremonies but denying that they had any protective power – except for those unlearned laypeople who continued to believe in them.

In this emerging world of scepticism, exploring magical avenues to knowledge and wealth increasingly attracted accusations of demonic conjuring. This would create problems for Dee, who from his student days followed Bacon in seeking divine revelations. Nearly forty years later he reminded God that 'I have from my youth up, desired and prayed unto thee for pure and sound wisdom and understanding of some of thy truths natural and artificial', hidden 'in the frame of the world'. Such 'radical truths' could not be learned through study but only by 'thy extraordinary gift', through angelic revelations 'of thy Secrets'. But soon after Dee wrote these words the devout Protestant William Harrison, whose close friend Christopher Carye had studied with Dee in the 1550s, denounced Bacon as a sorcerer, 'whatsoever John Dee our countryman either hath or will write in the defence of Bacon to the contrary'.[41]

In February 1546 Dee took his Bachelor's degree.[42] The increasingly dominant Protestant faction at St John's, encouraged by attacks on magical Catholic beliefs by reformers at Court and in the Church, then refused to elect him as a Fellow. However, Henry VIII made Dee a founding junior Fellow of Trinity College in December 1546, where he became Under-Reader in Greek.[43] Henry was enjoying one of his fits of conservatism. Besides Dee, all five Fellows chosen from St John's proved vigorous defenders of Catholic orthodoxy.[44] To deceive his critics, in 1570 Dee tried to attribute his reputation for 'conjuring' to 'vain reports' about his stage production of Aristophanes's *Peace* in Greek soon after entering Trinity. In fact Dee's use of pulleys and mirrors to create the illusion of 'the Scarabeus [beetle] flying up to Jupiter's palace, with a man and his basket of victuals on her back' derived from rediscovered classical treatises. Precisely because he could explain these stage effects naturally, Dee used them to distract attention from the real source of his reputation, his 'conjuring' magic on behalf of Princess Elizabeth in 1555.[45]

At Trinity College, Dee found a patron in the leading Greek scholar John Christopherson, a devout Catholic from St John's. He arranged for Dee to pursue his mathematical studies at the Catholic university of Louvain in the summer of 1547, supported by money from Trinity and Christopherson's commendatory letters. The Inquisition had purged Louvain of heresy in 1546, savagely executing evangelicals, issuing the first Index of prohibited books, and tightening control over university admissions. The great geographer Gerard Mercator had been imprisoned for months under threat of execution for heresy.[46] Dee spent the summer studying with Mercator, Gemma Frisius and Antonius Gogava at the leading European centre for astronomy and astrology. When Dee on his return presented Mercator's globes and astronomical instruments to Trinity, Christopherson conveyed the college's gratitude for these exceptionally beautiful and accurate gifts.

After graduating Master of Arts in May 1548, that summer Dee again left Cambridge for Louvain. The college once more financed his studies. To make his elevation to the Court seem more effortless, he later claimed that he never returned to Trinity. In fact he mostly resided there from October 1551 until April 1553, eking out his meagre Fellowship stipend of £8 a year.[47] Trinity epitomised the impoverished university's increasing dependence on royal patronage. Henry VIII had established the college to supply humanist intellectuals for political service, not intellectual speculation.[48] Thus, Dee developed in an intellectual culture attuned to the practical demands of the monarch and Court. His career would depend on how well he could attract patrons by tailoring his erudition and writing to address political needs.[49] This became particularly obvious after his father's catastrophe in 1547 demonstrated the crucial role of patronage in contemporary politics. In the short term this crisis explains Dee's second departure for Louvain in 1548, but its effects reverberated throughout his life.

While the imperious, terrifying Henry lived, the City had avoided directly challenging his Packer, Roland Dee. Until 1547 Roland shared the abundant rewards of his Packership with the mayor's appointee, William Brothers. After Brothers's death in mid-summer, Roland monopolised the profits for some months. Already by December 1543 Roland's growing wealth and status had earned him a place in the socially exclusive church Vestry of St Dunstan's.[50] Thanks to devoted parishioners, St Dunstan's possessed some of the richest chantry endowments in London, which supported regular Masses celebrated with an abundance of luxurious vestments and plate.[51] Roland exploited his political connections and parish authority to acquire these resources. Henry VIII part-funded his French war by seizing assets through the Chantries Act of 1545, which established a commission to identify lands 'wasted' on 'superstitious' Masses chanted for the dead. By 20 May Roland had obtained an advantageous lease for sixty years of chantry lands belonging to St Dunstan's.[52] In July he leased other parish properties near the Tower.[53] After Henry began seizing chantry lands, Roland leased a former chantry property in St Dunstan's from the Crown.[54]

On 8 July 1547 the Vestry elected Roland as junior churchwarden for a year. Nine days later the Vestry authorised Roland and the senior warden to sell £92 worth of altar vessels to repair the church roof.[55] During a time of rapid inflation many vestries resorted to this expedient to repair neglected churches. However, the sale process evidently gave Roland ideas, when his prospering career began to collapse a few weeks later. Following the death of Henry VIII, the accession of the nine-year-old Edward VI in January 1547 had shifted the balance of power between Crown and City. By the late summer the City felt able to reassert its rights, since the financially strapped government of the Lord Protector, the Duke of Somerset, needed London's money. In early August, Somerset's steward and adviser, Sir John Thynne, struck a deal with the City.

Thynne was a Russian oligarch of his day, ruthlessly exploiting his political connections to accumulate strategic positions and resources. He and his children would marry amongst the merchant princes of London. He squeezed his offices and vast estates to build Longleat House and founded the dynasty now represented by the Marquis of Bath. Thynne sent the Dees plunging in the other direction. The former suggested that Edward should issue Letters Patent restoring the Packership to the City's control. Thynne would then replace 'one Roland Dee' as Packer to the Strangers. He undertook to inform Roland personally that Henry's grant had been annulled. Both Thynne and Dee were Mercers, and Thynne was probably settling a personal score. Furthermore, Thynne undertook to obtain the King's written promise under his Privy Seal never again to appoint a Packer. Thynne then surrendered his office to the City, and received it again for life from the Corporation. The City probably paid the avaricious Thynne for the privilege. He would hold the Packership from the City against all political challengers until his death in 1580.[56]

Roland could not afford to go quietly. In 1548 and 1549 he continued to haunt the quays and warehouses along the Thames, bluffing some ill-informed foreign exporters into paying him the Packer's fees. Finally, Thynne appealed to the Lord Protector to crush the upstart.[57] Roland's experience of Thynne's persecution pushed him towards ultimately cata-strophic support for Somerset's emerging rival, John Dudley, Earl of Warwick. More immediately, Roland's loss of the Packership slashed his income, forcing him into desperate expedients that destroyed his standing in London mercantile society.

The senior Aldermen who had resented Henry's imposition of the upstart Dee now demanded that Roland fully account for his Packership. He tried to avoid accurately admitting his profits, particularly during his sole control of the books in the summer of 1547. Roland also tried to duck the £66 per annum rent that the City demanded for the Packership. Though he signed bonds to provide a final accounting, it took the City until November 1549 to force him into merely paying its legal costs, without settling his actual indebtedness.[58] While Roland ducked and dived to save his financial skin, for the first time John felt the cold wind of penury that would plague his life. For Dee, his father's crash reverberated in chronic financial insecurity, which undermined his self-perception as a leading European intellectual. The mismatch between his financial and intellectual status would provoke Dee into making overly ambitious requests for patronage and spending wildly whenever he came into money.

Robbed of his income as Packer, Roland took desperate measures to conceal his cash-flow problems and maintain his financial and social credit. The 1548 tax assessment still rated him at £200 in 'goods', meaning not real possessions but his general reputation or creditworthiness in the City.[59] To maintain this appearance of wealth, sometime after July 1548, Roland, by now senior churchwarden, purloined and sold further gold altar plate amounting to £94, 'without the consent of any of the parishioners', as the shocked St Dunstan's Vestry complained.[60] Despite the outrage in the parish, Roland kept the money and refused to name the purchasers of the stolen plate. His junior colleague, William Ansteye, blamed Roland entirely, before making an emergency inventory of the remaining plate on 11 August 1549.[61]

The age had witnessed much rapacious behaviour by the powerful, but Roland now lacked power. Just as he avoided accounting for his Packership, so Roland refused to submit his parish accounts after his term expired in July 1549. He had probably already fled the parish. John Dee later recalled that the calamity forced his mother to move home.[62] In June 1551 the parish could still not audit its accounts 'because of the great Hindrance and after deal of the said Rowland Dye and that he went out of London and dwelleth at Gravesend'. Roland fled to Gravesend, home to his wife's family the Wildes, because there he could shelter under the political protection of the local magnates, the Dudleys and Wyatts. This, and considerable bluff, enabled him to keep the money.[63] Roland's fraud, however, inevitably reflected on John Dee's reputation in mid-Tudor London, especially since, as the Vestry reminded the King's commissioners in 1552, John Dee had paid his father £5 5s for stolen brass candlesticks from St Dunstan's.[64]

CHAPTER 2

The Rays of Celestial Virtue

JOHN DEE responded to his father's crisis by leaving England and matriculating at Louvain University in August 1548. By then the little Netherlands town, famous for its beer, already sheltered many Henrician Catholic refugees, including several from St John's College, Cambridge. Dee arrived amidst a second wave of exiles from the Edwardian Reformation. The canon lawyer John Story, who signed the matriculation register just days after Dee, so vehemently opposed the Elizabethan Settlement of 1559 that he would be kidnapped from the Low Countries and executed for treason in 1571.[1]

Dee could have studied privately with Mercator, Gemma Frisius and Antonius Gogava. Instead he publicly swore allegiance to Catholic orthodoxy, which had been bloodily reimposed at Louvain just months earlier. Dee also swore to reject 'the doctrines of Martin Luther and all heretics, in so far as they clash with the teachings of the ancient Roman Catholic Church'. He had denied the Pope's authority when graduating from Cambridge, but now swore 'to live according to the Church's precepts and under the guidance of its supreme guardian, the Roman Pontiff'.[2] His later life would suggest he took neither oath particularly seriously.

Dee's matriculation enabled him to study Roman civil law at Louvain, bringing him into contact with particularly devout Catholic teachers, while equipping him for service at the English Court. Civil-law training qualified ambitious English intellectuals for the royal equity courts of Chancery, Star Chamber and Requests, as diplomats and Privy Councillors, and in the higher ecclesiastical courts. Under Elizabeth I politically powerful civilians would include Francis Walsingham and Thomas Wilson, her first Master of Requests. Trinity College supported Dee's civil-law studies at Louvain because Henry VIII's suppression of the Catholic Church's canon law had undermined Cambridge teaching in the closely related civil law.[3] Henry, and Lord Protector Somerset, had tried and failed to amalgamate Clare College with Trinity Hall to train civil lawyers.[4]

Dee later claimed to have astonished everyone at Louvain by applying his mathematical knowledge to reveal the 'deep judgement, and just determination of the Ancient Roman Lawmakers' in laws 'accounted very intricate and dark', particularly regarding inheritance and land rights. The science of numbers, by penetrating to the equity concealed within civil law, elevated it to the divine justice praised by Aristotle and Plato. In Dee's view, mathematics had even greater applications in canon law and English common law, both of which were inequitable.[5] Dee emerged from Louvain University clutching a Licentiate in civil law, being still too young for the doctorate. His civil-law training would inform his later advocacy of Elizabeth's imperial claims, since much civilian jurisprudence dealt with competing jurisdictions over land and sea.[6]

The difference between Dee's world and our own is revealed by the fact that his studies in astrology with Mercator, Gemma and Gogava also turned him into the kind of specialist useful at Court. His Cambridge training in arithmetic, geometry, perspective and astronomy enabled Dee to participate enthusiastically in his Louvain teachers' precise measurement of 'the heavenly influences and operations actual in this elemental portion of the world'.[7] A recently rediscovered astrological disc, covered in complex systems for measuring and calculating stellar influences, reveals Mercator's influence on Dee's distinctive method of astrology.[8] Dee believed that it was theoretically possible to measure the invisible 'rays of celestial virtue' that emanated from the stars alongside their light. Measured geometrically, stellar distances, magnitudes, aspects and movements would determine the power of these rays. Dee claimed to have invented while young a way of measuring 'those fixed Stars whose Operation in the Air, is of great might'.[9]

Dee's invention resembled the methods of Mercator's group, whose disc applied techniques developed for triangulating terrestrial geography to the precise measurement of heavenly influences. The disc enabled the student astrologer easily to measure 'from physical explanations ... what any planet signifies, what strength it has, what advantage or disadvantage it receives from elsewhere and in what order the planets mutually succeed each other in power'.[10] Like Dee, Mercator argued that a star's angle of incidence to the earth determined its power, perpendicular rays being the strongest.[11]

This precise method of astrology so excited Dee that he made thousands of 'observations of Heavenly Influences (to the Minute of time)' between 1547 and 1555, using instruments created at Louvain.[12] Later he would teach these methods to his students, including the well-known supporter of Copernicus, Thomas Digges. Mercator and Gemma tested their ideas by trying to measure the effects of the heavens on meteorology. Gemma left decades of weather notes. Immediately upon arriving in Louvain, guided he believed by Christ, Dee imitated this practice. We therefore owe to Mercator and Gemma's teachings that tantalising document often called Dee's 'Diary'. In August 1548 he picked up a medieval Arabic work on horoscopes, and in its blank pages started scribbling down notes about the weather.[13] Dee soon realised that he could more conveniently correlate the celestial influences to his weather observations by writing them in Johann Stoeffler's *Ephemerides*. Each opening of this book showed a month's worth of daily celestial positions, in the shorthand notation used by astrologers. The whole book covered many years, and in it Dee entered weather observations until 1556.[14]

More controversially, Mercator and Gemma traced human fates to the celestial influences prevailing at conception and birth. Gemma, who was also a physician, filled two vast volumes with nearly thirty years of astrological medical cases.[15] Dee's annotations in Ptolemy's *Four Books* also emphasised the geometric rules underlying the celestial influences on the human body.[16] He wrote that the moment of birth affected not only the future of the body but even of the soul. According to Dee, the changing angle of impact of celestial rays at different latitudes affected human reproduction.[17] Thus, when contemporaries referred to 'Doctor' Dee, they meant that he applied astrology to medicine, just as Gemma used the most refined instruments to measure celestial influences for horoscopes.[18] Many Cambridge students combined medical studies with mathematical astrology, and it gave Dee another string to his bow when seeking Court patronage. Therefore, he did not object to being described as 'Doctor and Mathematician' some years later, in published congratulations to Maximilian II on his coronation as King of Hungary in 1563.[19]

Gradually, Dee added to his weather notes records of nativities, which finally broadened into astrological interpretations of important and trivial events in his life, as well as of the mental and physical health of family, friends and clients. In accordance with Gemma's theories he carefully recorded his wife's periods and the times of their sexual intercourse, so that he could calculate the planetary influences when their children were conceived. He used three successive *ephemerides* in this way. Only the last two survive, their scattered marginalia since gathered and published several times as Dee's 'Diary', but not connecting occurrences to the astrological influences that Dee considered so important.[20] When Dee finally returned to England in October 1551, he tried to advance his career by writing no fewer than three hundred 'astrological aphorisms' about this Louvain application of mathematics to astrology.[21]

Dee also claimed to have taught the English courtier and diplomat Sir William Pickering in Louvain, 'in the use of the Astronomers staff, the use of the Astronomer's Ring, the astrolabe', and Mercator's globe. Like Dee, Pickering had studied at St John's, Cambridge, and was close to the Wyatts and Dudleys. His confidential servant Wyatt Wylde may have been related to Dee's mother.[22] Considered the handsomest English man of his time, Pickering lived very lavishly as Edward VI's ambassador to Charles V at Brussels. Dee 'began to eat' in Pickering's house there on 7 December 1549. Dee insisted that his teaching had made Pickering 'for skill in the Mathematical Sciences ... the Odd man of this land'. Unfortunately for Dee, early in Elizabeth's reign Pickering would withdraw from Court to husband his estates, so he could not advance Dee's Court career.[23] When Pickering died on 4 January 1575, unmarried and immensely rich, his house overflowed with luxurious clothes. He bequeathed Dee a mirror that produced optical illusions, another source of Dee's necromantic reputation, and the 'Glass so famous' that would draw Elizabeth to visit Dee on 16 March 1575.

In July 1550 Dee travelled to Paris. Clustered within its walls, particularly around the ancient and famous University, were some of the leading mathematicians in Europe. He carried Mercator's letters of introduction, but Dee had a knack for making intellectual friendships, amongst them now the renowned mathematical philosopher Pierre de la Ramée, or Ramus, who later sent his 'singular friend' Dee his 1567 *Introduction to Mathematics*. Dee later claimed to have made a splash by lecturing on Euclid's *Elements of Geometry* to an audience pressed against the windows and overflowing into the street. He demonstrated Euclid's first few definitions using paper models, like those in some copies of the *Elements* published in 1570 and described in his 'Mathematical Preface' to that book. He probably did not know that the University required all students to attend lectures on Euclid on those infrequent occasions when they occurred.[24]

More importantly for the development of his later occult philosophy, Dee encountered that miracle of learning, Guillaume Postel, also perhaps the most eccentric scholar in Europe. Postel had just returned from a tour of the Near East, where he had studied several Semitic languages. They confirmed his previous speculations that the profound mysteries of God's original language lay concealed within the alphabets, the very letter shapes of the ancient languages. While Dee lived in Paris, Postel began developing these kabbalistic theories about the mystical construction of Hebrew letters from 'points, lines, and surfaces'. Postel published his theories in broadsheets that Dee acquired. In his marginal comments on these, Dee accepted Postel's kabbalistic theory. He later used points, lines and circles to construct his mysterious Hieroglyphic Monad.

Postel's ideas appealed to Dee partly because Postel derived all the Hebrew letters, and eventually all languages, from the triangular letter

'Yod', the fourth letter of the Hebrew alphabet. Dee constantly harped on the triangular fourth letter of the Greek alphabet, 'delta', as the first letter of his name. It also signified alchemical fire. For Postel the number four connoted God, and Dee often Latinised his name as 'Deus'.[25]

Dee also visited the Court of Henri II, who had been trying to suppress Protestant heresy while maintaining the royal tradition of bountiful magnificence. Dee claimed that he refused a stipend of 200 crowns 'to be one of the French King's Mathematical Readers'. However, though Henri and his Queen, Catherine de Medici, notoriously relied on astrologers such as Nostradamus for political advice, the promise of a stipend seems as lightly given as any that Elizabeth I later made to Dee.[26] It may have been a polite compliment to the enormous, glittering English embassy to Henri II that summer, which included Pickering, Dee's patron, and young John Dudley, the Earl of Warwick's son and the great hope of his family, whom Dee met on this occasion.

Dee returned to Louvain and then embarked for England in the autumn of 1551. He braved the grey, chilly North Sea with a sense of triumph, exulting in Mercator's celestial globe and astrological disc carefully stowed in his luggage. One wonders how much credit he claimed for designing the disc when he returned to Cambridge.[27] Dee may have refused Henri's offer because he expected a place at Edward VI's Court. The downfall of Lord Protector Somerset in October 1549 soon led to the dominance at Court of John Dudley, Earl of Warwick. By October 1551 Dudley monopolised access to Edward, sparking dark legends about his lust for power. To mark Somerset's final disgrace, on 11 October John Cheke, William Cecil and Henry Sidney were knighted, Dudley became Duke of Northumberland, and William Herbert became Earl of Pembroke. The rest of Dee's life would be entangled with the Cecil, Sidney, Dudley and Herbert families.[28]

But in the autumn of 1551 he faced more immediate financial challenges. As on many later occasions, he was broke. Weeks after being feted and flattered at the dazzling French Court, Dee returned to his spartan scholar's cell at Trinity College so poor that on 31 October he had to borrow £4 in advance from his Fellowship.[29] Edward VI's Court offered an obvious solution. The Seymour affinity's influence at Edward's accession had dashed Dee's father to the dust. Maybe the rise of the Dudleys could now restore his son's fortunes. Opportunely for Dee, Edward's tutor, John Cheke, had become a Fellow of Trinity before Dee left for Louvain.[30] Cheke centred the young King's education around mathematics, astronomy and astrology, inviting leading Cambridge specialists to teach him. Yet Dee had many rivals for that opportunity, and after Henry VIII's lavish expenditure the Court chronically lacked money.

Dee bypassed these obstacles by attracting Cheke's, and in turn William Cecil's, attention with a new approach to a hoary astronomical subject – measuring the size of the universe. Dee applied Gemma's and Mercator's training to determine the distances of the planets, fixed stars and clouds from the centre of the earth, along with their arrangement and magnitude. Dee's treatise impressed Cheke when he read it in October, as Dee learned through their mutual friend, the Exchequer official Peter Osborne. Two long months crawled by before Osborne, Cecil's talent-spotter, invited Dee to meet Cecil, who had left St John's before Dee arrived. Barely thirty years old, Cecil wore his beard long and dressed in the bureaucrat's long black gown to add gravity to his enormous capacity for absorbing administrative detail. That and his sensitive political antennae had already made him indispensable to Edward's government, as he would be for Elizabeth's.

Thus began the long, tortuous relationship between Cecil and Dee, for despite his evangelical Protestantism, Cecil believed deeply in occult philosophy. Forty years later Dee still remembered Cecil's appreciation for his mathematical astrology at that first meeting. Later Cecil would find uses for Dee's astrology and alchemy, though when Dee's learning failed to serve his political agenda, he could just as easily dismiss it. He may also have been mending fences with the now-powerful Dudleys when he agreed to meet Dee, because Cecil was Sir John Thynne's lifelong friend, had worked closely with him in Somerset's administration, and knew what he had done to Dee's father.[31]

In fact the regime probably accepted Dee because of Roland's connection with the Dudleys, which was so close that it would finally ruin him in 1553. Between 1551 and 1553, while residing in Trinity, Dee became an occasional intellectual consultant at Edward's Court.[32] To keep up his profile he bombarded the King and the interlinked political families surrounding him with manuscripts on a variety of astronomical, astrological and cosmographical subjects. At some unrecorded date Edward rewarded Dee with a pension of £25.[33] Little evidence survives about Dee's time in Edward's household. He may have met Henry Sidney, the King's childhood friend brought up with Edward alongside Robert and Mary Dudley. Sidney was one of the principal Gentlemen of Edward's bedchamber and married Mary Dudley, Northumberland's daughter.[34] Both Henry and Mary later patronised Dee's alchemy, and Mary Dudley Sidney would be one of his conduits to Elizabeth's Privy Chamber. Their son Philip Sidney would study alchemy with Dee, though behind Dee's back Sidney joked to his smart friends about Dee's magical pretensions.[35]

Northumberland did not employ Dee, despite his interest in astronomy. He could not afford the household he already employed. Dee again met John Dudley, Northumberland's eldest son, lately made Earl of Warwick. Dee later noted Warwick's military and humanistic training for service 'both in England and France' and drew a vivid character sketch in his 'Mathematical Preface'. According to Dee, young Warwick condensed classical and modern rules for marshalling soldiers into a parchment of 'Rules, and descriptions Arithmetical' worn in a golden case around his neck. This detail suggests that Dee had some role in Warwick's mathematical education. John Cheke tutored the Dudley sons, another entrée for Dee into their household. Dee's 'Mathematical Preface' described the geometrical application of 'Stratarithmetrie' to arranging armies, and, more interestingly, to the military use of primitive telescopes or 'perspective glasses'. Even the perennially enthusiastic Dee admitted the latter needed improvement.[36]

Despite Dee's access to the royal and Dudley households, he actually entered the service of 'Black Will Herbert', Earl of Pembroke, on 28 February 1552. That day Pembroke buried his first wife, Anne Parr, sister to Henry's last Queen, Katherine, with a stately funeral in the echoing gothic gloom of St Paul's Cathedral. Pembroke took the opportunity to reshape his household staff.[37] Dee's claims to practise a new kind of precise mathematical astrology appealed to this avaricious, tough and violent soldier, not noted for scholarly curiosity. Even by contemporary standards Pembroke was an unprincipled opportunist, perennially anxious to back the right political horse. He needed all the foresight he could get. Dee noted the birth dates of Pembroke's daughter Anne, and his second wife, Anne Compton (née Talbot), whom he married in May 1552. In both cases Dee supplied the astrological assurances Pembroke demanded.[38]

Dee's Louvain training in precise measurement also enabled him to act as a navigational and geographical consultant at Edward's Court. Dee claimed that he advised Richard Chancellor on navigating the North-East Passage to Cathay in 1553. Thanks to his study of Mercator's 1541 globe, a splendid example of which Dee had brought back to England, he possessed important new knowledge that could solve the problems of navigation. A ship following a fixed compass bearing, or rhumb line, will create a 'loxodrome' that spirals into the pole the further north or south one sails, as the distance between degrees of longitude becomes compressed. Pedro Nuñez, with Portuguese experience of these paradoxes of high-latitude navigation, persuaded Mercator to draw correct spiral loxodromes on his 1541 globe. At sea loxodromic navigation required flat charts showing the spirals, and at Louvain Nuñez had possibly taught Dee how to draft them, centred on the North Pole.

Dee instructed Chancellor in an early form of this 'paradoxal compass' he claimed to have invented in 1552 and perfected by 1557. Despite its name, Dee's 'compass' was not an instrument but a circular polar projection chart, fifty inches across, which 'paradoxically' turned the supposedly straight rhumb lines into spirals.[39] The chart relied much more on Nuñez's ideas than Dee cared to admit. According to Dee's student John Davis, the 'paradox' meant it confounded belief, 'that such lines should be described by plain horizontal motion'. Davis, who as a boy attempted to contact spirits, would join Dee in a North-West venture in 1583 and would end as one of England's greatest explorers.[40] Dee also advised Chancellor on stellar navigation.[41]

Dee's pension of £25 may never have been paid, for a financial crisis in late 1552 forced rigid economies on Edward's government. As usual the government tried to shift the burden onto the Church. In March 1553 Edward appointed Dee as Rector of Upton-upon-Severn, Worcestershire, a rich living normally reserved for clerical high-flyers.[42] Dee's appointment while still a layman owed much to young John Dudley, Earl of Warwick and Lord of the Manor of Upton.[43] The appointment also precipitated a typically convoluted episode of Tudor ecclesiastical skulduggery that would cost Dee much time and money. The Crown obviously believed that it could present him to Upton-upon-Severn. On 29 March Edward's Letter Patent presented Dee, and two days later the Privy Council ordered John Hooper, Bishop of Worcester, to admit him to the Rectory.[44]

Unfortunately for Dee the right of presentation actually belonged to Bishop Hooper, notoriously stubborn over issues of principle. Hooper insisted that only those 'called and sent of God . . . to the edifying of the Church' could be ministers. Patrons who appointed 'such as cannot, or will not, feed with the word of God . . . shall die eternally'.[45] Political appointees such as Dee aroused his particular anger, for laymen could not be pastors of souls. Moreover, Hooper considered 'calculation by astronomy' the 'greatest and abhominable evil', violating the First Commandment, 'Thou shalt worship no God before me'.[46] In Hooper's view, those who attributed power over human lives to the stars worshipped them as deities. Still worse for Dee, Hooper remained in London, enabling him to lobby against Dee's appointment more effectively.[47] The bishop's opposition probably explains why Dee's presentation does not appear in Hooper's Register. A second Letter Patent dated 19 May seemingly forced Dee's presentation to the Rectory over Hooper's protests.[48]

Dee immediately rented out the Rectory's lands and tithe income for £30 a year.[49] His first tenant left a year's rent unpaid. The next caused even bigger problems. In May 1559 Dee leased the Rectory's income for sixteen years to Richard Smyth of Upton, at a rent of £27 a year. Smyth eventually refused to pay and withheld possession from Dee, forcing him to take a Chancery case for recovery. Smyth could refuse payment because

Dee remained a stranger in the county, where Smyth was 'greatly friended and allied'.[50]

Within months of being presented to Upton, Dee had to deal with more pressing issues. King Edward's unexpected death aged sixteen on 6 July 1553 precipitated another political crisis for the Dee family. When the King died, Dee's father Roland was at Gravesend, hiding out in a former chantry chapel that his wife's family had converted into a substantial dwelling house. He may have retained some Customs office, since the Port of London legally extended to Gravesend, where searchers examined all ships.[51] When that July the Privy Council mounted a desperate coup against Mary Tudor in favour of Queen Jane Grey, Roland Dee, Northumberland's man, occupied a politically crucial strategic position. Situated on a high ridge surrounded by the Thames marshes, Gravesend controlled both the quickest sea connection to Calais and the easiest access to the Dover road to Europe. Henry VIII's twin fortifications at Gravesend and Tilbury across the Thames, linked by an important ferry, commanded the sea approaches to London. The English commanders appreciated the position's importance in 1588 when they placed Elizabeth's army there to face the Armada.

More significantly, Northumberland had built his political power base just south of Gravesend in the Weald of western Kent. He had cemented the Sidney family's support by giving them substantial spoils from Somerset's fall, including their main Penshurst estate. They acted as his loyal lieutenants around Gravesend, which Sir Henry Sidney dominated politically. Roland's dependence on Sir Henry's and Northumberland's protection helps to explain John Dee's connection to the Sidney and Dudley families during Elizabeth's reign.

Roland's actions during Northumberland's coup remain unclear because it was hurriedly thrown together at Edward's death, and it left few documents. However, though the Duke's military effort suffered from lack of money, numbers and clear purpose, one fact consistently emerges – Northumberland's chain of command relied heavily on his personal supporters.[52] Roland may have assisted the Dudleys and Sidneys in what limited local preparations they had previously made, such as transferring cannon from Gravesend to the Tower in June 1553.[53] He could also have proclaimed Queen Jane in Gravesend, offending the robustly orthodox Catholics there.[54] He may even have helped Northumberland militarily. The Protestant Weald supplied many of Northumberland's troops. As the Duke headed towards Norfolk in pursuit of Mary, the most direct route from the Weald to his assembly point at Newmarket in Suffolk lay via the Gravesend-Tilbury ferry, a crossing that substantial armies used in the Civil War.[55]

After Northumberland's army collapsed at Cambridge, he and his officers had been imprisoned in the Tower on 25 July. A second group seized by Mary's army arrived on the 26th. Roland played a prominent enough role to be imprisoned in the Tower the very next day, along with Sir John Cheke, John Dee's friend and Queen Jane's Secretary, accompanied by the Chief Justice of the King's Bench and the Chief Justice of the Common Pleas, who had ratified Edward's deathbed testament in favour of Jane. Those arrested with Roland on the 27th seem to have been in London and the surrounding area.[56] His subsequent treatment confirms that he had made powerful enemies, for he remained in the Tower until 1 September, when the Privy Council, including Pembroke, John's ever-nimble patron, examined and discharged him under strict conditions. Roland may have breathed the air of freedom deeply, but the odour of treason still clung to him like the prison stink to his by now ragged clothes.

According to Protestant critics, Stephen Gardiner, Bishop of Winchester, who targeted a long list of Dudley supporters, ensured that Mary specifically exempted Roland and others from her coronation pardon. As the Protestant chronicler Richard Grafton complained about his own exemption, 'they that needed the same most, took smallest benefit thereby'.[57] The Privy Council established special commissions to purge the rebels from the body politic. Roland appeared before one such commission in the Dean of St Paul's house, at the west end of the great Gothic cathedral that loomed over the City, close enough for his aggrieved former neighbours to walk over from St Dunstan's to savour his ritual humiliation. Doubtless dressed in his finest, Roland had to listen while the grim-faced commissioners seized all his property for the Queen and imposed heavy fines. He was further charged the considerable sum of £13 to buy the Queen's pardon. His credit ruined, he took until 15 December 1553 to scrape this sum together, one of the slowest to purge his guilt.[58] Roland then disappears from history and probably died long before 1574, when John Dee reminded Cecil about the 'hard dealing' that broke him.[59]

By late 1553 John Dee faced multiple problems. Mary's regime was already purging the Church of married, Protestant or otherwise undesirable clergy. As a layman, Dee's claim to Upton-upon-Severn looked particularly shaky. The Catholics considered Hooper an illegal usurper and all institutions to churches under his episcopate legally void. Further darkening the outlook, Roland's actions had associated the family with treason, raising suspicions at a Court abuzz with rumours of plots and hypersensitive about political and religious loyalties.[60] John Dee's Dudley connections automatically increased those suspicions.

To make matters worse, if that were possible, Dee's patron the Earl of Pembroke had been deeply implicated in Northumberland's plot. Though as soon as Dudley's back was turned Pembroke had led the other Privy Councillors in turning their coats for Mary, she remained suspicious even after restoring him to the Privy Council. By then, Pembroke had so ostentatiously reinvented himself as a loyal Catholic that a Protestant pamphlet described him as a 'hardened and detestable papist'.[61]

Pembroke began to allay Mary's suspicions when he supported her plan to marry Prince Philip of Spain. The Earl finally earned her trust when, in contrast to several vacillating noblemen, he played a decisive part in defeating Sir Thomas Wyatt's Kentish rebellion in early February 1554. Pembroke's restored reputation made it correspondingly more pressing to tidy up some embarrassing connections with Northumberland's regime. One of them was John Dee. Quite apart from Roland's treason, through his mother's family John retained close connections with the Wyatts, at a time of heightened paranoia at Court. John's need to ingratiate himself with Mary's regime coincided with his patron's requirement for conspicuous orthodoxy amongst his servants. So with Pembroke's active encouragement, John Dee took the necessary step of becoming a

Catholic priest. His ordination has been overlooked, although Dee appears in Edmund Bonner's ordination register. Pembroke paid £20 towards Dee's taxes to the Pope. By taking Catholic orders Dee acknowledged that in the prevailing climate of rigid orthodoxy even Pembroke's influence could not preserve Upton for him if he remained a layman. He thus forestalled the danger posed to his income when Mary finally deprived Hooper of his bishopric on 15 March 1554.

Dee's ordination also conspicuously displayed his loyalty, as it took place during the week when Mary's government, badly shaken by Wyatt's rebellion, executed not only Wyatt but also Jane Grey, her husband Guildford Dudley, and her father the Duke of Suffolk. At some level Dee may also have been acting out of genuine conviction, judging by his upbringing and his close relationships with Catholics at St John's College and Louvain. The circumstances of his ordination signal an existing friendship with Edmund Bonner, the restored Bishop of London who possessed a keen nose for heterodoxy. Very unusually, Dee took all the six degrees from first tonsure to the priesthood on a single day, 17 February 1554, which required Bonner's personal approval.[62] Bonner may have pulled strings because he and Dee believed they were distantly related. Bonner's relatives the Bostocks of Cheshire had married Dees who bore the same coat of arms that John Dee acquired in 1576 and printed on several of his publications. In November 1555 Bonner publicly acknowledged Dee as his chaplain, though when he attained that position is unrecorded.[63]

As he knelt to accept the chrism on his freshly tonsured scalp, and then rose to don the priest's pure white alb and amice, the green chasuble, the stole, cincture and maniple, Dee must have believed that he had begun to restore his family's fortunes. In the short term he did, but in the longer term the connection his critics would draw between his priesthood, his magic and Bonner would prove disastrous.

CHAPTER 3

Conjuring the Future

THE UNCERTAIN political ground under Dee shook again in September 1554, when Queen Mary, desperate to produce a Catholic heir, convinced herself that she was pregnant at the advanced age of thirty-eight and began proudly showing off her unlaced stomacher in the Presence Chamber at Whitehall. Mary's marriage to Prince Philip of Spain (later Philip II) in July had created complex succession issues for the English political elite. Their marriage treaty specified that Philip could not interfere in the succession if Mary died childless, thus implying Elizabeth's succession. The announcement of Mary's pregnancy therefore transformed Philip's and Elizabeth's political prospects. Dee's patron, the Earl of Pembroke, an enthusiastic supporter of the Spanish Match, now tried to engage Philip in the daily management of government, seeing a future role for himself as a loyal chief minister.[1]

Philip's supporters introduced a Bill into the House of Commons in late 1554, proposing to give him guardianship of Mary's children in the event of her death. More importantly, in the event that Mary died without issue, his supporters even wished to make Philip king, thereby breaking the marriage contract and sidelining Elizabeth. After much debate, in January 1555 Parliament compromised, permitting Philip to govern the realm during the minority of Mary's child if the Queen died but reasserting English control over the succession under the marriage treaty. So in early

1555 Mary's conviction that she was about to provide England with a Catholic heir threatened to divide the political elite. By May Philip's English supporters needed the birth of that child to give him true royal authority.[2]

If Mary and the child both died, that would immediately destroy Philip's power in England. If the child died, Mary had little chance of bearing another at thirty-nine, and Philip's support in England would evaporate, leaving Elizabeth as the obvious successor. Advisers urged the Holy Roman Emperor Charles V to send troops to enforce his son Philip's rule, should Mary miscarry or die. Mary called Pembroke to Court to organise her forces.[3] On the other side Elizabeth's supporters began military preparations to oppose the hated Spaniards, published propaganda and wrote to France and Germany seeking support.[4] The possibility of her sudden succession required Elizabeth to walk a very fine line between being prepared for power and avoiding entanglement in traitorous conspiracy. She certainly recognised this quandary.[5] If Mary died in June 1555, prominent courtiers such as Pembroke, Arundel and Paget might well support Philip, a powerful king liberal with rewards, over an inexperienced woman likely to revenge herself against courtiers who had repeatedly tried to marry her off, assassinate her, or tar her with treason.

Facing an uncertain future, Elizabeth needed information in order to concentrate her forces for maximum effect. Therefore in April 1555 she turned to Dee to divine the future awaiting herself, Mary and Philip. Her choice suggests that Dee already had an established reputation as a seer, though not a scrap of evidence survives about any previous work. He performed his magic at Woodstock Palace before her auditor, Sir Thomas Benger, and two members of Elizabeth's household.[6] Since Elizabeth lived under tight security but attended Mass at Woodstock, Dee's Catholic priesthood may have been useful cover for his frequent visits.

Dee worked through April, when the Privy Council uncovered an obscure French-backed plot against Mary, though his vague hints mean we must guess at which of the many current methods he used. Elizabeth left Woodstock Palace for Hampton Court on 17 April, and Dee then performed divination at Great Milton in Oxfordshire, the home of auditor

Benger, when rumours that Mary had given birth caused spontaneous celebrations.[7] Back in London Dee tried to conjure the future in rented lodgings, where the Privy Council's pursuivants abruptly arrested him on 28 May, seizing his books and papers and sealing up his door 'for suspicion of Magic'.[8] He blamed two informers, George Ferrers and Thomas Prideaux. The fact that Ferrers, a confirmed Dudley opponent, denounced Dee indicates that he believed his magic served Dudley interests. Perhaps Dee hoped to enhance the Dudleys' standing with Elizabeth. Their subsequent gratitude might help him recover the family fortune that Roland Dee had lost.[9] The connections of Dee's other accuser, Thomas Prideaux, reveal the high political stakes involved in the campaign against him, for Prideaux was a trusted servant of Sir Francis Englefield, Mary's Privy Councillor.[10]

Englefield and Mary's Principal Secretary, Sir John Bourne, took over the questioning of Dee, showing that the investigation originated inside Mary's household, where her devoted servants constantly sought to implicate Elizabeth in treason. Dee cracked under pressure from Bourne, a notorious bully.[11] The Privy Council then arrested his chief astrological accomplice, John Field.[12] Pembroke attended the Council meetings on the affair and had his own reasons for persuading Dee to cooperate, given his hopes of serving Philip. The Privy Council confined Dee and Field on 1 June, but from Mary's point of view the real prizes that day would have been Benger, Elizabeth's auditor, and Christopher Carye, an Oxford medical graduate and Dee's former pupil. Carye could claim kinship with Elizabeth through the Boleyns.[13] Roping in Benger and Carye improved the chances of pinning the conspiracy on Elizabeth.[14]

Politics thus motivated the investigation of Dee, which initially focused only on the horoscopes that he had cast for Philip, Mary and Elizabeth. Within narrow limits, 'genethlialogy' of the mathematical type Dee had learned at Louvain seemed harmlessly conventional. Mary's own doctors applied commonplace ideas of lunar prognostication to argue that the birth 'unless it take place at this new phase of the moon [23 May] may be protracted beyond the full moon and its occultation on the 4th or 5th' of June.[15] However, astrologers courted danger when they drew up destinary or questionary horoscopes about princes. Destinary horoscopes required knowing the ascendant sign or planet upon the horizon at the moment of conception. From that and with considerable tedious labour a complete horoscope could be developed.[16] Dee's note in Stoeffler's *Ephemerides* that Philip and Mary's marriage took place at 11 a.m. on 25 July with Libra in the ascendant may be a fragment of such calculations.[17] Ultimately, even the immensely complex procedure required to forecast a time of death could be justified by Ptolemy's example in his *Four Books*, the fundamental text for Renaissance astrology, though those in authority considered such forecasts damnable.[18]

More controversial still were questionary horoscopes, though monarchs, nobility and commoners alike used them avidly. Drawn to answer specific questions, they were calculated from the questioner's moment of birth – Dee left many birth calculations – or from the time of asking the question. They were often used to locate lost or stolen property. However, the questionary horoscope could also be applied to high politics, because it assigned specific themes to the twelve houses of the destinary horoscope, including nativity in the fifth house, favour with the monarch in the sixth, and monarchs themselves in the tenth.[19] In normal times Dee and his fellows might have appealed to their patrons for protection, but the perilous childbirth of a reigning Queen in her late thirties was anything but a normal occasion. As time dragged on, Mary's anxiety about the success of her pregnancy transmitted itself to her courtiers and beyond. Rumours circulated in London that she was bewitched, sick, or dead.[20]

Ominously, within days of Dee's arrest, one of Ferrers's children died and another went blind.[21] This apparent exercise of magical revenge against Dee's accuser struck directly at Mary's fears for her unborn child and strung the Privy Council's nerves even tighter. By 5 June Dee and his three fellow prisoners had confessed to 'lewd and vain practices of calculing and conjuring'. The thoroughly panicked Council now feared a broader conspiracy. They demanded their investigators uncover it and added 'eighteen written questions', which Dee still remembered in 1592. Within two days the prisoners' answers raised the charges to full-blown accusations of 'conjuring or witchcraft', apparently confirmed by what happened to Ferrers's children. The French ambassador now reported rumours that the accused had practised enchantments against Philip and Mary, impaling wax images to kill them by sympathetic magic. Rumours spread that they had conjured a demon for advice. Though the Council sought to prove a necromantic conspiracy, the investigation had stalled by 9 June. The four 'obstinate persons' had refused to incriminate themselves, so the Council authorised the use of torture.[22]

For this purpose the questioners moved the prisoners to the Tower, nearly two years after Roland Dee had endured months there. The Tower dungeons housed the torture devices, especially the rack. Its system of pulleys stretched the prisoner's arms and legs, causing agonising pain in the joints and ligaments, which might never recover even if the joints did not dislocate. If Dee was racked, he never mentioned it, but for a man highly conscious of his princely descent and singular intellect, it would have been a humiliating as well as an excruciating experience. At this point the Privy Council record falls silent, but Dee recalled in 1592 that 'at length' he and his fellow prisoners were brought to the Star Chamber in August, where they were 'discharged of the suspicion of treason', after the Council finally resolved the political and legal problems of precisely what to do with them.[23]

Dee's vague 'at length' quietly skipped over the fact that in early July, soon after the Privy Council had authorised torture, he reappeared in Bonner's household as chaplain, weeks before the Council officially sent him there. Perhaps he had confessed all the Council required. John Foxe's *Acts and Monuments* (1563) places Dee in Bonner's garden at Fulham on 5 July. There the Protestant prisoner Robert Smith debated the Eucharist with 'one of my lord's chaplains, a conjuror by report', identified in the 1570 edition as 'Dr Dee'. Foxe described Dee's ingratiating 'sweet words'. Smith replied, 'Under the honey lies the poison'. Smith rebutted Dee's argument for transubstantiation, that Christ could be simultaneously in many places because He only possessed a spiritual body, as reviving the ancient Marcionist heresy. Foxe summarised Dee's response as 'many scoffings'. Protestants not versed in magic could not possibly grasp his spiritual theories.[24]

Dee believed that Christ's body could move through solid objects and hence that spirits could manifest themselves in this world. In the summer of 1555 he explored techniques for summoning spirits into crystals. Dee's interest in spirits supports the Privy Council's allegation that he and his accomplices dealt with 'a familiar spirit'.[25] The loose contemporary notion of magic made this a common accusation, since it had been practised since ancient times and condemned by the Church for a thousand years. Nonetheless, the circumstances surrounding Dee's arrest point to more complicated procedures than casting horoscopes. The Council's action in sealing up his London rooms and its interest in his books and papers suggests he was suspected of performing elaborate magical rituals tied to a specific place, requiring some paraphernalia. The most likely procedure for summoning spirits used 'Archemastry', the form of divination Dee had encountered at Cambridge. His 'Mathematical Preface' was carefully vague in describing it. Dee intimated that just as intellectual architecture surpassed manual building skills because it enabled 'mind and imagination' to perceive architectural symmetry instantaneously, so 'Archemastry' surpassed the 'Astronomer, and the Optical Mechanician' by its power of giving instant revelation to the imagination.

Some defended divination by natural causes. Contemporaries believed that all vision occurred when light beams emitted by the soul and imagination through the eyes encountered objects. So when constantly reflected from highly polished surfaces, those beams sent the soul, particularly the virgin soul, into a self-reflexive spiral of religious rapture in which visions appeared. Dee applied mathematical rules of perspective to take such terrestrial beliefs to the higher, celestial, level, arguing that one could use optical devices to manipulate celestial influences. The Archemaster could use light, 'that Divine Creature' that modelled the occult celestial influences, to achieve inner illumination. Before Dee dropped hints about 'Archemastry' in the 'Mathematical Preface' in 1570, he indignantly denied the slander that he was a 'Conjuror of wicked and damned Spirits'.[26] This rumour, which began spreading in 1555, still clung to him fifteen years later.

Within 'Archemastry', Dee alluded obscurely to three subordinate sciences, using esoteric names only recently decoded by Nicholas Clulee. They were 'Alnirangiat', the 'Art of Sintrillia' – divination by reflecting celestial rays onto liquid surfaces – and a third 'chief ... OPTICAL Science' that Dee left nameless.[27] The second and third of these sciences seem ideally suited to the needs of Elizabeth and her supporters. 'Sintrillia' enabled seers to divine the past, present and future, by using polished surfaces to reflect celestial rays onto semi-precious stones submerged in three different liquids.[28] Inducing visions by the use of gems and crystals, crystallomancy, like the 'chief ... OPTICAL Science', involved invocations of angels or spirits.

Crystal-gazing and raising spirits happened frequently at Renaissance courts. Many courtiers in 1555 could have recalled William Wycherley, who was examined for conjuring in 1549. Wycherley had told Lord Protector Somerset that he invoked celestial spirits into crystals, aided by a 'scryer' and several Catholic priests to bind them. The Privy Council's accusation that Dee, also a priest, had a 'familiar spirit' suggests that he employed crystals the same way in his magic. Despite his denials, when Dee began working with a new 'scryer', Edward Kelley, about twenty-five years later, he simply assumed that Kelley could perform rituals to command angels into a crystal. About twenty years after that a conjuror who visited Dee's Mortlake house beside the Thames copied a traditional 'call' he found there. It would allegedly bring angels into a reflecting surface, on which the conjuror had written the powerful name 'Hermely' in oil. This closely resembled methods found as far away as fifteenth-century Bavaria. Whatever his precise method, Dee believed that the 'Art of Sintrillia' offered a total understanding of the cosmos, and in 1555 this belief enabled him, or his accomplices, to forecast the outcome of current political crises.[29]

In early July, while Dee debated theology with Robert Smith in Bonner's garden, the surviving supporters of the Dudleys and of Sir Thomas Wyatt found new courage as Mary still failed to give birth. They began meeting openly in St Paul's Cathedral, then a fashionable promenade and gossip centre. The Lord Chancellor, Bishop Stephen Gardiner, fearing they would become a focus for Elizabeth's partisans, banished them to their country houses.[30] Mary's false 'pregnancy' had precipitated the conjuring crisis. However, once her delusion was perceived, the crisis evaporated, thus saving Dee. By early August even Philip had stopped believing that Mary would give birth to an heir, and everyone accepted that Elizabeth would succeed her.[31] Gardiner, ever the realist, gave his first loyalty to the House of Tudor. Therefore the embarrassing conjuring scandal needed to go away.

As Elizabeth's star rose, her auditor, Benger, and Dee's helper, John Field, disappeared from the Privy Council's books. Because Philip recognized Elizabeth's new status as heir apparent, a carefully stage-managed appearance in the Star Chamber cleared all the accused of treason, removing the stain from Elizabeth's reputation. The conjuring accusations remained, but Gardiner had no particular objection to conjuring – indeed, one of his chaplains practised it. On 29 August 1555 the Council released Carye and Dee on bonds for good behaviour until Christmas.[32]

CHAPTER 4

A Royal Occult Institute

JOHN DEE had jumped ship too early to benefit from Elizabeth's improved political status. His activities in Bonner's household later that year further distanced him from Elizabeth, her Dudley supporters and her household loyalists. They also severely damaged his long-term reputation amongst Protestants during Elizabeth's reign. By aligning himself with Bonner, Dee committed himself to the Dudleys' implacable enemy. Under Edward VI they had organised Bonner's mistreatment in the Marshalsea prison, an experience that was later used to excuse his violent assaults on Protestant martyrs.[1]

Dee may even have tried to ingratiate himself by helping Bonner finally to distance Catholicism from the world of charms and spells that had provided countenance for Dee's magic. In July 1555 Bonner wrote *A profitable and necessarye doctryne, with certayne homelies* 'with my chaplains'.[2] This comprehensive document of the restored Catholic Church in England condemned 'witches, Conjurors, enchanters' who forsook God by 'conjurations, to raise up devils' for 'any manner of cause'. That effectively condemned Dee's recent activities, despite his attempt to distinguish between his intellectual 'optical science' and vulgar necromantic 'mechanicians'.

However, Bonner went further, trying to defend Catholicism from Protestant attacks by distinguishing the folk religion in which Dee had grown up from the religion of the educated. Bonner silently dropped the power of the 'sacramentals' to ward off evil, as did all the Catholic primers issued under Mary, and cracked down on midwives using charms at child-birth, a practice formerly tolerated. He ordered his book to be read repeat-edly, chapter by chapter, from every pulpit in London diocese, and Cardinal Pole enforced the same teaching programme for the rest of England.[3] Now that the Catholic religion was determined to see the decline of magic, conjurors such as Dee would be increasingly left out in the cold, exposed to Protestant criticism.

Bonner did, though, share Dee's love of books and could ooze charm when he tried, especially for handsome young men.[4] By September, Dee considered Bonner 'my special friend'. Despite the storm of vituperation that fell on Bonner's head after Elizabeth's accession in 1558, when Bonner died in prison in 1569, Dee still called him 'friend'.[5] Under pres-sure from Mary and her Privy Council, Bonner had reluctantly begun prosecuting Protestant heretics in 1555. On 19 November Dee partici-pated in his friend's seventh examination of John Philpot, the former Archdeacon of Winchester. Confutation of heretics normally fell to epis-copal chaplains, though Dee proved theologically underpowered for that task. In Mary's first Church Convocation, Philpot had doggedly defended the Edwardian Protestant liturgy. His political and social prominence generated enormous public interest in his examinations: he ranked behind only bishops Cranmer, Latimer and Ridley in Protestant martyrology.[6]

Philpot smuggled accounts of his examinations to his supporters in wealthy, well connected London Protestant families. The leading Protestant exile Edmund Grindal read them at Strasbourg by late December, and in August 1556 John Foxe published them. At Elizabeth's accession these families' political influence and outrage against Bonner explain why Pembroke and Robert Dudley felt it necessary to stand beside Dee when recommending him to Elizabeth's service.[7] That occa-sion has the curious air of a strayed sheep being returned to the fold. At least one imagines Dee looking rather sheepish.[8]

Grindal, by then Bishop of London, republished Philpot's story in 1559, which did not help Dee's later search for patronage.[9] Worse still, in

1563 Foxe incorporated this text into *Acts and Monuments*, giving Elizabethan critics of Dee's 'conjuring' fresh ammunition, as we shall see in later chapters. Though Dee's service to Bonner would eventually blight his reputation under Elizabeth, his time in Bonner's bibliophile household stimulated Dee's desire to collect manuscripts and printed books. By late 1555 Dee owned sixty-eight printed books and eight manuscripts that survive, though many other books he then possessed have disappeared. Dee had purchased books for his undergraduate studies, his teaching as a Regent master, and especially for his advanced studies at Louvain from 1548. In Louvain, Antwerp, Paris and London, Dee seriously began collecting classical, Arabic, medieval and modern texts in astronomy and astrology, the related fields of angel magic, optics, geography, alchemy, and some Neoplatonic philosophy. They became the core of the largest library in Tudor England, though we still cannot explain how he found the money.

Analysing Dee's books hardly measures his restless intellectual ambitions. A new project suddenly appears on 15 January 1556, when he allegedly 'exhibited' a 'Supplication to Queen Mary for the recovery and preservation of ancient Writers' and manuscripts. Bonner doubtless arranged this royal audience, but the Court would not have found Dee's plan entirely novel. In the previous twenty years many scholars had complained that when Henry VIII suppressed the monasteries he enabled the destruction and dispersal of many precious libraries.

Henry had established a Royal Library, partly to compete with Francis I of France in collecting rare and magnificent books, and partly to collect monastic texts supporting his divorce and Royal Supremacy. The King showed little interest in the scholastic philosophy that Dee would later pursue, much of which disappeared. Henry had commissioned John Leland in 1533 to collect the finest monastic manuscripts. Leland chose chiefly British writers and British history, texts that Dee would scour for evidence about King Arthur and his own genealogy. Sadly, after Henry's death in 1547 privileged courtiers quickly filched Leland's choice selection from the Royal Library. The collection, roughly a thousand printed books and 450 manuscripts at Whitehall, a tiny fraction of former monastic glories, shrank further when the Privy Council purged 'superstitious' books in 1551.[10]

Obviously, when addressing the Catholic Mary, Dee took a completely different tack from Leland's plan to expose popish fables, corrupt doctrine and usurped authority.[11] Dee began by assuring Mary he worried that the loss of monastic manuscripts would undermine Catholic theology, and lamented the loss of classical texts, so dear to Cardinal Pole's heart. However, his actions soon revealed that he really coveted the manuscripts of scholastic philosophy, which everyone else had ignored. Dee promised Mary he would stop the unending destruction of the 'liberal sciences' by craftsmen who stuffed monastic manuscripts into the linings of hats, clothes and pie dishes. He sought her Letters Patent to procure copies of these manuscripts for a Royal Library.

Unlike Leland's historical texts, Dee envisaged the Royal Library as a national repository for natural philosophy. Since he would select which manuscripts to copy, occult philosophy would naturally dominate. Such *arcana* needed to be locked away from the vulgar gaze. In some ways Dee's outline for a Royal Occult Institute foreshadows Humphrey Gilbert's later proposal for alchemical teaching at 'Queen Elizabeth's Academy', Dee's own library 'for Itinerant Philosophers' at Mortlake, and Dee's plans to turn the College of St Cross near Winchester into an esoteric research centre. Grandiose paper schemes littered Tudor England, but Dee's proposal for a new national *scriptorium* seems particularly half-baked. He seemed oddly uninformed about the centralised Royal Library already at Whitehall. His ideas for funding also anticipated a lifelong pattern: he wildly overestimated contemporary willingness to invest hard cash in occult knowledge. Given three months, Dee insisted, he could collect enough sample manuscripts to persuade Cardinal Pole and the Church synod planned for May 1556 to finance a national scheme.[12] Mary and Pole remained unmoved. However, with Bonner's assistance Dee started borrowing manuscripts through his academic contacts. Instead of presenting his scheme to the synod in May, however, Dee travelled to Cambridge.

There, on 6 May, Peterhouse lent him four manuscripts. Within their massive bindings lay Dee's vast range of interests, from arithmetic to perspective, medicine, alchemy, crystals and occult divination.[13] Walking a few hundred yards north, he entered the familiar gates of St John's, pausing perhaps to wonder yet again at the 'yales' supporting the college arms, with their elephants' tails, antelope bodies, goat heads and opposing horns. There he borrowed works on perspective, astronomy, meteors, urines and Euclid's geometry from his friend the Regius Professor of Physick, John Hatcher, who would die owning two crystals for magic.[14] Dee then rode to Oxford, where on 12 May Bonner's secretary John Morren and Christopher Carye persuaded Queen's College to lend Dee a scientific manuscript. He also borrowed an Oriel College collection of medical, astronomical and geometrical works.[15]

Back in London by 18 May, in the sale of Leland's vast library, instead of items of history he bought five manuscripts of astronomy, astrology and alchemy. He also purchased a manuscript of Roger Bacon's alchemical works.[16] Dee listed all these amongst 'ancient written books' he possessed in 1556, which he had begun copying. Despite his protestations to Queen Mary and Cardinal Pole, his forty-five manuscripts included no history, theology or classical literature, but they do indicate what Dee considered to be a proper Royal Library: heavily focused on mathematics, geometry, Arabic and medieval perspective, astronomy, astrology and other forms of divination, alchemy and even 'the Art of Sintrillia'.[17]

After his exhausting journeys to rescue occult philosophy, Dee spent July 1556 sequestered in Bonner's household, absorbed in trying to reconcile the obscure imagery and cryptic instructions of fifty-five tracts on alchemy. Developing his Cambridge studies, he aimed to master an entire field of occult philosophy, from his newly acquired classic alchemical texts onwards. Some derived from the *Emerald Tablet* by Hermes Trismegistus. Most sixteenth-century scholars revered Hermes as the original alchemist, contemporary with Moses. However, Dee's reading course shows that he created his own alchemical synthesis from many ancient traditions.[18] The resonant names of Aristotle, Arnold of Villa Nova, Avicenna and Geber, founder of Arabic alchemy, gave authoritative weight to these complex, enigmatic descriptions of how to transmute metals and create the philosopher's stone. That astonishing universal elixir would restore mankind's physical and spiritual purity, which had declined since Adam's Fall.

Dee's reading included Bacon's popular *Mirror of Alchemy*, which described how Nature created the hierarchy of metals, from iron to gold, by varying combinations of two fundamental principles, mercury and sulphur. The elixir would rebalance those principles to purify imperfect metals into gold, remedying Nature's defects through a process imitating its own creative force.[19]

Dee connected his alchemical studies to his increasing fascination with optics, the mathematical measurement of celestial rays, and astrology. His synthesis pursued Bacon's vision of a comprehensive science explaining the unity behind Creation. Bacon believed that prolonged study, plus God's illumination offered to the virtuous, would restore the complete understanding of Creation that God had revealed to Adam, and which Adam's descendants taught to Aristotle. At one level, explaining Creation entailed understanding light's creative power, measured both optically and astrologically. At a still deeper level, recovering God's original wisdom required the adept to fathom the hidden grammatical reasons behind the ancient alphabets.[20]

Dee was following Bacon when he ventured into these dark speculative thickets, beginning to decode the Monad, a universal symbol Dee believed he received by God's direct revelation.[21] Over the next few years he used the Monad to pursue Bacon's ideal of unifying and rectifying all learning. Dee progressed from the optical measurement of astrological forces to the religious contemplation of the hidden grammar behind all languages – the geometrical Kabbalah hidden in alphabets.[22] This shift reflected Postel's ideas and also Dee's increasing acceptance of Neoplatonist claims that emanations from the Godhead sustained all Creation. Like Bacon, Dee believed that beneath the superficial babble of human languages could be heard whispers of God's original language, which communicated a unified revelation in the Monad.

Bacon's theories about optics had influenced the astrological teachings of the Louvain mathematicians. Yet Louvain had also exposed Dee to the empirical application of optics in the Low Countries' tradition of natural-istic painting. David Hockney has recently demonstrated how this tradi-tion originated with Van Eyck, quite suddenly, around 1420–30. Artists learned to use lenses and mirrors to project external scenes onto walls and canvases in darkened rooms, a miraculous effect that Bacon had described two centuries earlier. Using this projection technique, artists from the Low Countries harnessed the creative power of light to paint, apparently by 'magic', realistic landscapes and portraits. This tradition reached its height during Dee's time at Louvain, when Gemma Frisius learned about the effect.[23] Optical effects delighted Dee as they had Bacon, and in 1557–9 Dee wrote on 'the refraction of rays' through lenses and mirrors, and the secrets of artistic perspective.[24] He owned Albrecht Dürer's writings on the subject. Dee's experience of practical optics stimulated his acquisition of Bacon's works in the mid-1550s.[25]

Dee found ancient support for astrology in the Arabic philosopher al-Kindi's treatise *On Rays*, which taught that occult rays constantly pouring out of stellar bodies determined events and human actions. Dee's interest in al-Kindi probably dated from his time at Louvain, for like the Louvain group al-Kindi applied his ray theory to weather predictions. Reading Bacon convinced Dee that he could further vindicate astrology by systematically measuring the intersecting occult influences from all celestial bodies. Applying optical rules and mathematical calculations to celestial rays, in 1558 he produced *Propaedeumata aphoristica* (or 'An Aphoristic Introduction Concerning Certain Outstanding Virtues of Nature'), which merely sketched a staggeringly complex programme of geometric optics.

Like many of Dee's ideas, this worked better in theory than in practice. Even his 'very general' calculations became hopelessly involved, so that by Aphorism 117 the 'industrious workman' needed to measure the influ-ence of over twenty-five thousand different celestial conjunctions. Nor was the idea exactly new. Dee had no very convincing answer to critics who later accused him of plagiarising his aphorisms from the twelfth-century doctor Urso of Salerno. When Dee began casting horoscopes he reverted to traditional methods.[26]

The contrast between exalted theory and mundane reality became particularly obvious for Dee towards the end of Mary's reign and the beginning of Elizabeth's. To supplement his income from Upton, and whatever honorarium he received from Bonner, he worked as a jobbing mathematician and astrologer in London, judging by the mathematical treatises he later claimed to have written in these years. In 1554 he had turned down an offer from two impeccably orthodox Catholic academics to teach mathematics at Oxford. Apart from teaching terrestrial and celestial perspective, Dee now gave practical lessons on the astronomical instruments he had brought back from Louvain. In 1557 he applied Gemma Frisius's teaching to a typically ingenious treatise on a hundred additional uses for the astronomical ring, which was originally designed to tell time by the sun.[27] He continued to consult for the Muscovy Company, further developing the 'paradoxal compass' with a work on nautical triangles and the 'analogical compass'. He claimed to have invented a mathematical art he named 'Hypogeiodie' in 1560, to settle conflicting claims over unusually fractured coal seams. It actually applied German techniques for plotting underground compass bearings on the surface by spherical geometry.[28]

Dee's mundane consulting did not prevent him from more elevated theorising about the cosmos. His Monad, combining the symbols of all the planets and metals, appears on the title page of Propaedeumata, concentrating rays emanating from the sun and moon and connecting the four elements. Dee believed its comprehensive powers included 'whatever wise men seek'. Even when focused on astrological optics, in the Propaedeumata Dee remained mindful of his recent alchemical reading. For the celestial rays poured down upon practical alchemy. In Aphorism 52 Dee suggested that those skilled in 'catoptrics' could intensify rays through focusing mirrors. Such a boost to natural forces resembled Bacon's idea of alchemy as natural magic, harnessing hidden principles to perfect Nature's work.[29]

Dee sent Mercator a copy of his *Propaedeumata*, enclosing the alchemists' planetary symbols 'in a certain Monad', the symbolic key to the underlying unity of nature, encrypting profound alchemical secrets.[30] Contemplating the Monad over the next seven years, he would discover another approach to the underlying unity of Nature, through the kabbalistic study of language, writing and all Creation. He sketched the potential of this approach in his *Monas hieroglyphica* (1564). Yet even Dee's contemporaries, accustomed to enigmatic books of luxuriant eccentricity, would struggle to understand his allusive arguments in the *Monas*.

CHAPTER 5

The Kabbalah of Creation

JOHN DEE was fortunate that the circumstances surrounding Elizabeth's accession on 17 November 1558, plus help from powerful patrons, enabled him to recover from his disastrous choice to abandon her in 1555. Fundamentally he shared the new Queen's religious and philosophical outlook, and he could prove his usefulness in counteracting both French propaganda against her and the magical resistance of die-hard Catholics to her accession.

Elizabeth and Dee both practised an evangelical, Christocentric style of religion, venerating the sign of the cross in the private prayers that they much preferred over preaching. They shared the belief that Christ was really present in some form in the eucharistic bread and wine. Elizabeth easily accepted later suggestions, some made by Dee, that she could reconcile Protestants and Catholics as an ecumenical Last World Empress. In part this reflected her learning in occult philosophy. She believed Dee's interpretations of the celestial signs foreshadowing the coming Apocalypse. The means to bring about this final reconciliation included alchemy and the philosopher's stone, which like Dee she avidly pursued throughout her life, as we shall see.

More immediately, from late 1558, the French, again at war with England, stepped up their propaganda. They publicised Nostradamus's enigmatic prophecies of catastrophe for Elizabeth's anticipated religious changes. English writers had to acknowledge that these effectively stirred up popular anxiety.[1] Moreover, within days of Mary's death on 17 November the Privy Council arrested Anthony Fortescue, comptroller to the just deceased Cardinal Pole, Thomas Kele and John Prestall. They were accused of 'conjuring'. This was the first of several occasions when Prestall cast horoscopes or consulted spirits, predicting Elizabeth's imminent death and the succession of his Catholic near kinsman Arthur Pole, great-grandson of the Duke of Clarence and the Cardinal's nephew. Sir William Cecil, ever paranoid about Spanish plots, believed that the Poles had been egged on in their rebellious plans by the Spanish ambassador, in whose house they were arrested.[2]

An ambitious but spendthrift Surrey gentleman, Prestall spent the next thirty years alternately involved in magical conspiracies against the Elizabethan regime, seeking his recall from impoverished exile by informing on his fellow exiles, or buying his way out of prison by offering to apply his alleged alchemical skills. Several times his fate became entangled with John Dee's, and their continuing occult conflict from late 1558 partly explains the persistence of slanders that Dee conjured evil spirits.

Dee's patron the Earl of Pembroke attended those Privy Council meetings that ordered Prestall's arrest with his accomplices. Pembroke recognised the political threat their conjuring and prophecies posed to an infant regime bogged down in an unpopular war, a sluggish economy and an empty treasury. However, the Council still lacked legislation against conjuring, as they had when faced by Dee's similar activities in 1555. Therefore, they sent the culprits for 'severe punishment' under ecclesiastical law to the Bishop of London.[3] This was still Edmund Bonner, and Dee may still have been his chaplain. No record proves that Bonner punished Prestall.

However, this ironic situation does suggest how the Privy Council's need to counter Prestall helped Dee to recover Elizabeth's goodwill. He later recalled how in early December 1558 Elizabeth 'very graciously took me to her service', recommended by Pembroke and Robert Dudley, her rising favourite and leader of the Dudley clan, which both Dees had served. With their memories of 1555, Pembroke and Dudley appreciated how Dee's occult knowledge could be used against Nostradamus and Prestall's dangerous prophecies. Dee's biographers usually state that he chose Elizabeth's coronation date, but the Council seems to have settled on 15 January even before Dee's return to favour. Against the occult threats facing the new Queen, Dee performed a greater service at Dudley's suggestion, delivering an electionary horoscope about the day 'appointed for her Majesty to be crowned in'.[4]

Dudley would utilise the power of occult knowledge at Court until his death in 1588. However, Dee's electionary horoscope, based on Ptolemy and his numerous Arabic and medieval followers, did not 'elect' a time for Elizabeth's coronation but interpreted the horoscope governing her coronation day. Doubtless he foresaw a long and glorious reign, a useful counter to Nostradamus and Prestall's dire warnings of imminent catastrophe.[5] Yet as Elizabeth's coronation procession wound slowly from the Tower towards Westminster through a joyous, holiday crowd, pausing regularly for intensely loyal, but also intensely Protestant, pageants, neither monarch nor astrologer would have much appreciated the real future that lay before them.

Dee's first service as an astrological consultant to Elizabeth's Court received an ominously meagre reward. In 1559 he became rector of distant Long Leadenham in Lincolnshire. The fact that he found it necessary to reside there for the next few years emphasises the meagreness of the position.[6] The appearance of a second edition of *The Examination of John Philpot* in 1559 refreshed memories of Dee's assistance to Bonner, and Foxe's Latin translation spread the story throughout Europe.[7] Elizabeth, not for the last time, failed to keep her large promises of doubling Edward VI's pension when she received Dee. Therefore, he embarked on a scholarly tour from January 1562 to June 1564 that included Rome.[8] However, he headed first for Louvain and Antwerp, where he knew he could acquire books for his new interest in Kabbalah.[9]

Dee also planned to copy rare manuscripts of natural philosophy in great European libraries, particularly the Vatican and St Mark's, Venice. He left England intending to travel only for a year. He took just £20 in cash, supplemented by bills of exchange secured against his Church living. In mid-February 1563 he wrote from Antwerp begging Cecil for more time and money, announcing the stupendous discovery of a manuscript by Johannes Trithemius that offered ways to communicate through spirits and angels.[10] 'Steganographia', or 'Hidden Writing', described how to invoke spirit messengers to convey messages instantly. When he wrote, Dee knew that these spirits included the 'malicious and untrustworthy' Pamersiel, and that Trithemius openly identified many spirits as demons. Trithemius had a long-established reputation for trafficking with evil spirits, which evidently did not worry Dee. When he read Trithemius's claim that angels revealed arcane knowledge to men who served God in love and purity, he commented in the margin, 'God has given this to us sometimes'.[11]

Apparently Dee never realised that the incantations in 'Steganographia' could not invoke angels but contained encrypted instructions for concealing messages inside gibberish or inoffensive 'plain text'. Not until the *Key* to *Steganographia* (1606) could Books I and II properly be decoded, and Book III's numeric codes defeated all cryptanalysis until 1998.[12] Dee therefore continued to reverence Trithemius's authority on angelic matters and later pronounced his book *On the Seven Planetary Angels* conclusive proof for Arthur's great European empire.

Cecil's response to Dee's offer of demonic magical communication illuminates his general attitude to occult philosophy. He wrote supporting Dee's further travels, enabling him to remain abroad until June 1564. Cecil clearly rated 'Steganographia' highly. Like his keen interest in alchemy, this may have dated from his Cambridge days. Probably he sent Dee money, for Dee could hardly have travelled for another year in Europe only by teaching 'points of Science' to noblemen like the Hungarian who let him copy 'Steganographia'.[13]

Dee combined angelic studies with kabbalistic reading of the exceptional collection of books in Hebrew, 'Chaldean', Aramaic and Syriac that he now began collecting. Because he could barely understand these languages, like Postel he spent more time contemplating each letter of their alphabets as a profound hieroglyphic symbol or sign. His first purchase at Louvain promoted such contemplation. Jacques Gohory's

Book of the Use and Mysteries of Signs attributed magical powers to hieroglyphs, including a Monad created through numerology.[14] Dee also bought Johann Widmanstetter's groundbreaking Syriac New Testament (Vienna, 1555), with secret contributions by the learned Postel. Like the notorious Henry Cornelius Agrippa, Widmanstetter and Postel believed Syriac to be Christ's holy language, concealing profound meanings in the very shapes of its letters.[15]

In 1562, at Paris, Dee wrote an ambitious treatise, a now lost 'Compendious Table of the Hebrew Kabbalah'. It summarised his twenty years of hard labour in alchemy since his days at St John's.[16] He combined those alchemical conclusions with the results of the last five years' kabbalistic theorising about the hieroglyphic Monad's symbolic summation of Creation. Probably influenced by Postel, who was just then enjoying a brief interlude of freedom, and even sanity, in Paris, Dee applied Kabbalah not just to Hebrew but to all languages created by God. However, he tried to outdo even Postel's 'vulgar' Kabbalah, which only dealt with spoken languages. His Parisian treatise allegedly explored the still more profound 'real Kabbalah' hidden in the very framework of Creation, which God had revealed to Adam. To recover this lost 'alphabet', Dee derived the 'real' Kabbalah's 'signs and characters' not from alphabets but, by kabbalistic geometry, from visible and invisible things in Nature, which his *Monas* later called the Kabbalah 'of that which is'.[17]

Both Postel and Dee confidently expected an imminent 'restoration of all things' to their first perfection, partly because they believed they could apply universal mathematical principles to the reform of all knowledge. About the time of Dee's visit to Paris, Postel began describing himself as a 'cosmopolite', a French word he coined for a citizen of no country but Christ's imminent kingdom. Dee would use the same word for himself in his *Monas* and in his writings foreseeing Maximilian II's, and later Elizabeth's, apocalyptic empire.[18]

While Dee's European travels began shaping his later *Monas*, they also introduced him to the profound mysteries of Paracelsian alchemy. Paracelsus also prophesied a magical, apocalyptic restoration of debased human knowledge. Dee eventually owned ninety-two editions of books by Paracelsus or Paracelsians, grouped on his library shelves at Mortlake for ready reference, whether as a Paracelsian doctor or teacher.[19] Dee connected the reformed alchemy promised in his *Monas* with Paracelsus's claim to have revived lost Elect alchemy, first revealed to the Prophet Elijah. Thus Dee wrote into one of his earliest Paracelsian purchases the names of good angels who revealed Elect knowledge: 'Anchorus, Anachor, Anilos'.[20]

Supported by Cecil, Dee resumed his travels, visiting the famous physician and alchemist Konrad Gesner at chilly Zürich in April 1563.[21] From Zürich he rode south through Splügen, threading the rugged Lago di Montespluga pass between six-thousand-foot peaks to Chiavenna, noticing in the snow a giant wooden hand pointing to the warm sunshine of Italy. Arriving at Padua on 20 May, by early June he had reached Venice, the ancient republic secure in its lagoon behind its formidable navy. Travelling 150 miles further south across the stifling, unhealthy marshes between Venice and Ravenna, Dee visited Urbino about mid-summer. Along the way he studied alchemical books, consulted alchemists, and wrote copious notes about oriental alphabets.[22] By July another journey of 150 miles had brought him across the Apennines to Rome, to be introduced to scholars and shown the titanic western facade of St Peter's, newly completed by the aged Michelangelo, the dome still shrouded in scaffolding. As in Antwerp and Louvain, his Catholic priesthood helped to open doors.[23]

Dee laboriously retraced his steps through Ravenna and Venice to Graz, determined to witness Maximilian of Habsburg's coronation at Bratislava in early September as King of Hungary.[24] For eight centuries Europeans had cherished prophecies of an heroic Last World Emperor, increasingly identified with the Habsburgs. Many attending his coronation hoped that Maximilian would prove such an imperial 'cosmopolite', healing broken Christendom before ushering in global peace and prosperity. The celebrations made heavy use of apposite symbols, defying the reality that just a few miles away most of Hungary lay under Ottoman rule.[25]

Back in Antwerp, Europe's greatest trading city, his mind teeming with new alchemical and kabbalistic ideas, stirred by the aching desire amongst his new scholarly friends for some way to heal a divided Christendom and reform corrupt polities and societies, in January 1564 Dee sat down to write a remarkable book. For his *Monas* aimed at nothing less than the solution to all the world's problems. It offered Maximilian 'cosmopolitical theories' to usher in this 'fourth, great, and truly metaphysical revolution' of universal empire, an idea he borrowed from Postel.[26] *Monas* also proved Dee's philosophical superiority, at least to his own satisfaction, because he was the one man in a billion who could explain 'the supracelestial virtues and metaphysical influences' to a ruler already versed in 'the stupendous mysteries of philosophers'. Dee's blatant play for patronage also employed political flattery. His Monad combined Habsburg symbols representing the Sun, the Moon, the Cross and Aries, which had been displayed at Maximilian's coronation to symbolise his inheritance of universal empire.[27]

For twelve days Dee wrote feverishly, feeling that divine revelation offered him glimpses into the hidden secrets of Nature. His virtue meant that 'our IEOVA' had chosen him alone to receive 'this sacred art of writing', the Monad, knowledge that had been lost since God revealed it to Adam. Because all grammars expressed 'one science', one underlying truth, fundamental laws governed the placing of Hebrew, Greek and Latin letters in their alphabets, their ways of joining, their numerical values, and even 'the shapes of the letters'. Only the rarest philosopher could uncover these laws.[28]

The *Monas* certainly challenges modern assumptions about rational argument. The reader may choose whether to follow Dee in his flights of alchemical speculation, the particle physics of his time, or to read in the next chapter how Dee acted on his thoughts. Dee's belief that his hieroglyphic writing uncovered the divine language of things hidden in the world at Creation owed less than he claimed to divine inspiration. He derived it from his contemporaries, as he did the idea that his hieroglyphic writing transformed all supposedly different disciplines by illuminating their essential unity.

As so often, Dee was applying well-worn ideas in novel ways. *Monas* drew on centuries of learned speculation about the underlying unity of Creation, the geometry of alphabets, and recent kabbalistic teachings by

Agrippa and Postel that alphabets had divine, not human origins. It also incorporated his own musings about the Monad since 1557, including his 1562 first draft written in Paris. Superficially Dee's search for the original divine language seems far removed from the *Propaedeumata's* geometric optical study of rays. However, Genesis linked God's language and light at the Creation: 'And God said, let there be light' (Genesis 1:3). Moreover, Dee's reading emphasised this connection. Al-Kindi's *On Rays* claimed that magic could redirect the effects of celestial rays. Fully a third of *On Rays* applied ray theory to the 'power of words' in magical prayer, figures, diagrams, talismans and symbols.[29] Since everything resonated with 'rays', including people, writing and symbols, contemplation of a hieroglyph could produce magical effects.

Dee deeply admired 'Joachim the Prophesier', the twelfth-century mystic who, he believed, could foretell the future because he had penetrated to the 'formal numbers' by which God sustained Creation, and which gave rise to the profound meanings hidden in the very shapes of the Greek *alpha* and *omega*.[30] Dee collected books by Joachim of Fiore's many followers, who developed his diagrams and symbols into prophecies of spiritual triumph under a Last World Emperor.[31] Dee had been captivated by Postel's enthusiasm for Joachim's imminent golden age and his teachings about the hidden meanings within alphabets.

Agrippa had speculated about the intrinsic magical powers of languages, alphabets and numbers in his scandalous but influential *Three Books on Occult Philosophy*. Dee probably read *Occult Philosophy* quite early in his career.[32] Like many occult books it camouflaged knowledge aimed at adepts under verbiage designed to mislead the casual reader. The informed reader could uncover a hidden, carefully graduated programme of magic, as did Hugh Plat, the English occult philosopher and Dee's relative by marriage. Different levels of Agrippa's magic corresponded to the different forms of language powerful in the natural, celestial and divine worlds. Agrippa's Book III illustrated how Kabbalah and ritual could harness the language of demons and angels in the divine world, to achieve magical effects.

Along with Postel, Agrippa essentially founded Christian Kabbalah. From Jewish Kabbalah he took *gematria*, the numerological interpretation of words.[33] Because the ancient Hebrews represented numbers by letters, Kabbalah enabled diligent readers to decode hidden messages in the Torah. Agrippa took this search for hidden meanings several steps further. Like Joachim, he applied to language the ancient Pythagorean and Neoplatonist commonplace that God, the perfect number, had formed the world from 'formal' numbers.[34] Unlike commonplace numbers, these 'formal' numbers, through their proportions 'by lines, and points make Characters, and figures', and ultimately, letters.[35] Therefore the 'certain order, number and figure' of letters emerged not from 'the weak judgement of man' but 'from above, whereby they agree with the celestial, and divine bodies, and virtues'. In other words the Hebrew letters, for example, were diagrams of the heavens.[36]

Agrippa believed that he outdid Jewish kabbalists by applying their methods to all alphabets, a method Dee took further in *Monas*. Since alphabets derived from the framework of the world, Agrippa could relate them all to the four elements, the seven planets and the twelve zodiacal signs.[37] More profoundly still, since the very shapes of letters symbolised the cosmic structure, they became not just characters but hieroglyphic images. By contemplating these images the virtuous adept could experience sudden, divinely inspired, interpretive leaps to perceive their dense, hidden meanings.

Dee found two consequences fascinating. These powerful magic images symbolised truths inexpressible in fallen human language. Also, the hieroglyph harmoniously vibrated with its celestial influences. Properly constructed, it would draw down and concentrate them. From al-Kindi, Dee derived the consequence that altering the hieroglyph by changing its 'framing' would alter the stellar influences with which it vibrated.[38] The most powerful hieroglyphs resonated with the greatest forces. For example, the simplest Hebrew letter, 'Yod', signified that 'Unity' from which everything derived. From it Postel derived the entire Hebrew alphabet as cosmic diagrams. In Agrippa's 'exemplary' or highest world, 'Yod' connected to the 'One Divine Essence', the fountain of all virtue and power. Below, in the intellectual world of the angels, it harmonised with the 'soul of the world', and in the celestial realm with the sun's power. In the elemental world it represented the philosopher's stone, 'instrument of all virtues natural, and supernatural', in the physical world the heart, and in the infernal world Lucifer, the prince of rebellion.[39]

Therefore, Dee followed Postel and Agrippa when he showed how God had created the Hebrew, Greek and Latin alphabets from 'points, straight lines, and circles'. Humans had needed divine help to derive the Hebrew alphabet from the 'Chireck', or point, and the 'Yod', or line. However, he went further in demonstrating from the same fundamental ideas the mathematical and geometrical language underlying the structure of Creation. The same 'divine power' from 'our IEOVA' behind alphabets revealed to Dee the secret mathematical language of the cosmos.[40]

He further explained the Monad as possessing 'hidden away in its innermost centre' a terrestrial body. Dee claimed, like Agrippa, that the Monad hieroglyph taught symbolically, 'without words', what divine force should activate the 'terrestrial centre', to unite it with solar and lunar influences. The hieroglyph achieved this end by combining the rays of all the planets whose symbols it contained, as a talisman. Dee told his Parisian audience that his discovery of a unitary symbol combining all celestial rays had great cosmic significance, for it would produce a 'metaphysical revolution', metamorphosing the adept himself.[41]

As a divinely inspired writer, Dee wrote only for adepts. 'He who does not understand' must 'be silent or learn', warned the title page of Monas. Like many occult writers he reserved his mysteries for initiates. This fitted the work to Maximilian, since secret knowledge supported political power. Expecting the ignorant to criticise his 'lofty mysteries' as impious demonic magic, he could not be explicit.[42] No one could describe Dee's prose style as limpid, but in the Monas he became particularly opaque.

Applying 'the sacred art' of Kabbalah to this new realm of symbols, Dee found that the Monad's components, the 'common astronomical symbols of the planets', derived like letters from geometrical elements of points, straight lines and the circumferences of circles. Their proportions also evoked cosmic meanings, because he believed that the planetary symbols, like letters, were not mere human conventions but 'imbued with immortal life'. Dee asserted that 'any tongue' could express the symbols' 'special meanings' by 'hieroglyphic' writing that disentangled their geometric structure. Dee had restored these symbols' 'mystical proportions' by enclosing them in the Monad, which looked like the symbol for Mercury with the additional pointed hook of Aries. God had used Dee to restore astronomy, and indeed all disciplines, to original purity by this new kind of writing, the 'real Kabbalah'. It would reveal the meanings in the Monad hieroglyph by rearranging its component parts.[43]

Feeling inspired, Dee unfolded the Monad to reveal the divine secrets hidden in Creation. 'Real' Kabbalah thus used the Monad to explain to grammarians the reasons behind the shapes of Hebrew, Greek and Latin letters, their positions in the alphabet, and their numerical values. By rearranging the Monad, the 'real' kabbalist could show how numbers were not just abstractions but concrete entities: they derived their shapes from the structure of Creation. Geometers would be astonished to learn how to square the circle, while the Monad could yield celestial harmonies for the musician, the orbits of the heavenly bodies for the astronomer, and the perfect form of burning mirrors for the optical mechanic. In theory it also rearranged the traditional order of the elements, placing earth below air but above water and fire.

Dee claimed that his 'real' kabbalistic revelations would bring about the Apocalypse by converting the Jews. To prepare for this event the hieroglyphic Monad concealed at its centre 'a terrestrial body', Dee's coy allusion to the philosopher's stone. The Monad symbol instantly taught the initiated that the celestial bodies it collectively symbolised activated that concealed body by the perfect balance of their rays. A 'great compendium', the Monad also encrypted knowledge to perfect medicine and 'scrying', whether using reflections in water to perceive everything on earth or gazing into carbuncles or rubies to reveal the regions of air and fire.[44]

In the *Monas* Dee applied 'real Kabbalah' to reveal profound secrets through both constructing and deconstructing his hieroglyph. He constructed its 'head' from a point extended to a line then rotated into a circle. As in kabbalistic *notarikon*, where parts represent the whole, this circle with a central point represented the sun orbiting the Earth, while also symbolising the sun and gold. Adding a half-circle to the sun's orbit symbolised the moon and silver. The lower, elementary, part of the Monad shows not divine circles, but only straight lines forming a cross.

Dee analysed the four arms of the cross as kabbalists used *tsiruf*, rearranging words to discover other words. Dee, following Trithemius, replicated the Pythagorean 'tetractys', the equation $1+2+3+4 = 10$. The cross denoted the four elements (earth, water, air and fire), the four qualities (cold, hot, dry and moist), and many other Pythagorean fours. Dee frequently emphasised that his initial stood fourth in all three divine alphabets. Just as kabbalists interchanged numbers and letters in *gematria*, so Dee showed how the cross also includes 1 (the point), 2 (the line ended by two points), 3 (two lines crossing at right angles and their shared point). Therefore, the cross $(1+2+3+4)$ adds up to 10, meaning Unity, which explained why in Roman numerals X, a cross-shape, represents 10. Numerology also determined the place of the letter 'x' in the alphabet, because $(1+2) \times (3+4) = 21.$[45]

Dee constructed the 'foot' of the Monad from the astronomical sign of Aries, which symbolised fire, the alchemical art, and the 'fiery trigon', the formation in which the superior planets opposed each other as they passed through the three 'fire' constellations of the zodiac. Dee taught that a new world would suddenly emerge in the 'fiery trigon' in 1584.[46] He expected the Habsburgs to lead it.

Dee then revealed the Monad's 'kabbalistic anatomy' by removing components different from those he used to construct it. He derived the seven planetary symbols from it to demonstrate lunar and solar influences, continuing with a section heavy with subtle and unsubtle alchemical allusions to the making of gold and the philosopher's stone.[47] He then constructed other zodiacal hieroglyphs, indicating how to strengthen normal heavenly rays for alchemical effects.

Deconstructing the 'X' by *gematria*, Dee, like Paracelsus, turns it into 'V' and 'V'. Interpreting 'V' as the Roman numeral for 5, 'V' squared (5×5) becomes XXV, or 25, explaining why 'V' needs to be the twentieth letter of the Latin alphabet and the fifth vowel, interchangeable with 'U' in Dee's day. Turned slightly, 'V' becomes 'L', also the Roman numeral for

50. In Roman numerals, V times X (the letter with which Dee started) also produces L, or 50. Breaking the number '50' into the numerals '5' and '0', Dee then transposes them into letters. He combines 'E' (the fifth letter of the Roman alphabet) and 'L' (ten letters from both A and X) to make 'EL', one of God's scriptural names, hidden within the Latin alphabet.

At length, having shown how the Monad also concealed the shapes of alchemical laboratory vessels, Dee produced from 'X' the number 252, which he associated with the philosopher's stone. Like the shining crystal in the great cross at St Dunstan's that Dee had seen daily as a child, the stone lay where the arms of the cross intersected in the Monad. This position reflected its perfect temperate balance among all the elements and cosmic influences, and connected to Dee's veneration of the sign of the cross in prayer.[48] At this point even Dee's inspiration flagged and he addressed Maximilian directly about the philosopher's stone. Though Dee was obviously angling for patronage, like many other European 'cosmopolitan' alchemists he expected dramatic reforms from Maximilian.[49]

Dee proclaimed to Maximilian that in those perilous Last Days the Habsburgs should possess the 'Unity', that marvellous medicine capable of healing a divided and declining world. By kabbalistically observing every 'jot and tittle' of the elemental cross, Dee managed to make it refer to the philosopher's stone in other ways. He beseeched God to forgive him for publishing so great a secret, even to Maximilian. For the King or some other Habsburg ruler might become 'very great by this interpretation of mysteries'.[50] Within six months Maximilian became Holy Roman Emperor. Dee believed he was offering the potential ruler of the world a truly tremendous gift. As we shall see in the next chapter, when Maximilian proved unresponsive, Dee and others turned to Queen Elizabeth.

CHAPTER 6

'The Great Conjuror'

Maximilian ignored Dee's *Monas*, if he ever saw it. Therefore, in July 1564 Dee returned to England as medical escort to the dying Elizabeth Parr, Marchioness of Northampton. Her father George Brooke, Lord Cobham, was cousin to Thomas Wyatt, so Dee owed this appointment to family ties through the Wildes of Gravesend. In December the Marchioness used her friendship with the Queen to obtain a promise of the Deanery of Gloucester for Dee. However, Parr's death the following April contributed to another of Dee's many patronage defeats during the reign. Elizabeth kept the Deanery vacant so she could take the income.[1] A larger contribution to this setback was that Dee's absence had enabled his enemies to embellish his dark reputation as a persecuting Catholic 'conjuror', thanks to the events behind the Witchcraft Act of 1563. These events involved the political uses of magic, which have never been linked to Dee's biography before.

On 14 April 1561 the Gravesend Customs officers had arrested John Coxe, alias Devon, a Catholic priest trying to leave England for the Netherlands. Coxe carried letters to leading Catholic exiles, and his suspiciously timely arrest enabled Cecil to thwart Robert Dudley's hopes of marrying Elizabeth with Spanish support.[2] For Coxe's confessions enabled Cecil to assemble evidence of Catholic plots against Elizabeth, allegedly inspired by Coxe and other priests conjuring, yet again, 'how long the

Queen shall live'. Within weeks Cecil had convinced Elizabeth that they had predicted her imminent death and conjured demons to kill her.[3]

This supported Cecil's vigorous argument, which he would reiterate throughout the reign, that Catholic 'superstition' inevitably entailed traitorous magic. To destroy the reputations of several surviving Marian Privy Councillors, Cecil used interrogations designed to uncover an international Catholic conspiracy against Elizabeth.[4] He punished all the Catholic 'conjuring' priests with maximum publicity, displaying them in London pillories in June 1561, because he already had a larger aim in mind. Over the next sixteen months he carefully nurtured an even more dangerous version of this plot to fruition in October 1562. He possibly hoped to connect Robert Dudley with conjuring for political intelligence. Dudley had assured some courtiers that 'conjurators' were lawful, especially those who conjured 'good angels', though there is no proof he meant Dee.[5]

The Catholics arrested through Coxe's confessions included Lord Hastings of Loughborough and Arthur Pole, the nephew of Cardinal Pole. Hastings had encouraged Arthur Pole's hasty marriage with the Earl of Northumberland's sister, strengthening Pole's Catholic claim through his Plantagenet descent.[6] Elizabeth pardoned Hastings and soon released Pole. Cecil hoped that Pole, 'not very prudent, but spirited and daring' according to the Spanish ambassador, might implicate other Catholics in his schemes, even the most serious Catholic claimant to England's throne, and Cecil's perennial obsession, namely Mary Stuart, Queen of Scots.[7] Cecil knew that Pole's brother-in-law, Anthony Fortescue, had been implicated in November 1558 in John Prestall's conjuring about Elizabeth's imminent death, which Dee had been called in to counteract. Cecil inserted a spy into the group, Humphrey Barwick, later rewarded as 'the Queen's servant'.[8]

However, Elizabeth fell dangerously ill with smallpox in early October 1562, forcing Cecil to spring his trap prematurely on 14 October, when her disease reached crisis point. Frightened by the prospect of an uncertain succession dividing the Privy Council, Court and political nation, Cecil arrested the conspirators as an immediate argument against Catholic Mary's succession. Once Elizabeth recovered and called Parliament for the New Year, Cecil found further uses for his prisoners. He had captured Fortescue, Arthur Pole and his brother Edmund, Barwick, and two servants to Lord Hastings, just before they embarked for Flanders. Cecil alleged they were hatching a scheme whose boundless optimism typifies Elizabethan Catholic plots, at least those involving Cecil's agents when his political agenda required Catholic threats.

According to Cecil, the plotters intended to kill Elizabeth and make Mary queen, aided by Mary's French uncles of the House of Guise. On arrival in Flanders, Arthur Pole would reclaim his ancestral title of Duke of Clarence, marry Edmund Pole to Mary, obtain an army of six thousand troops from the Guise, invade Wales in May 1563, raise rebellion in England and enthrone Mary. Cecil claimed they sought papal assistance. As an added bonus Fortescue allegedly implicated the Spanish and French ambassadors, asking for aid from their Catholic sovereigns.[9]

There is little evidence that the Poles actively supported Mary then, and none that the Spanish would help the French to conquer England through her. But connecting the Poles with Mary perfectly suited Cecil's purposes. It immediately enabled him to quell Elizabeth's lingering doubts about aiding the French Protestants, newly revolted against their King. It also offered useful propaganda to sway the forthcoming Parliament. A month after their arrest Cecil informed Sir Thomas Smith that 'the matter of the Pooles here shall not be meddled withal until Parliament'.[10] Just before Parliament met, Cecil rekindled hysteria about the plot by accusing the Spanish ambassador of encouraging it.[11]

When Parliament opened on 12 January 1563, Lord Keeper Bacon's speech for the Queen told a packed House of Lords, with the Commons thronging at the doors, about the continuing threat from the Guise 'with a devilish conspiracy within our selves tending to the aid of the foreign enemy, and by their own confession to have raised a rebellion within this realm'.[12] Cecil hoped to use the plot to persuade Elizabeth to marry, or at least exclude Mary from the succession. Badly frightened by Elizabeth's narrow escape from death, the Privy Councillors combined with most of the Commons and Lords on 28 January to petition her to avoid civil war by naming her successor. They believed that Mary Stuart was now beyond the pale.[13] The petition reveals how Cecil used Arthur Pole's connection to Mary Tudor's former Privy Councillors to emphasise that the magical plot threatened Protestantism. The Commons knew that the traitors not only hoped 'of the woeful day of your death', but 'to advance some title', to renew their persecution against Protestants.[14] When Elizabeth refused to settle the succession, Cecil used the plot to kick-start his cherished anti-Catholic legislation.[15]

According to the official indictment, on 10 September 1562 John Prestall had invoked 'false evil spirits' to ask 'the best way to carry out their treasons'. Cecil privately revealed that Prestall had also inspired the plotters with another prediction that Elizabeth would die, this time in March 1563.[16] The fact that she had nearly died in October 1562 made Prestall's actions seem even more sinister. Conjuring did not constitute a felony, because that statute had been repealed in 1547, but Cecil's plans for the Parliament of 1563 included penalising conjuring.[17] This was why Cecil arranged the show trial of the conspirators on 26 February in Westminster Hall, mere yards from the Parliament chambers.[18] All the accomplices were duly condemned, despite claiming they intended to act only after Elizabeth's prophesied death. Yet none was actually executed, according to the historian William Camden, 'for reverence of the blood Royal', despite their reliance on 'the unlawful Arts of cunning Wizards'.[19] Cecil's timing helped push the Witchcraft Act through a legislative logjam, criminalising conjuring evil spirits, including to find buried treasure and lost goods, and conjuring love.[20]

Yet his triumph remained incomplete. Prestall had left for the Netherlands on 10 October 1562, just days before Elizabeth's smallpox forced Cecil to scoop up the other plotters. Outlawed and broke, in late 1563 Prestall grovelled to Cecil for the Queen's letters of protection before returning to England to answer the charges. On arrival he was immediately thrown into the Tower and condemned as a traitor.[21] Prestall nursed a lifelong grudge against Cecil, but direct attack would cost him his head. Against Cecil's oppression of himself and his kin through the somewhat imaginary conspiracy, he could only mount an indirect attack against one of Cecil's clients. Prestall could even call upon another kinsman to carry out this attack. The target was John Dee, who had countered Prestall's predictions in 1558–9, and whose letter from Antwerp of February 1563 expressed his dependence on Cecil. Prestall's chosen weapon was the first edition of John Foxe's *Acts and Monuments*, published in 1563.

Foxe's book reprinted the anonymous *Examination of John Philpot*. Thus *Acts and Monuments* widely publicised Dee's participation in Bonner's seventh examination of John Philpot in November 1555. Dee's brief appearance in that debate was undistinguished, at least in Philpot's version, which was smuggled out to the London Protestant underground, published in Europe in 1556, republished in 1559 and now again by Foxe. Consciously organised as dramatic confrontations, Philpot's 'tragedies' used Dee to connect unlawful magic with the Catholic clergy, a theme that Elizabethan Protestants, especially Cecil, would hammer home despite Bonner's attempt to distance his Church from folk beliefs. Philpot recounted Dee's hesitant, nervous attempt to prove the Pope must be Supreme Head of the Church. He rejected Dee's divinity as 'nothing but scoffing' and dismissed him as a novice in the subject 'though you be learned in other things more than I'.[22] Philpot's subsequent account made it obvious that those 'other things' involved conjuring.

During his imprisonment Philpot exchanged smuggled letters with the London faithful. One letter sent to him reported the treatment of Barthlet Green, a young lawyer held in Bonner's household. When searched, Philpot attempted to destroy the letter, but Bonner reassembled it, and read that Green had been committed to the care of 'doctor Dee the great conjuror'. This was just months after the great conjuring scandal that summer, in which Dee had faced charges of high treason. Reading the letter to John Christopherson, Dee's Cambridge patron, Bonner claimed Philpot had written it and dishonestly chose 'to belie me, and to call my chaplain a great conjuror'.[23] Subsequently published in the *Examination*, and especially in *Acts and Monuments*, after Elizabeth's accession this letter became crucial evidence to influential London Protestants, confirming Dee's reputation as a 'conjuror'. It associated him closely with Bonner and other leading Catholic hate-figures, such as the virulently anti-Protestant

Dr John Story, Dee's fellow student at Louvain, and the exiled propagandist Nicholas Harpsfield, another former chaplain to Bonner.

The new regime also brought the 'Cambridge Connection' back into power. So those continually reminded of Dee's activities in 1555 numbered many of his university predecessors and contemporaries.[24] Their leaders included Edmund Grindal, who initially conceived 'a book of English martyrs' and had closely read Philpot's account while at Strasbourg.[25] Grindal could not have missed the references to Dee the 'great conjuror'. When Bishop of London and confronted with Coxe's 'magic and conjuration' in 1561, Grindal demanded 'extraordinary punishment' for such grievous offences against God. His visitation articles denounced these 'devilish devices'. Grindal's later reluctance when Archbishop of Canterbury to permit Dee to hold two church livings reflects his distaste for the conjuror.[26]

Philpot's *Examination* also recorded that Bonner showed the letter about 'doctor Dee the great conjuror' to Barthlet Green. The story of his martyrdom followed Philpot's in *Acts and Monuments*, revealing new details about Dee's participation in Bonner's persecution. *Acts and Monuments* printed Green's own long letter describing his treatment by Bonner, including that he 'was committed to master Dee, who entreated me very friendly', and whose bed he shared.[27] Although Bonner's chaplains often used friendliness to 'soften up' Protestants before aggressive examinations and disputations, this hardly reflected badly on Dee.

However, Foxe underlined Philpot's pastoral importance by printing several previously unpublished letters between Philpot and the London godly underground. They included an unsigned letter, purportedly from a friend of Philpot, giving a very different version of Bonner's treatment of Green. All the details in this letter could have been gleaned from the already published *Examination*, including the fact that Green shared a chamber with Dee. Yet the sinister interpretation this letter placed on that fact would come to assume apparently disproportionate importance to Dee. He traced all later slanders about his occult philosophy back to the letter's words that Bonner had 'since committed [Green] in chamber to Doctor Dee the great Conjuror: whereunto conjecture you'.[28]

Dee attributed such importance to this letter because it became the kernel of a campaign of manuscript and oral slander against him, justified by its appearance in the authoritative *Acts and Monuments*. In the political, religious and cultural context prevailing after 1563, this accusation of conjuring put him outside both the law and mainstream opinion. The 1563 Witchcraft Act had recriminalised 'conjurations and invocations of evil spirits'. Cecil's carefully timed prosecution of the Poles had indelibly identified Catholic priests and traitors with conjuring demonic powers against Elizabeth.[29]

Acts and Monuments therefore inspired the wider circulation of gossip and manuscript libels that enlarged upon its relatively brief mentions of Dee the 'conjuror'. The writings have long disappeared, but Dee knew that the peculiar atmosphere of the Court magnified their effects. As the 'fount of honour' where the monarch distributed rewards, the Court seethed with gossipy, backbiting rivalry. The Crown's relative poverty during the 1560s, the uncertain succession and religious divisions, only exacerbated that hierarchical society's intense sensitivity about issues of reputation and good name. All this made slander an exceptionally sharp weapon when strategically employed against a competitor.[30]

Dee's compromised past put a keen edge on that weapon. Thus he complained in his 'Mathematical Preface' in 1570 about 'Vain prattling busy bodies' gossiping about his ability to conjure spirits, and 'Fond Friends' exaggerating his occult powers to thrill their listeners and enhance their own importance. Trying to distract attention from Foxe's evidence about 1555, his 'Preface' first tried to trace his sinister reputation to his theatrical illusions at Trinity College over twenty years previously. He defended those 'marvelous Acts and Feats, Naturally, Mathematically, and Mechanically' contrived as utterly different from his reputation 'as a Companion of the Hellhounds, and a Caller, and Conjuror of wicked and damned Spirits'.[31] This misleading explanation for his conjuring reputation is too often believed.[32]

In fact his theatrical natural magic had been forgotten, as Dee's manuscript 'General and Rare Memorials' acknowledged in 1576, when he abandoned this diversion. Instead, 'Memorials' directly rebutted the

'Malicious Ignorant' who attacked Dee's occult knowledge to support their relatives and friends amongst his rivals at Court.[33] These devilish liars, Dee wrote, claimed that he did not serve with God's aid like a good subject and Christian, but used 'wicked and ungodly Art . . . by the help of Satan'.[34] The manuscript 'Memorials' then proudly demanded that Elizabeth throw out crafty Satan. The *Memorials* as printed in 1577 wisely replaced this reflection on the Queen's failings with a humble request that she suppress this 'very Injurious Report . . . Spread and Credited' that Dee was not just a conjuror of devils but '*The Great Conjuror*: and so, (as some would say), *The Arch-Conjuror*, of this whole kingdom'.[35] So finally, in 1576, Dee admitted that his reputation as the 'Arch-Conjuror' really began with his forecasting for Elizabeth in 1555 and with Philpot's *Examination*.

However, he attributed its propagation by *Acts and Monuments* to his enemies inserting forgeries into Foxe's book. The 'Memorials' claimed that 'divers impudent lies are placed (long since) among the Records' of the martyrs, and blamed Foxe and his assistants. The printed *Memorials* shifted responsibility to the forger who had deceived that editorial team with 'divers untrue and Infamous Reports'. These lies 'Credited, by reason of the Dignity of the place wherin they were installed' then enabled the 'Devilish Cozener' to fabricate even more 'Counterfeit letters, or Discourses, answerable to the foresaid foul untruths, unadvisedly Recorded'.

Dee's enemies had exploited the brief description of 'doctor Dee the Conjuror' in *Acts and Monuments* to concoct numerous documents, convincing the credulous that Dee dealt with devils and so was an unfit member of the commonwealth. These 'Cozening forgeries' probably circulated at Court and in London, but their disappearance makes it difficult for us to appreciate the true extent of the hostile campaign. However, Dee's reference to forgeries inserted into *Acts and Monuments* in 1563 points to the anonymous letter, which had ostensibly invited Philpot to 'conjecture' how 'Doctor Dee the Great Conjuror' would treat Barthlet Green, as the first of these 'Counterfeit letters', because of the counterfeiter whom Dee identified.[36]

Dee's 'Memorials' names him as Vincent Murphyn, in Dee's eyes a low-grade 'cunning man' performing 'Devilish horrible facts' and 'fraudulent feats' for money. Independent evidence confirms that Murphyn was one of those creatures who inhabited the shadowy Elizabethan underworld, making a living of sorts out of casting political horoscopes and spreading political prophecies, conjuring with nail clippings and hair, and dealing in spirit magic. Murphyn also had a habit of forging letters and other documents to support his invented stories, ingratiate himself with the powerful and to blacken his enemies, including Dee.

According to Dee, even after Murphyn conned John Foxe by fabricating letters about Dee's conjuring with devils, he attached himself to Dee's coat-tails. Murphyn then forged letters allegedly written by Dee, letters that not only supported Murphyn's 'ungodly and unlawful' magic but also confirmed 'the foresaid foul untruths' in *Acts and Monuments*. Murphyn also deceived his 'miserable' clients by claiming to have discussed their cases with Dee. Murphyn thereby threatened to entangle Dee's occult reputation with the lowest kind of popular 'conjuror'. More importantly, Murphyn did all this because he was John Prestall's brother-in-law.[37]

Murphyn's forging of the anonymous letter in the 1563 *Acts and Monuments* greatly incensed Dee because by identifying Dee as the 'Great Conjuror' it indirectly attacked Cecil for his treatment of Murphyn's kin. Murphyn's prolonged and successful slander campaign against Dee highlighted Dee's activities since 1555, thus distracting attention from Prestall, while exposing the hypocrisy of the Elizabethan regime's attack on Catholic magic in the trial of the Poles and the Witchcraft Act of 1563. So long as Dee, with his Catholic priestly orders, his ambiguous record under Queen Mary, his connection with Bonner, and his conjuring reputation enhanced by Murphyn's forgeries, enjoyed the Elizabethan Court's patronage, he threw an unwelcome light on Elizabeth's regime. Murphyn's attack partly explains Dee's inability to secure major appointments in the 1560s and later, as his rivals for patronage exploited Dee's reputation as the 'Arch-Conjuror' created and disseminated by Murphyn.[38]

This context made it easy for Dee's rivals to present all his actions in a sinister light. When he sent copies of his *Monas hieroglyphica* from Antwerp in 1564, Elizabeth had to defend him against 'University-Graduates of high degree, and other Gentlemen' who through 'malicious fantasy, willfully bent against him' devised 'Strange and undue speeches ... of that Hieroglyphical writing' as a form of conjuring. After Dee's return to England in June, Elizabeth's interest in 'the secrets of that book' helped to suppress criticism by her 'little perusal of the same with me'. She encouraged his 'studies philosophical and Mathematical', despite being baffled by the *Monas*.[39]

Dee's immediate response to his failures in gaining patronage and countering Court gossip accurately reflected his diminished prospects – he decided to marry in 1565. As an ordained Catholic priest, Dee could not have lightly abandoned his oath of celibacy. If Catholicism returned to England he would face the heavy punishment that married priests had endured under Mary. Dee's marriage certainly scandalised English Catholics in Rome, who later warned everyone against helping 'John Dee, a married priest, given to magic and uncanny arts'.[40] Dee's choice of wife reflects his lowered expectations, for she could hardly be considered a suitable companion for the descendant of Welsh princes. Katheryn Constable, a respectable City matron, lacked the polish and pedigree to appear at Court with Dee. Her first husband Thomas Constable, a general trader whose business and parish careers resembled Roland Dee's, had been closely associated with him.

Thomas had served as churchwarden of St Dunstan's-in-the-East beside Roland.[41] The parish audited his accounts with Roland's in 1552, suggesting they were business partners. However, after Roland fled to Gravesend, Thomas remained active in the parish until October 1562.[42] Thomas must have died before September 1563, when the parish register refers to 'Mistress Constable's' house.[43] Dee possibly lodged with the Constables in 1555. Katheryn brought a modest legacy, including a house in Marlborough and some lands in Wiltshire.[44]

She may have been older than Dee, who was already thirty-eight in July 1565, because Constable had made her sole executrix of his will, and she died in March 1575 without bearing children by Dee. They initially settled at Long Leadenham in Lincolnshire, where in 1565 Dee rebuilt part of the Rectory for his new wife. He inscribed over the lintel a significant verse from Psalm 88:2, notably choosing the Latin Vulgate text over

Protestant versions. The verse alluded to his angelic magic: 'O Lord God of my salvation, I have cried day and night before thee'.[45]

Dee spent part of the year in his mother's house, which was more convenient to get to Court, since his legal cases described him as 'of Mortlake' about 1565. It soon became a landmark for the magical underworld. Jane lived very simply, for as late as 1576, the year before she died, she paid minimal tax compared to her neighbours. Her property probably included the rambling house and two adjoining gardens that Dee mortgaged in 1583. Dee established his library there, but also sued to recover relatively small amounts from Thomas Constable's debtors across East Anglia and Lincolnshire.

Dee's career was going nowhere. The Queen's support could not counter Murphyn's cunning slanders against the 'conjuror', provoked by the contest between occult philosophers. Moreover, from the moment of Elizabeth's accession, the destabilising claims of Mary Queen of Scots to her throne helped to intensify this occult rivalry, to an extent the modern world seems to have forgotten. The Protestant preacher William Harrison firmly believed that Mary practised sorcery and that she hastily married Lord Darnley in 1565 partly because 'witches and sorcerers' had yet again promised that Elizabeth 'is but a dead woman and to end her life before the last of July'.[46]

Ironically, such beliefs enabled Mary's Catholic supporters to use Dee's established unsavoury reputation amongst godly Protestants to denigrate his abilities. In 1569, by which time she had fled Scotland for what amounted to an English prison, Mary's claims to succession helped create the deepest political crisis of Elizabeth's reign. Several overlapping conspiracies swirled around the imprisoned Queen and Thomas Howard, fourth Duke of Norfolk. The crisis of one of these failed conspiracies in the summer of 1569 provoked Murphyn and Prestall to intensify their slander campaign against Dee. His claims to non-conjuring forms of occult wisdom did enable him to counteract their attacks, particularly during the craze for alchemy that swept through the Court in the 1570s. However, he never entirely succeeded in shaking off his conjuring reputation, partly because he failed the Court as a practical alchemist.

CHAPTER 7

Hunting for the Philosopher's Stone

To UNDERSTAND the fluctuations in Dee's career we need to appreciate the Elizabethan Court's deep interest in occult philosophy, particularly alchemy. That interest explains how Prestall, imprisoned in the Tower for high treason in 1564, soon won his release. Almost immediately he began to outshine Dee as an occult philosopher. In fact, Dee struggled to make headway not so much because of his reputation as a 'magus' but rather because the particular kind of occult knowledge he offered did not meet the Court's practical alchemical needs. His rivals claimed that they could meet those needs.

Dee's *Monas* offered the dazzling prospect of reforming the world through the philosopher's stone, but the Court showed more interest in solving its chronic financial problems by transmuting base metals into gold and silver. Despite his intellectual aura, Dee's practical alchemical skills proved ordinary. But his rivalry with alchemists making bolder claims, particularly Prestall, explains why Vincent Murphyn's slander campaign persisted. The dark thread of their rivalry runs through the glittering fabric of early Elizabethan politics.

Elizabeth's celebrated education made her fluent in several languages, adept in humanist belles-lettres and a model of evangelical piety. Yet she also set the tone for her Court in her pursuit of alchemy, thanks to the prominence of Sir John Cheke and Sir Thomas Smith amongst her brilliant teachers. Cheke's contemporaries knew of his fascination with alchemy and astrology, while Smith's almost frenzied quest to find the elixir added lustre to his Cambridge and Court career in the 1540s.[1] After Elizabeth's accession in 1558, her knowledge of 'all parts of Philosophy' and 'favour for science', including alchemy, became known throughout Europe. Alchemists dedicated books to her, and she received at least one New Year's gift of an alchemical book. Later a flattering emblem built into a Whitehall palace window described her as the 'true elixir'. That acknowledged her investment in distilling houses at Hampton Court, which were run throughout her reign by William Huggons, Robert Dudley's relative, and a Cambridge contemporary of Cecil, Thomas Smith and Richard Eden. Millicent Franckwell also distilled in her Privy Chamber for an equally generous £40 per annum. Their products included what alchemical recipe books described as 'the Queen's medicine' and 'Queen Elizabeth's potion', a purgative she used twice a year.[2]

Elizabeth openly revelled in her reputation for philosophical profundity, wide-ranging enough potentially to conflict with evangelical religion. Speaking from the throne, dressed in her jewel-encrusted finest as the Virgin Goddess, she told the 1585 Parliament that 'I am supposed to have many studies, but most philosophical. I must yield this to be true that I suppose few (that be no professors) have read more'. She quickly emphasised that she observed scriptural limits to her enquiries, thus implying their occult direction.[3] To the end of her life courtiers appreciated how to use her alchemical interests to manage the Queen's moods: 'I was all afternoon with her Majesty', Sir Thomas Stanhope wrote to Robert Cecil in 1598, 'and then, thinking to rest me, went in with your letter. She was pleased with the philosopher's stone, and hath been all this day reasonably quiet'.[4]

In this context Elizabeth's carefully controlled iconography suggests previously unnoticed alchemical significance in her 'Pelican' and 'Phoenix' portraits, painted by Nicholas Hilliard between 1573 and 1576. Hilliard later made remarkable artistic objects from alchemically transformed mercury, claimed a secret process for making the brilliant enamelled colours in his miniatures, and intervened to save his workman Abel

Fecknam from execution for alchemical coining.[5] His portraits began a fashion for associating the pelican and phoenix images with Elizabeth. After Lady Mary Dudley Sidney's gift in 1573 they repeatedly featured in New Year's jewels.[6]

This sudden innovation in the Queen's iconography has never been explained, but it coincided with the period from which we know much about Elizabeth's alchemical interests. Conventionally, the pelican symbolised Elizabeth's charitable care for her people, since the pelican allegedly fed its young with blood from its breast.[7] However, to many the pelican also symbolised the penultimate stage of making the philosopher's stone, when the potency of the red elixir was multiplied a thousandfold by repeated dissolution and coagulation, using a vessel resembling a pelican piercing its own breast.[8] In 1572 Elizabeth's secretary Sir Thomas Smith continually recycled his distillations in 'the pelican' vessel.[9] This meaning of the imagery became widely known. Many Londoners believed in 1599 that the pelican kills its young and then 'tears open its breast and bathes them in its own blood' to restore them to life, recalling the circular processes of putrefaction and regeneration central to alchemy.[10]

The red phoenix, a Renaissance emblem of the uniqueness and self-renewal of hereditary monarchy, also represented the red powder, or elixir, the last of the four colour changes during the Great Work to create the philosopher's stone. It thus represented the stone itself.[11] In 1574 several courtiers presented Elizabeth with rich jewels featuring a phoenix.[12] In 1577 Dee's friend and Elizabeth's 'servant' Samuel Norton wrote from St John's, Cambridge, offering her, as one well practised alchemist to another, a complicated method of making the stone. He expected her to achieve it.[13] Hilliard probably understood such resonances in his portraits.[14] Dee's preface to Maximilian II in Monas described the promise of his philosophy as a metaphorical phoenix, 'from the wings of whose charity alone we have extracted with fear and love all those speculative feathers against the nakedness brought down on us by Adam'.[15]

Elizabeth's alchemical learning attracted attention from English alchemists outside Court circles. Thomas Charnock offered from remotest

Somerset to transmute gold for her and in 1566 presented Cecil with a book on the philosopher's stone dedicated 'unto the Queen's majesty'.[16] Charnock envisaged himself as 'the Queen's philosopher', a title sometimes claimed for Dee. Charnock hoped to follow other royal alchemists, such as Thomas Norton under Edward IV, and his own uncle, another Thomas Charnock, philosopher to Henry VII.[17] His book shares Dee's apocalyptic expectations, which are often depicted as drawn from a more purified, exalted philosophy. They both struck their neighbours as 'no better than a conjuror'.[18]

Charnock pretended to attack the common belief that perfecting the stone would show 'that the end of the world is at hand', when 'all secrets shall be opened'. Yet the Last Judgement 'shall be by my astronomical judgement' about 1581 – an accurate forecast of his own death.[19] Charnock read widely in the kinds of occult knowledge found in Dee's library, rising from 'false' alchemy through face-reading and palm-reading to astrology, cosmology and medicine, which like Dee he practised, and ultimately to the true natural philosophy of the stone.[20] Therefore, Charnock praised the ancient royal pursuit of the philosopher's stone by adepts steeped in the wisdom of Roger Bacon, George Ripley, Albertus Magnus and Raymond Lull.[21] According to Charnock, Henry VII had possessed the purest stone by 1504.[22] Charnock staked his head on making the stone and pure gold for Elizabeth in seven years. It would prolong the Queen's life and restore her coinage to its medieval quality, when monarchs had coined pure alchemical gold.[23] He offered Elizabeth two copies of his treatise, and later believed that one copy had been placed in her library.[24] In fact William Cecil kept it, another sign of his alchemical interests. It joined an English translation of Geber and other essential alchemical texts, still in Cecil's library at Hatfield House.[25]

Elizabeth and Cecil refused Charnock's offers of alchemical riches only because, he claimed, 'the Queen and her council had set one a work in Somerset place in London before I came and had wrought there by the space of one year'.[26] Charnock had been forestalled by Cornelius de Lannoy, or de Alneto, from a prominent Low Countries family. De Lannoy promised Elizabeth almost instant riches, yet ironically it was

Dee's highly intellectual *Monas* that introduced the Queen and Cecil to ideas that persuaded them to accept his rival's offers.[27] Dee's *Monas* promised that his alchemical Theorem XXI about the 'great secret' hidden in the Monad would please the *Voarchadumicus*. This alluded to Joannes Pantheus's description of the philosopher's stone in his book *Voarchadumia*. De Lannoy wrote to Cecil from Bruges in December 1564, offering his thirty years' experience in the art of 'Boarhchadamia' derived from the ancients. He also signed himself 'Boarchado' to Elizabeth, which would have seemed nonsense to her unless he assumed she knew what that meant.[28]

Like Pantheus's method, de Lannoy's embraced both medicine and transmutation. He could distil a compound called 'pantaura' which incorporated the virtues of 'the soul of the world' to heal diseases instantly. His method involved multiplying his 'medicine' through progressive multiples of ten, to which Dee attributed such kabbalistic significance in his *Monas*. As Thomas Tymme later interpreted the *Monas*, 'By the DENARIE is meant the Multiplication of Gold and Silver, by the perfection of the Medicine, from 1 to 10, from 10 to 100, & so by the Number to a Number infinite by Arithmetical proportion'. Dee still believed this in 1607.[29] De Lannoy similarly offered to use one part of his 'medicine' to transmute ten or a hundred or a thousand parts of pure gold into medicine of the 'second order', a ruby stone like the phoenix, 'having besides many other colours'. Ground to fine powder, this would turn a hundred or a thousand times as much molten lead into pure gold.[30] He could also make pure gold worth annually £33,000, and diamonds, emeralds and other precious stones. Ten pieces of gold could multiply into one thousand within four months.[31]

Cecil's enthusiastic response again suggests that beneath the grave exterior of his stuffy official portraits beat the excitable heart of a speculator in occult philosophy. His retention of Charnock's book, like his enthusiasm for de Lannoy, attests to his lifelong fascination with alchemy, which, as with Dee, began during his education in Aristotelian natural philosophy at St John's, Cambridge. He acquired the texts of Geber and others after 1545. That shared experience partly explains his patronage of

Dee. In 1552 Cecil employed as secretary the geographer Richard Eden, who had spent the previous three years seeking the philosopher's stone.[32] When Eden successfully sought Cecil's patronage in 1562, he appealed to Cecil's 'pleasure in the wonderful works of Art and nature', the standard euphemism for alchemy, 'wherin doubtless shineth the spark of the divine spirit that God hath given you'.

Eden enclosed a treatise describing a model of the universe 'moved by the same spirit of life wherby . . . all nature is moved'. This derived from 'The Material of the Philosopher's Stone'. He concluded that his alchemical discoveries would have delighted their old Cambridge friend Sir John Cheke, 'As I know the divine spark of knowledge that is in your Honour partly received of him, will move you to do the like'.[33] Cheke was Dee's connection to Cecil, Elizabeth's teacher, and Cecil's brother-in-law and tutor. Cheke doubtless instilled the same 'divine spark' in Elizabeth. This accounts for the treatise on the philosopher's stone amongst Cecil's papers and explains why he carefully filed away offers of alchemical medicines to cure his chronic illnesses.[34]

In fact, though de Lannoy has been dismissed as a plausible conman, his reception demonstrates how the prospect of alchemical transmutation fascinated Elizabeth's inner circle. Faced by an empty royal treasury, Elizabeth and Cecil willingly believed de Lannoy's promises to transmute gold worth £33,000 a year. The Queen supplied him with Somerset House, another house in the country, all his materials, and expensive equipment, plus monthly living expenses for his family and servants. By March 1565 Cecil had paid their travelling expenses, and Elizabeth awarded de Lannoy the enormous pension of £120 per annum, which Cecil ensured he received each quarter, in advance. Dee spent much of his life vainly petitioning for such support.

By August, despite Elizabeth's pressure for quick results, de Lannoy was complaining about shoddy English glass and pottery vessels, and sending to Antwerp and Kassel for specialist alchemical replacements. To modern eyes this looks like delaying tactics. Yet Armigall Waad, who managed de Lannoy for Cecil, reported that de Lannoy was using the elixir only to transmute gold for himself.[35] Elizabeth visited the laboratory at Somerset House and demanded de Lannoy's copy of an alchemical manuscript. She practised her own alchemy in her Privy Chamber – de Lannoy assumed that she knew how to proceed.[36] When in July 1566 Waad reported de Lannoy's boast that he had omitted crucial sections from the manuscript, Elizabeth demanded that he provide another copy to check against her own.[37]

All this suggests that Elizabeth, Cecil and Dudley, now Earl of Leicester – whose interest in occult philosophy matched the Queen's – believed the elixir really worked. Even Waad considered that de Lannoy's complaints, delays and evasions were a cover not for fraud but for the alchemist's self-enrichment. De Lannoy's growing reputation gave him fabulous lines of credit. In mid-January 1566 Princess Cecilia of Sweden, currently visiting Elizabeth, borrowed £10,000 from de Lannoy, who had formerly served the King of Sweden, and a further £13,000 in early March, and these transactions were quickly revealed to Cecil. By the end of March, Waad believed de Lannoy and the princess were plotting to escape to the Netherlands together. But Waad still promised Cecil the greatest gift ever given to a Queen, 'the projection of the medicine to be done before her highness, first by me and afterward by her Majesty's own hand'. The most fanciful stories about Elizabeth have not dared to conjure this real vision of her moving restlessly among her alembics and pelicans, endlessly seeking the elixir to repair the ravages of the smallpox, fight the decay of her aging body, and halt time itself, as in her motto *semper eadem*, 'always the same'.[38]

The prospect of losing the elixir, rather than suspicion about de Lannoy's claims, explains why Elizabeth first restricted his movements, then removed him with his laboratory to the Tower.[39] For Waad had uncovered de Lannoy's escape plans and firmly believed that he had 'The Medicine or Elixir [which] he will carry with him upon his own person together with the book of the art'. If the Queen arrested him en route, 'her Majestie shall come by the Art and the thing itself'.[40] De Lannoy still exuded great confidence in late May 'and speaketh words every inch of a foot and a half long' when Waad forestalled another escape plot.[41] Waad continued to suspect de Lannoy of defrauding the Queen by trying to keep the gold. In July he interrogated him in the Tower about his method.

It involved multiplying the 'medicine' as in 'Voarchadumia'. However, Waad calculated that this would produce not just the Queen's £33,000 but almost £825,000, four times the annual income of the Crown.[42]

Therefore, Cecil continued to pay de Lannoy's expenses in August 1566, when he removed his furnaces to the Tower. But in early 1567 Cecil lost patience and transferred de Lannoy to a cell. From there the prisoner desperately petitioned Cecil and Leicester, promising to transmute lead with the red powder in just two days.[43] Cecil's disgusted diary entry for February 1567 that 'Cornelius Lanoy, a Dutchman, [was] committed to the Tower for abusing the Q[ueen's] majesty in Somerset House in promising to make the Elixir' and 'to convert any Metal into Gold' should not be taken as evidence of general scepticism about alchemy. Rather it reflects Cecil's disappointment with this specific alchemist, upon whom he had pinned great hopes. He kept de Lannoy in the Tower until at least 1571.[44]

In 1568 Cecil questioned the English ambassador to France about an Italian alchemist who had written asking to be 'entertained', even though the Queen 'will in no wise hear of any such offers, which she thinketh are but chargeable without Fruit'. Elizabeth may have been burnt by her experience with de Lannoy, but Cecil remained an inveterate gambler regarding alchemy's ability to restore the royal finances and 'had earnestly moved her Majesty to have adventured some small piece of Money upon such a man'.[45]

Dee may have partly inspired Elizabeth and Cecil's patronage of de Lannoy. However, the Court fashion that the Queen and her Secretary thus encouraged seriously affected Dee's career, because Prestall seized the opportunity to obtain his release from the Tower by trumpeting his own alchemical abilities. Armigall Waad's first extant report to Cecil about de Lannoy in August 1565 passed on Prestall's request: 'to remember your honour of his suit. He sayeth that being granted that he might at liberty be conversant among us he would do great service.'[46] One of Prestall's many get-rich-quick schemes had required a licence 'for to make gold of other metal (which I can do) as is well known'.[47]

Dee may have failed to fulfil the Earl of Pembroke's alchemical demands, for Pembroke took up Prestall's case. Over the next eighteen months he repeatedly petitioned Cecil and Elizabeth for Prestall's pardon, undertaking Prestall would keep his alchemical promises. Pembroke claimed to be motivated by Prestall's 'great offer' to restore Pembroke's declining health through alchemy, but Cecil knew better. Prestall's pardon of 6 January 1567 for treason, conspiracy and 'all conjurations of evil spirits', Cecil drily noted, represented the Queen's New Year's gift to Pembroke after 'Prestall's offers by Ar[migall] Wade to convert silver into gold'. By that time, de Lannoy's refusal or inability to keep his agreement with Elizabeth made Prestall seem a plausible alternative.[48] Dee evidently felt unable to compete with Prestall in making gold, for he responded to Pembroke's patronage of his bitter rival by once again addressing his *Monas* to Maximilian II.

By 27 January 1567, within weeks of Prestall's release, Dee had translated the 1564 *Monas* into German, including the long dedication to the now Emperor Maximilian. Dee intended this previously unknown manuscript as a presentation copy, since the book was written out in a careful German hand. Its current location in Heidelberg suggests that Dee sent the manuscript to the Emperor, though there is no record of any response.[49]

Later in 1567 Dee therefore revised his *Propaedeumata aphoristica*, exploiting the current vogue for alchemy by inserting key alchemical ideas from his *Monas* into *Propaedeumata*, which had focused on the measurement of occult rays. His additions included an example of kabbalistic *notarikon* from Pantheus's *Voarchadumia*, which he claimed would be understood by 'pyrologians', or alchemists.[50] He also added a discussion of talismans and of how catoptrics, the science of mirrors, could concentrate the 'hidden virtues of things' to advance alchemy. He referred to his *Monas* to explain all the alchemical symbols enclosed in the Monad.[51] He also re-emphasised the correspondences between supercelestial, celestial and terrestrial events. He cited Biblical numerology to sanction the sevenfold purgations and compoundings by which the 'Holy Art' made the philosopher's stone, explaining the added hint about prolonging human life.[52] Altogether the revised *Propaedeumata* shows how the alchemical focus of Dee's *Monas* had increased his belief in the celestial influences.

Dee hoped that the revised book would secure him patronage by addressing the current Court fascination with alchemy. It appeared on 9 January 1568, and the next day Dee hurried to present the first copy to Cecil. Again his timing was off, since the de Lannoy fiasco had temporarily dampened Elizabeth's interest in alchemy and 'Voarchadumia'. So Cecil cleverly suggested that Pembroke should present a copy to the Queen. Three days later Pembroke assured Dee that Elizabeth had liked the book. Yet she was in no mood to reward his efforts, and he had to make do with £20 from Pembroke.[53]

The revised book did, however, bring Dee to Elizabeth's notice again, and late in February they had 'very gracious talk' in the Privy Chamber at Westminster. This exceptional access also seems connected with alchemy. Dee's European travels had acquainted him with Nicolaus Nicolai Grudius, former secretary to Charles V, who now administered the Order of the Golden Fleece, a symbol laden with Habsburg alchemical resonances. According to Dee, his conversation with Elizabeth concerned 'the great secret for my sake to be disclosed unto her Majesty' by Grudius.

Undoubtedly this unexplained 'secret' concerned alchemy. Yet 'God best knoweth', complained Dee, what caused the whole scheme to fall through. In fact, Grudius was in deep financial trouble, and like de Lannoy probably saw Elizabeth's money as his solution. However, badly burnt by de Lannoy, Elizabeth issued no invitation. Later that year Grudius fled to Venice to escape his creditors, leaving the finances of the Order in chaos.[54] Dee's attempts at securing patronage for his intellectual version of alchemy never quite succeeded, though he would persist, even when the greatest political crisis of the reign soon revived slanders against him.

CHAPTER 8

War Amongst the Alchemists

In FEBRUARY 1570 Dee complained in his 'Mathematical Preface' about Vincent Murphyn's intensifying slanders. This reflects Dee's involvement with high politics in the previous year. When Mary Queen of Scots escaped to England in June 1568, she further destabilised a Court already worried by Elizabeth's reluctance to marry and by the threat of an uncertain succession. Cecil still schemed to exclude Mary, but Thomas Howard, 4th Duke of Norfolk, imagined he could solve Britain's dynastic problems by marrying her, expecting that their children would rule the united British Isles.[1]

By February 1569 an aristocratic group supporting Norfolk, including Leicester, and under his influence Pembroke, appeared ready to press this solution, which would break what they considered Cecil's monopoly over Elizabeth's counsels. Elizabeth, appreciating that such a marriage threatened her authority and survival, faced down Cecil's opponents. The immediate crisis passed. Yet in that turbulent summer of 1569 Mary's supporters, the Earls of Northumberland and Westmoreland, began gathering their followers.[2] Prestall became caught in the middle, just like Pembroke, the patron he shared with Dee, though it seems unlikely that Pembroke ordered Prestall to help the rebels.[3] Official propaganda later accused him of practising a 'great treason with certain persons', suggesting he joined Mary's English Catholic partisans in madcap plans to seize the

Tower and overthrow Elizabeth.[4] However, with the rising tension over the succession, Prestall's abilities in divining the future again came into play. He seems to have made yet more predictions about Elizabeth's imminent death, which were quickly taken up in political prophecies designed to encourage the rebels. Years later, William Camden, one of the few to mention Prestall in print, explained that in response loyal courtiers began the glittering Accession Day Tilts on 17 November 1570, to defy the 'light-believing Papists' who swallowed the illusory predictions of 'Wizards' such as Prestall. Under pressure, in late 1569 Prestall again had to flee abroad just ahead of Cecil's agents, this time to Scotland.[5]

However, he left behind many who believed in his prophecies. In September 1569 Lord Wentworth, the Privy Council's eye on the Duke of Norfolk at his power base around Norwich, informed Cecil that Richard Cavendish, Leicester's go-between to Mary, had been spreading rumours that 'it is concluded by Astronomy that the Scottish Damsel shall be Queen, and the Duke the Husband'.[6] After Elizabeth disgraced Norfolk in 1571, Cecil's investigators pursued this line with the Duke and his intimate servants. They asked whether Norfolk's servants had heard of Englishmen 'who travailed by Astronomy, or Art Magic . . . to understand what should become of the Scottish Queen, of her marriage, or of the Person that should succeed the Queen's Majesty that now is'. The answers prompted the Privy Council to ask Norfolk himself 'What Prophecy or Writing have you seen', that '*The moon [Mary] shall be exalted and the Lion [Elizabeth] cast down?*' Though Norfolk dismissed 'foolish Prophecies', he admitted he had seen 'above sixty' of them.[7] This blizzard of political prophecies, connecting Norfolk with the Earls of Northumberland and Westmoreland's Northern Rebellion of November 1569, continued to worry senior royal servants. Investigators questioned one of the diehard rebels, seeking to learn 'What Books of Prophecies hath he seen touching the late Rebellion, and the Duke's Imprisonment?'[8]

In Scotland, Prestall obtained protection from Lord Maxwell, Mary's devoted supporter and a key figure behind the Northern Rebellion. Cecil considered Prestall enough of a threat to contemplate a cross-border raid to seize him. However, Prestall ingratiated himself by coining alchemical gold and silver, not only buying Maxwell's protection but that of Maxwell's enemy the Regent, the Earl of Moray, normally Cecil's ally against Mary.[9] Northumberland and Westmoreland's disorganised rebellion quickly collapsed, sending them with many of their Catholic supporters across the border to join Prestall. All were condemned in their absence in early 1570, and the following June, threatened by repeated English raids across the border against Maxwell, Prestall fled with other rebel leaders to Spanish-controlled Antwerp.[10] Dee's role in forcing Prestall into another embittered exile remains murky. He could have informed Norfolk about Prestall's plots through Pembroke and especially Edward Dyer, who corresponded with Norfolk during the latter's imprisonment in the Tower in 1569.[11] Norfolk tried to buy himself some goodwill with Elizabeth by revealing Prestall's designs. Dyer remained Dee's most important knowledge broker to the Court for the next thirty years.[12]

Vincent Murphyn seemingly blamed Dee, perhaps again hoping to deflect attention from Prestall. George Ferrers, who had accused Dee of sorcery in 1555, remained an active partisan of Mary in 1569, suggesting another possible reason for Murphyn to redouble his verbal slanders against Dee.[13] He used the line favoured by later Catholic propaganda. Alleged plots against Elizabeth had been invented by Cecil and Leicester, the real 'conjurators' or plotters, whose 'conjuration' bewitched the Queen by 'sorcery', so that even she, 'of so rare wisdom, for a woman', failed to penetrate their self-interested policies.[14] Similarly, barely six months after Prestall fled, Dee's 'Mathematical Preface' complained how 'the Common peevish Prattler' and 'malicious scorner', Murphyn, forged slanders 'by Word and print' that Dee was 'A dangerous Member in the Common Wealth: and no member of the Church of Christ' but followed the Devil.[15]

Unfortunately for Dee, the death in prison of his former friend and patron Edmund Bonner on 5 September 1569 revived memories of the Marian persecution right in the middle of the crisis. An immediate wave of publications excoriated Bonner's bloody cruelty. For a while he became a stock monster on the popular stage.[16] Murphyn was riding this wave for all he was worth. Foxe's 1570 *Acts and Monuments* not only retained Philpot's contemptuous dismissal of Dee's theological learning but included a new marginal comment that 'M[aster] Dee slippeth away', emphasising his learning in 'other things'.[17] Although Foxe retained Green's mention of Dee's friendly treatment, he still included amongst Philpot's pastoral letters the contradictory view of 'Doctor Dee the great conjuror' in Murphyn's forged anonymous letter.[18] If memories of Dee's actions under Mary had ever faded, this republication brought them to the attention of a new generation of Protestants and explains Dee's vehement self-defence in the 1577 *Memorials*.

Dee's search for patronage through his occult philosophy also became more complicated. Prestall remained in exile, plotting to assassinate Cecil and Elizabeth by magic, trying to persuade the Spanish to invade England, or selling out his fellow exiles to curry favour with Cecil.[19] Pembroke died in March 1570, leaving Dee without an obvious patron. His indirect response again places some well known features of Elizabethan Court culture in a new light.

About 1570 the courtier-explorer Humphrey Gilbert proposed the 'Erection of an Academy in London for education of her Majesty's wards and other the youth of nobility and gentlemen'. Besides the traditional rhetorical and physical exercises, the teaching of humanities and letters, Gilbert proposed practical training for future Crown servants. These included applying arithmetic and geometry to fortification and gunnery, cosmography and astronomy, 'the art of Navigation', and the 'rules of proportion and necessary perspective and mensuration' for drawing maps and charts. Dee had taught all of these and more to students at Mortlake since 1566 and had advocated their use in his 'Mathematical Preface' to Euclid's *Elements of Geometry* in February 1570, which helped to advertise his teaching. The connection between Gilbert's suggestions and Dee's advocacy has not been noticed before. Such parallels might be expected, since Dee advised Gilbert on his scheme for exploring the North-West Passage to Cathay in 1567, and they remained close.[20]

Moreover, Gilbert proposed staffing his 'Academy' with a natural philosopher and physician, two of Dee's many roles. They would teach alchemy, and Gilbert may have been trying to create a job for Dee. Gilbert's confidence that training in alchemy would prepare the next generation of England's leaders seems so alien to the modern world that historians have ignored it, but Gilbert was part of a large network of nobility and gentry who avidly pursued the philosopher's stone. He therefore expected a positive response from the alchemical devotee Cecil, who just happened to be Master of the Queen's Wards, to the idea that, like Elizabeth, they would 'by the fire and otherwise . . . search and try out the secrets of nature'. The alchemical teachers would write annual reports on 'their proofs and trials', 'without Equivocations or Enigmatical phrases'. Most importantly, they would record both successes and failures, to enlighten others about 'both the way of their working and the event thereof, the better to follow the good and avoid the evil'. This important step towards a scientific method would 'bring great things to light if in Alchomistery there be any such things hidden'. Gilbert fully expected the adepts to transmute metals into gold.[21]

Gilbert's alchemical reporting exactly parallels one of Dee's few surviving alchemical notebooks, for July to October 1581. Dee's notes reflect the mathematical element in his alchemical thinking, buried under the cosmic allusions of the *Monas*. He later complained to Landgrave Moritz of Hessen-Kassel that 'Mathematical studies are certain' and follow 'a plausible method', but that vulgar alchemical studies require us to grasp 'enigmas and metaphors'. His alchemical diary therefore records precise quantities and avoids enigmatic, metaphorical descriptions of substances. It thus marks Dee's belated recognition of the Court's utilitarian requirements. He plainly named and quantified his materials, the dates and times of putting them to the furnace to assess the astrological influences upon them, their changes in appearance, and his procedures. Just as the 'Academy' proposals required, Dee reported both successful and unsuccessful experiments, and attempted to explain his failures.[22]

Projected annual running costs of £3,000 meant Gilbert's 'Academy' remained another paper gathering dust in Cecil's bulging files. However, it indicates the Court's general acceptance of alchemy. The 'Academy' would have enabled Dee to expand his practical alchemy further at Mortlake, which required three alchemical laboratories by 1583. The 'Academy' would also have provided Dee with the institutional independence from patronage that he would seek at St Cross College, Winchester, in the 1590s, where his 'works Philosophical' under Elizabeth's protection would attract 'special men' from all over Europe.[23]

The year after Gilbert's proposal, Dee undertook alchemical work for Henry and Mary Sidney. His connection with the Sidney clan had possibly begun at Gravesend. Henry had discussed alchemy at length with Cornelius de Lannoy in November 1565, when Sidney's finances were more than usually chaotic.[24] Twenty years later Dee still kept Mary (Dudley) Sidney's 'many letters' from 1571 'inviting me to Court'. Mary gave Elizabeth a pelican jewel in 1573, and her alchemical experiments, assisted by Adrian Gilbert, Humphrey's brother, were common knowledge. Adrian became notorious as 'a great chemist, and a man of excellent parts', though 'very sarcastic, and the greatest buffoon in the nation'. Adrian later assisted Mary's daughter, Mary Sidney Herbert, Countess of Pembroke, with her alchemy. Her brother Philip Sidney studied alchemy alongside Edward Dyer under Dee.[25] That did not prevent Philip from privately sneering at Dee's belief in his hieroglyphic monad.[26]

Until 1573 the Sidneys controlled extensive ironworks in the Weald and Wales. Dee had amassed a complete modern library on ironworking.[27] Like Pembroke, Cecil and Leicester, Henry Sidney held shares in the Mines Royal, from which Dee later leased mines.[28] However, in late March 1571 Henry returned to Court from Ireland facing political and financial ruin from his failure as Lord Deputy. He had won the position by offering to subcontract the government of Ireland on the cheap. Unfortunately, his strategic and political blunders provoked rebellion, which the Crown only suppressed at staggering expense, devastating Sidney's fortunes. Mary Dudley Sidney had already complained of poverty and debt, and in May 1572 Henry felt too poor to accept Elizabeth's offer of a peerage.[29] Mary's several letters to Dee, now lost, probably discussed her hopes of restoring her family's financial and political fortunes by alchemy.

However, as de Lannoy had complained, English glass makers could not produce the specialised clear-glass vessels that Dee needed to observe the successive colour changes of alchemical processes. So within weeks of

Henry's return to Court, Dee left for Lorraine, guided to specialised manufacturers there by skilled workers from Lorraine recently settled in London. He returned via Paris, where on 31 May 1571 he purchased two of Guillaume Postel's books on mankind's first language.[30] Elizabeth supported the journey with a generous passport. Dee travelled with her highly regarded Chancery clerk, Thomas Powle, a venerable fifty-seven years old. They returned with cart-loads of 'purposely made vessels' of pottery, metal and glass, some intended for the Queen.

When Dee returned seriously ill, Elizabeth sent her own physicians with Mary Sidney to check on his condition and the success of his mission. By now Dee was notorious enough for rumours of his death to reach distant Worcester by June, from where a client of Leicester's begged for Dee's living of Upton-upon-Severn.[31] Twenty years later English alchemical vessels had improved, for Dee would seek appointment to St Cross partly to be close to the glasshouses of Sussex for 'my exercises in Perspective and other works Philosophical'.[32]

Dee's illness may have prevented him from performing alchemy for the Sidneys; no evidence about it survives. Nonetheless, they probably enlisted Dee's expertise, since at the time other leading courtiers were investing in what came to be called 'The Society for the New Art'. This promised great riches by performing alchemy on an industrial scale. The intrigues that surrounded the 'Society' explain Vincent Murphyn's continuing attacks on Dee as the 'Arch-Conjuror' in the 1570s. For Murphyn's circle attacked the 'Society' through the same words and methods he used against Dee. Murphyn's accusations about Dee's 'conjuring' are part of wider disputes amongst Elizabethan occult philosophers, which have been forgotten until now.

Murphyn's extraordinary allegations against Dee throughout the 1570s and 1580s reveal that he was still fighting the battles over alchemy and other occult knowledge that had swirled around the Catholic plots of the 1560s. Even the incorrigible Prestall reappears. Dee remained a target because he had developed something of a reputation amongst other alchemists. His distant relative Hugh Plat recorded Dee's recipe for a lamp oil suitable for long, gentle alchemical heating, and alchemists passed around instructions for 'Mr John Dee his black lute most excellent', a cement to join alchemical vessels.[33] Furthermore, during the 1570s the whole issue of transmutation became central to Court gossip because about April 1571, as Dee prepared to depart for Lorraine, William Medley initiated a venture to transmute iron into copper that attracted several of Dee's Court patrons and connections – including Elizabeth, Cecil (newly made Lord Burghley), Leicester, Sir Thomas Smith and Sir Humphrey Gilbert, and eventually the Sidneys, Edward Dyer and Sir Francis Walsingham.

Part of the reason the modern world believes that Elizabeth's Court had little time for alchemy is that in 1698 the Enlightenment historian John Strype dismissed Medley's irrational enthusiasm and broke off his story in 1576, with Medley allegedly languishing in prison for debt, a caricature of the con-artist outsider exploiting gullible courtiers.[34] In fact, both Medley and his short-cut method were legitimate. Chemically, his process worked. He proposed making copper – valued for industrial uses, coinage and ordnance, but also an important stage towards the Great Work – by dissolving copper ores in boiling sulphuric acid to make copper sulphate, then throwing in iron to condense the copper from solution by cementation onto the iron. This technique of hydrometallurgy required lower temperatures than smelting, and had been published in Georgius Agricola's *Of Metals* (1556). Manufacturers used it right up to the nineteenth century.[35] Medley successfully demonstrated the process to Gilbert and Smith.

Medley attracted financial backers by describing this cementation as 'transmuting of iron into copper with vitriol'. He ultimately failed to produce copper economically because the process cost so much, not because it was fraudulent.[36] Despite believing Medley's demonstration, Smith doubted sufficient cheap sulphuric acid could be produced to make the process profitable. Therefore, Medley spent many months searching for 'earths' suitable for making acid.

Nor was Medley a low-born outsider. He was a gentleman, and his distant relative, Lady Burghley, had recruited him for 'daily attendance' in Burghley's intimate service, where he was 'bred up'. He served until

Burghley's death in 1598, probably in some alchemical medical capacity, given their shared alchemical interests and Burghley's chronic ill health.[37] Even though Medley's eventual failure to make cheap copper turned Leicester against him, he retained Burghley's confidence.

The conflicting stories by Smith and Medley about what happened next agree on one thing – there was considerable courtly interest in the enterprise.[38] After initial trials that summer at Winchelsea, Medley shifted production to Canford Manor near Poole in Dorset. Having allegedly discovered how to make copper more cheaply without vitriol, he persuaded Gilbert and Smith to lease ore-bearing grounds and production facilities there from Lady Mountjoy for £300 a year.

Medley's 'alchemical' production techniques at Canford may explain Dee's surprising venture into copper mining in 1583, an episode only briefly mentioned in his 'Diary'. Like Medley, Dee possessed descriptions of transmutatory hydrometallurgy in Georgius Agricola's *On Metals* and two copies of Vanoccio Biringuccio's *Pyrotechnics*.[39] Dee also possessed Lazarus Ercker's *Mineworks* (1574), whose title page showed the occult rays emanating from JHWH, the Name of God, 'seeding' the earth with diverse metals that grew under occult stellar influences. Lazarus Ercker's book vividly described metallurgical techniques for processing these divine gifts. It described the transmutation of iron into copper in the presence of vitriol as an essential part of 'the Great Work'.[40]

Dee certainly knew how metalworkers purified their ores with acids, but he had no direct experience of mining.[41] Therefore, after leasing a Devonshire copper mine, on 10 July 1583 he hired 'Thomas Hoke of Cranford [sic]' to work with him, an identification that suggests Dee's familiarity with that remote Dorset manor. The Hoke family were native to Canford. Thomas probably had experience in working Lord Mountjoy's mines, though he departed within two weeks, perhaps unable to perform the transmutation process that chiefly interested Dee.[42]

Medley informed Burghley that since he began at Canford in September 1571 he had successfully made 'nature ripe by art', a euphemism for alchemy. He repaid his investors partly from money supplied by his friend Thomas Curtess, of whom more anon. Sir Thomas Smith and Sir

Humphrey Gilbert then revealed that Elizabeth had stayed their patent for 'The Society of the New Art', which included Burghley and Leicester but excluded Medley.[43] Unprotected by a legal monopoly, Medley therefore refused to make copper at Canford 'for fear my Lord Mountjoy [will] get knowledge of the secrets thereof', which he and his friends 'go very indirectly about'. Mountjoy was soon boiling dissolved copper ores with iron to 'transmute' the iron into copper.[44] Burghley promised to persuade Elizabeth to include Medley in the patent and tried to extend their lease from Mountjoy. When he failed, Medley left Canford and washed his hands of Gilbert, offering to join Burghley and Leicester under a new patent, promising a hundred tons of perfect copper a year.[45] Medley also curried favour with Dee's alchemical patrons, the Sidneys.[46]

Sir Thomas Smith reveals Elizabeth's close personal interest in their enterprise. He assured Medley that his inclusion in the patent had been agreed 'both by her majesty and my lords'.[47] Elizabeth implicitly trusted Medley's promises, not only taking her usual cut from the deal but proposing that after twenty years she could 'enjoy or occupy the said new art, by her self', an arrangement the investors refused.[48]

However, appointed ambassador to the French Court in late December 1571, Smith soon fumed impotently from France that Medley 'doth as Geber, Ripley and the other alchemists do, that leadeth a man from this to that and so through so many gates that at the last they come through never a one right, and in fine, find nothing'. On the other hand, Smith's alchemical learning, his many distillations and Medley's demonstration persuaded him, he assured Richard Eden, that 'that art' could produce 'most strange, wondrous and incredible things'.[49] Smith sent home part of a treatise by the medieval alchemist Raymond Lull, 'worth the weight of pure gold'. He ordered his assistant in England to follow two Lullian experiments and celebrated their success in bringing alchemical mercury and sulphur to one step before the elixir.[50] Yet when Smith returned to England in August 1572 he found Gilbert departed to the Netherlands war, Medley gone and Burghley now partnered with Leicester in a 'new society', which left him saddled with debts and rent obligations to Lady Mountjoy.[51]

We might assume this marked the end of Medley's schemes, but that would underestimate the Court's belief in his alchemical abilities. By late 1572 he had commenced working on the copper deposits at Parys Mountain, Anglesey, where in 1574 he demonstrated a new method, bankrolled by Sir Henry Sidney and Sir John Wynn of Gwydir. Medley boiled powdered 'iron' in local mineral waters emerging from copper deposits, producing 'crocus' of copper that tested about 10 per cent pure. This created a sensation, and 'part was sent to the Lo[rds] of the Council that were partners in the work, part to others of the nobility; and every gentleman of quality there present had part to carry in his pocket'. Medley even persuaded Burghley, Leicester and Walsingham to make the arduous journey to Anglesey, although doubts remained whether the process could turn a profit.[52] Emboldened by his success, in October 1574 Medley demanded funding from Burghley and Leicester for the under-taking in Anglesey, offering Sidney's testimonial and a 'plat' or design of the work.[53]

As usual when confronted with investment proposals, Burghley sought expert advice.[54] William Humphrey, Warden of the Mint, interviewed Medley, observed his procedure, and assayed his product. Humphrey initially confessed himself mystified that Medley could produce more weight of copper than the iron he started with, but soon reached a start-ling conclusion.[55] God's providence, Humphrey reported, had blessed England with Medley's 'honourable and marvelous' work. It should be secretly rewarded, while publicly left 'in discredit with the world as now it is'.[56] This suggests that some contemporary criticisms of alchemy should be taken with a large pinch of salt, because successful experiments could become a state secret. Smith now hinted that Burghley and Leicester should stump up some cash, if they expected to share the profits.[57]

Burghley and Leicester's patent dated 14 February 1575 included Medley.[58] Yet he still delayed, demanding money upfront, angering Smith because Medley's Anglesey demonstration had made the technique common knowledge, and 'My L[ord] Mountjoy hath gotten one of Mr Medleys chief workmen to him'.[59] Medley next turns up as Leicester's prisoner in the Wood Street Counter on 1 September 1576 – but not for debt as Strype assumed. In fact, rival alchemists had raised questions about Medley's loyalty, especially to Leicester. These attacks parallel the assaults on Dee in several respects. Medley's failure to meet Leicester's expectations of returns on his investment left him vulnerable to criticism from two surprising sources – his erstwhile friend Thomas Curtess and John Prestall.

Dee's rival Prestall kept bobbing up like a cork on the turbulent waters of Elizabethan politics, because his occult knowledge, plus his willingness to spy on his fellow Catholics, made him especially useful. Prestall had been indicted again in 1571 for having 'conspired, compassed and imagined the death of the Queen' by sorcery in 1570.[60] He later claimed that Philip II, who patronised alchemists, appointed him to his Council, and that he made alchemical wildfire for use against the English navy.[61] Yet despite Prestall's public threats to kill Burghley and Elizabeth by magic, he maintained a secret correspondence with the former and was allowed to return to England in late 1572.[62] Despite his treason the Privy Council released him under large bonds for good behaviour in July 1574, much to the disgust of that loyal Protestant William Harrison.[63]

Prestall denigrated Medley's loyalty and abilities in order to emphasise his own alchemical expertise. Curtess tried to distance himself from Medley's fall by turning against him. This seemed obvious to Medley's lone defender, Dee's patron and Leicester's sister, Mary Dudley Sidney, who maintained close contact with Medley. Burghley warned her off, but Lady Sidney insisted on defending Medley against 'continual malicious prosecuting' by men guilty of 'so many false and traitorous crimes to their prince, country and friends'. They had even tried 'to bring my name in with his in all these brabbles'. Evidently Prestall's gang had extended their campaign against Dee to Medley and Lady Sidney, using methods bitterly familiar to Dee since the 1560s.

For years Medley's accusers, just as they spread tales about Dee around Court, had brought Lady Sidney groundless tales about his misdemeanours against her. She believed that Curtess and Prestall's false accusations had persuaded Leicester to imprison Medley against his better judgement. They had also tried to blacken Medley's reputation with Burghley.

She reminded Burghley that while Medley dutifully submitted himself, 'his accusers be so monstrous, vile and wicked themselves, and would do others, and his betters, no less hurt if they could'.[64] Prestall's accusations against Medley entailed forged letters, the same method that Vincent Murphyn had used against Dee. Leicester received a letter apparently signed by Thomas Wotton, one of his Devonshire clients and Medley's cousin, accusing Medley of infamous but unspecified words and deeds. Leicester sensibly checked with Wotton, who protested that he had not written the letter and could not imagine Medley doing things that 'I have a long time much disliked'.[65] We shall see how Dee eventually turned the tables on Murphyn and Prestall and helped Medley's rehabilitation.

Medley's copper transmutation enterprise dissolved not because investors doubted his industrial alchemy but because in 1581 Joachim Gans, an experienced German industrial alchemist, began producing cheaper copper at the Mines Royal in Cumberland. His method resembled Agricola's and Medley's, whereby powdered 'right Iron ore, being by roasting, brought into the perfection of Iron, is by the water and strength of vitriol converted into copper'.[66] The subsequent improvement in investment returns from the Mines Royal, thanks to what everyone believed was an alchemical process, removed the incentive to invest in Medley's schemes.

Yet Medley remained Burghley's trusted servant, in close attendance on his lord.[67] Through Burghley's patronage Medley would acquire rich leases in the vacant diocese of Ely.[68] He became the Queen's surveyor there by 1590 and ultimately Keeper of the imprisoned Catholic priests at Wisbech Castle.[69] Medley's imprisonment in 1576 demonstrates the importance for Dee and other occult philosophers of meeting their patrons' expectations. Failure to do so left them vulnerable to the backbiting of courtly politics and jealous rivals. Success gave them leverage against those rivals. We can see this process most clearly in the dramatic revisions made to Foxe's account of Dee in the 1576 edition of *Acts and Monuments*. Foxe essentially abandoned Murphyn's attacks on the 'Arch-Conjuror' and accepted Dee's version of events. He did so because at that date Dee was gaining kudos by writing advice about the British Empire that suited Leicester's political agenda.

CHAPTER 9

Recovering the Lost Empire

JOHN DEE's reputation for inventing the concept of an American 'British Empire' is only part of the story. He did coin the term, which to him meant the restored Empire of Arthur, King of the Britons. However, to uncover the full story we must set Dee's writings about an Atlantic 'British Empire' in the context of Elizabethan Court politics and contemporary European events.[1] That context enables Dee's *General and Rare Memorials Pertaining to the Perfect Art of Navigation* (1577) and his manuscripts, 'On the Limits of the British Empire' and 'Of Famous and Rich Discoveries', to shed new light on the Elizabethan Court and Dee's contemporary world. For those writings were actually advice aimed at Elizabeth and her Privy Councillors on how to deal with a domestic and international crisis in the 1570s and 1580s, which would determine English history for centuries to come.

Those intervening centuries have persuaded the modern world to associate the British Empire with the spread of forward-looking Protestantism, first through American discovery and colonisation, and then throughout the globe.[2] There was, however, nothing very Protestant about Dee, or his 'British Empire', which looked back to the ancient past. He used civil-law arguments to reassert Elizabeth's sovereignty in America, because he believed that Arthur's colonies still existed there. However, influential Protestant courtiers found far more interesting Dee's coherent arguments for Elizabeth's rights to recover Arthur's lost British Empire in Europe. Putting Dee's 'imperial' writings into their proper historical context also shows that they emerged less from legal and political theories than from his fascination with occult philosophy. Nor did Dee's 'imperial' writings have much to do with Martin Frobisher's contemporary search for the North-West Passage in 1576–8.[3] Neither the Queen nor her Privy Councillors respected theoretical limits when Frobisher's discoveries suddenly required flexibility in making actual policy.

We can observe Dee's mind working through theories of empire in his copy of Ferdinand Columbus's *History of the Life and Deeds of the Admiral Christopher Columbus* (1571). As so often, Dee turned the book into an organiser for his own ideas, busily jotting notes and comments in the margin.[4] He confuted Ferdinand's claims for Spain's sovereignty over America, based on his father Christopher's discoveries, legal arguments and ceremonies 'establishing' possession. Dee denied Columbus's priority. In Ferdinand's descriptions of Indian customs and languages Dee found support for his pet theory that the Welsh prince Madoc ap Owen Gwynedd had discovered America in 1170. Moreover, Welsh-speaking Indians confirmed his descendant Elizabeth's prior claims. Madoc featured prominently in Dee's own genealogy.[5] Dee also denied the Pope's authority to grant the New World to Castile.[6]

Dee read Ferdinand Columbus alongside Giovanni Battista Ramusio's great collection of *Navigations and Voyages* in 1577–8, the very time of Frobisher's second and third voyages. Allegedly searching for the North-West Passage, these voyages really sought American gold.[7] Dee's marginalia reveal that he read Ramusio to discover the rights and rites of possession in new-found lands.[8] Dee's interest in 'the customs of acquiring dominion' stemmed from his obsessive search for traces of Madoc hidden within Spanish descriptions of America.[9] For, since '1. Discovery 2. Conquest 3. Quiet possession', as Dee summarised it, conveyed sovereignty, Madoc had bequeathed his descendant Elizabeth the Caribbean and Mexico.[10] The Pope, Dee scribbled angrily in the margins of Ramusio's book, had no intrinsic authority to award America to Spain, for he 'was chosen arbiter: he could not make himself so'. Therefore, 'If the ancient title were good', then England did not need the Pope's licence. 'But', he concluded with a flourish, 'that is nought and ours more certain, therefore our Title is more truth than the King of Spain his title', whichever way the Pope claimed to divide the world.[11]

Dee's patriotic conclusion supported his other marginalia in Ramusio's publication about the North-West Passage to Cathay.[12] He heavily marked evidence of the Indians' cultivation of fertile soils and European level of civilisation. Dee found most exciting reports of 'white men arrayed with cloth as in France'. These confirmed his belief that Arthurian colonies still survived along the North-West Passage, confirming Elizabeth's inherited rights over that gateway to the fabulous East. In early 1578 he used these pages in 'Limits of the British Empire'.[13]

Yet Dee was not writing simply to promote Frobisher's voyages.[14] Nor was he merely applying his Louvain education, using civil-law definitions of imperial 'Dominion' to place new English discoveries under Elizabeth's absolute prerogative.[15] Those were not sufficient reasons for important politicians and courtiers, such as Edward Dyer, Leicester, Sir Humphrey Gilbert, Sir Christopher Hatton, Sir Philip Sidney and Sir Francis Walsingham to see to it that Dee obtained audiences with Elizabeth, merely to persuade her to grant Letters Patent empowering Frobisher to settle territory in America.[16] Elizabeth did not depend solely on Dee's legal expertise. If the Queen needed advice about civil law she could turn to experienced civil lawyers on her Privy Council, such as Walsingham and Thomas Wilson. Nor did Tudor concepts of 'empire' depend solely on Dee's writings. Elizabeth believed her Atlantic sovereignty rested on her Crown's inherent prerogative.

Philip and Mary had asserted as much in Letters Patent of 1555, granting the Muscovy Company the power to 'subdue, possess and occupy' and 'get the Dominion' over all lands 'of infidelity'. These privileges, confirmed by Parliament in 1566, covered all northern seas. Richard Hakluyt printed both texts in his *Principal Navigations* (1589). Contemporaries believed long before Dee wrote that the Crown's imperial power and the authority of statute law controlled overseas trade and new-found lands. Dee knew this through his close connections with the

Muscovy Company. When he petitioned in 1583 to monopolise the North-West Passage, under the Muscovy Company's patent, he expected to make laws there modelled on 'the religion and laws of this realm'.[17]

Dee's audiences with the Queen discussed more than her Atlantic imperial titles. At Windsor in late November 1577 Dee declared Elizabeth's 'title to Groecland [believed west of Greenland], Estotiland, Friseland'.[18] This had no connection to Frobisher's Letters Patent, issued six months later,[19] because Dee went to Windsor primarily to reassure 'men of no small account' that, despite their fears, the great comet of November 1577 would not harm the Queen. His drawing of the comet still streams across the top of this page in his manuscript 'Diary'. His reference to Elizabeth's Atlantic titles seems to have been added later. He recalled in 1592 that, after three days closeted with him, Elizabeth promised to defend him against attacks on 'any my rare studies and Philosophical exercises'. This clearly refers to his magical and alchemical practices. Dee's astrological expertise, not his civil-law training, persuaded influential courtiers to rush him into an audience with Elizabeth. His alchemical 'exercises' shared with the Queen also remind us that, like other occult writers, Dee's 'imperial' treatises addressed more than they appeared to on the surface. Dee believed, for example, that the philosopher's stone would recreate Elizabeth's empire.[20]

The Elizabethan 'state' did not decide on a single policy and then co-opt Dee to justify it intellectually. Policy emerged through vigorous debates among Elizabeth's Privy Councillors, and between them and the Queen, which required courtiers and politicians to draw upon accumulated wisdom both in and outside the Court. Leading Privy Councillors daily consulted intellectuals and men of practical experience, using their expertise to shape detailed policy in response to events.[21] This process had stimulated Dee's earlier writings on British 'empire' and economic development. In 1566, at the request of the knowledge-broker Edward Dyer, he wrote 'Atlantical Discourses'. Just then Humphrey Gilbert and Anthony Jenkinson were seeking backers for voyages to Cathay via the North Atlantic, while the Muscovy Company was asking Parliament to confirm its exploration monopoly.[22] In 1570 at Dyer's request Dee rewrote his 1565 outline of 'commonwealth' reforms, 'A Synopsis of the British Republic'.[23]

Nor did Dee's advice follow modern understandings of political calculation. When a supernova appeared in the constellation Cassiopeia in 1572, Dee told Edward Dyer that it might 'signify the finding of some great Treasure or the philosophers stone', a prediction he felt confirmed by Frobisher's apparent discovery of gold in 1576.[24] We need to remember such occult connections when assessing Dee's ideas about empire. Intellectuals could also submit uninvited papers on current events to the policy-making process, as when Dee dedicated the 1576 manuscript of 'Memorials' to Dyer. However, the influence these 'devices' had on actual policies depended on how Privy Councillors responded to events, sometimes at odds with the Queen.

The chief evidence for the case that Dee wrote exclusively about American empire is his involvement in the Frobisher voyages. Yet the processes of Elizabethan government make it unlikely that Dee wrote 'Memorials' in August 1576 to support Frobisher's first voyage. By then Frobisher had long disappeared over the horizon. Dee wrote 'Memorials' to address more pressing current issues than a possible Arthurian empire in the north-west.[25] After Frobisher returned in October boasting about his route to China, Burghley's draft charter gave the 'Company of Cathay' a monopoly over that trade but notably failed to mention occupying American territory. Dee's belief in an Arthurian America was irrelevant to Burghley's policy.[26]

However, in early 1577 claims by alchemists to have found gold in a stone brought back by Frobisher transformed the government's agenda. Burghley's March 1577 instructions for Frobisher's second voyage now required him to fortify places for 'possessing of the Country' and its presumed gold mines.[27] The Privy Council claimed a territorial empire in America without Dee's input. In fact, his 'Memorials' dealt only tangentially with Arthur's American empire. We shall see that the powerful politicians who read 'Memorials' and persuaded Dee to rewrite it were only interested in its solutions for domestic and European problems.

Therefore, we need to reassess Dee's connection with the Frobisher voyages. Dee became increasingly involved in organising the later voyages, thanks partly to his geographical knowledge about Arthur's empire. Yet others possessed that same knowledge, and new evidence reveals other reasons behind his increasing prominence in organising the voyages. The common assumption that Dee cooperated with Frobisher and Michael Lok, the chief financial backer of the first voyage, seems based on Dee's earlier involvement with the Muscovy Company. He devised his 'Paradoxal Compass' in the 1550s for the Company's pilot William Borough, who drafted the two 'round charts' listed amongst Frobisher's navigation equipment.[28] However, Lok and a dissident group of Muscovy merchants were using political connections to circumvent their own Company's statutory monopoly over northern exploration.[29] Lok teamed up with Frobisher in early 1574, but by Lok's account Dee learnt of their plans only sixteen days before Frobisher sailed in June 1576.[30]

Dee tried to hijack the arrangements, offending Lok's possessiveness about his cherished venture. In May 1576 Sir Humphrey Gilbert had published his supportive *Discourse for a new Passage to Cathay*.[31] Lok claimed he appreciated Gilbert's support, but 'without giving any offence', he said – before doing precisely that – everything Gilbert had written was 'known to us long before'. Dee also spotted flaws in Gilbert's *Discourse*, but outlined 'another voyage of Discovery' superior to Lok and Frobisher's: 'God send them good speed'.[32] Then, tactless as ever, Dee sought out Lok to announce his '18 new and very strange Articles of Consideration'. Lok took his revenge in November 1581. By then incarcerated in the Fleet prison for huge debts run up by the voyages, he naturally blamed everyone else for the disaster. Even so, he still denied that Dee made any contribution to the first voyage, instead claiming full responsibility for his own Atlantic research.[33]

Lok's denial reminds us that the sheer bulk of Dee's surviving writings, books and manuscripts have created the false impression that he alone amongst Elizabethans knew about Atlantic geography. Lok remembered Dee breezing into his house on 20 May 1576, expecting his erudition to dominate. However, for once Dee had to listen silently while Lok 'laid before him my Books and Authors, my charts and Instruments', encompassing Christendom's knowledge of New World navigation, gathered at huge expense over twenty-five years – but now entirely lost.[34]

In 1581 Lok recalled in his freezing prison cell how he had confounded Dee. For, like Dee, he expected that Frobisher would encounter an advanced civilisation in the North-West Passage. Where Dee imagined Arthurian colonies, Lok used the same travellers' tales to prove that 'the new found lands' were as 'full of people and full of such commodities and merchandize' as Scandinavia.[35] By 1581 Lok knew enough about the barren reality of Baffin Island to have abandoned hopes of any lingering Arthurian outposts. However, his assumption in 1576 that Frobisher would establish another Muscovy trade explains the emphasis of the first voyage on trading opportunities.

Flattened by an enthusiast whose claims for the duration and cost of his researches for once matched his own, Dee bounced back by offering to teach polar navigation to Frobisher and Christopher Hall. For this, Lok recognised, 'he deserveth just commendation', though not as much as he thought. William Borough, Dee's pupil with actual experience sailing in high latitudes, had long been preparing Frobisher for his journey. In the sixteen days of frantic last-minute preparations for their first voyage, Frobisher and Hall had little leisure to grasp Dee's *'Perfect Art of Navigation'*, by which he meant practice with his 'Paradoxal Compass'. *Memorials*, showing Dee's characteristic tactlessness, printed their letter claiming that they tried to follow his instructions, but, 'for want of learning', could not understand the art.[36] A short-tempered bully who chose to be portrayed clutching a pistol, and who left his wife and children to starve while he haunted the glamorous Court, Frobisher had little interest in complex theories and sailed by traditional dead reckoning. Lok purchased the elementary English books on the sphere best suited to his extremely limited arithmetic.[37]

The most compelling evidence that Dee and Lok happily cooperated, is that Lok apparently put up £100, a full share, for Dee's investment in the gold-hunting second and third voyages.[38] Also, the Privy Council nominated Dee to a commission that would smelt the ore from the second voyage and organise the third. However, Dee only became an 'investor' after three ships returned from the second voyage in October 1577 groaning with allegedly high-grade gold ore. Before this, Dee could waste neither money nor his limited credit on such high-risk speculation, despite reports of gold from the first voyage. Lok was willing to include new venturers after the second voyage because he needed ready cash to pay off the ships.[39] However, Dee's 'investment' owed less to his abilities than to his connection to the previously unknown story behind the financing of the second and third voyages.

Lok's enthusiasm for the voyages effectively bankrupted him. By 1580 he had invested about £2,200. He was also personally liable for £2,500 owed by the 'Company of Cathay', because the 'Company' was never legally incorporated.[40] Lok borrowed much of this money on personal bills of exchange, which he claimed cost £500 in interest alone.[41] But having raised £800 for the first voyage, Lok's credit eventually ran out, especially when successive assays after the second voyage failed to find gold. He later tried to fob off his creditors by reminding them 'by whose hands I have taken up the money'. By this he meant Richard Young, another Muscovy merchant, who had known Lok since the 1560s and had invested before the second voyage.[42] Young had risen through the Customs service since the 1550s, using the Customs fees he collected to run a lucrative money-lending business, which was well established by 1577.[43] Young's excellent credit rating enabled him, after Frobisher's second voyage, to counter-sign 'many Bills of Exchange ... for the said Michael Lock amounting to £1600' and to pay the principal and interest on Lok's outstanding bonds.[44] Young effectively took over the stumbling 'Company of Cathay'.

This explains Lok's unusual generosity in paying for Dee's share, undoubtedly a condition of Young's financial support, for Dee was Young's brother-in-law.[45] Dee's involvement in the Frobisher venture dates only from the time that Young began underwriting Lok's borrowings.[46] Dee was therefore advancing his new financial self-interest in advising Elizabeth of her title to 'Meta Incognita' in his audiences of November 1577. Yet, though alchemical assays convinced Elizabeth that Frobisher's ore contained gold, the Privy Council disagreed over its value.[47] At this stage Dee remained a passive investor. His eventual appointment as a commissioner owed as much to Young's financial influence as to his own alchemical expertise.

The Privy Council added Young to the commission overseeing the smelting at Dartford on 8 January 1578. Eleven days later they added Dee, after other commissioners came up with excuses to withdraw.[48] Young and Dee sat on the commission for several years, but Young's financial resources gave him greater say over the 'Company of Cathay'.[49] In November 1578, after the third voyage, he solved another cash-flow crisis, lending the Company a staggering £400 in coin to pay off the Queen's ship, the *Aid*. In return, Young received the first fragments of gold and silver that the smelters coaxed from the ores in 1579.[50]

With 'great difficulty' Young forced Lok to guarantee his loans by mortgaging his Cheapside and Tottenham properties to him for £1,000 on 3 February 1579. Young thus secretly financed Lok's attempt to buy up all the north-west ore over the following weeks. Most other investors had given up, but Lok believed that the ores would produce sufficient gold to redeem the mortgage before it fell due in June. However, when the ores proved worthless, Lok defaulted. Young claimed the properties in July, provoking an epic legal battle that rumbled on until Lok died in early 1621.[51]

Therefore, Dee's apparent prominence in the Frobisher voyages only reflected Young's financial clout. This underlines the fact that Dee's 'imperial' writings were not simply concerned with American exploration. The real purpose of Dee's 'imperial' writings – applying his magic to advance the 'Protestant cause' during the central crisis of Elizabeth's reign, the Netherlands Revolt – opens new vistas onto that European political crisis, to which we now turn.

CHAPTER 10

'More is hid, than uttered': The Philosopher's Stone and Empire

From about 1576 to 1583, Dee's occult philosophy became entangled with the politics of the Elizabethan Court as it struggled with a European crisis. Two significant features of that Court explain why. The first characteristic all Renaissance courts shared with modern politics. Courtiers inhabited a political hall of mirrors, officially reflecting their sovereign's dazzling light, but more often enabling politicians to present their rivals in unflattering postures, by exposing their activities from unexpected angles. What we now see as discrete events resulting from various causes, courtiers could weave together for ideological ends, presenting them to the monarch as evidence of a coherent threat. Dee would feel the force of this distortion.

In England's particular religious and strategic crisis during these years, this general political 'spin' interacted with a feature specific to the Elizabethan Court. The line of ideological difference ran not between Leicester and Burghley but between outright Protestant Privy Councillors and a far more conservative Queen. Burghley struggled to convince a reluctant Elizabeth of the reality of an international popish plot, which since the first moments of her reign had tried to subvert true religion and her people's obedience, kill her and place Mary Queen of Scots on her throne. The papists knew, Burghley insisted, that they must destroy her to succeed in their determined assault on the 'Protestant cause'.

On the other side, conservatives emphasised that tolerating what they stigmatised as 'puritan' disobedience to the Church established in 1559 would subvert due order and usher in 'popular' or 'anabaptist' government. Anti-Catholicism and anti-Puritanism, like modern 'wedge-issues', therefore enabled courtiers to 'spin' events in ways targeted at the Queen's anxieties and prejudices. At moments of delicate balance, contingent events could therefore disproportionately influence her decisions. Even Dee understood this. Coming across Fernandez de Oviedo's bitter reflection on the 'problem of counsel' in his *General and Natural History of the Indies* during these years, Dee wrote in the margin 'NOTE: Either Truth is kept from Princes or They will not believe it, being told'.[1]

This did not just affect the Queen's notoriously fickle policy decisions but also affected the man to whom Dee dedicated his *Memorials*, Christopher Hatton, who at that very moment in 1576–7 was making his delicate transition from handsome favourite to trusted counsellor. Hatton knew his best course lay in tracking closely to Elizabeth's twists and turns, but more outspokenly Protestant advisers could apply the anti-Catholic 'wedge' to force him away from his conservative instincts. It affected Dee, not only determining his access to Elizabeth at crucial moments for the 'Protestant cause' but also what he wrote: when politicians 'spun' events to suit their ideological agendas, the intellectuals they co-opted had to 'spin' their writings to follow suit.

Therefore, Dee's imperial writings contained hidden messages. Like the courtiers for whom he wrote, their surface appearances often concealed underlying purposes. One of Dee's drawings for the highly symbolic title page of *Memorials* claimed that 'more is hid, than uttered', an acknowledgement phrased in discreet Latin in the printed version.[2] To unearth the hidden messages of his 'imperial' writings we should read them as one collective text, since Dee constantly reiterated earlier ideas in later works. Broadly speaking, his writings show increasing interest in Arthur's European conquests. Their apparent concern with American empire conceals Dee's deeper interest in recovering Britain's empire in mainland Europe, in the unusual circumstances of the late 1570s, 'Wherof *in this place*, or of the foresaid means, how to bring this royal purpose to pass farther discourse is not to be holden'.[3]

Dee's hidden agenda emerges when we listen closely to his stated intentions for, and descriptions of, his writings. Finding that agenda restores their connection with Dee's practice of magic. This context, perhaps surprising for the modern reader, actually explains his perspective on Elizabeth's ecumenical empire. Far from marginalising Dee from the Elizabethan Court, his reputation as a 'magus' along with his 'philosophical' knowledge and practices helped to shape his imperial vision. In the right circumstances they made him more useful to politicians seeking to advance the 'Protestant cause'.[4] Yet when conservatives pushed back with their own 'spin' on affairs, he was cut out of policymaking.

We can begin recovering Dee's wider imperial vision by tracing the connections between his writings, which Dee collectively entitled 'The British Monarchy'. 'Limits of the British Empire' reveals Dee's magical imperial perspective, because that manuscript, written only for Elizabeth and her Privy Councillors, could openly discuss the hidden meanings of *Memorials* and 'Discoveries', which carefully screened Dee's magical ideas from a wider public. In 'Limits of the British Empire', Dee revealed to the inner circle that lately he had been 'strangely, and vehemently stirred up' by the Holy Trinity and 'ordered, to pen divers advices, and Treatises, in the English Language', that is, *Memorials* and 'Discoveries'. Only if Queen and Privy Council permitted would her 'British subjects' understand and 'practise' those works, because in *Memorials* 'the method ... covertly proceedeth (occasion so served)', though most could be understood 'vulgarly'. This confirmed Dee's warning about *Memorials* that 'more is hid, than uttered'. *Memorials* in turn warned that 'in the Secret Centre' of 'Discoveries' there 'is more bestowed, and stored up than I may, or *(in this place)* will express'.[5]

So both *Memorials* and 'Discoveries' hid meanings accessible only to the elite, from which 'many more [meanings] may consequently be thought upon, and inferred'. Such hidden meanings explain why, although it was printed in fifty copies by September 1577, Elizabeth commanded Dee not to distribute *Memorials*, which in August 1578 was 'yet stayed in my hands'. In return for his occult advice, Dee required free access throughout Elizabeth's dominions under her 'protection absolute' to perform mysterious future services for the 'British Empire'. These would follow not human policy but 'the Almighty his will and direction'. They recall Dee's offer to Burghley in 1574 to find buried treasure by spiritual means. Dee's advice directed by God would recover Elizabeth's northern and western British Empire and, more intriguingly, the 'homage and arrearages' of 'your Easterly and Southerly disdainful Vassals and Tributaries' – because Dee's advice also pertained to areas '*besides* that portion of the world', meaning besides America.[6]

These mysterious allusions point to the hidden meanings of *Memorials* and 'Discoveries'. For, amongst the writers verifying Arthur's empire, Dee considered 'none, of greater name and crediting than Johannes Trithemius', in his book *On the Seven Planetary Intelligences*.[7] 'Discoveries' also made that book, 'so great, as lightly it can not of any man be rejected', central to proving Arthur's empire over thirty kingdoms.[8] Dee's respect for Trithemius suggests why he felt 'strangely stirred up' by the Trinity to write about the magical restoration of the British Empire 'Easterly and Southerly', on mainland Europe.

Trithemius had long been notorious for the invocation of demonic spirits. In 1563 Dee had excitedly promised Cecil a copy of Trithemius's 'Steganographia', which superficially taught methods of conjuring angels for communicating messages. Those rituals Trithemius drew from the medieval conjuring tradition attributed to Solomon, Peter of Abano and Honorius of Thebes. Dee possessed Honorius's *Sworn Book* detailing the elaborate preparations, in a manuscript later owned by the playwright Ben Jonson, who lampooned Dee and his 'scryer' Edward Kelley in *The Alchemist*.[9] Agrippa continued the tradition, and the angels later instructed Dee and Kelley to use Honorius's design of the *Seal Aemeth*, which became the centre of their angelic rituals.[10]

Dee's emphasis on Trithemius is striking evidence of his perspective on empire. He may have been signalling to courtiers familiar with angelic magic that they should perceive Arthur's empire within a magical, cosmic religious framework. Trithemius's book did not discuss Arthur's history or address questions of empire; rather it described how the angelic spirits governing the seven planets controlled history. Each angel ruled successive periods of 354 years and four months, giving each epoch distinctive characteristics, including Arthur's empire. The cataclysmic political and religious changes that marked each new period formed steps towards the Second Coming of Christ, the Eschaton.

Dee accepted Trithemius's scheme so wholeheartedly that he recalculated his periods. Unlike Trithemius he believed that Anael, the angel of Venus, governed the remarkable concentration of female rulers in mid-sixteenth-century Europe. The November 1572 supernova, which his calculations placed within the sphere of Venus, increased that angel's influence. God was signalling through the new star, he told his Court connection Edward Dyer, that a decaying world would be restored by angelic magic and by the discovery of the philosopher's stone.[11] Therefore, he dated *Memorials* to the year of the world 5540, 'The Fifth Year, of the Star Sent from Heaven and Returning Directly There'.[12]

Like his dedication of his *Monas* to Maximilian II, Dee's belief in Arthur's empire shows that, together with his ecumenical generation of European intellectuals, he believed in the centuries-old vision of a reformed world, unified politically and religiously under a Last World Emperor.[13] Dee saw Arthur as part of his search 'for the pure verity, understanding, and recovering of divers secret, ancient, and weighty matters' of universal knowledge. His first Arthurian studies at Louvain with Gerard Mercator and Gemma Frisius, sometime cosmographer to the Emperor Charles V, had introduced him to Habsburg court culture at nearby Brussels, where Charles celebrated Arthur as the model for a Habsburg Last World Emperor.[14]

For centuries, the default position in English foreign policy had been to maintain good relations with whoever controlled the Netherlands, the primary outlet for England's most important export trade, woollen cloth. Until the 1570s, that meant good relations with the Habsburgs. However, the Netherlands Revolt beginning in the mid-1560s caused a watershed change in Elizabethan policy, to an effectively anti-Habsburg position. This persuaded devotees of the 'Protestant cause' that Elizabeth should become a Protestant Last World Emperor. The 'learneder sort' now applied the ancient prophecies to her. After the collapse of Spanish control in the Netherlands in late 1575, some Privy Councillors encouraged her to accept the proffered sovereignty of Holland and Zealand.[15] One enthusiast believed she would thus become 'sovereign of the sea', able to advance Christ's Kingdom and resolve religious differences 'in all Christendom'. Importantly, this would advance 'the exploits towards the coast of the Indians', thanks to Dutch information about the northern passages.[16] The States-General of Holland and Zealand offered her election as Countess through her descent from Philippa of Hainault, but Leicester's followers broadened this into claims to the whole Netherlands.[17] They tried to persuade the House of Commons to petition Elizabeth to accept Dutch sovereignty in early 1576. Hatton blocked their efforts, demonstrating his new political importance as a potential conservative leader.[18]

In 1576 even Elizabeth imagined herself bringing peace to the whole of Christendom.[19] Dee's associate in magical learning, James Sandford, another Leicester client, that year dedicated a book to Hatton which gave Elizabeth the cosmic apocalyptic role previously reserved for the Habsburgs. Plagiarising Cyprian Leowitz's predictions that the great 1583 conjunction of Saturn and Jupiter would bring abrupt imperial changes, Sandford added for good measure the widespread expectation that either the world would end in 1588 or 'at least governments of kingdoms shall be turned upside down'. Elizabeth, in whom 'there must needs be some diviner thing . . . than in the Kings and Queens of other countries' would lead humanity in the 'End Times'.[20]

Sandford dedicated his translation of Giacopo Brocardo's *The Revelation of St John Reveled* to Leicester. Following Joachim of Fiore, Brocardo foresaw Christ's religion dominating 'the whole world. No other religion, no other law, and rule to hear than that of the Gospel'.[21] Soon the belief that Elizabeth would usher in world peace permeated the excitable underworld of popular prophecy. Manuscripts circulated declaring that 'Elizabeth now Queen of England is ordained of God to be Queen of Jerusalem'.[22] It was in this context of prophetic excitement that Dee's

General and Rare Memorials appeared in September 1577, urging Elizabeth to recover Arthur's vast European empire, to the 'south, and east'. It was a time when, Dee later recalled, 'great hope was conceived, (of some no simple politicians), that her Majesty might, then, have become the Chief Commander, and in manner Imperial Governor of all Christian kings, princes, and states'.[23]

Therefore, Dee's assertion of 'your hi[ghness] just Arthurian claim, and title Imperial' made an important contribution to the Elizabethans borrowing, or rather stealing, an ancient imperial mythology from the Habsburgs. However, Dee never defined the British Empire as particularly Protestant. He dedicated his now lost treatise on converting the American Indians partly to Elizabeth and her Privy Council, partly to Philip II and the Pope, since all imperial authority must spread universal piety.[24]

By the 1570s Dee believed that the feminine angelic influence of Venus pointed to Elizabeth's special role in the sudden change of empire. This was because he felt that angelic revelations inspired many of his ideas, not just global restoration. Since his Cambridge years Dee had regularly prayed for revelation of God's 'truths natural and artificial ... bestowed in the frame of the world'. His desire for angelic teaching of 'radical truths' by God's 'extraordinary gift' had been answered in 1555. He later encountered a spirit, 'Prince Befafes', who had been with no human since King Solomon but 'preserved me ... from the power of the wicked' on that occasion.[25] Though he indignantly denied Vincent Murphyn's accusations that he was a 'Conjuror of wicked and damned Spirits', Dee wrote '1567' in the margin where he read about demons deceptively promising wealth.[26]

Dee also convinced himself that he channelled the Holy Spirit because *Monas hieroglyphica* contained kabbalistic mysteries revealed by the angel Michael.[27] By psychological means that lie beyond historical explanation, Dee believed that *Propaedeumata aphoristica* had been God's 'extraordinary gift'. The Catholic exile Robert Turner wrote to William Camden in 1574, attacking Camden's friend John Dee for plagiarising much of *Propaedeumata* from the twelfth-century Urso of Salerno. When Camden questioned Dee, he conceded that superficially 'our aphorisms are indeed one and the same (only different in order and phrasing)'. He blamed angelic illumination for their 'admirable divinely influenced consensus'.[28] Even if their books 'were literally word for word', God's complete knowledge explained 'such miracles'.[29]

Dee connected both *Monas* and *Propaedeumata* to *Memorials*. His enigmatic title-page design for *Memorials* includes cryptic symbols derived from his Monad, while the Archangel Michael leads the ship of state. His 'Preface to the Reader', omitting the claim to divine inspiration for the public, insists that *Propaedeumata aphoristica* had been proved original against 'the slanderous opinion' of plagiarism.[30] He explained that he published *Memorials* anonymously because of the 'Strange and undue speeches' against his *Monas*.[31] Dee spent pages in *Memorials* denying Murphyn's lies that he was a 'Caller of Devils'.[32] He did so because crucial parts of *Memorials* 'from above only', by angelic revelation, not human reason, 'hath gratuitously streamed down into my Imagination'.[33] He claimed the book was 'directed' by 'the Omnipotent Spirit of Verity'.[34] This was why Dee confided to the inner circle in 'Limits' that the Holy Trinity had 'strangely, and vehemently' stirred him up to write about the 'British Monarchy', and why parts of his advice had to be reserved for the Queen and Privy Council.[35]

Angelic magicians were no strangers to the courts of Renaissance princes. On the contrary, Trithemius dedicated *On the Seven Planetary Intelligences* to the Emperor Maximilian I, who saw himself as the Last World Emperor.[36] After seeing Maximilian II's coronation, adorned with Habsburg global symbolism, Dee dedicated his *Monas*, and its German translation, to that notably ecumenical Emperor.[37] The Monad's 'real cabbala' would help Maximilian achieve the 'perfect piety and religion' envisaged by prophecies of the Last World Emperor, part of 'still greater mysteries ... described in our cosmopolitical theories'.[38] This did not merely echo Postel's dreams of cosmic reform. Wandering European alchemists regularly earned the epithet 'cosmopolitan', and *Memorials* also alluded to Dee's application of natural philosophy 'in sundry affairs Philosophical, and Cosmopolitical'.[39]

Memorials used the same apocalyptic language as *Monas*, because restoring the British Empire required divine assistance. Dee carefully concealed this in additions to the printed *Memorials* in 1577, under language intended for the inner coterie familiar with angelic magic. This subtext explains why the printed *Memorials* especially emphasised that John Foxe had been forced to remove accusations against 'the Arch-Conjuror' from his 1576 *Acts and Monuments*. If retained, they would have made Dee's important 'intended exploits' appear diabolical, not inspired by 'the Blessed Trinity'.[40] In other words, Dee believed that *Memorials* recorded what angels had revealed about restoring the British Empire.

This included his central idea that a revamped Royal Navy would restore the imperial authority secured by King Edgar's navy in the tenth century. For 'the self same *Idea*' as Edgar once had, had 'gratuitously streamed down into my Imagination'. In magic, angels were *ideas* that streamed down into crystals.[41] Thus, like magical secrets, Dee could only reveal some of the secrets in *Memorials* verbally to Privy Councillors or Elizabeth, 'in convenient Time and Place'.[42] Little time remained, felt Dee, writing as 'Cosmopolites', citizen of the 'Mystical City Universal' medi-tating on 'the Cosmopolitical Government' under God, which was moving swiftly towards the apocalypse.[43]

While echoing the apocalyptic tone of *Monas*, *Memorials* also offered Elizabeth the philosopher's stone that Dee had offered to Maximilian. Dee connected angelic revelation with a purified alchemy, which would enable Elizabeth to become the Reforming Empress of the Last Days. Therefore, he added a proposal to *Memorials* in the summer of 1577, that revenue raised for his proposed 'Petty Navy Royal' should also support an alchemical research institute hosting 'Four Christian Philosophers'. This proposal outdid his plans for Gilbert's 'Academy' and fuelled wider expec-tations that Elizabeth would acquire the philosopher's stone in 1577.[44] By hiding his proposal under allusions to the alchemical King Khalid, Dee signalled to courtiers 'whose Insight, is Sharp, and Profound' the connec-tion between producing the philosopher's stone and restoring the British Empire. Such veiled language again illustrates the many layers of meaning in his imperial writings.[45]

Connecting Dee's angelic magic with his imperial vision also recovers the hidden purpose of his 1577 'Famous and Rich Discoveries'. The first thirty folios of this manuscript, declaring Dee's intentions, are lost. Parts appeared in Samuel Purchas's *Hakluytus posthumus* (1625), which quoted from 'Discoveries' how the Earth seemed lost in the immense Heavens, so Dee would go 'far above all Heavens ... and thence with a spiritual and heavenly eye look on earth'.[46] This angelic perspective encouraged Dee into a typically Renaissance display of copious justifications for the North-East Passage to Japan and India, and evidence 'confirming' the North-West Passage.[47] This fulfilled the claim in *Memorials* that 'Discoveries' established Elizabeth's title to 'very large Forrein Dominions', since Arthur's empire had controlled both northern passages to Asia. Yet the surviving manuscript of 'Discoveries' does not reveal how God's Providence 'will benefit all of Christendom, and Heathens' by restoring Arthur's empire. Nor does it justify the assertion of *Memorials* that 'the Secret Centre' of 'Discoveries' hid more 'than I may, or (in this place) will express'.[48] Obviously, the lost part of 'Discoveries' contained these mysteries.

Dee's first surviving angelic 'action' of 22 December 1581 shows that the missing pages of 'Discoveries' applied Trithemius's angel magic. Dee began with a traditional invocation, asking God to send his 'holy and mighty Angel, named Anael', the 'steward of the orb of Venus: and also Chief governor General of this great period, as I have Noted in my book of Famous and rich Discoveries'.[49] Clearly, Dee began 'Discoveries' by announcing Elizabeth's global leadership in the current Age of Venus. However, another 'secret' in 'Discoveries' required that Elizabeth establish her empire soon. For in a manuscript neglected until now Dee reveals the 'secret' in 'Discoveries': the imminent, abrupt shift to the Age of Jupiter. The spirit 'King Bynepor' told Dee, 'Thou beginnest new worlds, new people, new kings, and new knowledge of a new government.' Dee responded in the margin, 'New Worlds: perhaps a new period doth begin, as I have set down in the Volume of famous and rich Discoveries' where the 'great period' of Jupiter followed Venus. Elizabeth, however, would hardly welcome such threatening news, which Dee omitted from subsequent drafts.[50]

A late marginal addition to *Memorials* shows how Dee used the imminent Age of Jupiter to press Elizabeth to exploit England's temporary
imperial opportunity. For the incredible 'Privilege by God, and Nature,
Appropriate to this British Monarchy' will only last 'for a While'. Dee saw
himself as the prophet of this 'Incredible Political Mystery', the coming
new age. He scattered his Jupiter symbol throughout his books and manuscripts, including an account of Frobisher's third voyage.[51]

Dee felt apocalyptic pressure to warn Elizabeth about her prophetic
imperial role. His angelic revelations and offer of the philosopher's stone,
would not have alienated Elizabeth. On the contrary, she always proved
receptive to his occult philosophy. Whether Dee would gain an audience
to tell the Queen what God and His angels had revealed depended on
other factors. Most importantly, it depended on how politicians could
exploit the other hidden messages in his writings on the 'British Monarchy'
to advance the 'Protestant cause'.

CHAPTER 11

Rehabilitating 'The Arch-Conjuror'

ON 1 AUGUST 1576 Dee began dictating his 'Memorials' to an amanuensis. We can imagine him every inch the magus, striding up and down between the packed shelves of his library at Mortlake in his black robe and skullcap, his long beard waving, his arms gesticulating as he groped for the right expression. We can still hear his pauses in the occasionally impenetrable prose, full of fractured phrases, incomplete allusions and digressions. In six days of dictation he never even broached his ostensible subject, the art of navigation. Dee believed that 'Memorials' solved current political and strategic problems. He hardly mentioned Frobisher. When he finally stopped talking, he dedicated the text to Edward Dyer.[1] Dee expected Dyer to take his proposals to the Privy Council. In the short term he would be disappointed. In the medium term 'Memorials' would have a curious life, exemplifying the struggles that more Protestant Privy Councillors had in convincing a conservative Queen of the dangers she faced.

Busy Privy Councillors received policy advice while dealing with a stream of contingent events. As social subordinates, writers of advice had to accept that circumstances determined the reception of their ideas.[2] Therefore, whether anyone applied Dee's ideas to policy depended on how well 'Memorials' fitted the specific policy needs of Elizabeth's government in August 1576. For Dee's treatise grappled with the latest in the unremitting economic, political and military crises spinning out of and feeding into the larger, perpetual crisis we now call the Revolt of the Netherlands. Elizabeth's government faced multifaceted geopolitical problems in north-west Europe: warfare in the Low Countries, the recurrent French Wars of Religion, the shaky authority of England's clients in Scotland, and simmering Irish unrest.

Persuading Elizabeth to deal with these challenges exacerbated domestic political tensions between politicians of varying opinions, from convinced Protestant to open Catholic, because they differed widely over what the Queen should do in fluid circumstances. So did she. Dee's reputation, badly tarnished by Murphyn and Foxe's 1570 *Acts and Monuments*, depended upon how successfully his advice addressed these difficult challenges, in the midst of constantly shifting debate over policy.

This explains why 'Memorials' addressed European and domestic problems, not an American empire. Dee's dictation turned into eighty printed pages, which in part explained how to fund, supply, organise and deploy a 'Petty Navy Royal', not an ocean-going fleet but sixty ships for patrolling home waters. This was not a new topic for Dee, somehow stimulated by Frobisher's voyage. His 'Synopsis of the British Republic', started about 1565 and rewritten for Dyer in 1570, outlined how reforms could 'make this kingdom flourishing, triumphant, famous and blessed'. Later he retrieved the manuscript from his files, scratched out 'kingdom' and inserted 'British Monarchy'. Strength, he wrote in 1570, required a coastguard of fifty ships, half the Queen's and half hired merchant vessels.[3] By 1576 he considered a royal coastguard of sixty ships the 'onely Master Key, wherewith to open all Locks, that keep out, or hinder, this Incomparable British Empire' from power, peace and prosperity.[4]

Now Dee's navy would address the problems filling the State Papers and Privy Council register for these years: prevent foreign invasions; protect English merchant ships from piracy; train more navigators and seamen; stop the illegal export of victuals and munitions; suppress domestic rebels; selectively recruit English pirates; protect that nursery of seamen, the English fishing industry; and force foreigners to respect the English Crown and merchants. Dee's navy would enforce 'the Royalty and

Sovereignty of the Seas . . . environing this Monarchy of England, Ireland, and (by right) Scotland, and the Orkneyes also', because that naturally belonged to 'the Imperial Crown of these British Islands'.[5] Applying his civil-law training, Dee extended Elizabeth's authority to 'the Middle Seas over'. Eventually, he suggested still wider sovereignty for Elizabeth, because her Arthurian and Plantagenet descent entitled her to claim substantial parts of Europe.[6]

Dee believed that enforcing Elizabeth's sovereignty over the Narrow Seas would solve political problems reaching crisis point by August 1576. Public order depended on reliable food supplies, so the unlicensed export of food was illegal.[7] However, the poor harvest of 1575 drove prices sky-high, encouraging more and more English and Dutch profiteers to smuggle expensive victuals into the Netherlands war zone.[8] They also carried munitions, which encouraged a little piracy on the side, now that the Netherlands Revolt and French wars of religion had destroyed govern-ment control over the north-west European coast. By 1576 county piracy commissions had failed to suppress piracy.[9] The English fishing industry struggled against the more technologically advanced Dutch.[10]

However, Dee's solutions for these *chronic* policy problems do not explain his insistence that 'Memorials' directly addressed the *acute* polit-ical crisis facing Elizabeth on 1 August 1576. He emphasised the hurry in typically breathless phrases. Right now there existed 'a Little lock of Lady Occasion, Flickering in the Air, by our hands, to catch hold on: whereby, we may, yet once more (before, all, be utterly past, and for ever) discreetly, and valiantly recover, and enjoy, if not all our Ancient and due Appurtenances, to this Imperial British Monarchy, Yet, at the least, some such Notable Portion thereof, As . . . this, may become the most Peaceable, most Rich, most Puissant, and most Flourishing Monarchy of all else (this day) in Christendom'.[11]

Dee symbolised this end-of-times imperial moment in his hand-drawn title-page illustration, showing Empress Elizabeth steering the ship of Christendom, supplicated by the British Republic, 'to arm ourselves with a war machine' that will 'guard our security against all enemies'. Dee's navy would produce incredible commodities, unto which God had provided 'even now, the Way and Means', because militarily 'our Friends are become strong: and our Enemies, sufficiently weak', 'though their accustomed Confidence, in Treason, Treachery and Disloyal Dealings, be very great'.[12] This last directly responded to current events, for after completing the main text on 6 August, Dee wrote this comment on a slip of paper inserted between the manuscript's pages. It allowed him to put a cosmic prophetic 'spin' on the recent collapse of Spanish power in the Netherlands. Philip II had unilaterally rescheduled his debt repayments in September 1575. That instantly destroyed his credit, so by July 1576 armies of mutinous unpaid Spanish troops had begun looting the provinces. The Netherlands Council of State declared them enemies of the state on 26 July.[13] Days later this news reached London, sparking Dee's decision to begin dictating 'Memorials' on 1 August.

Less obviously, Dee's weak 'Enemies' referred to the current confrontation with the rebellious provinces of Holland and Zealand over the piratical Sea Beggars of Flushing. Dee's 'Petty Navy Royal' would not just force the Spanish to respect English merchants.[14] The Sea Beggars also challenged Elizabeth's maritime sovereignty.[15] More importantly, they had threatened England's economy by seizing the Merchant Adventurers' wool fleet bound for Spanish-held Antwerp. Escalating reprisals stymied negotiations, and Elizabeth ostensibly commanded the Privy Council to blockade supplies to the Dutch on 1 June, and again in early July.[16] This pragmatic order closed international waters, by a fleet enforcing Elizabeth's sovereignty over the Narrow Seas.[17]

On the day Dee began dictating 'Memorials', the Privy Council ordered that fleet to sweep the Flushing pirates from the English Channel. They toughened these orders on 6 August, the day Dee stopped dictating 'Memorials'.[18] Apparently, the angels were inspiring Dee to advise Elizabeth how to enforce her current policy more thoroughly. More likely, Dee's 'scryer' transmitted angelic 'revelations' inspired by Court gossip about that week's decisions. Therefore, 'Memorials' argued that the 'Petty Navy Royal' would force 'France, Flanders, Holland, Zealand, Denmark, Norway, Scotland, [and] Spain' to observe 'their sworn, or pretended Amity'.[19]

Unfortunately for Dee, the Privy Council's posturing to defend Elizabeth's honour was all bluff.[20] None of the Council seriously wanted to weaken Holland and Zealand, assisting a Spanish reconquest that would inevitably prelude the invasion of England. Burghley emphasised this consequence while meticulously demolishing the case for blockading the Dutch. He insisted that public statements of outrage against the Sea Beggars should accompany secret negotiation with William of Orange.[21] The Privy Council's anti-piracy orders carefully exempted ships holding William's commission, and they barely enforced the embargo on supplies.[22] Since March Walsingham had been secretly coaching William through negotiations with Elizabeth, despite the embarrassments caused by the lawless Sea Beggars. On 7 August, after Dee had completed 'Memorials', Walsingham and Elizabeth secretly advised Orange of her terms for a settlement.[23] The Privy Council quietly countermanded its orders before the punitive fleet sailed in August.[24] Edward Dyer would have found 'Memorials' hard to broker to the Privy Council, hence it initially failed as a 'politic plat'.[25]

In this version, perhaps appropriately given his religious upbringing, Dee's advice most resembled the programme of Catholic courtiers, who when Dee wrote 'Memorials' believed they 'possess the Queen's Majesty's ear, to egg her on to the utter ruin of the Protestants beyond the seas'.[26] The Earls of Arundel, Surrey, Northumberland and Rutland, Lord Henry Howard and Charles Arundel, shared deep attachment to the old religion, close family relationships, and burning resentment against the upstart Leicester. Modern hindsight too easily underestimates their influence at Court. With their friends such as the erratic Earl of Oxford, they enjoyed privileged access to Elizabeth through their female relatives in the Privy Chamber.[27] They appealed to Elizabeth's ingrained aristocratic and anti-puritan prejudices by portraying the upstart Dutch and the Sea Beggars in the worst possible light. Burghley, Walsingham and Leicester barely preserved secret support for the Dutch from Elizabeth's public outrage and demonstrations of naval strength. This suggests that Dee had been 'stirred up' and 'ordered' to write the treatise by a scryer connected to conservatives at Court.

However, comparing the manuscript 'Memorials' with the version of Dee's advice printed in the *Memorials* a year later reveals that careful editing transformed the first version's conservative attack on Holland and Zealand. The printed *Memorials* now supported an aggressively Protestant policy to support the provinces militarily. This transformation occurred because Dee's writing became entangled in the great crisis for the 'Protestant cause', the disgrace of Edmund Grindal, Archbishop of Canterbury. As a reward for making these changes, Dee could strike back against Vincent Murphyn and try to restore his reputation.

Elizabeth had reluctantly appointed the zealous Protestant Grindal to Canterbury in January 1576. In early June, when her Privy Councillors were trying to mitigate Elizabeth's orders against the Dutch, she, or someone close to her, retaliated by recalling another example of 'puritan' excess where Privy Councillors had evaded her commands. This concerned the 'exercises', regular training seminars for unlearned preachers, supervised by bishops or senior clergy. To reassert her authority, Elizabeth would ensure her archbishop obeyed her by suppressing these unauthorised meetings.

Probably those Catholics seeking just then to 'ruin the Protestants beyond the seas' played on her frustration. They had a discreet ally in the conservative Hatton, whose clients John Whitgift and John Aylmer would rise to power in the Church by demanding complete conformity to the Elizabethan Settlement of 1559. That envisaged no place for 'prophesy-ings'. Critics preferred that name to 'exercises' because it supported their 'spin' that 'puritans' used these 'popular' assemblies to agitate for further Church reform, and even scandalously allowed the low-born to 'prophesy' from the Scriptures. Elizabeth agreed that the subversion of all authority could only come next.[28]

When Elizabeth had tried to suppress the prophesyings in 1574, bishops and Privy Councillors had studiously looked the other way. Now she meant business. Leicester, Burghley and Walsingham warned Grindal in early June about approaching storms, and on 12 June Elizabeth flatly ordered him to suppress the exercises. He defended them as firmly under control, but when their reports came in some bishops expressed doubts that critics could seize on. A few even agreed with Aylmer that 'prophesy-ings' were a Trojan Horse for popular presbyterianism.[29] In December 1576 Grindal refused Elizabeth's renewed command to suppress the exer-cises, insisting that Scripture authorised them. She threw him out, and the stubborn archbishop sealed his fate in a six-thousand-word letter, defending himself by daring to limit the Queen's authority in ecclesiastical matters. After inconclusive negotiations, Elizabeth sequestered him from office and placed him under house arrest in May 1577.[30]

Grindal's restoration to favour and leadership of the Church became a central objective of the 'Protestant cause', because zealous Protestants believed that his downfall immensely encouraged Catholics and their fellow travellers. Hatton's star rose still further, and through his influence Whitgift became Bishop of Worcester and Aylmer became Bishop of London. Both began punishing 'puritan' like 'papist' disobedience. Elizabeth's treatment of Grindal depended on the fluctuating influence of those urging her to support the Dutch. In October 1577 circumstances inclined her to help them, and there was talk of Grindal's release from house arrest. By late November, however, new developments pulled her back, and she planned to humiliate Grindal before the Star Chamber.[31] This pattern would continue until his death in 1583.

Dee's writings became tangled in this web of intrigue. After Bishop Thomas Cooper of Lincoln began proceedings to deprive Dee of Long Leadenham on 27 September 1576, Hatton secured Elizabeth's dispensa-tion for Dee's ecclesiastical pluralism, but Grindal avoided signing it.[32] This suggests that at that date Dee had still not rewritten 'Memorials' to encourage aggressive support of the Dutch. Dyer probably proposed this revision. The Pacification of Ghent in November 1576, which seemingly confirmed William of Orange's political authority in the Netherlands, made an aggressive policy plausible. Dee's change of advice has left no direct evidence, but we can trace it indirectly through his successful riposte to Murphyn.

In August, Murphyn's slanders had provoked Dee into hours of bitter digressions, filling over 10 per cent of 'Memorials' with denials that he dealt with any 'wicked and ungodly Art'. Abandoning his earlier attempt in the 'Mathematical Preface' to blame his stage effects at Trinity College, Dee now acknowledged that his work for Elizabeth in 1555 had earned him the title of 'The Great Conjuror'. However, he also sought to defuse that charge by rewriting history, insisting that he had not been Bonner's persecuting chaplain but 'also a prisoner himself: (and bedfellow, with one master Barthlet Green)'.[33]

Surprisingly, John Foxe personally inserted this fabrication into his 1576 *Acts and Monuments* to make Dee look like an innocent victim in 1555.[34] In return, by the time it appeared *Memorials* had toned down the manuscript's criticism of Foxe for publishing 'Devilish and malicious' lies 'under the Cloak of good and sound Religion'.[35] *Acts and Monuments* now recorded that it was not Dee whom Philpot dismissed as learned in 'other things', but only an anonymous 'Doctor'. Foxe's description of the letter to Philpot omits 'Doctor Dee the great Conjuror'. Foxe printed that letter, which according to Dee was forged by Murphyn, without the reference to Green sharing a chamber with the great conjuror and the invitation to 'conjecture' about what that meant.[36] Foxe, however, retained Green's comment to Philpot that Dee had been 'very friendly'. Foxe even added a new marginal comment to support Dee's story that the Privy Council had ordered him to Bonner's household on bail for good behaviour. Thus Dee turned from persecuting Catholic chaplain to sympathetic fellow prisoner, Foxe meekly agreeing with Dee's claims in 'Memorials'.[37]

Dee's long, close relationship with John Day, the printer of *Acts and Monuments*, might explain these changes,[38] except that John's son Richard controlled the printing of the 1576 edition, while the 1583 edition, which John very closely supervised, included some new criticisms of Dee for 'conjuring'. It is more likely that someone Foxe respected had a quiet word with him, and that the removal of Dee the 'Arch-Conjuror' from the 1576 *Acts and Monuments* reflects the way Dee tweaked *Memorials*. As published in 1577 it covertly advocated Leicester's Netherlands policy, on the basis of Elizabeth's rights to European empire.[39] Dee's service to a powerful patron gave him temporary political clout. Thus *Memorials* emphasised that Foxe had removed the conjuring accusations from the 1576 *Acts and Monuments* because they would make Dee's 'intended exploits, of great importance' seem diabolical, rather than divinely inspired support for a Reforming Empress.[40]

In mid-January 1577 rumours of aborted negotiations between the Dutch provinces and the new Spanish governor, Don John of Austria, made military intervention seem vitally necessary to Leicester and his followers, including Dyer and Philip Sidney. They revived earlier dreams that Elizabeth would lead Protestant Europe to reform Christendom, beginning by accepting the sovereignty of Holland and Zealand and then assuming the mantle of the Last Reforming Empress. Also that month, alchemists found gold in Frobisher's ore sample from his first voyage, galvanising courtiers into supporting a second one. That excitement took place amidst the struggle over Grindal and the Netherlands. Dee certainly perceived the Frobisher voyages from this cosmic perspective, since he now held that the supernova of 1572 had signalled the gold discovery.[41]

All this fuelled his apocalyptic vision of restored empire. On 16 January 1577 rumours of the failed negotiations reached Court, and Dee met with Leicester, Sidney and Dyer. Probably they discussed Frobisher's next voyage, but also Sidney's forthcoming embassy to Frankfurt, where the German princes would attempt to resolve divisions amongst Protestants over the Eucharist.[42] The same day Dee wrote to his friend the Dutch geographer Abraham Ortelius, asking for confirmation of the northern passages. However, Dee also told Ortelius that geographic knowledge needed reform so that 'great and unexpected changes in the affairs of all States will be made', words which echo Postel and Leowitz, 'and then the last and desired end of human affairs'.[43] To Dee, inspired by angelic revelations, events in Europe and Frobisher's explorations seemed to be leading to the 'Last Empire'.

Perhaps even stranger to us, Dee believed that his 'Petty Navy Royal' would hasten 'unexpected changes' by dramatically restoring Elizabeth's European empire. In early 1577 this proposal now dovetailed neatly with the Leicester group's agitation for Elizabeth to support the Dutch with an army. Sidney met William of Orange on his return journey from Frankfurt. They planned to exploit the power vacuum left by the Spanish withdrawal from the Netherlands.[44] On his return in late May, Sidney wrote a paper, perhaps with help from Dee, emphasising how the combined navies of England, Holland and Zealand could enforce Elizabeth's sovereignty over the Narrow Seas.[45] This supported Orange's June offer to Elizabeth of a naval union for mutual defence against Spain. In this new political context Dee's 'Petty Navy Royal', because its relatively small ships suited Dutch coastal conditions, could clear a path across the Narrow Seas for Leicester's Protestant army to aid the Netherlands. Though Elizabeth refused Orange's offer, it remained Leicester's objective.[46]

Dee's new political clout impressed Foxe but failed to silence Murphyn. In fact, Dee's closer association with Leicester's 'forward' Protestant policy provoked Murphyn's renewed attacks. In late May and mid-June 1577, Dee learned of Murphyn's 'abominable misusing me behind my back'.[47] These attacks probably originated amongst the Catholic courtiers opposing Leicester, who from exile would attack Dee as the Earl's 'conjuror' in *Leicester's Commonwealth* (1584). Therefore, before 'Memorials' went to print in August, Dee completely changed its strategic arguments by removing Flanders, Holland and Zealand from his list of 'false friends', and by adding new complaints, echoing Sidney and Orange, about supplies smuggled to 'our Secret Mortal Foes, or unassured Friends', the French and the Catholic Flemings.[48]

These and other changes to the printed *Memorials* confirm Dee's statement that he did not write in intellectual isolation, but at 'the earnest request of my countrymen', as a member of the 'commonwealth' within the Elizabethan monarchy.[49] A long section of *Memorials*, hitherto overlooked because it focuses on domestic issues, shows how the City of London, aware of Dee's rising influence through Leicester's patronage, used his writing to persuade the Queen to solve 'commonwealth' problems. Dee's 'Diary' noted that on 26 May 1577, while rewriting 'Memorials', he met the City's water bailiff, responsible for Thames navigation and fishing. The section of *Memorials* that emerged from their discussion would influence royal policy more than all the rest of the book.

Dee's rambling house at Mortlake stood right beside the Thames. So every day his celebrated library, his alchemical laboratories, his private rooms for angel magic, his gardens and outhouses that sustained a large household, his many visitors and students, were permeated by the miasmic smell of the Thames shore 'vilely stinking, at the Ebb'. Therefore, he was easily persuaded by the water bailiff to add 'a little digression' of eight pages, fully 10 per cent of *Memorials*. This attacked the destruction of the Thames and its fishing by 'Trinker-men' whose fixed nets on 'Trink-boats' caught enormous quantities of immature fish, only to be wasted as pig food and fertiliser.

Dee lamented the incredible 'Public loss' to England's economy. Fixed 'Timber-nets' and over a hundred artificial weirs blocked river traffic and destroyed enormous numbers of fry. This un-Christian pursuit of self-interest abused God's gifts and ignored the law. 'Costly Suits' failed to stop official corruption. Therefore, Dee dutifully trusted that the Queen and Privy Council, once 'they understand the causes', would enforce justice against 'Trink-Net-Men', because 'the PROFIT-PUBLIC' must prevail over 'Private Gain'.[50] Dee would find official responses more complicated.

Events also forced Dee to revise 'Memorials' further to support intervention in the Netherlands. Don John provoked renewed hostilities in July. Convinced that he lacked men, munitions and especially money, Leicester and Walsingham pressured Elizabeth into committing Leicester with an army, thus exploiting Burghley's prolonged absence from Court.[51] To highlight the threat from Catholic subversion they played up the case of Cuthbert Mayne, a Catholic priest arrested with a papal bull in Cornwall in June. On 4 August the Privy Council decided to consider Mayne the tip of a very large iceberg, and began surveying Catholic recusant numbers in mid-October.[52] They needed this 'proof', not just to push for Edmund Grindal's restoration as Archbishop. As the Spanish reconquered Flanders that summer, hemming in Holland and Zealand, Orange again offered Elizabeth the sovereignty of Holland and Zealand.

Hatton had scotched this proposal in 1576, but Dee had grounds by August 1577 for changing the dedication of *Memorials* from Dyer to the far more influential Hatton. Leicester and Walsingham used the Mayne case to raise the bogeyman of a full-blown Catholic conspiracy, helped by the Earl of Oxford's foolish dallying with the idea of revolt that summer. Anti-Catholicism thus became their 'wedge-issue' to redefine loyalty, splitting Hatton from the Catholics at Court and pushing him into supporting Leicester's 'forward' policy. Hatton also had personal reasons for switching, having lost a fortune in goods when Spanish troops sacked Antwerp in November 1576.[53]

Current events also explain why Dee insisted on the special relevance of *Memorials* to 'these dangerous days', when Elizabeth's empire to the 'south and east' must be recovered by closing the sea lanes and rolling back the Spanish tide in the Netherlands.[54] For he later recalled that other hidden political reason for publishing the *Memorials* in September 1577, when sophisticated politicians had great hopes of Elizabeth as the Last World Empress, 'Imperial Governor of all Christian kings, princes, and states' – especially states where the English could easily land or who must trade through 'any of her Majesty's appropriate and peculiar Seas'.[55] Leicester seems to have envisaged Elizabeth recovering her Netherlands empire preparatory to becoming the Last Reforming Empress.

The recovery of Elizabeth's ancestral European empire required Dee's writings to become increasingly explicit in describing Arthur's empire. However, besides historical doubts about Arthur's existence, such claims invited opposition, because Leicester identified himself with Arthur. In July 1575 Leicester staged elaborate Arthurian pageants for the Queen at Kenilworth, where poets celebrated him as Arthur's descendant. Edmund Spenser's *Faerie Queene* echoed these pageants. Spenser's Arthur receives Mercilla/Elizabeth's immediate permission to rescue 'Belge' and her 'seventeen goodly sons', or provinces (V, x–xi), before achieving her imperial destiny.[56] Leicester's triumphal entries into Netherlands towns in 1586 drew heavily on Arthurian themes.[57] Such claims made some Protestants nervous about their European implications. William Patten satirised the Kenilworth fantasies in *Laneham's Letter* (1575). Patten shared his patron Burghley's worries that foreign adventures could imperil the defensible Protestant 'Empire' of the British Isles.[58] Some Court opinion, therefore, opposed Dee's increasingly detailed claims for Arthur's European empire.

Memorials merely alluded to Arthur's empire beyond the British Isles, referring to 'Discoveries', which claimed that Arthur had ruled 'Hollandia'.

'Limits of the British Empire' more explicitly added for the inner circle 'Zelandia, Brabantia, Flandria, et Picardia' as parts of that British Empire to be reclaimed 'where no Christian Prince hath presently possession, or Jurisdiction Actual' – that is, where Spanish control had collapsed after 1576.[59] 'Limits of the British Empire' therefore implicitly supported Elizabeth becoming 'Imperial Governor of all Christian kings'. Though unnamed advisers urged peace with princes who had 'usurped your Majesty's ancient royalties', this disgraced 'your Majesty's honour Imperial'. Dee therefore fervently begged Elizabeth 'by entry and reentry to recover again' the British Empire in Europe.[60]

Dee believed that 'within these few years' Elizabeth would rule a global empire through God's 'Gracious Direction, and Aid thereto', already begun 'by means not yet published'. This meant sudden apocalyptic change, angelic direction and the 'cosmopolitical' philosopher's stone. Even so, Elizabeth must seize her opportunity: whether she would depended on the constantly shifting contexts for Elizabethan policy debates.[61] Elizabeth hoped to reconcile the Netherlands provinces to Philip's obedience while restoring their ancient liberties, demilitarised and free from French inter- ference. This blithely ignored years of bloody, brutalising warfare. Herself flexible in her religious attitudes, she also underestimated Philip II's messianic fixation on imposing Catholic orthodoxy in the provinces.[62]

However, more often Elizabeth oscillated between cutting off support to the Dutch, joining a defensive international Protestant league, confronting Spain by militarily supporting the Dutch, or in the last resort accepting their sovereignty.[63] Depending on international religious poli- tics, courtly struggles between conservatives and zealous Protestants to influence her thinking, and the daily tide of events, Elizabeth flirted at any moment with all of these policies. Timing therefore decided whether or not Dee's imperial writings would prove influential. For Dee remained a client, subordinated to the interests of the powerful. Even his belief in the apocalyptic truth of his imperial ideas could not overcome that reality.

CHAPTER 12

Defending Elizabeth against the Dark Arts

MEMORIALS EMERGED in early September 1577, in seemingly propitious circumstances. Under increasing military pressure, the Netherlands States-General had begged Elizabeth to send an army under Leicester.[1] In mid-September Leicester was confident he could overcome Elizabeth's resistance to his departure. Court gossip expected Hatton, Thomas Wilson and even Dyer to be sworn as Privy Councillors, along with several lawyers to manage Elizabeth's extended sovereignty. Yet at the last moment she cancelled the promotions.[2] Burghley's return to Court partly explains this cautious turn of events.[3] However, the latest French war of religion had concluded in early September, closing the window of opportunity, and releasing both the French King's younger brother, the Duke of Anjou, and his rivals the Catholic Guise family, to intervene in the Netherlands. Protestants believed this made intervention even more vital, but Elizabeth's Catholic courtiers used it to counsel inaction. They could argue that dishonourable support of rebels would now unite France and Spain against England.[4] In these circumstances Dee's vision of Elizabeth as Empress of Europe became confrontational, so Elizabeth prevented Dee from distributing *Memorials*.

However, Leicester continued to bring Dee into audiences with Elizabeth at crucial moments for his policy, sometimes taking advantage of Burghley's absence. For the next few years Dee became closely identified with an aggressive Netherlands policy and opposition to Elizabeth's proposed marriage to the Catholic Duke of Anjou. This explains the timing of Vincent Murphyn's continuing slanders against Dee. It also explains why *Leicester's Commonwealth*, written in bitter defeat and exile by Catholics in 1584, insisted that Leicester had kept the 'atheist' Dee for 'figuring and conjuring'.[5]

This charge held some truth for the next few years while the Court obsessed over the Anjou marriage negotiations, linked with Grindal's fate and Netherlands affairs. The very few public events Dee noted in his 'Diary' included several key moments in Anjou's courtship.[6] In mid-October the Privy Council began hurriedly surveying Catholic recusants, to quantify the popish fifth column it believed the Anjou negotiations were encouraging. Some Privy Councillors assured Grindal of his release, expecting that the survey would demonstrate the need to restore him to lead the Church. On 12 November the Council decided to execute Cuthbert Mayne for treason, with maximum publicity.[7]

Yet the 'forward' Protestants met resistance. To overcome it they needed to exploit Elizabeth's receptiveness to Dee's occult philosophy. By November, Anjou had guaranteed to protect Elizabeth's interests in the Netherlands, and, on the day the Privy Council decided Mayne must die, she made Hatton her Vice-Chamberlain and a Privy Councillor. Hatton's promotion rewarded his reversion to Elizabeth's cautious tactic of using Anjou as her surrogate in the Netherlands, though Elizabeth still vacillated about sending Leicester with an army. Dee now contributed passages to Humphrey Gilbert's 'Discourse how her Majesty may annoy the King of Spain' that repeated his attacks in *Memorials* on the same 'doubtful friends' and again urged Elizabeth to exploit Spain's temporary weakness.[8]

Murky manoeuvres stirred up 'a sudden contrary tempest' on 26 November when Elizabeth ordered Grindal to appear before the Star Chamber three days later. Only illness prevented his submission and probable condemnation.[9] Leicester used Dee to try to fend off this prospect. Dee spent a week at Windsor countering 'great fear and doubt' spread by 'Men of no small account' about a comet whose tail pointed to the Netherlands, presumably Catholics anxious to discourage Elizabeth from intervention in that direction. He advised the Queen on the 22nd, again on the 25th, the day before Grindal's summons, and the 28th, the day before his scheduled appearance. Dee demonstrated the extent of Arthur's empire, including the North-West Passage, and perhaps reassured Elizabeth about the Last Days, signalled by the comet. At least she courageously faced up to another comet in 1580. On 30 November he spoke with Walsingham and on 1 December with Hatton, when Elizabeth knighted both men.

Dee never recorded these conversations. But during his audiences Elizabeth promised Dee her protection against anyone seeking 'my overthrow' because of 'my rare studies and philosophical exercises'. This suggests that Dee's occult advice implicitly criticised the Anjou match by emphasising Elizabeth's apocalyptic imperial destiny. He thus confirmed his reputation amongst Catholic courtiers.[10] Several pamphlets, one by Dee's friend the Kent physician Thomas Twyne, claimed that the comet signalled miraculous alterations in Netherlands politics, but the crypto-Catholic Lord Henry Howard was probably thinking about Dee when he criticised even 'the better sort of Princes' for consulting 'Astrologers and Conjurors'.[11]

Dee's place in the midst of these important political consultations explains how he came to marry Jane Fromoundes on 5 February 1578. Just months after Katheryn Dee died on 16 March 1575, Dee had obtained letters from Elizabeth, Leicester and Hatton supporting a marriage proposal. Jane was then twenty, a gentlewoman servant to Lady Katherine Howard, Elizabeth's closest female friend to the end of her life. So Jane was a well-placed member of the Court and probably the object of Dee's proposal. The fact that Dee sought traditional character references not from friends but from the Queen, her favourite, and Leicester suggests that he expected some resistance.

So it proved, for Jane's father, Bartholomew Fromoundes, was a Catholic recusant, who married his children amongst other recusant families. He clearly resented the demand that he allow Jane to marry a lapsed priest. His will, dated 3 August 1577, when Dee was basking in Leicester's favour and no doubt fancied his chances of marrying Jane, provided £100 for his other daughters at marriage, but not a penny for her. The following months, when Leicester made heavy use of Dee's occult philosophy against Catholic interests, only increased the pressure to accept the 'conjuror', and one can imagine Bartholomew's feelings when Dee finally married Jane on 5 February 1578, just days before the prohibited season of Lent. Bartholomew died of a stroke the day after Arthur, their first child, was born.[12]

Let us return with Dee to the Court and its problems. Recognising the apocalyptic significance of the Netherlands conflict helps to highlight Dee's intentions in 'Limits of the British Empire'. He began writing 'Limits' by November 1577, expanded it before 4 May 1578, when Anjou's marriage negotiators arrived, and again before 22 July 1578, when negotiations resumed. Dee's involvement with Frobisher's voyages from November 1577 onwards might lead us to expect that 'Limits' justified Elizabeth's 'Arthurian' empire in the north-west Atlantic. Part of it does. However, most of the manuscript asserted Elizabeth's sovereignty over Europe, particularly the section written in July 1578 detailing Arthur's European conquests. Neither the third Frobisher voyage, long departed, nor Humphrey Gilbert's Letters Patent for colonising America, already issued in June, needed Dee's support.[13] Dee remained astonishingly ignorant about Gilbert's real objectives in August, believing that Gilbert aimed 'toward Hochelaga', now Montreal, rather than his real objective, the West Indies.[14]

The contents and timing of 'Limits', like the occasion when Dee tried to present it to Elizabeth, fit much better with Leicester's attempts to subvert Elizabeth's marriage negotiations. Leicester's pressure behind Dee's writing emerges in an important contradiction. Dee's contemporary annotations in Ferdinand Columbus's *History* and in Oviedo's *Navigations* firmly denied the Pope any authority to award Castile the New World. However, 'Limits' now accepted the Pope had this authority, because Dee dramatically concluded that work with the assertion that Elizabeth was 'the Lawful successor of Castile'. Her Plantagenet ancestors had been illegally deprived of that crown centuries before. Elizabeth's pedigree thus

redoubled her right to the Netherlands and entitled her to America –
another imperial angelic revelation concealed within *Memorials*.[15]
Contemporary politicians took genealogy very seriously. Hence the stress
before the 1576 Parliament on Elizabeth's inherited right to the sovereignty of Holland and Zealand.

Dee's 'Limits' therefore addressed Leicester and Walsingham's central
preoccupation in that summer of 1578 – the sovereignty of the
Netherlands, which they feared Anjou would seize. Anjou used marriage
negotiations to reassure Elizabeth that he would protect her interests in
the Netherlands, nullifying Leicester's interference. So although Dee
claimed to have written 'Limits' at Elizabeth's command, Leicester probably floated the idea. Dee believed that 'Limits' demonstrated her sovereignty over foreign kingdoms 'and provinces', meaning 'Zelandia,
Brabantia, Flandria, et Picardia', once possessed by Arthur.[16]

Despite Walsingham's incessant warnings from the Netherlands in July,
when Dee wrote the last section of 'Limits', Elizabeth remained blind to
Anjou's ambitions. However, by 9 August Walsingham's startling news
that Anjou would shortly become sovereign over the provinces reached
the Court, on its summer Progress at Bury St Edmunds. Leicester seized
upon the nightmare prospect of the French controlling England's
economic lifeline through Antwerp to panic Elizabeth into immediately
agreeing to send him with an army.[17] No one, especially Leicester, trusted
Elizabeth to maintain this policy, as Catholic courtiers immediately
regrouped to reverse it and advance the Anjou marriage.[18]

Therefore, Leicester again turned to Dee, at one of the most crucial
moments of the reign. The tensions over policy between the Queen and
her Privy Councillors had never been greater, the decisions never more
pressing. No Privy Councillor could be certain how seriously Elizabeth
took the marriage negotiations, though Protestants feared the worst. With
Anjou busily stirring the pot, events in the Netherlands looked more than
usually chaotic. Grindal still languished. Above all, the current Progress
daily exposed the Court to disobedient subjects, both Catholic and
'puritan'. The Queen initially favoured an equally hard line against both.[19]
Privy Councillors desperately tried to muzzle the 'puritan' preachers, to

make Elizabeth focus on the popish threat. By the time they reached Norwich in mid-August, they had compiled a hit list of disobedient Catholic recusants requiring severe punishment.[20] But would Elizabeth allow this partisan approach?

The Privy Council were lucky. Dee left Mortlake with 'Limits' on 15 August to meet the Court at Norwich.[21] Leicester probably hoped that Dee's demonstration of her Arthurian inheritance would help solidify Elizabeth's intervention in the Netherlands. Dee could also thwart Anjou's courtship by reminding Elizabeth how the marriage threatened her prospective European empire. But when Dee rode into Norwich, weary and mud-stained after a hundred miles of almost incessant rain, things had changed again. The French ambassadors had soothed Elizabeth's anxieties before Dee gained an audience, and Leicester's Netherlands ambitions dissipated.[22]

The Privy Council now had more urgent need of Dee's magical learning. In mid-August the commissioners charged with London's security uncovered three wax images under a dunghill, one inscribed 'Elizabeth' and two, according to Mendoza the Spanish ambassador, dressed like Privy Councillors. All three were 'transfixed with a quantity of pig's bristles', apparently witchcraft meant to kill, as the dunghill's gentle heat melted the images. On 15 August the commissioners sent them to Norwich, Dee arriving just afterwards. Mendoza claimed that this 'augury' disturbed Elizabeth.[23] The panicking Privy Council demanded that Dee speedily 'prevent the mischief' they 'suspected to be intended against her Majesty's person'.[24] That morning Dee, 'in godly and artificial [technical] manner', did something he never defined. Contemporary magic included charms against witchcraft and questionary horoscopes to identify malevolent witches. Of the badly spooked Privy Council, only Secretary Thomas Wilson found the courage to observe Dee's 'godly' magic and report to Elizabeth.[25]

Dee's activities over the next few months brought him great influence, because he was meeting Leicester's need, to find evidence of Catholic sorcery against Elizabeth, which he could use against his Catholic rivals at Court. The Progress had already turned up evidence of Catholic idolatrous 'superstition' in East Anglia. Now Privy Councillors could put a potent anti-Catholic 'spin' on events, especially for contemporaries increasingly willing to identify Catholicism with 'conjuring'. This justified hard measures against Catholic recusants and forced conservatives such as Hatton back towards the political centre. The ironies here, given Dee's Catholic orders and 'conjuring' history, are best left to himself.

On 20 August the Privy Council demanded that the London commission hunt down likely suspects. Two days later they sent Dee hurrying back to London to assist. Meanwhile, the Privy Council at Norwich used the wax images to justify punishing their hit list of Catholic recusant gentlemen.[26] Elizabeth still balked at helping the Dutch, but correspondents reported that 'by good means' the Queen had been persuaded to revise her opinion of 'zealous and loyal' Protestants in Suffolk and Norfolk, and to countenance the papists' disgrace.[27]

If Dee had not yet guaranteed Elizabeth would follow a thoroughly Protestant policy, he had certainly raised the hopes of Privy Councillors.[28] A week after Dee's return to the capital the London commission arrested the young Catholic Henry Blower.[29] The Privy Council demanded more results. On 10 September the commissioners arrested the Catholic Henry Blower the elder, and moved his son to the Tower.[30] Under harsher interrogation there the younger Blower accused Thomas Harding, the Protestant Vicar of Islington, of making the wax images.

Harding had form. The previous April he had been accused of conjuring, though in those more relaxed times investigators found insufficient proof. The commissioners had arrested him by 18 September, trying to placate the increasingly grumpy demands of the Privy Council.[31] By late September the interrogators had lost patience with Harding's refusal to confirm Blower's accusations, especially regarding his secret papistry, and had begun torturing him. The sufferings of the prisoners over the following weeks demonstrate Leicester's commitment to uncovering a Catholic conspiracy. The Privy Council used the putative conspiracy to press Elizabeth into tougher measures against papists, ordering the bishops to apprehend Catholic missionaries seducing the people from their allegiance.[32]

However, ultimately the prisoners' predicament originated in Dee's occult abilities. While the screams of the tortured echoed through the

Tower dungeons, Dee's stock at Court rose higher than ever. Secretary Wilson briefed Elizabeth about Dee's contribution to the investigation at Richmond on 28 September.[33] Dee used her gratitude not to advocate an American empire but, as a civic humanist, to solve a domestic problem raised in *Memorials*. That very day, Wilson summoned the Lord Mayor, the City's Commissioners of Sewers and its water bailiff, before the Privy Council. The Council now demanded that the weirs in the Thames beside Richmond Palace 'be put down forthwith'. The City's indirect strategy of using Dee had worked.[34]

Three days later the Privy Council conveyed Elizabeth's anger that the Lord Mayor had failed to destroy the weirs. He quickly replied that 'the officers and purveyors for her Majesty's household' had thwarted the City's efforts. In 1569 they had imprisoned the water bailiff for destroying their weirs. Since then successive mayors had done all they could 'or dare'. In 1574 household officers had threatened the Lord Mayor and his officers, while declaring fourteen weirs inviolable. However, by September 1578 many more had been erected to supply eels for the Court.[35] Echoing the words they had inserted in Dee's *Memorials*, the City complained that the weirs destroyed 'the brood and fry' of fish and blocked navigation. Having with the Council's authority silenced the household officers, in early October the water bailiff, accompanied by a flotilla of Aldermen, destroyed thirty-three weirs, but left the Queen's.[36] Typically of Tudor government, this intervention failed to end the matter.

Meanwhile, in early October the Privy Council tried to tie the conspiracy to the Catholics by arresting John Prestall, four years after releasing him under bonds for good behaviour. Were they 'rounding up the usual suspects', or was Dee settling old scores? Earlier in the year the Council had ignored accusations of coining against Prestall. But on 8 October Dee enjoyed a two-hour audience with Elizabeth after a week when pain had incapacitated her. On 13 October he marked another audience in his 'Diary' with an 'E' surmounted by a crown, which usually denoted some magical practice for the Queen.[37] About then someone reminded the Privy Council about Prestall's 1571 indictment for treasonous conspiracy to kill Elizabeth by necromancy. The Council badgered Burghley to hunt down any surviving papers.[38]

In this highly charged political atmosphere Prestall's track record of 'magical devices' against Elizabeth encouraged Leicester to stake his political credit on proving a popish conspiracy.[39] That would prejudice the Anjou match, advance the 'Protestant cause', and provide a deadly weapon against Catholic courtiers. Leicester spread rumours that Anjou's supporters were using 'amorous potions and unlawful arts' to make Elizabeth fall in love with him. The Queen's ill-health since the summer made accusations of witchcraft more likely to stick. She felt unwell in mid-September and by early October was suffering constant facial pains that defied diagnosis by London's best physicians.[40] Everyone remembered the wax images that had killed King Charles IX of France in 1574.[41] Only weeks later did some doctors blame her rotting teeth and infected gums.

Two days after Dee performed magic for her, Elizabeth commanded Leicester 'to examine these fellows at the Tower'. The Earl, dressed immaculately and expensively as usual, personally interrogated the suspects: his cold hauteur, revealed in the dark, heavy-lidded eyes which stare out of his portraits, was unmoved by their agonised writhing on the rack.[42] Was Dee coordinating with Leicester? Though the Earl now desperately needed to prove Prestall's involvement in a Catholic conspiracy, after a month of torture Secretary Wilson had to admit defeat.[43] The Privy Council then sent for Prestall's brother-in-law, Vincent Murphyn. Whether Dee or Prestall provided his name remains unknown.[44]

By then Dee had left for Germany. He had attended Elizabeth for her illness in late October. Her diagnosis remained unclear, so in early November Leicester and Walsingham dispatched Dee on an arduous mid-winter journey to consult the Paracelsian physician and alchemist Leonhard Thurneysser at Frankfurt on the Oder. They quickly provided £100, the kind of income for which Dee vainly petitioned throughout his life. He spent it in travelling fifteen hundred miles before he returned in February. Such elaborate precautions enabled Leicester and Walsingham to milk the crisis for all they could against the Catholics.[45]

Dee politely omitted from his later account the important detail that Leicester and Walsingham had entrusted him with a flask of Elizabeth's urine. Thurneysser had invented a famous device to diagnose by urine distillation. This consisted of a square glass bottle divided into twenty-four horizontal bands, each corresponding to a part of the body. When filled with the urine and set in a lukewarm bath, steam settled on the band corresponding to the diseased part. This and other magical inventions had brought Thurneysser a huge salary from the Elector of Brandenburg. Dee sought but never achieved such patronage.[46] After meeting Thurneysser, on 4 January 1579 Dee consulted the angels about Elizabeth but did not describe their response.[47]

By now Leicester had used pamphlets and ballads to stir up a national scandal against the Catholics and their 'conjured images'.[48] The French lawyer Jean Bodin gave the affair European publicity in his *On the Demonmania of Sorcerers*.[49] The Privy Council began seeing conspiracies everywhere. In January 1579 they obsessed over some Windsor witches, worryingly close to the Court, who used wax images like those used against 'her Majesty's person'.[50] For the Privy Council had still not established who made them. Leicester had both Harding and Prestall condemned to death for high treason in early 1579.[51] However, in April the Privy Council quietly moved the younger Blower from the Tower and released him altogether in July.[52] This change of heart reflects Leicester's eclipse after Anjou's supporters revealed his secret marriage to the Countess of Essex, which accelerated Elizabeth's marriage negotiations with Anjou. Her increasing interest in Anjou and disinterest in the 'Protestant cause', or supporting the Dutch, almost brought Catholic courtiers onto the Privy Council by October.[53]

The Privy Council also eased the younger Blower out of the picture at least partly through embarrassment that innocent men had been tortured. The conspiracy, Catholics gleefully recalled, 'being a little too foolishly handled by the accusers at the beginning, was for very shame in the end, let fall and sink away'. Leicester lost all credibility when the notorious conjuror Thomas Elkes confessed that he had created the wax images to enable a wealthy young client to obtain a woman's love.[54] Elkes became a marked man, condemned to death in November 1580 for conjuring buried treasure and stolen goods. Someone, probably a Catholic, obtained his reprieve from the Queen.[55] Dee suffered from the fallout. The Court knew about his angel magic, for in June 1579 Hatton sent him a new 'scryer', Bartholomew Hickman.[56] What courtiers thought of Dee's error we do not know. The implications for his imperial advocacy are clearer – he became vulnerable to Vincent Murphyn's revenge.

CHAPTER 13

'The winking eye of Achitophel'

ELIZABETH EXCLUDED Leicester and Walsingham from Court until early 1580. Leicester could not promote Dee's access to Elizabeth until later that year – leaving him vulnerable to Murphyn's accusations. Murphyn certainly had strong motives this time, apart from his own arrest and interrogation. Following his torture and condemnation, Prestall remained in the Tower under sentence of death until July 1588. He later claimed he was prepared three times for execution.[1] Therefore, in 1580 Murphyn accused Dee of being involved in a complicated Catholic plot, which mingled distorted memories of the Pole plot of 1562 with elements from the Northern Rebellion of 1569. Murphyn wanted to revive Dee's reputation as a Catholic 'Arch-Conjuror', which the 1576 *Acts and Monuments* had attempted to bury.

This story emerges from a previously overlooked letter from Murphyn to Burghley. Ultimately, Murphyn aimed to incriminate the Hastings family, often targeted by Catholic propaganda because of their Yorkist claim to the throne. The godly Henry Hastings, Earl of Huntingdon and Leicester's loyal brother-in-law, had been Leicester's preferred successor to Elizabeth when she contracted smallpox in October 1562. On that occasion Prestall narrowly escaped Cecil's net. Huntingdon's younger brothers, Sir George and Walter Hastings, both discreet Catholics, avoided politics.[2] Murphyn's accusations connected Dee with the

Hastings. They also connect to Huntingdon's stealthy, protracted and ultimately successful attempt to take over Lord Mountjoy's copper deposits at Canford, Dorset. Murphyn's claims add something to the belief that Dee participated in the industrial alchemy there.

During the late summer of 1580 suspicion began building about a Catholic plot involving coining. Hurried investigations led to the arrest in London in late August of the Irish alchemist Richard Stanihurst. These developments triggered Murphyn's allegations, forcing Dee to clear his name by initiating legal proceedings against Murphyn on 14 September 1580. Politics took an exceptionally dangerous turn that September. The recent peace between French Catholics and Huguenots, and Anjou's treaty with the Low Countries, revived Elizabeth's fears about France controlling the Netherlands. Leicester played upon those fears, pressing her to send English troops. Dee's evidence for her rights to a European empire formed the capstone of this campaign, so Murphyn may have been a stalking-horse for Leicester's Catholic opponents.

Some measure of the heightened tensions at Court can be gained from Elizabeth's well-known visit to Dee three days after he began his case against Murphyn. Doubtless encouraged by Leicester, she declared her confidence in Dee by giving him her hand to kiss and by pointedly commanding him to 'resort oftener' to her Privy Chamber, thereby both showing him her support against Murphyn and reviving hopes for Leicester's 'forward' policy. Over ten years later Dee could still vividly recall the details of this significant visit.[3]

Dee's conflicts with Murphyn over the following weeks counterpoint disagreements within the Privy Council over how best to respond to the rapidly changing situation in the Netherlands. On 22 September Dee put his 'declaration' against Murphyn into the London Guildhall court. His hand had been forced because Murphyn had told anyone who would listen that Dee had practised traitorous magic against the Queen and Privy Council. The next day Murphyn responded from prison by writing to Burghley. Murphyn sent his letter through his fellow prisoner William Herle, Burghley's agent in the murkiest depths of the Elizabethan political underworld. Herle forwarded Murphyn's letter on 26 September, calling it 'the discovery of certain ill practices' by 'men of some note ... shrewdly affected to her Majesty's person, and ... dealers against the state'.[4] The letter claimed that Dee sought £666 in damages through his court action, which revealed the 'spite and malice' of a man whom, Murphyn protested, 'I never knew in all my life'. He asked to meet Burghley to reveal 'the winking eye of Achitophel' a reference to King David's traitorous counsellor, declaring he would only reveal that 'insolent conspiracy' personally.[5]

Murphyn's letter carefully kept the plot vague. Some details can be reconstructed from his interrogation in August 1582, after he renewed his allegations. Murphyn then admitted that in late 1579 he had begun plotting with Sir George Hastings, Walter Hastings, the Earls of Desmond and Westmoreland, and many unnamed Catholic noblemen and gentlemen. They recruited Murphyn to coin money in Ireland by alchemy. The money would raise an army to invade the north of England, deliver Mary Queen of Scots from captivity, unite with Sir George Hastings's English army at Nottingham and march on London, already secured by an odd collection of London merchants and Catholics, including Richard Stanihurst and other financial backers of Murphyn's alchemy. After murdering the Queen and Privy Council, Sir George would marry Mary, becoming the first King of the restored house of Pole, from which the Hastings brothers descended. Murphyn later claimed that Sir George used him to conjure whether he would outlive the Earl of Huntingdon and become King, and had shown him an old book prophesying all these events.[6]

Murphyn's story resembles, especially in its magical aspects, the allegations that Cecil had unblinkingly presented against Prestall in 1563 and had later reused against other Catholics as a generic Popish Plot when he needed one.[7] Contemporaries would therefore have found it quite plausible, which gave Murphyn another reason for using it against Dee, 'the Great Conjuror'. According to Murphyn, Dee's action for slander itself confirmed the conspiracy's existence. Murphyn claimed that in 1580 he escaped to London to reveal the plot, pursued by the conspirators. When he survived their assassination attempts they 'suborned false accusers against him, whereby he was indicted and arraigned at London.'[8] In Murphyn's account, Dee's prosecution proved that Dee was secretly a Hastings stooge. Murphyn claimed that he had revealed the entire story in court against Dee 'when he was arraigned in the Guildhall' in October 1580.

Those Guildhall trial records have disappeared, but such incendiary testimony might explain why the jury found for Dee only after 'much ado', and why, if Murphyn had told the truth for once, Dee demanded £666 in damages but only 'had by my jury at Guildhall £100 damages awarded me against Vincent Murphyn the cozener'. Perhaps Dee's lingering conjuring reputation inclined the jury to believe some of Murphyn's story.[9]

Moreover, Murphyn did get to tell his story to Burghley, who in this tense period could not overlook the unlikeliest security threat. Their interview took place during a crucial week when, prompted by Leicester, Elizabeth wrote to Dee desiring 'to understand ... her title to foreign countries'. At Richmond early on Monday, 3 October, Dee presented her with two large vellum rolls, a draft of 'Limits of the British Empire' describing her genealogical claims to Arthur's extensive European empire. That afternoon he continued his imperial lecture in the Privy Chamber. However, this time Burghley made sure to attend. From his immense genealogical learning he immediately doubted 'the value of the work', questioning Elizabeth's Arthurian 'Title Royal' in Europe, and particularly her claims to Castile and Leon. In part he did so because Dee had compiled the work without his knowledge. Yet he also feared the costly foreign-policy implications of Dee's claims.

At Elizabeth's command, on Tuesday and Wednesday Dee continued to explain the evidence to Burghley, who 'used me very honourably' and who took notes from Dee's treatise. But he could not be moved from his belief that, genealogically, Philip II had a stronger claim to descend from the House of Lancaster than Elizabeth.[10] However, when Dee returned on Friday, 7 October, Burghley, 'being told of my being without, and also I standing before him at his coming forth', simply brushed past Dee and 'would not speak to me, I doubt not of some new grief conceived'. The most likely 'new grief' to make the normally courteous Burghley cut Dee dead was Murphyn's allegations. For although they eventually 'fell out to be but cozenage', at first sight they might well have given him pause for thought about Dee, given Burghley's own knowledge of his activities since 1555.[11]

Elizabeth tried to smooth things over at Mortlake the following Monday, passing on what she said was Burghley's praise for Dee's historical arguments.[12] Though perhaps a polite fabrication, Dee would have especially welcomed her clear signal of support after his public humiliation, and he recalled it in detail in 1592. A few weeks later Burghley patched things up with a gift of venison, perhaps a sign that he no longer believed Murphyn.[13]

Indeed, when political conditions changed Burghley would find Dee's 'Limits' more persuasive. In 1585, after the assassination of William of Orange, the Dutch again offered Elizabeth their sovereignty. Burghley's secretariat drew up 'Declarations of the Reasons of granting aid to the Low Countries', quickly rushed it through the redrafting process and then into print.[14] In the first draft Burghley interlined the claim that Elizabeth could show 'some good pretence of title by lawful descent to some of our progenitors to some part of the low countries'. He included this in the second draft text. But though Elizabeth agreed to send an army, she declined the offer of sovereignty, so he deleted it before publishing the book.[15] This was the closest Dee ever came to seeing his imperial advice enshrined in policy. In 1589 he still insisted that the Low Countries owed Elizabeth 'due and true obedience'.[16]

Elizabeth may even have joined Dee's action against Murphyn, for two years later Murphyn claimed he had been falsely arraigned 'for slanderous speeches against the Queen', not just Dee. Burghley also kept Murphyn under close observation. Dee's Guildhall judgement sent Murphyn to the City's debtors' prison, the Counter in Wood Street, until he paid up. Dee never saw his £100 and claimed to have released Murphyn on 9 February 1581, calculating that the daily fees demanded from prisoners in the Counter had sufficiently punished 'the cozener'. By March 1581 Burghley had removed Murphyn to the King's Bench prison. After August 1582 he would disappear from history.[17]

Elizabeth and Burghley awarded Dee something of a consolation prize in October 1580. Burghley again called the Lord Mayor and Aldermen in to upbraid them about the state of the Thames. The City reported twenty-five weirs still standing. Burghley blamed them for the mess. The weirs had particularly incensed the Queen because her barge had just run aground on one. Elizabeth vaguely recalled Dee's criticism in *Memorials* of 'Trinker-men' and their 'Trink-boats', so Burghley commanded the City to remove 'certain things which her highness called Trinkers'. Burghley clearly had no idea what she meant. The Lord Mayor and Aldermen also shrugged their shoulders and looked blankly at one another. They ordered the water bailiff to report, 'And for the matter of Trinkers he shall ... certify this court of the quality of those Trinkers'.[18] In the long run private interest would always trump civic humanism.

October 1580 was the high-water mark of Dee's imperial advice to Elizabeth. In late 1580 the tide went out, taking Dee with it. As he spoke to Elizabeth and Burghley early that month, news reached London that Philip II had marched into Portugal, made himself King, and added that empire's resources to his vast inheritance. His was the first empire on which the sun never set, and Spanish power backed the new English Jesuit mission carrying the Pope's Bull of excommunication. In Scotland, Morton, the English-backed Regent, fell from power, again exposing England to Catholic invasion from the north. Inept English diplomacy fumbled an alliance with the German Protestant princes, ensuring Elizabeth would not become Dee's imagined 'Imperial Governor' over Christendom. The Duke of Parma continued his inexorable advance in the Netherlands.[19] These changes left Elizabeth dependent on France, so handing the initiative to the Duke of Anjou.

Therefore, in late 1580 Leicester and Walsingham began to covet a French political alliance. Eventually, they reluctantly agreed to the French price – Anjou's marriage with Elizabeth. Anjou then demanded a free hand in the Netherlands and became 'Defender of Belgic Liberties' with Elizabeth's implicit approval. Elizabeth and Leicester welcomed his inauguration as sovereign of the Netherlands in early 1582 through gritted teeth. So from late 1580 Leicester no longer needed Dee's European

British Empire and abruptly dropped him. By August 1582 Murphyn felt Dee was weak enough to be attacked again, though he overplayed his hand by also attacking the powerful Hastings brothers. Until the 1590s Dee recorded no more discussions with the Queen about alchemy, magic and his apocalyptic imperial vision. When Leicester sponsored Edward Fenton's unlucky voyage to the East Indies in 1582, he ignored Dee's erudition about that region but welcomed other Frobisher veterans.[20]

Dee also had to contend with increasing scepticism about King Arthur's conquests. Frobisher's failure to discover remnants of an Arthurian civilisation shattered Dee's assumptions about the North-West Passage. He failed to mention Arthur in July 1582, when Sir George Peckham asked about 'the title for Norombega [Labrador] in respect of Spain and Portugal parting the whole world'.[21] Peckham financed Humphrey Gilbert's second American voyage to find a site for colonisation.[22] After Gilbert's death in September 1583, Peckham tried to revive his plans by publishing a *True Report* of Gilbert's recent discoveries. Peckham echoed Dee's belief that Gilbert's plantations would restore 'her Highness ancient right and interest in those Countries', yet did not claim those rights began with Arthur. Like Dee, he now relied on Prince Madoc and the Cabot voyages under Henry VII to prove Elizabeth's title southwards to Cape Florida by 'prescription of time'.[23]

In June 1578 Dee had assured Richard Hakluyt the elder that 'King Arthur and King Malgo' had conquered 'Friseland' in the north-west. However, the younger Hakluyt's *Divers Voyages* (1582) urged Englishmen to possess 'those lands, which of equity and right appertain unto us' without reference to Arthur, despite reprinting the entire travel story of the Zeno brothers to the North Pole, which to Dee proved Arthur's conquests.[24] Hakluyt's 'Discourse of Western Planting' in 1584 based Elizabeth's title on Madoc. Not until 1589, after Elizabeth committed troops to the Netherlands, did Hakluyt's *Principall Navigations* include 'Flanders' amongst Arthur's traditional conquests. Hakluyt also found in 'Famous and Rich Discoveries' Gerard Mercator's letter to Dee, quoting a text Mercator assigned to one Jacobus Cnoyen and printed on his great world map of 1569, which text he then lost. According to Mercator,

Cnoyen mentioned Arthurian colonists amongst the northern islands, suggesting English rights by prior conquest.[25] However, even Dee's friend Thomas Blundeville, a popular writer on navigation, dismissed Arthur's northern conquests as 'mere fables'.[26]

The final blow to Dee's Arthurian empire came from George Abbot, later one of Dee's scholarly correspondents.[27] In 1605 Abbot, a rising star in both Church and Court, dismissed 'one of some special note' who awarded Elizabeth sovereignty over America through her descent from Arthur. Abbot's patron was Thomas Sackville, Lord Buckhurst, who had served in Elizabeth's Privy Chamber in the 1570s, when Dee often visited, and who was also a client of the Cecils. It seems Abbot learned from Buckhurst that 'the wisdom of our State hath been such, as to neglect that opinion' because built upon 'fabulous foundations'.[28]

Excluded from Leicester's schemes and Elizabeth's presence, Dee nevertheless continued to advise explorers. In May 1580 he worked with William Borough, advising Arthur Pet and Charles Jackman on their north-east voyage to Cathay. Borough taught them practical navigation, using Dee's 'Paradoxal Compass' or 'plat of spirall lines'. Dee, in contrast, obsessed about Pet and Jackman measuring known landmarks by 'the distances and points of the Compass'. This required surveying on a heroic scale, and like many of Dee's suggestions worked better in his imagination than in practice.[29] Also in 1580 Dee prepared a chart, showing the entrance to the North-West Passage, perhaps connected with Michael Lok's attempt to restart the venture.[30] Dee's continuing fascination with north-west discovery persuaded him to join Humphrey Gilbert's company in December 1582. He drew another polar projection map for Gilbert, which was decorated with his imperial Monad.[31]

Dee's Court reputation seemed to be recovering. Yet in 1583 he would fall victim to two Court machinations. One concerned reforming the calendar, the other concerned Albrecht Laski, a Catholic Polish prince whose relationship with the Queen would raise the hackles of Protestant Privy Councillors. The results of both would be calamitous for Dee.

CHAPTER 14

'Misbegotten time': Reforming the Calendar

D<small>EE'S</small> <small>EXCLUSION</small> from the Queen's counsels did not sever his Court connections – he still found godparents for his children amongst second-rank courtiers and the Queen's intimate servants. He continued to discuss exploration with navigators and travellers, to be consulted as an interpreter of dreams, and to have some success in alchemical projection with salts of metals, which were early stages towards the great elixir itself.

However, in March 1582 a new relationship pushed Dee's life in an ultimately disastrous direction. He had continued to consult angelic spirits, using Bartholomew Hickman and Barnabas Saul as 'scryers'. In May 1581, when prompted, he even believed he saw a spirit in a crystal. A record of his angel magic with Saul survives from December 1581, but on 6 March 1582 Saul suddenly announced that he had lost his spiritual insight. He was probably under some pressure from one Edward Talbot, who wanted to join Dee's household. Talbot's mysterious previous career has attracted all sorts of legends, but he later confessed that an unnamed person had originally sent him to trap Dee in 'dealing with wicked spirits'. There was certainly less difference between Dee's earlier angel magic and common ritual magic than Dee liked to pretend. He believed that specific angels would 'answer' to his crystal stone, burnt the names of evil spirits with brimstone, stood in magic circles, used magic seals, and received from the angels a very traditional 'Solomon's Ring' to summon spirits.

Talbot's name certainly resonated with Dee, who cherished his distant kinship with the Talbot earls of Shrewsbury. But Talbot appealed more directly to Dee's vanity by revealing 'from a spiritual creature' that Saul, like Murphyn, had been slandering Dee behind his back. Dee therefore began using Talbot as a 'scryer' on 10 March. Dee's second wife Jane disliked Talbot on sight, and when he was unmasked as Edward Kelley in May, she was incandescently furious, fearing that Kelley was a spy, but Dee was already so dependent on him that he continued to believe in Kelley's cosmic significance. He claimed that the 1572 supernova in Cassiopeia had foreshadowed Kelley's revelation of the philosopher's stone, which would 'astonish the world'.

At first glance Kelley did appear an unlikely harbinger of apocalyptic global reform. At twenty-six already running to fat, he used a staff to support a crippled leg and carefully covered his ears, which had been cropped in punishment for forgery. Yet though prone to drunken rages, Kelley could concoct for the angels, out of the English Bible and magical texts, the most sonorous, majestic, apocalyptic language, sufficient to overawe Dee's occasional doubts. The fact that sometimes Kelley became psychologically disturbed enough to believe he actually *saw* angels also helped to convince Dee. However, Kelley's weak grasp of political realities meant that at crucial moments the angels' commands he transmitted badly misled Dee in dealing with the powerful.[1] For example, in late 1582 the Elizabethan government co-opted Dee to advise on the reformed Gregorian calendar. Applying his previous expertise in measuring time, while also advising on the North-West Passage, Dee temporarily boosted his Court career in early 1583 but failed to appreciate the real situation.

Pope Gregory XIII's calendar reform aimed to reassert papal authority over Christendom by establishing a single date for Easter. The sun's orbital year was actually slightly shorter than the Julian calendar year, so that, minute by minute over the fifteen centuries since Christ, eleven extra days had accumulated as the sun failed to keep up with the calendar. For political symbolism, Gregory removed just ten days, counting solar time back only to the Council of Nicaea in 325. The papacy claimed to have guided that first general Council of the Church, which had decreed the formula to calculate Easter. Many European scholars agreed with Dee that eleven days should be removed.[2]

Before the Privy Council consulted Dee in December 1582, several Catholic countries had already obeyed the Pope. France and the Low Countries omitted the last ten days of December, thus foregoing Christmas. That month Dee observed the change in his 'Diary', renumbering the 15th the 25th of December. However, calendar reform provoked decades of Catholic-Protestant strife. Most Protestant states retained the Julian calendar, symbolically denying papal authority.[3]

Elizabeth seriously considered adopting the papal calendar in 1582–3. Dee's part in its eventual rejection reveals much about the Elizabethan Court, how his calendar work became entangled with his requests for patronage, and his dubious reputation in Church circles. Above all, the story exemplifies how Elizabeth's ministers sometimes thwarted her commands while ostensibly fulfilling them and used Dee for that purpose. Control over time had been part of the Royal Supremacy since Henry VIII purged 'superstitious' saints' days in the 1530s.[4] However, the Gregorian reform needed careful handling, because its growing European adoption meant it could not be ignored. The problem therefore preoc-cupied Walsingham, Burghley and Elizabeth herself.

The government's need for Dee's expertise rescued him from ongoing financial crisis. On 16 November 1582 Dee asked the angels, in another very traditional invocation, to help him find 'some portion of Treasure hid, to pay my debts withal and to buy things necessary'. Though rebuffed, on the 22nd Dee revealed his growing alienation from Elizabeth's Court. He sought angelic help to 'have the King of Spain his heart to be inclined' to receive Dee's Latin treatise of 1581 on evangelising the American Indians, a treatise in part dedicated to Philip II. The angels advised commonplace ritual magic to secure his patronage.[5]

Through Kelley they also promised Elizabeth's increased favour, because 'thou shall do wonderful and many benefits (to the augmenting of God's glory) for thy country'.[6] Even so, two nights later Dee experi-enced an appalling prophetic nightmare. His disembowelled body talked with many, including Burghley, 'who was come to my house to seize my books' and 'looked sourly on me'.[7] Dee's anxiety about seeking Philip's favour had provoked visions of a traitor's death, though the source of that anxiety, his scholarly library, would soon appear his salvation.

In turning to Dee, the Privy Council once more tapped intellectual expertise to solve a policy problem. Dee's mathematical studies at Louvain had trained him in the exact measurement of astronomical bodies for astrological and horological purposes. At any location the precise length of the solar year, and the times of solstice and equinox, varied through irregularities in the earth's orbit, and could only be determined by multiple observations of the sun's height at that meridian.

Beginning in London in 1553–5 Dee had made thousands of observations, recorded in a lost *Ephemerides,* using the five-foot-long quadrant of his close friend the navigator Richard Chancellor.[8] After Chancellor drowned on a Muscovy voyage in 1556, Dee kept this quadrant until 1583. He also used a ten-foot-long *radius astronomicus,* set in a frame that enabled precise 'heavenly observations', timed by a clock accurate to the second. He taught his mathematical student and friend Thomas Digges with these instruments, and together they published mathematical treatises on measuring the nova of 1572. In December 1582, therefore, Dee defined the Gregorian change as adjusting to 'the sun's place' in its annual revolution.[9]

Dee's obsession with astronomical time explains his collection of books on horology, all now lost, including the Jesuit Christopher Clavius's massive *Eight Books on Sundials* (Rome, 1581), which he had acquired about 1582.[10] Clavius had driven the Gregorian reform. His peerless calculations of the solar year still astonish modern scientists. Dee's horological books brought him paying pupils in 'dialing', or constructing sundials, a thriving luxury trade in an age with few and very expensive clocks.[11] Dee's advice to Elizabeth summarised his reading about earlier attempts to reform the calendar.[12] Walsingham supplied the perpetual Gregorian calendar, published at Venice in 1582 and listed amongst Dee's books in 1583, as well as 'the summary of the order of the Pope's new corrected calendar' sent from Paris on 4 November 1582.[13] Dee worked closely with Walsingham and Burghley through January, while also negotiating with them about his north-west plans.

On 26 February 1583 Dee presented Burghley with a sixty-two-page illustrated 'Plain discourse and humble advice for our Gracious Queen Elizabeth', allegedly completed in just twenty days.[14] Typically, Dee used his so-called 'Plain discourse' to display his voluminous learning, taking thirty-two pages just to reiterate that the calendar had advanced eleven days ahead of the true solar years since the time of Christ. After more copious display he concluded from Copernicus's calculations that exactly eleven days and fifty-three minutes should be removed. He pointed out that the Gregorian reformers also used Copernicus, though he passed over the astronomer's heliocentric hypothesis.[15] However, Rome's ten days were only acceptable for 'public or vulgar accounts'. Rome must accept Dee's calculation of eleven days as astronomically more accurate, 'will they, nill they'.

Dee appealed to the Privy Council's prejudices, explaining how the Gregorian error reflected Rome's growing corruption until today's 'hideous and monstrous . . . mass of misbegotten time'. The Incarnation marked the true epoch, therefore Elizabeth could lead Europe into a truly Christian calendar reform.[16] Dee described this opportunity in words echoing the apocalyptic expectations of *Memorials*. Elizabeth could again grasp the 'most beautiful flower of opportunity' as the Last Reforming Empress restoring harmony to Christendom by reforming time. He concluded with verses describing her as 'Caesar's peer, our true Empress', and 'ELIZABETH, our Empress bright', who 'made the truth to come to light, and civil year with heaven agree'.[17]

As in *Monas*, Dee saw calendar reform as another divine gift, part of the required reform of all knowledge, and as in *Memorials*, historical parallels beckoned, like the thirteenth-century Catholic calendar reformers Simon Bredon, a Welsh subject of 'the British Sceptre Royal', and especially Roger Bacon, whose name before he took religious orders, Dee believed, had been David Dee. He quoted Bacon extensively, concluding that reformed time would truly reform religion, lived 'in newness and sincerity of life'.[18]

Dee offered two revised almanacs. One removed eleven days from May to September 1583 without affecting Church festivals or the law terms.

The other, 'Queen Elizabeth's perpetual Calendar', would guide Christendom for centuries.[19] Based on the London meridian, this offered her control over time itself, just as Dee's earlier writings offered her control over Arthur's empire. Harmonising human with divine knowledge served the greater cause of Elizabeth unifying Christendom. However, Dee wrote with even greater apocalyptic urgency than in 1577. His 'Mathematical Preface' quoted from Genesis 1:14 that God had ordained precise astronomical study from the Creation. Astronomy enabled 'high Mystical Solemnities holding' and the 'Consideration of Sacred Prophecies'.[20] The former might mean both astral magic and settling the date of Easter, but his belief in sacred prophecies drove his calendar reform.

His opening flourish about sundials illustrated all time since Adam as a sundial face, leaving a tiny sliver after 1583 until the circle closed.[21] Burghley, whose Protestant sensitivity to prophetic signs, like his alchemy, has been underestimated, shared Dee's awareness of a looming Apocalypse.[22] Burghley noted that Dee's calculations 'may serve for a hundred or two hundred years … if the sins of the world do not haste a dissolution'.[23] Like Dee, Burghley expected imminent dissolution. Dee begged Elizabeth to reform the calendar before November 1583 'upon a very weighty consideration'. After hearing Dee's reasons, Burghley agreed that 'a secret matter' required calendar reform 'before November'.[24] Why this urgency?

Dee and Burghley shared the widespread expectation that the conjunction of Saturn and Jupiter in Aries in March 1583 heralded dramatic changes. This great conjunction, seen only six times previously, always signalled a cosmically significant event, including Noah's Flood and the Ten Commandments. Contemporary astrology divided the twelve zodiacal signs into the fiery, earthy, airy and watery 'trigons'. The conjunction in March 1583 paralleled Creation, which had occurred in the first moment of Aries, the first sign in the 'fiery trigon'.[25] Only once every millennium did Jupiter and Saturn re-enter the fiery trigon in conjunction. The common belief that the world would end after a week of millennia made this seventh such conjunction appear even more ominous.

Dee's copy of the influential book *On the Great Conjunction* (1564) by the Bohemian astrologer Cyprian Leowitz still shows where he underlined many prophecies of Habsburg and Bohemian apocalyptic events. Leowitz prophesied the revelation of Antichrist in eastern Europe and the Second Coming. Dee's friend James Sandford plagiarised Leowitz's expectations for 1583: 'undoubtedly new worlds will follow, which will be inaugurated by sudden and violent changes'.[26]

The angels assured Dee in 1582 that he would begin 'new worlds, new people, new kings, and new knowledge of a new government'. Dee's astrological students, the brothers Richard and John Harvey, reveal that Dee and Burghley expected these cataclysmic changes in November 1583.[27] Richard foresaw political tumults in eastern Europe that November, creating 'a new world, by some sudden, violent and wonderful strange alteration'.[28] Early in 1583, while Dee hurried to reform the calendar, John published *An Astrological Addition* to Richard's work, foretelling the coming Turkish Antichrist and the Elect's final battle under the Last Emperor, when 'a great new Monarchy' would enthrone one pastor to preach 'the true Gospel of the kingdom . . . throughout all the world'. John combined this with an idea from Dee's reading of Trithemius's *On the Seven Secondary Intelligences*, foreseeing the third age of the angel Gabriel, when God would punish the neglect of His truth.[29]

Such prophecies explain Dee's willingness in September 1583 to follow the impoverished Polish nobleman Albrecht Laski to Poland. Yet to this apocalyptic pull the calendar reform added considerable push, for it became combined with Dee's attempt to revive exploration of the North-West Passage. Despite Frobisher's failure, Dee convinced himself that north-west discoveries could restore his finances. In fact, the combination of enterprises destroyed his standing at the Elizabethan Court.

On 23 January 1583 Walsingham found Dee discussing the North-West Passage with Adrian Gilbert, another member of his brother Humphrey's company. The next day Dee, Gilbert and John Davis met Walsingham at the house of Robert Beale, Secretary to the Privy Council. There 'all charts and rutters [sailing maps] were agreed upon in general'.

From them Dee wrote a 'Geographical or Hydrographical Description of the Northern Hemisphere' supporting the project.[30] Walsingham backed Adrian Gilbert, Dee and Davis's application to sublease the Muscovy Company's exploration monopoly over the North Atlantic.[31] Dee drafted a grant of discovery to the north of 'Atlantis' for 'The Collegiate of the Fellowship of new Navigations Atlantical and Septentrional'.[32] Dee's service in advising on calendar reform helped to gather official support for the voyage. His spectacular recovery from recent poverty and neglect was marked by another visit from Elizabeth in early February. She privately asked about the Duke of Anjou's future. Dee pronounced he was 'Biothanatos', born for a violent death.[33]

The voyage and calendar reform became linked when Dee presented his 'Plain Discourse' on 26 February. Burghley discussed it with him and condensed its arguments into a letter for Walsingham to read to Elizabeth, including the threatening prophecy about November.[34] Burghley acknowledged the need to remove eleven days but persuaded Dee to accept ten 'for conformity with the rest of the world', so long as Elizabeth retained the option to lead 'the Romanists and other parts of Christendom' to remove the extra day. Burghley checked Dee's calculations with leading mathematicians. Yet the looming Apocalypse in November gave 'great cause to have this conference accelerated', either to remove the days from March to November, or all immediately.[35]

On 17 March the Privy Council summoned Dee to explain his almanac and 'Queen Elizabeth's Calendar' the following week. Burghley reported on 25 March that the mathematicians agreed that eleven days should be cut but accepted ten. He also recommended Dee's plan to drop several days each month between May and November, to protect the Church and legal calendar.[36] That same day Walsingham summoned Dee to Richmond Palace to advise Burghley when he consulted the judges about the law terms. They accepted the plan, but from this moment both the north-west scheme and Dee's calendar reform began to fall apart. The increasing disparity that resulted between Kelley's angelic revelations about Dee's momentous future and his floundering Court career would help to provoke their departure from England.[37]

Walsingham's summons included an ominous postscript asking to discuss the Muscovy Company's grant to Adrian Gilbert. The letter also passed on Burghley's response to Dee's request for a 'privilege' for the voyage. Burghley would grant the request 'in substance' but 'in some other form'. He meant that Elizabeth refused to allow Dee and Gilbert freedom from customs duties and to charge fees for sharing in their discoveries.[38] This eliminated the potential profits of the 'Collegiate of the Fellowship' and made it impossible to attract investors.[39]

This disappointment further increased the tension between divine revelation and successful Court politics. Adrian Gilbert may have been the problem – courtiers universally disparaged him as a fool. When the angels announced on 26 March that Gilbert should hear their revelations and that he was God's choice to measure the 'straits of the earth', even Dee doubted Gilbert's abilities 'in common external Judgment'. Eventually he submitted to God's power to make 'the dumb' reveal His glory, and felt angelically inspired to prophesy that Gilbert 'shall carry the name of Jesus among the Infidels'. However the Queen and Court thought otherwise.[40]

A similar contrast emerged about calendar reform. On 26 March, the day after Dee showed his almanac to the Privy Council, the angels confidently prophesied that 'Time shall be altered'.[41] Yet some of the goings-on at Elizabeth's Court might have puzzled even God. It might be thought odd that Burghley and Walsingham supported the hated papacy's calendar reform. Always anxious about papist subversion, Burghley's *Execution of Justice in England* in December 1583 condemned the 'tyrant' Gregory XIII, whose 'vermin' Jesuits and seminary priests aimed to extend the Pope's 'absolute authority over all Princes and Countries' to England.[42] Therefore, wrote Burghley, Elizabeth had excluded papal bulls, and though monarchs for political reasons 'can endure the pope to command' where they pleased, they forbade papal usurpation over 'any part of their dominions'.[43] The Royal Supremacy included control of the ecclesiastical calendar. Walsingham exhibited even greater paranoia about popery. Why then were they both so 'uncharacteristically naïve' in trying to stampede the bishops into this reform?[44]

The answer was the Queen herself. Elizabeth's most perceptive biographer has described her as 'pre-Protestant', venerating the cross that many of her Protestant subjects denounced as a popish idol. She had made no bones about outwardly conforming to the Mass under her sister Mary.[45] Like Dee, Elizabeth lacked Burghley and Walsingham's visceral fear of Antichristian popery.

She could also impose her will when she chose. Walsingham probably told Archbishop Grindal the literal truth on 18 March, that 'her majesty thinking it meet' to accept the calendar reform, had personally decided to consult Dee and publish his 'new calculation'.[46] The kudos of 'Queen Elizabeth's Calendar' may have attracted her, but her decision raised problems for Burghley and especially for Walsingham. Burghley might have accepted the prophetic need to change the calendar before November, but he still hated popery. Walsingham may have wanted no part of the popish calendar, but as Elizabeth's Secretary he had to execute her commands.

The Privy Council's dilemma appears in the draft proclamation of the new calendar in late March.[47] Its very drafting shows that Elizabeth accepted Dee's proposal. Burghley had recommended to the Council that once the Queen made her decision the reform should be proclaimed 'as thereto advised and allowed' by the bishops, who had always determined 'the causes belonging to ecclesiastical government'.[48] The draft ignored the Pope and instead claimed Elizabeth's own connection to Nicaea through her ancestor the Emperor Constantine, who convened that Council. It justified the change as aligning the principal Church feasts with the 'course of the Sun', and facilitating England's European trade. While noting Dee's protest about the eleven days, it stated that Elizabeth had ordered his almanac to be published, removing ten days from late May to late August while preserving the Church and legal calendars. It further claimed that Elizabeth had consulted both astronomers and bishops, the matter 'being partly ecclesiastical', and that they had accepted the need for reform.

This would have surprised the bishops, whose agreement had obviously been anticipated.[49] Indeed, Walsingham's dealings with the bishops seem carefully calculated to provoke their resistance. As with his earlier failure to suppress the 'exercises', this enabled him to be apparently carrying out Elizabeth's instructions while actually sabotaging them. He began by carefully framing the issue for Grindal on 18 March. Announcing that Elizabeth had decided to reform the calendar using Dee's calculations, he acknowledged that the Church of England's Convocation would normally debate 'things of this nature'. Yet he asked for the few bishops currently near the Court – Grindal, Aylmer of London, 'and him of Lincoln if he be not departed' – to rubber-stamp the change quickly because the Privy Council meant to proclaim Dee's calendar before 1 May.[50]

After eleven days of ominous silence from the bishops, Walsingham again demanded their expected agreement to keep to this schedule.[51] Walsingham knew what buttons he was pushing. Grindal's archiepiscopal authority had been sequestered since 1577 over precisely this kind of boundary dispute. He had refused to suppress the 'exercises' because they were apostolic, even if unauthorised by the Royal Supremacy. Grindal consciously modelled himself on Bishop Ambrose, who had resisted the Emperor Theodosius's encroachments on the autonomy of the Church. Daringly, Grindal had asked Elizabeth not to pronounce 'so resolutely and peremptorily' on matters of faith such as the 'exercises'. He demanded that she not merely consult her bishops for form's sake but obey their decisions about doubtful matters concerning 'discipline of the church'.[52] Walsingham now re-emphasised that the bishops lacked autonomy in such essential ecclesiastical matters as when to observe Easter. Once Elizabeth had pronounced, they must simply submit, even on matters 'partly ecclesiastical' in the proclamation's words. Walsingham's other actions, however, suggest he expected and welcomed the bishops' vigorous response.

Burghley's letter of late February summarising Dee's 'Plain Discourse' for Walsingham to read to Elizabeth prompted Walsingham to connect calendar reform with Grindal's disgrace. The letter also revealed that Grindal had agreed to resign on 25 March, obeying Elizabeth's recent demand.[53] Walsingham thus chose to send his peremptory letter of 18 March to Grindal in the hands of John Dee. Superficially this seemed logical, since Dee could explain his 'Discourse'. However, it would also remind Grindal that the reformed calendar was a power-play by the Antichristian papacy and would underline the insidious conjuring forces Rome deployed.

This was why Walsingham's letter suggested that Grindal consult 'him of Lincoln', meaning Thomas Cooper, Bishop of Lincoln. Again this appeared reasonable, because Cooper had published a universal *Chronicle* and therefore presumably knew something about chronology.[54] Yet Cooper was also industriously reforming his clergy by rooting out closet Catholics, whom he despised for their 'Necromancy' and 'Apparition of spirits' to confirm their Antichristian doctrines.[55]

This included John Dee. On 20 August 1576 Cooper's officials recorded the verdict on Dee's ministry at Long Leadenham: 'does not reside; neither is he in holy orders; vehemently suspected in religion; an astronomer [astrologer], not a theologian'. Therefore, Cooper demanded Dee's proof of holy orders, and a properly signed dispensation for also holding Upton-upon-Severn, against the canon law.[56] Dee could hardly admit his Catholic ordination to Cooper, who detested those priests who under Mary had 'revolted from Christ to the *Mammon* their Mass' and who also revered Philpot's memory.[57] Worse, although Elizabeth had told Hatton to write in support, Grindal had refused Dee's dispensation in late 1576. His reluctance probably reflected Dee's conjuring reputation. Grindal's diocesan visitations attacked clergy using 'charms, sorceries, enchantments, witchcraft, soothsaying, or any such like devilish device'. He had demanded 'extraordinary punishment' for a Catholic priest using 'magic and conjuration'.[58]

Lacking his dispensation, Dee exploited the labyrinthine appeals process until 1581.[59] He again petitioned for his dispensation in June 1582. Grindal's sequestration invalidated any document he signed and sealed, so Dr William Aubrey acted as his administrative vicar-general. Luckily for Dee, Aubrey was his cousin, and though sickness that summer allowed Grindal to procrastinate further, Aubrey sealed the dispensation in late 1582.[60] Ironically, reforming the calendar so preoccupied Dee that he missed the deadline to secure Elizabeth's Great Seal ratifying the document.[61] The process ground on until Dee was finally deprived of Long Leadenham on 15 June 1584.[62]

In March 1583 Dee escaped an embarrassing confrontation with Cooper, who had left London. However, he still had to face Grindal, who resented the pressure over Dee's dispensation. Certainly, Dee blamed personal animus by 'the Bishops' for his consequent loss of £1,000 in rent from his two rectories.[63] The deprivation does seem vindictive, especially since, unusually for the Elizabethan Church, his long-standing curate at Long Leadenham, Richard Lange, became rector.[64] As for his calendar work, 'I had small thanks at their hands ... nay, great hindrance'. He connected that refusal with Grindal's foot-dragging about 'her Majesty's absolute intent' for his dispensation.[65]

For Walsingham well knew that Grindal had intimate knowledge of Dee's persecution of Philpot in 1555. He had carefully scrutinised Philpot's account smuggled out of England, before passing it to John Foxe.[66] Therefore, Grindal knew about Dee's Catholic orders, his chaplaincy to the hated Bonner, his reputation as the 'Great Conjuror', and the scandal whipped up by Murphyn's forgeries. The frail, blind archbishop's reaction to Walsingham's commands – that he must both accept Dee's 'Plain Discourse' from its author and use his assistance in approving the revised calendar – can be imagined from the vehemence with which Grindal and his fellow bishops rejected the innovation as Antichristian.[67]

Their reply on 4 April 1583 deplored the hasty imposition of the new calendar. Because the change particularly affected 'the service of the church', their opinion should prevail, especially since accepting the Pope's device would split the English and European reformed Churches. Such profound alteration in God's worship required careful discussion, not only with Convocation but also with all the foreign reformed Churches. Moreover, only another Church general council could alter Nicaea's Church calendar. The popish Council of Trent had excluded much of Christendom. Parliament must also revise the Book of Common Prayer legislated in 1559.

However, the bishops mainly rejected Gregory's innovation because of its origins. Obeying 2 Corinthians 6, they refused to communicate in anything with 'the Church of Antichrist'. Nothing could be received from Antichrist without making it appear that England would receive other papal innovations. They particularly wanted to avoid the impression that they feared the Pope's Bull threatening to excommunicate anyone who refused the Gregorian calendar. Giving that impression, when papal Bulls had presumptuously excommunicated Elizabeth, would encourage English papists and 'offend the weak brethren'. Nor could any pretence that Elizabeth acted independently avoid the implication that she merely obeyed the Pope.

We can only speculate how much Grindal's knowledge of Dee's compromised past encouraged this focus on Antichrist's wily subversion. But in one respect the bishops directly rebutted Dee's justifications. His insistence that the new calendar must be enforced before the Apocalypse in November they simply turned on its head. Dee might have astrological grounds for his fears, but since 'the latter day' indeed approached, the new calendar was of 'no great importance' because there could not be much further alteration 'in the order and course of the year'. Dee wanted to harmonise time with Nature, but the bishops faced the Apocalypse with dismissive contempt for worldly concerns: 'the Pope might very well have spared his labour'.[68]

Unlike her crushing response to Grindal's resistance about the 'exercises', Elizabeth quickly backed down over the calendar. She probably dismissed the appeals to international Protestant opinion and vapourings about Antichrist's wiles. The need for parliamentary changes to the Prayer Book probably hit home. Her fury against the 'exercises' had been partly because the Prayer Book had not authorised them. Therefore, she accepted the need to legislate for a new calendar, though an attempt in 1585 became bogged down in attacks on Archbishop Whitgift's authoritarian stewardship of the Church.[69] In April 1583 Walsingham could shift the Queen's attention to the complex negotiations around Grindal's resignation, which were still incomplete when he died on 6 July.[70]

Elizabeth dropped the new calendar within a week of Grindal's reply, destroying Dee's hopes of reward. On 11 April he complained to the angels that 'her Majesty will not reform it in the best terms of Verity'.

Worse still, she had refused the privileges for Adrian Gilbert's voyage. The angels tried to use his collapsing Court reputation to confirm Dee's Elect status: 'Whom God commonly chooseth, shall be whom the Princes of the Earth do disdain'. Dee's guardian angel, Raphael, revealed the unsurprising fact that Court flatterers 'have dissembling hearts, and privily do they shoot at thee, with arrows of reproach'. Yet when the prophesied miseries descended on England in late summer, Dee would prevail 'yea even against the mightiest'.[71]

Energised by confirmation of his special status, but more critically £300 in debt and desperate, Dee sought Elizabeth's help through Walter Raleigh, currently enjoying the most spectacular rise to favour that seasoned courtiers had ever seen.[72] As the Queen mounted her horse at Richmond on 18 April, Raleigh, Adrian Gilbert's half-brother, spotted Dee hovering behind a crowd of courtiers and drew him forward. She allowed Dee to kiss her hand but merely said 'what is deferred is not refused'. In contrast, the angels that afternoon assured him he was 'chosen by God to an end' and relayed divine commands to leave England before the Apocalyse.[73]

What Elizabeth referred to remains mysterious. The north-west venture was now defunct.[74] Dee's lease of Devon mining rights from the Company of Mines Royal did not require royal approval. His belief that the 'extraordinary working of God' secured this lease suggests he expected to find the buried treasure that the angels now promised him.[75]

More likely, Elizabeth had deferred Dee's suit for a pension. Since he promised Edward Kelley £50 a year from this for 'scrying', he probably asked for £200, the enormous sum he also required in 1592.[76] This totally unrealistic suit epitomises the contrast between Dee's exalted sense of his prophetic importance, stoked by Kelley's angelic 'scrying', and his much lower actual value amongst hardheaded politicians. By 1 July Elizabeth had refused his petition, accelerating Dee's alienation from Court. In part this resulted from Walsingham's use of Dee's dubious past to provoke Grindal's resistance.

Even in death, Grindal's long friendship with Foxe enabled him to remind the world of Dee's real activities under Queen Mary. The 1583

Acts and Monuments added the Privy Council's record from 1555 that 'John D.' had been released under bonds for good behaviour. However, it reversed the impression given in 1576 that Dee had suffered persecution for true religion, for the Council record correctly attributed his arrest to 'lewd and vain practices of calculating or conjuring'.[77] By early summer 1583 Dee's declining hopes enabled his increasing trust in the angels to overpower his limited political grasp. When Kelley transmitted angelic commands to accompany the ambitious but impoverished Polish nobleman Albrecht Laski to his dazzling destiny, Dee had no alternatives left. In September he would follow Laski to the millennial grounds of eastern Europe.

CHAPTER 15

Called to a King's Office:
Laski and the Second Coming

JOHN DEE could be forgiven for believing that God had sent Laski, the Palatine of Sieradz in Poland, in answer to his prayers. On 18 March 1583, like Elizabeth, Leicester and Burghley, he received Laski's letter announcing his imminent arrival.[1] Laski had known Philip Sidney since 1573 and carefully nurtured relationships with Leicester's circle, so he knew about Dee's angel magic and alchemy.[2] Laski's flattering testimony to Dee's European reputation fostered a relationship that was to wreck Dee's career at Elizabeth's Court.

For months the angels had been commanding Dee to flee England before the prophesied Apocalypse. But in April he still lacked money and faced huge debts. Kelley fed Dee's belief in his prophetic importance, which encouraged Dee's assumption that God had sent Laski to restore his reputation and finances.[3] Kelley merely had to connect Laski with the prophesied Apocalypse in eastern Europe.[4] Unfortunately, Dee's belief in Kelley's revelations exacerbated his curious blind-spot about Court politics. He attributed his misfortunes to the malicious envy of his critics, not to the political calculations of his hoped-for patrons. Tying his fortunes to Laski ensured his failure, because Laski's English sojourn became an embarrassing problem for Burghley. When Burghley finally removed that embarrassment, Dee suffered accordingly.

Laski had written an elegant Italian letter to Burghley as early as December 1581. He already enjoyed a European reputation as a warrior-humanist. Idolised by patriotic Polish poets, he published in Latin on warfare and religious politics.[5] However, his letter received in March 1583 worried Elizabeth. He called her 'the refuge of the disconsolate and afflicted', implying that he was a disgruntled exile from Stephen Bathory, King of Poland. Elizabeth's government expected years of careful diplomacy to soon pay off in a treaty whereby Poland would protect England's vulnerable source of strategic naval supplies in the Baltic. Welcoming Laski might derail those delicate negotiations. Therefore, Elizabeth asked Burghley about Laski's 'quality' and reason for visiting.[6]

After consulting Leicester, Burghley reassured Elizabeth about Laski's high status, 'such as few are subjects to any Monarch in Christendom'. A sovereign prince, he 'carried great authority' under King Stephen. Burghley and Leicester recommended that Elizabeth should receive Laski like royalty and lodge him in a palace.[7] Persuaded by Burghley and by court gossip about Laski's magnificent open-handedness, Elizabeth put Winchester House in Southwark at his disposal. She received him with princely salutes of artillery. The Venetian ambassador in Paris reported on the seemingly endless round of expensive entertainments that followed. Presumably relying on Sidney's recommendation, Leicester immediately became Laski's bosom friend.[8]

Laski certainly looked the part. Tall and handsome, his hosts thought he had 'an English complexion'. He dressed spectacularly in red, while his yellow boots with curling toes evoked Chaucer's time to his hosts. He was sinfully proud of his gigantic white beard, worn tucked into his belt.[9] Elizabeth was charmed by his royal lineage, military reputation, physical prowess, intellectual attainments and splendid display.[10]

However, once settled, Laski wanted angelic revelations about his political future. On 5 May Dee asked the angels how to deal with this 'victorious captain'. They prophesied great journeys for Dee and Kelley. Dee finally met Laski in Leicester's chambers at Greenwich Palace on 13 May. Ten days later he put Laski's questions to the angels. Would Laski succeed Stephen Bathory, and would he rule Moldavia?[11] The angels promised

Laski a kingdom within a year. By 28 May Laski's dazzling courtly reception and his 'great good liking of all States of the people' convinced Dee that Laski would 'suppress and confound the malice and envy of my countrymen against me', restoring his personal and financial credit.[12]

This conviction epitomises how Dee's belief in the angels' pronouncements prevented him from hearing the subtle undertones of Court politics. By now the Pole's reputation at Court was already coming under attack. Despite Burghley's assurances to Elizabeth, nagging questions remained. Spanish and French diplomats described the Court's puzzlement about Laski's motives for visiting England.[13] Within days of Laski's arrival, the ever suspicious Walsingham asked for a briefing from Lord Cobham, Elizabeth's ambassador in Paris, where courtiers of Henri III, briefly elected King of Poland 1573–5, knew Laski well.

Cobham's reply arrived in mid-May and devastatingly exposed Burghley's embarrassing blunder. Laski had enjoyed great wealth and power in Poland, reported Cobham, but squandered both in bids for the Polish throne. While in Paris to conduct Henri to Poland, he married 'a young Italian woman of mean condition and bad reputation'. When Henri fled Poland for the French throne in 1574, Laski supported the Habsburg Emperor Maximilian as his successor. In retaliation the successful candidate, Stephen Bathory, seized Laski's estates. Laski fled to Italy, where he revealed himself as 'a Papist', sponging on a succession of princes. Only in 1581 had Stephen restored him to favour, returning his lands and relieving him with money, though insufficient to maintain his profligate lifestyle.[14]

Much of this information lay in Burghley and Walsingham's files, if they had bothered to check.[15] In London, Laski attended Mass with his Italian servants, and his March correspondents had included the imprisoned Mary Queen of Scots.[16] Therefore Laski's 'popularity', which so impressed Dee, alarmed the Privy Councillors, who were currently negotiating conditions for Mary's release while, to entrap Elizabeth's remaining Catholic courtiers, covertly encouraging Francis Throckmorton's plot to kill the Queen.

Cobham's letter forced Burghley to reverse his earlier advice and now try to persuade Elizabeth to see Laski as a dubious renegade exile. When

Laski returned from staying with Dee on 19 May, Hatton sent the informer William Herle to enquire rather pointedly whether Laski would attend the imminent Polish Parliament. Elizabeth also sought his intentions.[17] However, even though Laski broke his promise to depart, Elizabeth now refused to listen to his critics and in early June she staged a jousting tournament in his honour.[18]

Such public splendour masked Burghley's private struggle to change the Queen's opinion. It may therefore have deceived Kelley into revelations that turned Laski from a courtly embarrassment into a political threat. Laski arrived claiming descent from the medieval English Lacy family and bearing what he called their ancient arms. Thus he implicitly claimed political power. Dee's library contained hundreds of medieval deeds relating to the Lacys' Irish lands. These stimulated Kelley's angelic utterances on 28 May connecting Laski with the Earls of Chester and Lincoln, through a Peter Lacy who allegedly migrated to Poland generations earlier.

Moreover, said the angels, though 'many witches and enchanters, yea many devils' threaten 'this stranger', Laski, Dee and Kelley would prevail, for 'your names are in one book'.[19] Further angelic promises on 2 June, coinciding with Elizabeth's tournament, that Laski 'in Election ... shall govern him a people', being called 'to a King's office', further stirred this heady mixture of ambition, magic and politics.[20] Laski's prophesied royal status would certainly have appealed to Dee, whose struggles had made him acutely sensitive about his own reputation.

For two weeks the angels fell silent about politics, while Laski enjoyed fashionable entertainments. They included a state visit to Oxford University. Rowed up the Thames in the royal barge under Elizabeth's cloth of state and heralded by the Queen's trumpeters, a glittering retinue of courtiers, including Sidney, surrounded Laski. Oxford put on fireworks, orations, exercises, plays (including special effects such as Dee's at Trinity College, Cambridge), and academic disputations about astrology. The gaudy procession broke the return voyage at Mortlake on 15 June.[21]

That evening the angels again forecast England's troubles, but Dee was more interested in whether Laski had 'prevailed to win me due credit: and in what case standeth my suit' for a pension?[22] Their answer pushed deeper into dangerous territory. Dee would recover, because Laski would govern twenty-one kingdoms and be King within a year. However, 'his Counsel shall breed Alteration of this State; yea of the whole world'. Even more audaciously, the angels prophesied two kingdoms for Laski: Poland 'and the other he seeketh as right'. Dee then drew an imperial crown in the margin. His next question suggests this signified the English Crown. The angels had previously prophesied an invasion, and Dee asked whether Laski should return to Poland or remain in England during 'the troubles of August next'.[23]

By now willing to believe anything of Laski, Walsingham and Burghley likely learned of these dangerous ambitions through Charles Sled, currently in Dee's household. Sled, a self-proclaimed 'gentleman', had earlier spied for Walsingham at the English College at Rome. In November 1581 his testimony had condemned the Jesuit Edmund Campion and his companions for treason.[24] Dee first mentioned Sled in September 1582 as someone who knew international finance and could influence the Customs searchers, suggesting he knew about his intelligence work.[25]

Sled abused Kelley at Dee's table in April, and Dee later had to lecture him on 'virtue and godliness'. Sled's pressure may reflect an attempt by Walsingham to blackmail Kelley into spying on Laski, through false accusations of coining. Sled's continuing presence and rivalry with Kelley owed something to the fact that 'he used the crystal, and had a very perfect sight.'[26] It owed more to Dee's poverty. His household depended for its daily survival on the £56 he had borrowed from Sled over the year to September 1583. Dee left with the debt unpaid. Significantly, Sled enlisted Walsingham's support when trying to recover it from Nicholas Fromoundes, Dee's brother-in-law and trustee.[27]

Whether or not Sled informed Walsingham about Laski's English claims, when Laski returned to Mortlake on 19 June the angelic conversations took a dramatic turn. Kelley offered to conjure evil spirits for Laski, but Dee forbade it. The angels then told them that they must 'hide nothing from him, for you belong unto him.'[28] Laski now revealed his long experience of living on princely handouts, for he had detected, despite the endless courtly junketing, growing resentment that he had outstayed his welcome. He informed Dee that Burghley's increasing grudge against him would poison Court opinion. Therefore, he wanted to know whether he should return to Poland. Dee asked the angels whether Laski could be present at the next 'scrying' hours later.

Burghley's animus owed much to Laski's combination of Catholicism with unprincipled political adventuring. But it also reflects Burghley's chagrin at his initial error, which fuelled the Court's growing uneasiness that Laski had failed to match his advance billing for noble open-handedness and 'great revenues'. He had refused the Queen's initial offers of money, but his profligacy outstripped his credit. The longer he stayed the faster his reputation declined. In fact, Laski was penniless. Camden later recalled how Laski eventually fled in secret, leaving mountainous unpaid bills.[29] In itself this might not have counted against him. Flashy coves such as Laski survived on their wits at all the courts of Europe, and courtiers who habitually lived beyond their means, relying on credit and the forbearance of their tailors, could hardly complain.

However, an increasingly desperate Laski had dangerously politicised his grandiose ambitions, misguided by the angels. He persuaded a young Inner Temple lawyer, John Ferne, to trace the Lacy genealogy in a Latin treatise. Ferne later claimed he had also been enticed 'by a worshipful friend and alliance of mine'. This was Dee, whose library contained those Lacy deeds. Ferne certainly accepted Dee's Arthurian theories, proclaiming his loyalty to the 'mighty Empress of Great Britain, and the north Islands'. Unfortunately for Ferne, Burghley's mastery of genealogy enabled him to recognise the threat in Laski's claims, for the Lacy lands had descended to Elizabeth's Plantagenet ancestors in 1321.[30]

Laski was therefore claiming a blood relationship with the Queen, which gave a new and sinister meaning to his practice of wearing royal crimson every time she received him. This embarrassing connection was bad enough, but Laski had a record of raising private armies to pursue his ends.[31] He also sponsored propaganda trading upon his 'popularity'. In early July, Dee bought several pamphlets printed in London praising Laski.[32]

Critics began to slander Ferne's 'wandering affection', finding his research 'sinister'. Rumours multiplied that he had invented genealogical evidence for Laski, a politically lethal charge. He later protested that his treatise contained nothing 'which might give so strange a guest, occasion or colour, to challenge a kindred'. When finally printed, his book conspicuously omitted the two hundred and fifty years after 1321, and any Polish connections.[33]

Therefore, when Kelley and Dee brought Laski into their angelic conversation on that critical evening of 19 June, the revelations shifted to Laski's European destiny. Laski learned about his guardian angel, 'Jubanladaec', who prophesied that within a year Laski would lead the Cross to victory over the infidels. Jubanladaec anointed Laski and confirmed that Burghley 'hateth him unto the heart, and desireth he were gone hence'. In contrast, Elizabeth 'loveth him faithfully' and quarrelled with Burghley about him, while Leicester merely 'flattereth him'.

Jubanladaec then instructed Dee and Kelley, 'When this Country shall be invaded, then shall you pass into his Country', to make 'his Kingdom be established again'. The Second Coming would soon make Laski 'wonderful'.[34] The prophesied invasion may reflect Kelley's awareness of Catholic invasion plans for Lancashire, the core of the former Lacy estates, plans well known to Walsingham and Burghley.[35] No wonder Herle kept tabs on Laski for Walsingham, and Walsingham tried to insert his agent Thomas Watson into Laski's household. Also, Henry Howard's *Defensative Against the Poison of Supposed Prophecies* attacked Dee that summer. Howard deplored traitorous prophets who presumed to forecast 'how long the Prince shall reign', 'who shall succeed and by what mean' and 'what houses shall recover or decay'.[36]

Laski began spending longer at Mortlake and on 26 June addressed the angels in his soldier's Latin. They predicted Stephen Bathory's imminent death and that Laski would rule Poland and Moldavia.[37] Dee's dawning understanding that by attaching himself to Laski he had ruined himself increased his willingness to accompany Laski to eastern Europe. On 1 July, Dee learned that his suit for a pension of £200 had been rejected. The next day the angels confirmed his shocked realisation that Walsingham was 'marvellously alienated'. They had overheard Walsingham agreeing with Burghley that Dee 'would go mad shortly'. They both meant to trap him on charges of treason and would search his house once Laski, now labelled 'inwardly a Traytor', left England. Kelley was pressurising Dee, but real grounds existed for these warnings. On 6 July Walsingham noted that Laski still postponed his departure, 'which is found strange'. Though a skilled courtier of 'many good parts', his excuse that he came merely to see the sights was wearing thin.[38]

Laski then announced plans to depart in mid-August, but lacked money to travel. The angels could not conjure up cash, but did offer a magical talisman to destroy his enemies.[39] Dee had exhausted his credit by 4 July, when the angels evaded his question about future patronage from Burghley, Walsingham and Raleigh. They wisely clammed up about Laski's dangerous genealogy. Dee now feared that Kelley meant to abandon their scrying and leave with Laski.[40]

There follows a gap in the manuscript of the angelic conversations until after 21 September, when Dee, Kelley and their household accompanied Laski to Poland. Later evidence reveals that all three considered the angelic conversations of these weeks crucially important. They may have gathered them in a special volume, now lost. On 12 July Laski promised Dee 200 dollars annually, very roughly £50, but twice as much to Kelley, the first sign of a power-shift in their relationship. By 30 July Dee found both his financial and political credit at rock bottom. That day Elizabeth passed by Mortlake, but unlike previous critical moments for Dee she made no public demonstration of support, merely waving distantly to him. The next morning, despite receiving Raleigh's written reassurances about Elizabeth's 'good disposition', Dee raced to Court to salvage his reputation, calling first on Leicester.[41]

Leicester invited himself and Laski to dine with Dee two days later, perhaps to investigate the rumours. Embarrassed, Dee confessed that without selling plate or even pewter he could not entertain them, so Leicester quickly persuaded Elizabeth to send Dee £20. This grant, however, could not restore his long-term fortunes. The next day someone sent John Halton, a London clergyman with a deformed left hand, whom

Dee considered 'a wicked spy', to greet Kelley, his fellow Worcestershire native. Dee 'feared nothing being an innocent', which meant he was not, but realised that 'he was sent to E.K.' to gather information about the angelic conversations.[42]

As sinister forces began gathering around the house at Mortlake, at Court on 7 August William Borough, Dee's former pupil and friendly collaborator on northern voyages, 'passed by me'. Like Burghley's cutting Dee in October 1580, this gross breach of etiquette signalled Dee's diminished status. By attaching himself to Laski he had sunk beneath the Court's notice. No wonder the 'Diary' petered out on 18 August with a brief glimpse into a deeply stressed household, in Dee's veiled Latin note recording Kelley's furious anger with his wife.[43] Dee's last hopes in England had gone.

The four weeks before their departure proved busy in both mundane and cosmic matters. Their decision to leave meant Jane Dee had to dismantle a domestic economy she had spent five years organising. Dee also had to close his domestic alchemical research institute, dismantle the paraphernalia for his angel magic, make arrangements for his students, and pay off a large household and research staff, about which we get only fragmentary glimpses.[44] Laski was broke, so Dee also had to hire two ships to transport the Mortlake household, much of his library, and Laski, his servants and horses. Dee selected eight hundred printed books and almost a hundred manuscripts to take with him, enough to fill several large carts. In Europe this entourage required up to four coaches, at hideous expense. Dee therefore borrowed £400 from his brother-in-law, Nicholas Fromoundes, secured by his only assets: his house, its four gardens and its 'goods and chattels', including his remaining books.

Then he employed Andreas Fremonsheim, his London bookseller for European books, to catalogue the library. Dee still owed Fremonsheim £63 for some of those books.[45] He could only reward him with his copy 'Of Famous and Rich Discoveries', which later passed to Robert Beale, Secretary to the Privy Council. This gift signalled that Dee was severing his ties with the Court and exploration voyages.[46]

Meanwhile, the apocalyptic deadline loomed. On 2 September a spectacular meteor shower lit the night sky above London, provoking the inevitable pamphlet demanding repentance, because Nature's decay heralded the Second Coming.[47] Dee was too busy to comment on heavenly chaos, but on 6 September he began making a fair copy of Fremonsheim's catalogue. All this contributed to a heady atmosphere, in which the following day a profound event sealed Dee's departure with Laski. At 10 a.m. on 7 September God made a covenant with Laski, promising him kingship over three wicked nations, a promise solemnised by Kelley's vision of an angel holding a crown above Laski's head.[48] We merely glimpse this scene momentarily, through Dee's later recollection. However, it convinced Dee to depart.

Despite angelic predictions of imminent global alteration, Dee obtained passports valid until mid-1585. On 21 September in a carefully planned flit, the household took boat, met Laski on the Thames, and quietly slipped through London 'in the dead of the night' to avoid their creditors. They found their ships moored below Gravesend. After five days windbound on the coast of Kent, they finally escaped towards Holland.[49]

According to hoary legend, a furious mob, incensed by Dee's conjuring, immediately sacked his library at Mortlake, destroying his books of magic, smashing his delicate alchemical equipment and expensive navigational instruments. In fact, no such riot occurred. Dee's associates, some of them thwarted creditors, removed many of the books. Some pillaged with Nicholas Fromoundes's compliance. The navigator and occasional pirate John Davis, who as a boy had 'scryed' for Humphrey Gilbert, chose books randomly. Nicholas Saunder, a student at the Inner Temple in 1583, removed large numbers.[50] He probably gained access through Fromoundes, because Saunder belonged to a prominent Catholic family at Ewell, Surrey, about ten miles south of Mortlake. Jane and Nicholas Fromoundes's recusant relatives lived at Cheam, barely a mile from Ewell. The families moved in the same local Catholic circles and appeared on the same government recusancy lists.[51] Saunder was currently squandering his inheritance on the way to turning pirate, and his access to Dee's books indicates Fromoundes was seeking a quick return on his loan. Dee complained that Fromoundes 'unduly sold' his house contents as soon as he departed.

Dee's angry creditors also besieged Fromoundes for Dee's unpaid debts. Fremonsheim sued Fromoundes in the Court of Requests in November, when Charles Sled filed a Chancery suit for his £56. Sled's connections to Walsingham's spy network may explain how the angels at Lübeck in mid-November could twit Dee about Fromoundes's troubles. Sled and Fremonsheim both claimed that Dee had entrusted Fromoundes with his goods to clear his debts. Though Fromoundes had in fact been selling Dee's goods and receiving his rents, he defeated both suits. Dee only began repaying Fremonsheim in late 1595, and Sled's debt remained outstanding in 1598.[52] Fromoundes informed Dee in April 1584 that Sled, Adrian Gilbert and Fremonsheim had used Dee 'very ill'.[53] Probably all three helped themselves to Dee's collections. Gilbert seized Dee's alchemical instruments and remaining alchemical books with Fromoundes's help. Fromoundes sold Dee's alchemical equipment for about 80 per cent of its value, including vessels that Dee had brought from Lorraine in 1571.[54]

While vultures circled at Mortlake, the angels continually urged Dee and Laski forwards. Their arduous winter journey traversed the Netherlands and northern Germany to Silesia. Dee constantly fretted about his decision to leave. Even when windbound off Kent he had had second thoughts, nervously questioning the angels about the Queen and Council's reaction. A cold coming they had in Germany, with small towns such as Bochum unfriendly and the English merchants at Hamburg hostile, itching to return the notorious conjuror under arrest to England.[55]

The angels revealed that England considered Dee a renegade who despised his prince. There seemed no alternative to the travellers pressing on, though money ran short. In late October they kicked their heels in Bremen for a week while Laski touched the Earl of Friesland for a loan.[56] They finally limped into Lübeck on 7 November, where they took a month to recuperate, appropriately lodged at the 'Angel Michael'. A week later Kelley transmitted revelations that the Privy Council had interrogated Fromoundes about Dee's secrets, seized his books and planned to burn his house. This backfired when Dee asked for confirmation of God's command to accompany Laski, only to receive thundering angelic rebukes.[57]

While Dee's party struggled along the dismal winter roads of northern Germany, making short journeys from Lübeck to Rostock to Stettin, with long pauses for recovery, Laski travelled in style between noble house-holds. To silence Dee's doubts, an evil angel several times attacked them for presuming to seek perfect divine knowledge. In mid-January at Stettin the angels resumed the apocalyptic tone familiar to Dee's generation. The Books of Esdras and Revelation, they announced, prophesied these actions. All rulers would be overthrown by January 1587, when Antichrist would be revealed, the Turk replaced by Satan and the prophets Elias and Enoch returned to earth. Kelley would become 'a great Seer' and supreme alchemist, 'looking into the Chambers of the earth: The Treasures of Men'.[58]

When the group finally staggered into Lasko in western Poland on 2 February 1584, the angels reassured Dee that God had chosen them for this 'end of harvest'. They would receive instruction in the angelic language, 'that holy mystery' and 'CABALA of NATURE' that underpinned Creation itself. This would establish Christ's Kingdom on Earth, and 'then cometh the end'. Dee therefore ordered a new Holy Table for the reflective obsidian show-stone, the crystal, and other paraphernalia.[59] However, money problems soon re-emerged. Laski's heavily mortgaged estates could not support the Lord's labourers, and his Italian wife made it clear that she resented these threadbare intruders. On 18 February (Julian calendar) the angels commanded them to move to Poland's ancient capital Cracow, for the end times would soon bring bloodshed to Lasko.

Yet they needed money to reach Cracow. Four days later, racked by fever, Dee's questions reflect their desperation and their harsh welcome. He asked for remedies for his sickness and how long Lady Laski would live. Laski had expected Kelley's alchemy to solve his financial problems, but Kelley had failed. Dee therefore asked how to use the 'red powder' that Kelley claimed the angels had led him to in England. He asked them instantly to transport buried Danish treasure they had been promised in

England, to save Laski's estates and political credit. Above all, appalled by their sufferings, he now wanted to abandon Laski and asked whether Elizabeth or her Council 'do intend to send for me again'.

The angels confirmed their move to Cracow but emphasised the bloody future, describing England's coming civil war and the insignificance of worldly treasures beside 'the wisdom that judgeth NATURE'. Kelley had failed because the red powder was not the whole philosopher's stone. Days later the angels vaguely confirmed their promise that Laski would rule over Moldavia, though his financial problems were overwhelming his political ambitions.

By mid-March Dee and Kelley had somehow scraped together a year's rent on a house at Cracow.[60] The city had long sheltered unorthodox religious thinkers.[61] The Jagiellonian University's European reputation for Paracelsian alchemical learning attracted Kelley.[62] Dee sought to join the university community, presenting the library with a manuscript of Boethius in November 1584, which remains there today.[63] After almost a month of silence, in mid-April the angels returned to dictating the angelic language, vouchsafing forty-eight invocations.

Derived cryptologically from the tables of the *Liber Logaeth* revealed in 1583, these 'Natural Keys' would open the 'Gates of understanding', enabling Dee to invoke specific angels to reveal the secrets of Nature. This knowledge would be complete before 1 August, to comfort the world against Antichrist's assaults.[64] The angelic language was so powerful that the calls had to be dictated backwards, lest 'all things called would appear', as had happened once before. The angels selected letters individually from grids, a process Dee soon found tedious, baffling and prone to numerous errors. The angels also had to teach exact pronunciation of the words, vital for their desired effect. The first call took three days to deliver.[65]

Despite these problems, that summer Dee became convinced that Kelley's 'scrying' gave him better contact with God's messengers than the Old Testament prophets had enjoyed. He believed that 'these Actions' finally taught the wisdom he had prayed for since his youth. Kelley reinforced this conviction by refusing to 'scry' after the first few calls, claiming evil spirits deluded them. This forced Dee to demonstrate the orthodoxy of the revelations. Once Kelley consented to return, the angels explained the superiority of the angelic language over human language.

The difference involved manipulating letters and numbers in the 'CABALA of NATURE'. Human language garbled the letters of God's original creative language. Therefore, they must be kabbalistically restored to their original place by being assigned numbers. Every letter signified part of the substance of which it 'spoke'. When properly reorganised, the words they composed signified both that substance's essence and a greater number, kabbalistically derived from the original divine word. The first 'secret and unknown forms' of things were easily distinguished by their numbers, which signified letters, which made words, 'signifying substantially the thing that is spoken of in the centre of his Creator'. Just as ordered speech persuaded man's mind, so were God's creatures 'stirred up in themselves, when they hear the words wherewithal they were nursed and brought forth' by God, their true names.

Adam before his Fall spoke this language with God and the angels. Sharing God's power and spirit, he therefore knew all things 'and spoke of them properly, naming them as they were'. But when 'Coronzon', Satan's true angelic name, seduced Adam he lost 'his understanding' of the angelic language. Therefore, he spoke the first Hebrew, through which his posterity learned 'of God and his creatures'. However, modern Hebrew lacked 'the true forms and pronunciations', and therefore the power, of Adam's language. Still less could Hebrew now compare with the angelic language, hidden from man 'till now'. Through this 'tongue of power' God would give true wisdom.[66]

Dee found this angelic language compelling. His *Monas* had proposed that the letters of the ancient alphabets derived mathematically from the hidden structures of Creation. The angels who had taught Abraham now taught Dee and Kelley the secret keys to Creation, the root of all languages.[67] The excitement of grasping this root distracted Dee's attention from Kelley's ongoing problems with alchemy. By 21 April Kelley believed that his projections proved the red powder to be the philosopher's stone, though Dee received no angelic confirmation.[68] Therefore, they pressed on with the angelic calls. When translated these revealed Kelley's deep familiarity with the solemn cadences of Old Testament prophecy. Even so, Kelley's invention was exhausted, and from early May 1584 the dictation occurred only on Mondays, interspersed with enigmatic visions in the stone.[69]

Meanwhile the political situation in Cracow turned against Laski. Emboldened by the angelic prophecies, he joined a conspiracy against Stephen Bathory. Unfamiliar with Polish politics, Kelley proved slow in appreciating the danger. Stephen struck quickly against the conspirators. His Chancellor paraded the renegade Samuel Zborowski through Cracow on 7 May, and Laski was quickly implicated. When Dee asked the angels that day for news of Laski, Kelley reported an enigmatic vision of a man overcoming obstacles. Almost immediately they heard from Laski that 'he was in some cumber and hindrance'. He escaped punishment only with support from Cracow's citizens.[70]

Zborowski was beheaded in Cracow's marketplace. Out of his depth, Kelley could give only confused responses to the increasing danger. On 21 May the angels again promised Poland to Laski if he served God, because 'The King and Chancellor have sold the people of this land, and are sworn Turks'. Yet at the same time they commanded all three to flee to the Emperor Rudolph II at Prague. Local opinion thought Dee and Kelley's situation to be precarious. One of Walsingham's correspondents reported that some citizens believed Dee had quit 'a certain estate for an uncertain hope' but 'will repent of it at leisure'. Another Englishman who had witnessed Laski's magnificent entertainment in England now found him 'very bare' in Cracow.[71]

While the political situation remained confused over the next two months, the angels continued to dictate invocations. There remained calls for thirty heavenly princes and governors of kingdoms, who 'vary the Nature of things'.[72] As these began on 21 May, Dee's fears burst out in his questions whether Elizabeth still lived and how Laski should deal with the Chancellor. The angels fudged the latter question but again urged them to take Laski to Prague.[73] As a long-established Habsburg partisan, Laski could give Dee and Kelley entrée to Rudolf's inner circle. The angels repeatedly promised they had prepared Rudolf's heart for Dee's warnings. However, if Rudolf remained 'willful', he would die on 19 September, when the world would suddenly alter. This date agreed with John Harvey's prognostication that the solar eclipse of 30 April 1584 would particularly affect Bohemia. It presaged the Sultan's death in September 1584 and the collapse of the Ottoman Empire. The forecast would encourage Dee to inform Rudolf that September of his future triumph over both Turk and Devil, and of the Empire of the Last Days.[74]

Though God had chosen Laski as another Joshua, the angels revealed that 'the King's Enchanters' had impoverished him, using wax-image magic. This prevented them leaving for Prague, and in late June Dee again pressed for angelic guidance to buried treasure.[75] However, Kelley placed his hopes in alchemy. In late June he began a new course of dictation, again using grids of angelic letters. These contained all human knowledge, including the alchemy of stones and metals. When apparently illuminated by divine light, Kelley easily used the grids to construct angelic words. These holy names gave the adept power over evil angels to transmute metals. They also offered foreknowledge about Christ's Kingdom on Earth, the coming of Antichrist, that Dee was destined to set up the Cross in Constantinople on 15 September 1585, and that the angels obeyed when they were called by God's hidden names.

As Kelley pointed out, 'this is somewhat like the old fashion of Magick'. Indeed, alongside Kelley's apocalyptic visions of these weeks the angelic guidance reveals his long experience in traditional *grimoires*, books of ceremonial magic that bound spirits by magic circles, ritual spells and incantations.[76] Dee acquiesced in these suspect rituals, because of the great privilege the two men were receiving, the language through which they shared God's angelic knowledge.

Dee also knew they needed money to escape their precarious political situation. The angels promised money 'by Art'.[77] Kelley used both arguments in early July, when Dee began to notice human errors in his revelations. Kelley reiterated that only Enoch received the language to constrain the angels. Like Adam, he conversed with God and the angels in the original tongue.

By 23 July 1584 (Gregorian calendar) the final call of the forty-eight 'keys to God's storehouses' had been delivered, and Kelley belatedly grasped local political realities. In a shattering assault, an angel accused Dee of disobedience for not departing for Prague without Laski. God had abandoned Laski, who should no longer receive the divine secrets. Dee was forgiven when he pointed out their poverty. Further instruction in the Book of Enoch, the angels promised, would be given in Prague. By 31 July, through mysterious means, Dee and Kelley managed to raise sufficient money for the journey. After a tedious eight-day coach ride they arrived in Prague on 9 August, now expecting Laski to follow after God forgave him.[78] They brought with them the angelic promises of the Last Days and the Book of Enoch, the key to all the world's mysteries. Surely the Emperor must listen, or be cast down from his throne.

CHAPTER 16

'Chief Governor of our Philosophical proceedings'

THE HABSBURG Court at Prague shone as the European centre of prophetic expectation. The Habsburgs had long attracted cosmopolitan intellectuals aching for universal reform and religious reconciliation. Thinkers who rejected rigid orthodoxies moved restlessly across the religious spectrum, seeking mystical resolution of their spiritual uncertainties. Dee's transition from Catholic priest to conforming Elizabethan layman, to participant in angelic revelations, eventually to dutiful confessor and recipient of Catholic Communion, seems almost conventional by comparison with men he would encounter in Bohemia, such as Francesco Pucci and Christian Francken.[1]

The 'Catholic' and 'Protestant' labels imposed by us in hindsight hardly fit many of those attracted to Rudolf II's Court. In the relative anonymity of Prague their spiritual pilgrimages could end in extremely heterodox beliefs. Kelley's emotional instability and eclectic mishmash of ideas in the angelic revelations reflect the city's religious atmosphere. His denials of Christ's divinity and claims for the transmigration of souls provide a fleeting glimpse of a lost, exotic religious landscape.[2]

These cosmopolitan thinkers sought universal conciliation from Habsburg emperors, such as Maximilian II, who resented Rome's increasingly strident orthodoxy and refused its last sacraments on his deathbed. Dee had dedicated *Monas* to Maximilian, believing that its revelation of the universal secrets of Creation would support the House of Austria's universal rule. As 'Cosmopolites' Dee knew of Laski's attempt to recover Greek Christendom with Maximilian's implicit support. So Dee and Kelley expected Laski to assist them in pressing apocalyptic reformation on Rudolf at Prague.

They had some grounds for expecting a positive response. Rudolf's ecumenical outlook arose from his increasing alarm that Rome's Counter-Reformation undermined his imperial sovereignty. Yet he also feared Protestant aspirations to political independence. His melancholic spiritual uncertainty led him to pursue divine certainty through occult philosophy, especially alchemy.[3] Dee and Kelley would discover that Rudolf's uncertainty made him vulnerable to the powerful forces buffeting his throne in the late 1580s, particularly from Rome.

Dee's host in Prague in 1584, Tadeus Hajek, an accomplished alchemist, astrologer and astronomer in touch with moderate thinkers across Europe, had been personal physician to Charles V, Maximilian II, and now Rudolf, whom he counselled on his universal aspirations. Hajek probably met Dee at Maximilian's coronation in 1563, after which Dee had returned to Antwerp via Bohemia. All Hajek's sons studied in England, and he befriended Philip Sidney. Dee owned Hajek's book on the supernova of 1572, another reason for Hajek to correspond with Dee.[4] Hajek had collaborated with Laski on Habsburg plans to unite Christendom against the Turk. As Rudolf's confidant in cosmology, astronomy, medicine and alchemy, Hajek potentially gave Dee and Kelley access to the Emperor. Other circumstances encouraged them. They began angelic conversations in Hajek's house, where the study walls painted by a previous seeker after 'the holy stone' featured six alchemical vessels. They read his traditional summary of alchemy as 'a child's game and the toil of women.'[5]

The angels stressed that the angel of Revelations 16:12 was pouring out the sixth vial, presaging unclean spirits working miracles. Therefore, they commanded Dee to warn Rudolf that the Angel of the Lord rebuked him for his sins but also promised him universal rule if he listened to Dee in 'this last time.'[6] Even Dee balked at this presumption when he wrote to

1 Title page of John Dee's *Monas hieroglyphica*, 1564. The Monad hid 'in its innermost centre' the philosopher's stone, perfectly balancing all celestial rays (pp. 56–7).

2 Unfolding the Monad to reveal alchemical vessels (p. 59).

3 William Cecil, 1st Baron Burghley. 'Beneath the grave exterior of his stuffy official portraits beat the excitable heart of a speculator in occult philosophy' (p. 75).

4 Nicholas Hilliard, The Phoenix portrait of Elizabeth I (*c.* 1575). 'The red phoenix represented the red powder or elixir, the last of the four colour changes during the Great Work to create the philosopher's stone' (p. 73).

5 Nicholas Hilliard, The Pelican portrait of Elizabeth I (*c.* 1575). The Pelican was an alchemical vessel. The Queen 'was pleased with the philosopher's stone', reported Sir Thomas Stanhope (p. 72).

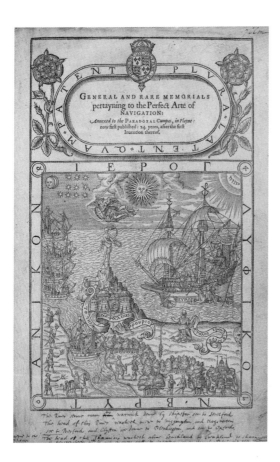

6 Title page of John Dee's *General and Rare Memorials Pertaining to the Perfect Art of Navigation*, 1577. In this work, Dee said, 'the method ... covertly proceedeth (occasion so served)', and 'more is hid, than uttered' (p. 105).

7 The dark, heavy lidded eyes of Robert Dudley, Earl of Leicester, stare out with cold hauteur. He betrayed no emotion when witnessing the torture of John Prestall in the Tower (p. 135).

8 Sir Francis Walsingham believed in transmutation but not in every adept, and consulted Dee about two London alchemists alleged to have made the philosopher's stone (p. 206).

9 The Seal of Aemeth, two smaller seals, Dee's obsidian disc, his crystal ball, and a golden talisman – all part of the elaborate paraphernalia required by Kelley to contact the angels.

SIGILLVM DEI; ÆMÆTH: EMETH
nuncupatum ∴
DEI
אמת } *hebraicæ*
אמת

10 The Seal of Aemeth was a means of generating the names of angels, based on the medieval conjuring treatise attributed to Honorius of Thebes (p. 106).

11 Emperor Rudolf II's spiritual uncertainty led him to pursue divine certainty through occult philosophy, especially alchemy (p. 180).

Rudolf II., deutscher Kaiser.

Geb. d. 18. Juli 1552, gest. d. 20. Jan. 1612.

12 'Kelley claimed from Prague that Hatton had inspired a whispering campaign against him and also made "divers reproachful speeches even afore her majesty"' (p. 215).

13 Dee went to John Whitgift, Archbishop of Canterbury, and 'talked with him boldly of my right to the parsonages, and of the truth of Sir Edward Kelley his Alchemy' (p. 212).

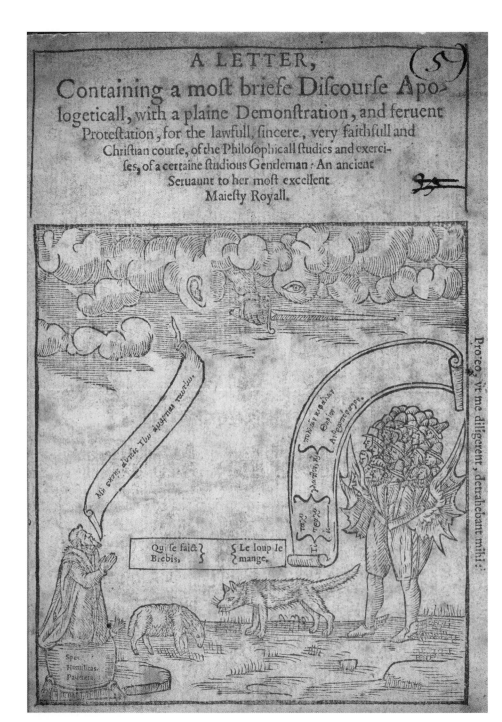

14 Title page of John Dee's *A Letter, Containing a most briefe Discourse Apologeticall*, 1599. Dee assured Whitgift that he studied only as part of 'that holy and mystical body, Catholicly extended' over the globe, under the 'illumination' of the Holy Trinity (p. 245).

Rudolf on 17 August. Instead he emphasised the 'divine plan', bringing them together through incredible patterns like the kabbalistic patterns revealed by his *Monas*, which he enclosed. He claimed that three successive Habsburg emperors had valued his learning: Charles V, Ferdinand and Maximilian II.

Dee's previous Habsburg connections underlined the divinely inspired prophecy in Theorem XX of *Monas*, which promised that numerological unfolding of the alchemical mysteries within the four elements would exalt either Maximilian 'or else some other member of the House of Austria'. The numerological correspondence between Dee, the fourth letter of all divine alphabets, and the Emperor, the fourth Habsburg he would serve, fulfilled that prophecy in Rudolf. Theorem XX also presaged this apocalyptic moment, which offered Rudolf a place among the twenty-four elders gathered around God's throne in the vision of Revelation 4:4.[7]

Even so, Dee kept his letter for another week, while the angels reiterated their special election as vessels for God's wisdom, the privilege Dee had claimed in *Monas*. God also renewed with Dee the covenant He had made with Seth, Noah and Abraham, to multiply Dee's seed, and, more surprisingly, to give him many houses in Prague. The guardian angels of Dee and Kelley even opened to them the greatest mystery, the dates when they would die, already entered in the Book of Life: 1601.[8] Such divine favour encouraged Dee to send his letter through the Spanish ambassador, Guillen de San Clemente. His choice underlines Dee's cosmopolitan outlook, despite Spain's increasing confrontation with England. San Clemente claimed descent from the Catalan mystic Raymond Lull, who he believed had also received divine insights into Nature, including the philosopher's stone. He remained Dee and Kelley's influential friend at the Habsburg Court.[9]

While they waited nervously for Rudolf's response, Kelley buckled under the stress. Through him the angels began to contrast God's Kingdom with the Catholic Church. Satan also seduced Kelley into getting fighting drunk, the day before Rudolf interviewed Dee on 4 September. In Bohemia's tense atmosphere of barely restrained religious sectarianism, Kelley's instability would create problems. Heterodox religious opinions, generated by decades of religious and social conflict, challenged the Catholic Church's attempts to reassert control over the Protestant nobility and town bourgeoisie.[10]

Dee walked to his interview in the Hradschin Castle through the Old Town, picking his way past steaming piles of manure and channels of filthy water. He carefully skirted the many gangs of street criminals in the newly booming city, crossed the Charles bridge over the Vltava, and ascended to the Castle, outwardly a gigantic, aloof setting for the Emperor. Yet Rudolf's Court had barely arrived in Prague, and inside Dee found an enormous building site, teeming with craftsmen creating display spaces for the vast array of exotic objects and pictures assembled by Rudolf, the greatest art patron in the world. The chamberlain led Dee from the Guard Chamber through the Dining Chamber, into the Privy Chamber, where Rudolf sat in his customary richly embroidered black doublet, his pronounced Habsburg jaw in his heavy, fleshy face emphasised by his full beard. Before him lay Dee's letter, his *Monas*, and 'A great chest and Standish of silver.'[11]

Rudolf had granted Dee an audience on San Clemente's assurances about Dee's scholarly standing, his zeal for Rudolf's reputation and desire to benefit him. Unfortunately, like Elizabeth, Rudolf could make little of the *Monas*. Frequently kneeling during the hour-long audience, Dee reviewed his forty-year quest for insights into the hidden springs of Creation, revealing that since Kelley had arrived in early 1582 angels had answered his prayers, bringing him a crystal stone worth more than earthly kingdoms. Tragically for his hopes, Dee then abandoned the emollient tone of his letter and followed Kelley's line, announcing firmly that 'The Angel of the Lord ... rebuketh you for your sins'. If Rudolf refused the admonition, God would cast him headlong from his throne. But if Rudolf forsook his wickedness, God would make him outshine all emperors and imprison the Devil, whom Dee identified with 'the Great Turk'.[12]

Rudolf responded mildly, because he deeply believed in his messianic destiny to destroy the Ottoman Empire, and because he was accustomed to hearing universalist prophecies. He had also been taught by Philip II to enhance his majesty by suppressing public displays of emotion. However, when Dee revealed God's command that Rudolf should read the angelic conversations and see 'the holy Vision' in the stone, he evaded the offer. Though Dee thought he heard Rudolf's offer of protection, 'he spake so low' that the audience petered out into awkward silence until Dee belatedly realised it was over.

Dee felt the anticlimax keenly. God alone knew, he told the angels later that day, how his words had affected Rudolf. It later emerged that Rudolf had understood them as Dee's personal rebuke for his sins, not God's admonition. But before this confusion could be remedied, the damage had been done.[13] The angels, offended by Kelley's recent drunkenness, refused to help. They did, however, reaffirm Dee and Kelley's superiority, as God's chosen prophets, over the Catholic clergy. They also confirmed the popular forecast of the world's end in the 'year eighty eight'. Dee felt confident about Elijah's return on that 'great day of the Lord'. Adding Christ's lifespan to 1588, he thought Christ's kingdom would return in 1621, unorthodox speculation that he justified with numerous scriptural passages emphasising divine revelation.[14]

Bolstered by angelic assurances, Dee tried through San Clemente to show Rudolf the records of the angelic conversations. Rudolf delegated the task to his confidant Jacob Kurtz. Dee anxiously asked the angels whether he should include Kurtz and Rudolf in their 'actions'. Disturbed, for once Dee actually felt the presence of 'my good Angel' and the 'wicked tempter', Pilosum. At this point, Kelley's fragile psychological state produced the first of many angelic instructions to reconcile himself to Rome, despite his criticisms of its clergy.[15]

The angels permitted Dee to show Kurtz his Latin translations of eighteen books of revelations. For six hours on 15 September, Dee guided Kurtz's skimming through the books and showed him the crystal brought by the angels. Kurtz claimed to know Dee's scholarly fame in Germany and he promised to report favourably to Rudolf. Yet, thanks to Kelley's 'scrying', Dee soon became convinced that Kurtz was slandering him at Court as 'A bankrupt Alchemist, a Conjuror, and Necromantist', who had been defrauded by Laski and intended to con Rudolf.

Kurtz's high standing encouraged someone to throw these accusations in Dee's face at San Clemente's table. Though the ambassador defended him, Dee again had to protect his 'name and fame', this time at the premier court of Europe. Unfortunately, he and Kelly were again penniless and desperately waiting for money from Laski. Kelley wanted to leave for England, while Jane Dee was pregnant and seriously ill. Somehow Dee learned 'of the Queen's displeasure for my departure' and that Aylmer, the rigorously conformist Bishop of London, intended to accuse him of conjuring with the 'secret assistance' of the Devil.

No wonder the angels commanded Dee to offer Rudolf the philosopher's stone, ironically confirming those recent slanders.[16] By early October, broke and disheartened, Dee abandoned hopes of becoming 'Caesar's philosopher and mathematician', and they all left for Hungary. His sense of his prophetic importance had again clashed with the ruthless competition at princely courts. For over two months he disappears from view, because one of the angelic books seems to be missing.[17]

In late December, Dee suddenly reappeared in Cracow, somehow able to afford a coach and horses to take his entire household, including Kelley, to Prague. At New Year 1585 he rented a house there in Old Town. He also wrote to San Clemente and Kurtz, re-energised to confront the slanders and prove his value to Rudolf.[18] As so often Dee's financial affairs remain mysterious, though he probably made his brave re-entry to Prague on borrowed money. In mid-January, Kelley began to see alchemical visions promising the philosopher's stone. Even Dee wondered how pursuing transmutation fitted their mission to proclaim reforms leading to the end of time. Moreover, he had no idea how to make the stone. The angels promised inspiration but now warned him against Rudolf and Kurtz.[19]

The following confused 'actions' marked two important changes. First, Kelley embarked on alchemical work that eventually seemed to succeed in making gold, and princes who once ignored Dee would soon compete to employ his former scryer. Secondly, the Catholic hierarchy began demanding they prove their orthodoxy. They were repeatedly questioned about transubstantiation, receiving Communion in the wafer only, and veneration of the Host, all disputed issues in Bohemia.[20] Fortunately for Dee and Kelley, the angels supported Catholic teachings on the Mass, since, like Man himself, the Host was an alchemical creation. Accordingly, the angels promised revelations about the philosopher's stone once they were reconciled to the Catholic Church.[21]

By late February the angels were commanding that Dee and Kelley embrace the Church's rigorous new confession and the priesthood's power to absolve sins. This raised Dee's stress levels, so that during an action on 23 February he again felt a spiritual presence, 'a heavy moving thing' on his head. The angels confirmed 'some treachery was devised against me'.

Days later Dee and Kelley suddenly panicked, pawned their belongings and fled south. At nearby Limburg, Kelley claimed to see angelic visions outside the show-stone, announcing that Stephen Bathory would replace Rudolf within a year, because Rudolf had refused the angelic revelations. God also encouraged Kelley's alchemy. Thus reassured, they returned to Prague.[22] Remarkably, two weeks later Dee's son Michael received Catholic baptism in St Vitus Cathedral, sponsored by San Clemente and two senior courtiers.[23]

By mid-March the angelic revelations had become exceptionally erratic. The angels either failed to appear or uttered such impenetrable mysteries that even Dee and Kelley sat looking blankly at one another. In late March, after the Pope's Nuncio accused them of challenging the Church's authority, Kelley refused to proceed until he had confessed to a Catholic priest. His anxieties, and Dee's increasing focus on the philosopher's stone, reflected their dire poverty, which was now common gossip. Jane Dee could no longer buy food on credit and petitioned the angels to relieve their wants. God alone could restore 'the credit of the actions' against the 'wicked slanders' of Prague's citizens.[24]

The angels promised the stone would restore their reputation and provide an entry for 'supernatural force and wisdom'. However, their recipe for the stone, called 'Darr, in the angelical language', followed surprisingly traditional methods, using the solid residue in fortified wine barrels to tint metals golden. Yet, even this unpromising beginning prompted Dee into a flurried week of letter writing to the English Court, in hopes of being rescued.

Dee requested that Elizabeth send 'an expert, discreet, and trusty man' to Bohemia to witness 'what God had sent unto me and my friends'. Dee suggested his friend the mathematician Thomas Digges, whose alchemical interests have been forgotten until recently.[25] Kelley sent a sample of transmuted metal. Yet Elizabeth ignored Dee's 'faithful letters'. Nor would the angels provide news from England, and he could make nothing of the seal and angel of Britain, 'Tedoand' in the Book of Enoch. Dee again wrote fruitlessly to the Queen and Privy Council in November.

One reason the Court ignored them was gossip about Dee's real attitude towards his English patrons. From Prague these stories spread through the German courts, whence correspondents gleefully relayed them to those concerned. In January 1586 Stephen Powle, whose father had accompanied Dee to Lorraine, and who had visited Dee at Mortlake, reported malevolently to Burghley. According to Powle, when asked why he had left England, Dee had blamed Burghley's niggardly patronage in many 'vile speeches', intended to 'dishonour ... your Lordship'. Powle promised to repeat these speeches personally to Burghley, who pretended to bear patiently with attacks on his 'monopolising' power in England. However, his vigorous defence on this occasion reveals that Dee's own philosophical self-confidence partly explains his lacklustre Court career. Burghley denied forcing Dee and Kelley's departure. He did not know Kelley, but 'Mr Dee I know well, who seldom came to me' to pay court. Like many intellectuals Dee mistakenly assumed that pure intellect would gain him reward, not appreciating that in the Court, that most human of institutions, personal relationships carried more weight than mere intellectual worth. Burghley would take his revenge for Dee's criticism and neglect, after he employed his philosophical abilities one last time in 1591.[26]

Worse still, as Dee later realised, 'I was chief Governor of our Philosophical proceedings' only until March 1585. From then on, Kelley's alchemical expertise enabled him to dominate their relationship. First the Bohemians, then the Italians and finally 'some of my own countrymen' plotted to marginalise Dee, until he separated from Kelley and made his slow, disconsolate return to England.[27]

More immediately, God sent them back to Cracow in April, after Laski finally replied to their begging letters. By now Stephen Bathory and Laski had reconciled. Within days of Dee's arrival Laski secured a royal audience, where Stephen offered his protection. Perhaps anticipating better luck, Dee now labelled the recipe for the philosopher's stone 'Mysteria Stephanica'.[28]

Prolonged debate with Kelley and pressure from the Catholic hierarchy had persuaded Dee to reconcile himself to Rome at the new Gregorian Easter. That year Easter Sunday fell on 21 April, ten days later than the Julian Easter. He chose a congenial confessor, the Franciscan friar and professor of divinity, Hannibal Rosseli. He had recently begun publishing an enormous edition of the *Corpus Hermeticum*. The second volume, just out, dealt with the Holy Spirit and Angels. Dee, like almost everyone, believed that Hermes Trismegistus had been contemporary with Moses. Hermes gave ancient sanction to the calling of spirits. How much did Dee tell Rosseli about the angels, under the seal of the confession that Good Friday?[29] The next day, Saturday 20 April, Dee received the Sacrament from the Observant Franciscans. Kelley also confessed, to a Jesuit, and 'very devoutly' took communion on Easter Monday, to Dee's 'unspeakable gladness and content'. Did Dee still believe in the Sacrament as a magical medicine against the evil spirits that troubled Kelley? Dee confessed and received the Sacrament twice more that Easter.[30]

Having established their orthodoxy, Dee might have expected more stability from Kelley. Yet although the angels now exalted Stephen Bathory's prospects, Kelley soon turned against Laski, who had never paid his promised annuity, and demanded that they return to Prague. When Dee demurred, his 'friend and partner' Kelley broke out into terrifying blasphemies. This dispute reflects the shifting psychological balance in their relationship, for the angels now forbade Dee to require their presence, until Stephen had been rebuked for his sins.

When Kelley resumed scrying on 20 May, the angels threatened to kill Dee's son Michael, because Dee kept the angelic knowledge from Stephen.

Keeping Dee off balance, once Laski had joined them, Kelley switched to prophesying Laski's triumph over Stephen 'for his wickedness'.[31] The next day, 23 May, Stephen gave Dee an audience. A devout Catholic, Stephen emphasised his doubt that God would secretly visit men nowadays. Dee responded with the Catholic doctrine that the Holy Spirit permeated the universe, like Christ in the Mass. He offered to demonstrate it from their twenty-four books of godly instructions, exhortations and prophecies.

Stephen consented to join an angelic action on 27 May, when the angels demanded that he purge his sins. Then Bohemia, that is Rudolf, would be afflicted and Stephen exalted. On 28 May prophecies of the imminent Apocalypse left Stephen unmoved, since Kelley delivered them in English. The angels then instructed Dee to offer Stephen the philosopher's stone. A brief note of Dee's speech records their utter failure to persuade the King. In early June the angelic revelations again stuttered to a halt, so we lack the 'divine orders' that sent Dee and Kelley to Prague in July.[32]

However, we do know that Dee returned to Prague with Francesco Pucci, whose erratic psychological state resembles Kelley's. Ordained a Catholic priest in Florence, Pucci's spiritual quest had covered much of Europe, including England, where he proceeded M.A. at Oxford in 1574. Dee first mentioned him at Cracow in July 1585. Pucci enthusiastically participated in the actions, believing that the 'renovation of all things' by God's chosen vessels would create a new world in 1600.[33]

On 6 August Pucci heard Kelley's visions of the end of time, that the Holy Spirit always guided the Church, and that Luther and Calvin roasted in hellfire. The angels confirmed Pucci's special calling, once he reconciled to the Church. However, he became convinced that to obtain papal forgiveness he must betray Dee and Kelley to the Jesuits.[34] The main record of the angelic conversations then suddenly breaks off until 30 April 1586. But we know what unfolded during the intervening period because Dee wrote a Latin pamphlet for a cosmopolitan European audience, defending himself and Kelley against Jesuit accusations of necromancy. He claimed that their treatment would scandalise 'all pious and true Catholics'.

Dee's pamphlet tried to establish their innocence by recounting dramatic angelic confirmation of the same angelic books that aroused Jesuit suspicions. These events also confirmed 'the great catastrophe overhanging the world'.[35] Dee described how the new Papal nuncio, Malaspina, revived suspicions about Dee and Kelley's angel magic once they returned to Prague in July 1585. Malaspina began requesting a 'friendly conversation'. Dee politely stalled, pointing out England's conflict with the papacy and hinting that Malaspina planned to ambush them.

In late March 1586 Malaspina lost patience and, through Pucci, commanded their attendance at his Prague residence. On 27 March Dee and Kelley finally obeyed, ostensibly to discuss the state of the Church. The nuncio lamented its current weakness. God's revelations to pious Catholics provided no remedy, being only private counsels of reformation. Dee and Kelley must disclose any angelic revelations that would rescue the Church.

Dee admitted that God's angels instructed them, but he avoided Malaspina's trap by denying they received angelic advice about reforming the Church, a topic beyond his authority. He felt great joy at receiving many divine mysteries, a million times greater than humans could imagine. Yet God commanded them to keep these private. According to his pamphlet, he then loudly protested his loyalty to Elizabeth.

However, Kelley immediately launched into the dominant theme of their recent actions – the contrast between the Catholic clergy's faith and its works, which required speedy reformation. They must learn to 'teach and live Christ'. Malaspina smoothly agreed, though Dee later learned that he had wanted Kelley killed on the spot (by defenestration, a Prague tradition).

According to Dee, in early April, Kelley's Jesuit confessor then demanded that Kelley confess the 'very great crime' of conversing with God and his angels. Kelley denied that the Church Militant could judge angels of the Church Triumphant and defended their Catholic orthodoxy. He refused to hand over 'our introductory lessons in a celestial school'. He also denied that they were accounted 'very odious' in England. The confessor eventually barred Kelley from the Easter Sacrament and the angels then forbade any 'action' for six months.[36]

Dee's pamphlet now described the most dramatic of the angelic conversations, on 10 April 1586. After reiterating that God revealed His mysteries to the lowliest, the angels promised destruction for the Catholic clergy. Dee and Kelley must give external obedience to the Church but internally obey the spirit. To the nuncio's demand to see their revelations, the angels answered that restoring the Church meant extirpating a devilish priesthood, unable to judge the angelic revelations. Obedience to God demanded disobedience to earthly rulers. Kelley would foretell the final harvest of Revelation 14:15, Dee would write the revelations, but Pucci would preach the apocalyptic news.[37]

The angels then demonstrated their awesome power. They reminded Dee and Kelley how they had rescued them 'from the accursed tribe' of 'innovators' in England, who resisted Christ's Holy Church. They had instructed them in 'the science of all things', revealing matters hidden even from the Church. Yet more remained.

The angels ordered Dee to gather the angelic conversations, starting with Kelley's appearance four years earlier, manuscripts that still exist.[38] They filled twenty-eight folio volumes, 'four times seven' as Dee could not resist kabbalistically noting. They included one that God held more valuable than the world; the forty-eight angelical calls; a short book of the still unexplained 'Mystery of Mysteries'; and Enoch's wisdom, in sum 'all sacred books, full and perfect'.[39]

The angels ordered Kelley to burn all of these, together with their two books of alchemy, and the 'powder', the philosopher's stone given by God, in the large tiled stove next to Dee's oratory. With Dee in the next room, in Dee's narrative Kelley suddenly saw an angel walking amongst the flames, collecting the books and powder. Dee later sacrificed loose charts and papers to the fire.[40] The angels finally promised to prove that only God's Elect received heavenly mysteries, by miraculously restoring the books. Dee and Kelley should dismount their show-stones and hang up their holy table as a memorial. The angelic conversations had ceased.[41]

Dee probably wrote his pamphlet soon after these events, because it ended with a peroration on God's power but omitted the astounding restoration of all the books on 29 April. That afternoon Kelley observed a 'gardener' pruning trees below, who invited Dee to come down before mounting up to Heaven in a biblical 'great pillar of fire'. They searched the garden and found three of the books they had 'burnt', untouched by the flames, as they appear today.[42]

The spiritual 'gardener' reappeared, apparently visible to Dee, because as the angel led Kelley back into the house 'his feet seemed not to touch the ground by a foot height', and the doors opened before him. Reaching into the stove, the angel passed most of the books over his shoulder to Kelley, before disappearing in 'a little fiery cloud'. Kelley returned the books to Dee, still waiting in the garden.[43] Other books and the 'powder' were returned on an unrecorded occasion.[44]

Of all the episodes in these manuscripts, the sixteenth-century's most remarkable account of angelic magic, this most defies historical explanation. History cannot account for what Kelley did and what Dee believed he saw. It can only describe the consequences. The next day the 'actions' abruptly began again when Dee requested that Vilem Rozmberk should be admitted to their holy fellowship.

Fifty years old, as Burgrave of Bohemia, Rozmberk held extensive but vague powers. Though a devout Catholic, he supported a broad-minded, moderate and anti-papal religious policy, as did his Protestant brother, Peter. With other culturally cosmopolitan magnates, they considered toleration the only basis for national solidarity, given Bohemia's complexities. Dee had again found patrons religiously and intellectually open to the possibilities of angel magic. Rozmberk had been friends with Dee's idealised Maximilian II, avidly collected alchemical, kabbalistic, astrological and apocalyptic books, and probably read Dee's pamphlet.[45] For decades Rozmberk had employed alchemists in Prague, on his southern Bohemian estates, and in Silesia, all places that Dee and Kelley visited.

The fact that Rozmberk's participation appears so unheralded emphasises that the angelic records give only a limited insight into Dee and Kelley's relationship with Rudolf's Court. On the same day the angels restored the books, the Papal nuncio reported that Dee and 'the cripple', Kelley, were creating 'a new superstition, not to say heresy' known 'to the Emperor and all the Court'.[46] The Venetian ambassador reported from Prague that though Dee 'did not profess a Christian life' but claimed angelic revelations, 'he has a following'.[47] The papal attacks themselves indicated how much their apocalyptic reform drive, verified by their alchemical successes, strongly impressed the Court, Rozmberk and even the Emperor, despite gossip against them in Prague.

Just how strongly can be seen from the angelic action of 30 April. God promised a covenant with Rozmberk, who would purify the Empire where Maximilian and Rudolf had failed. On May Day 1586, Dee revealed this offer to Rozmberk, who devoutly promised to reform himself and Rudolf through the angelic instructions. Rozmberk also prayed that Rudolf would grant Dee another audience and be 'restored to the favour of God'. He promised to protect Dee, having been made his patron by God.[48]

Believing his place in Bohemia to be secure, Dee travelled to the famous glasshouses at Valkenaw, renowned for producing alchemical vessels, and then on to the great trading city of Leipzig in Saxony. He hoped to find replies to his letters sent to England in November 1585. Disappointed, he wrote to Walsingham on 14 May 1586, intending his message also for Elizabeth. He acknowledged that his previous letters might have been ignored 'for the strangeness of the phrases' and because many Englishmen construed his godly actions 'to a contrary sense'. Dee carefully wrote nothing about his reconciliation with Rome. Seeking Walsingham's attention, he alluded to a vague Catholic alliance against England, and claimed that he had sent Malaspina packing to Rome 'with a flea in his ear' that terrified 'the whole State Romish and Jesuitical'. He again asked Walsingham to send Thomas Digges to witness their alchemical success, because God had not yet 'utterly cut off' his merciful purposes from Elizabeth.[49]

For obvious reasons, Dee pretended to be the victim of popish tyranny. However, for once his predictions came true. On 23 May, after Dee and Kelley's return to Prague, the new nuncio, Filippo Sega, announced that during their absence he had denounced them to the Emperor Rudolf for heresy, 'necromancy and other prohibited arts'. On 26 May they appealed to Rozmberk, but he intervened too late. The irresolute Emperor had crumbled under heavy papal pressure and decreed their banishment on 29 May. Sega had demanded Dee and Kelley's condemnation during his first audience, meaning that Pope Sixtus V had personally targeted them. Sega insisted they be sent to Rome, where Dee's dabbling in forbidden arts had been censured twenty years earlier. Despite second thoughts Emperor Rudolf could not rescind the order. Dee and Kelley had six days to leave the Habsburg lands.[50]

CHAPTER 17

The Magnificent Master Alchemist

Before Dee and Kelley left, all states had been warned against Dee's 'religious innovations'. The city of Erfurt in Thuringia refused them leave to stay, despite Rozmberk's request.[1] Pucci trailed behind them, beseeching them to submit to the Pope, under the nuncio's protection. Dee's repeated failures in Court politics show how poor he was at reading character. Only on 11 July 1586 did he realise that Pucci, as the angels had warned, was conspiring with Sega. Dee eventually persuaded Pucci to return to Prague on 17 July, taking with him a letter to Sega restating their orthodoxy and another to Rozmberk.[2]

Dee and his household turned west, towards the Court of Landgrave Wilhelm IV at Kassel, on the direct route from Prague and Erfurt to England. Dee had visited there in 1563–64 and later corresponded with Landgrave Wilhelm, yet another princely mediator between religious extremists. He corresponded on natural philosophy with Dee's intellectual circle, patronised mathematicians, and maintained precise instruments for astronomical observations like Dee's.

Dee owned several technical treatises by Wilhelm's experts. The landgrave shared Dee's belief that the 1572 supernova appeared in the sphere of Venus and portended great changes. He had also made careful calculations about the 1584 Great Conjunction of Saturn and Jupiter, believing it presaged global cataclysms. Dee arrived at Kassel to find the Landgrave and his research team preoccupied with using Tycho Brahe's improved instruments for an enormous series of solar and stellar observations, like Dee's of the 1550s. They would eventually catalogue a thousand stars.[3]

Wilhelm showed less interest in alchemical medicine and the philosopher's stone. Dee knew he dismissed the 'infinite numbers of sophists' who promised 'mountains of gold'. However, Dee still found his reception at Kassel that summer disappointing.[4] Within months Stephen Powle relayed to Walsingham gossip he had picked up at Kassel about Dee's pretensions and apocalyptic notions. These raised further questions about Dee amongst conservatives at Elizabeth's Court.

Years later Dee claimed that he had hired a single coach for his family. But he arrived at Kassel, Powle maliciously related, in a train of four coaches. Trying to save face after his expulsion from Prague, Dee claimed to have abandoned Rudolf because of his 'slender entertainment'. To 'show his greatness', sneered Powle, Dee also asked official permission to stay at Kassel, an unnecessary ostentation.[5] Powle informed Walsingham that Dee publicly claimed he lived on Elizabeth's financial support, and again attributed his departure from England to the 'envy of some of the nobility'. Worse still, Dee gave the impression that he was possessed by a 'proud and fanatical spirit'.

Dee presented Landgrave Wilhelm with his new Latin pamphlet 'About God's Secrets and Mighty Works, called in the Apocalypse Alpha and Omega'. This described the nuncio's tyranny and defended the angelic revelations about 'the great catastrophe overhanging the world'. It showed how Dee kept returning to the kabbalistic and apocalyptic preoccupations of his *Monas*. The first page bore the Monad symbol, with the same alchemical verse from Genesis 27:28 that appeared on the title page of the *Monas*: 'May God give thee of the dew of heaven and the fatness of the earth'.

Powle reported that Dee blasphemously signed the work 'Deus Londinensis', taken to mean, ambiguously, Dee or Saint or God of London. Overall, Powle assured Walsingham, Dee disliked all religions. He proclaimed an alternative apocalyptic vision, allegedly revealed by the angel Gabriel, that 'there must forthwith be a restorer of the house of

Israel' to its former terrestrial glory. This exceeded even the revelations at Prague but recalls his expectation in *Monas* about the conversion of the Jews, the Joachimite prophecy that Elizabeth would rule from Jerusalem, and Dee's exchanges with the mystical prophet Roger Edwards in July 1580, when they agreed on the 'paradoxal Restitution Judaical' of Israel. Dee was always drawn to paradox.[6]

Dee was probably unaware that Edwards had already cornered the Kassel market for such revelations. Edwards traversed Germany in the late summer of 1585, interrogating leading divines about his treatise on Israel's restitution. Like the English bishops, most had fobbed him off.[7] Edwards had harangued the Court at Kassel about restoring the Jews to their 'glorious estate', ushering in a new world without sin until the Elect were translated to heaven like Enoch and Elijah. Edwards received a cool reception, and since Dee agreed that the Elect would be 'translated from life to life as Enoch and Elijah were', probably the Court at Kassel also dismissed him.[8]

Fortunately for Dee, by 8 August Rozmberk had persuaded Rudolf to allow Dee and Kelley to reside on the Rozmberk estates in southern Bohemia, well away from the Court. They spent most of the next two years at Trebon, one of the Rozmberks' less important towns, though with good fishing for Kelley in the recently constructed local ponds. Marking their more settled life, from his arrival at Trebon on 14 September 1586, Dee began recording events in a different *ephemerides*, using the Gregorian calendar. Though discreetly removed hundreds of miles from Rudolf's Court and political influence, Dee and Kelley received visits from Rozmberk and Laski.

The angelic actions resumed on 19 September, after the six-month hiatus the angels had commanded. Dee placed the angelical stone in its gold frame on the Holy Table 'with its appurtenances', wax seals with mysterious symbols, tin seals with more magic circles inscribed with angelic names, and the Ring of Solomon. But Kelley had lost interest in cosmic revelations about Nature's secrets and the coming Apocalypse. The angels tried to interest Rozmberk in his political prospects. On 14 October they prophesied his triumph in the political turmoil that would hit Bohemia within three years. However, Rozmberk discouraged such fantasies, and henceforth the angels largely abandoned political prophecy.[9]

In fact, with one important exception, the angelic conversations rather fizzled out from here. Dee recorded them at long intervals. Those that Kelley found time for largely dealt with alchemy, reflecting Kelley's growing reputation, which increasingly attracted visitors to Trebon. From early October 1586 Dee made many cryptic references to successful alchemical processes, expeditions for alchemical vessels, and Kelley's visits to Rozmberk's laboratories in his palace at Prague.

This accelerated the power shift in their relationship. In December the English Muscovy merchant Edward Garland finally tracked Dee down to present Tsar Feodor's opulent offer of employment. Dee declined, but on 19 December Kelley 'made a public demonstration of the philosopher's stone' before Garland and his brother Francis. A grain of the stone transmuted an ounce and a quarter of common mercury to almost an ounce of gold. Dee and Kelley divided the gold and gave Edward Garland the crucible. It was a gift with consequences.[10]

Dee and Kelley naturally expected Francis Garland to inform Burghley and Walsingham. Francis then became a courier between Dee and Walsingham, and inevitably the latter's informant.[11] The months of January to March 1587 passed with Dee and Kelley carrying out alchemical procedures and undertaking mysterious journeys searching for materials. Rozmberk gave increasing rewards to Kelley, who passed a smaller share on to Dee.[12] The angelic actions on 4 April chiefly related to using the philosopher's stone to make gold for Rozmberk to purchase weapons for use against rival clans, who had turned Rudolf against Kelley.[13]

The angels informed Kelley that he remained childless because he had defied their commands in marrying. Suddenly they insisted that Dee and Kelley should 'participate one with another'. Apparently scandalised by the sexual implications, Kelley withdrew from scrying, demanding that Dee's son Arthur replace him in the pursuit. When Arthur failed to 'scry' anything, Kelley resumed scrying, but the sexual topic reappeared.[14] On 18 April the angels contrasted God's infinite mercy, which could turn apparent sin into virtue, with man's corrupt judgement. After rambling somewhat, they declared that obedience to God and resistance to Satan required 'unity amongst you'. Dee hoped this meant spiritual love, but Kelley believed it meant carnal love and demanded angelic clarification.

To Dee's amazed grief the angels confirmed they meant 'common and indifferent using of Matrimonial Acts amongst any couple of us four'.[15] Initially, Kelley may have invented this as an excuse to get rid of Dee or at least to abandon the angels and concentrate on alchemy. But in a typically unstable outburst, he then claimed a contrary spiritual visitation lasting four hours, one of several crucial occasions when he saw visions outside the show-stones.

A spirit called 'Ben' warned them that unless they obeyed the sexual injunction immediately, the powder of transmutation would become useless. Kelley became increasingly disturbed. He rambled wildly until 2 a.m., telling Dee he did evil to demand proof of this doctrine and would be led prisoner to Rome, that Elizabeth and Philip II would be destroyed from Heaven, that the Pope would die and his successor be the last for some years. Furthermore, a Habsburg would conquer England until ejected by a native king; parts of the Book of Enoch were false; Antichrist would appear soon; Elijah and Enoch would return from Paradise; St John the Evangelist still lived, invisibly, and had killed Julian the Apostate; and at Rome they would meet four others who received angelic revelation.

The only lucid revelation identified Francis Garland as Burghley's spy and warned that when sent for from England, they should refuse. Dee remained sceptical because of Kelley's previous lying. Yet, he told a distressed Jane Dee, he accepted that their 'cross-matching' must be done for God's secret purposes. Meric Casaubon's printed text of 1659 discreetly omitted Jane's condition, still in the manuscript, for yielding to God's command: that they share one chamber 'that I might not be far from her'. Casaubon also omitted prurient angelic questioning about sexual details after the event.[16]

Kelley finally convinced Dee on 20 April, through the angel Raphael's revelation of the spiritual cipher hidden within the Tables of Enoch. Raphael demanded they obey or receive God's plague. Dee now submitted to God's unfathomable will. The next day he drew up a covenant stressing that they obeyed as did Abraham when he sacrificed his son Isaac. Kelley's version minimised his role in the actions, stressed his doubts about the doctrine, and blamed Dee for the pact. Dee's zeal, he claimed, had overcome his reluctance, though he refused their wives' request for fresh angelic confirmation.

On 1 May Kelley prompted Dee to see the Archangel Michael, thus again confirming the new doctrine. On 3 May Dee, Kelley, Jane Dee and Joan Kelley signed the covenant, which was confirmed by the angels on the 6th.[17] After further angelic confirmation and some legerdemain with the crystal by Kelley, on 21 May they swapped wives. After a month of Kelley's manipulation, Dee uncritically accepted all Kelley's visions.[18]

Dee kept detailed records of the actions for a while longer. On 23 May the angels reiterated that only God could judge sin and that He 'will shortly visit the earth'. Dee and Kelley were 'the chosen of this last days'. The apocalyptic timetable would unfold within a hundred days, giving them complete understanding of all the angelic revelations and humbling critics who called them 'sorcerers' and 'vagabonds'. In a week the use of the powder would be explained. In ten months Muscovy and Tartary would unite, then fall upon Poland, Bohemia, Germany and Italy. Within two years Rome would be destroyed. Antichrist would arise in the north, 'and vengeance shall be on all the earth'.[19]

Dee's manuscript of the angelic conversations ends with questions from Rozmberk. Perhaps impressed by Kelley's alchemy and its associated apocalyptic prophecies, he eventually wanted to know the political future in Poland after Stephen Bathory died, and how he should advise Rudolf on imperial affairs and relations with the papacy. Kelley asked the angels about the philosopher's stone and whether Joan Kelley could conceive. Dee added a question on his wife Jane's health. More poignantly, he asked about the condition of England and Elizabeth.[20] For though his 'Diary' referred to later angelic actions, and even to repeated performances of the 'holy pact', they are lost to us.[21]

For the next two years Dee recorded only the burgeoning interest of the powerful in Kelley the master alchemist, and their complete disinterest in Dee's insights into the hidden structures of Nature. Elizabeth,

Burghley and Walsingham began trying to entice Kelley back to England to make gold for the Queen, who was now facing the overwhelming forces of Spain. If Dee expected to resurrect his career in England, it could now only be as Kelley's assistant. Would Kelley return with him?

This seemed unlikely as Dee became more dependent on Kelley's alchemical abilities. Kelley's increasing authority exacerbated tensions in the household. That in turn compounded the emotional turmoil created by the intermittent sexual 'cross-matching', or wife-swapping, until 1587. The associated stress further destabilised Kelley's already uncertain psychological state. Dee's cryptic 'Diary' shows Kelley guiding Dee in their alchemical experiments but easing him out of Rozmberk's favour, until a household emerged that was now led by Kelley.

Dee's growing fears about being marginalised can be seen in the increasingly complicated code he used to disguise sensitive 'Diary' entries. From writing English in Greek letters, he changed to writing English backwards in Greek letters, and finally to writing in Latin using Greek letters. Above all, by late 1587 Dee found himself uneasily poised between contrasting loyalties. Kelley increasingly sought Rozmberk and Rudolf's patronage. They ignored Dee, who wanted to return to England but realised that appearing there without Kelley's alchemical skills would be pointless. He had never been able to control Kelley, who no longer needed him. Therefore, when Kelley finally eased him out in early 1589 by excluding him from their shared alchemy, he could only procrastinate en route to England, hoping that Kelley would join him.

In the summer of 1587 Kelley began working with mercury in Rozmberk's mansion at Trebon. Dee initially shared the distillation and made the astrological observations to concentrate beneficial influences.[22] Dee and Kelley divided the 'mercury animal' they created. However, household relations were fraught. In July 1587 Jane Dee and Joan Kelley, and Edward and John, grudgingly reconciled, but as on previous occasions Kelley reverted within weeks to 'most terrible threats'.[23]

After having ignored Dee's letters for two years, the first sign of English interest in Kelley appeared in late August 1587. An English spy, Edward Whitlock, using the cover name John Basset, appeared in Trebon. He taught Dee's son Arthur for a year before absconding.[24] In late October Rozmberk built additional furnaces. For a while Dee and Kelley followed a traditional alchemical regime based on Kelley's writings and Dee's two books on the philosopher's stone, one translated from French by Dee at angelic command, the other extracted by Kelley from the 'Book of Dunstan', Dee's alchemical patron saint.[25] Yet Kelley chafed at having to collaborate with Dee and began turning the household against him. After the regular six-monthly angelic action in late October, Kelley, backed up by Joan, told their servants that Dee dealt with the Devil. Jane was now pregnant, but whether by Dee or Kelley they could not know. At his birth on 28 February 1588 they named the child Theodore, 'Gift of God'.[26]

In late November 1587 Francis Garland brought letters from Edward Dyer and Richard Young, enclosing Elizabeth's command to return to England.[27] Facing an imminent Spanish invasion, Elizabeth and Burghley had convinced themselves that they must harness Kelley's ability to make gold. Sending a royal letter would attract unwanted attention, so Elizabeth used Dyer and Young as cover. A month later other couriers arrived at Trebon, 'thinking we were ready to come into England upon the Queen's letters sent for us'.[28]

In February 1588 Kelley showed Dee how he distilled antimony, following George Ripley's 'Bosom Book', which Dee read aloud during their procedures.[29] Dee may have been anxious to return to England, but only now, after Theodore's birth, did he and Kelley reply to Elizabeth via Dyer and Young. More messages were sent back to England in April, because Kelley temporised about returning, as his demonstrations of transmutation became bravura displays of alchemical expertise, beyond Dee's knowledge and skill. Relations deteriorated further, and Dee had to ask the Kelleys for 'mutual charity', so that he and Jane could receive Easter Communion, a request that harked back to Dee's childhood religion.

Dee finally understood that Kelley would abandon him for Rozmberk's patronage. Yet in May Kelley revealed 'the great secret' to Dee, 'God be thanked'. This brought Edward Dyer out to visit them in July, the first of his several attempts to persuade Kelley to return to England. That he travelled in the midst of frantic preparations against the Armada testifies to how seriously Elizabeth and Burghley took Kelley's alchemy.

When Dyer arrived he immediately snubbed Dee and focused on Kelley. Though the two men then reconciled, Dee had now had a clear demonstration that his future at Elizabeth's Court would depend on Kelley. Dyer left in August, convinced that Kelley could perform transmutation, through 'the divine water' Dee saw in late August, thanks to 'the magnificent master and my incomparable friend Mr Edward Kelly', thus revealing a significant elevation in Kelley's status. That continued in September when something mysterious, possibly transmutation, was delivered by 'the gift of God and Master E. K. '. Yet days later Dee finally perceived 'the rancour and dissimulation' when Kelley excluded him from his alchemical work. 'God deliver me', he added, because this left him completely isolated and far from home.[30]

When Dyer's servants returned in November to recall Kelley, Dee had to pretend the invitation included him, though after Dyer's report only Kelley's alchemy interested Elizabeth. Dee replied to the Queen in a formal letter, carefully written in his exquisite italic hand. He naturally omitted the information that Kelley had no intention of returning. He rejoiced at Elizabeth's Armada victory and alluded to the apocalyptic language of *Memorials*, happy to obey 'a most secret beck of the most mighty Lady, Opportunity'. He praised her clemency in calling 'me, Mr Kelley, and our families' home 'into your British Earthly Paradise' and promised to 'untangle ourselves' as soon as possible.[31]

Dee even spent Rozmberk's rewards on a new coach for the journey. Yet he knew he could not return without Kelley. By December Kelley had begun to attract alchemical devotees and was offered great friendship and money for 'two ounces of the thing' – the philosopher's stone.[32] Kelley now gave Dee the mercurial water they had been working with, perhaps because he found the powder a more direct route to transmutation.[33] The gift signalled their imminent parting.

In early December, desperately trying to curry favour, Dee gave Kelley his perspective glass, a primitive telescope that 'could make things far off, to seem near, small things to seem great'. Symbolically, Kelley immediately handed this to Rozmberk, who presented it to Rudolf, who had long coveted it for his *kunstkammer*, his enormous collection of curiosities. It purchased Kelley's readmission to Rudolf's favour.[34]

Dee began to postpone his departure in letters to Rozmberk, who would not hear of him staying. In January 1589 Rozmberk told Kelley that Dee must depart. In fact, Kelley reported, cruelly twisting the knife, Rozmberk now wished 'that I should not have come hither, from the very beginning of our coming'.[35] Dee kept dragging his feet, so Rozmberk abruptly gave him forty days to leave and took Kelley away. On 4 February Dee symbolically acknowledged Kelley's alchemical superiority, handing over 'the powder, the books, the glass' for Rozmberk. On 16 February Dee watched Kelley ride away, accompanied by the majority of their servants.[36] He never saw him again.

Once more outmanoeuvred in the patronage stakes, Dee had few options in his apparently bleak future beyond returning to England. He left Trebon with his family in mid-March, heading northwest through Germany. If he were to secure new patronage he had to protect his European reputation, whatever the cost of keeping up appearances. The family travelled in some state in Dee's new coach and four. Two other coaches for the servants followed, with Rudolf's military escort to ensure they left. Behind them toiled wagons groaning with Dee's library, their household goods and clothes. The convoy wound its way via Kassel to Bremen near the German coast. Dee later claimed the whole journey cost the staggering sum of £600.[37]

They arrived at Bremen on 9/19 April 1589, Dee's use of both Gregorian and Julian dating systems suggesting his divided loyalties. His last hope was that Kelley would relent and come back to him, so that they could return to England together. He rented a house in Bremen in May, intending to sit tight until Kelley remembered where his true allegiance lay. Located on the fastest route from Prague to England, through the nearby port of Stade, Dee could theoretically monitor Kelley's communications with England and correspond quickly with him. The presence of the notorious conjuror disturbed the Bremen city council until Landgrave Wilhelm wrote Dee a testimonial.

Dee tried to ingratiate himself with Walsingham by becoming a listening post on affairs in the Low Countries.[38] He reported on the 'Archtraitor' Christopher Parkins, a Jesuit sent from Rome to assassinate Elizabeth, whose schemes 'my great friend' Edward Kelley had uncovered at Prague. This must finally silence the old canard that Dee somehow spied for Walsingham. Parkins had abandoned the Jesuit order and was actually Elizabeth's accredited diplomatic agent in Germany, Poland and Bohemia.

In August Dee heard the bitter news that Rudolf had created Kelley a Baron of Bohemia. He relayed this to Walsingham, again accused Parkins of treason and analysed Low Countries politics. He remounted his hobby horse of the *Memorials*, insisting once more that Elizabeth should be 'Queen over all their Provinces'.[39]

All this was merely marking time until Kelley reappeared. Dee kept from Walsingham the decision he had already revealed in a letter to Richard Young, that he had by now given up on Kelley and intended to return before winter, because Jane was three months pregnant.[40] In mid-September she complained bitterly about their poverty. Dee sulked, in 'low spirits' because of her 'ingratitude'. Their landlord gave them notice, probably for unpaid rent, and yet another of Dee's servants departed to seek better fortune with Kelley.[41]

Kelley meanwhile, judging from the stream of messengers through Stade recorded by Dee, had been haggling with Elizabeth over the conditions for his return. By early November, Walsingham's letters gave Dee some reason to hope that Kelley might actually reappear. He still hoped to intercept him at Stade. Instead, on 17/27 November 1589 he encountered Edward Dyer at the port, again hurrying to Prague, either to persuade Kelley to return or to learn from the alchemical master. Clearly the game was up. Dee and his family took ship for England two days later. They landed on 3 December (Julian calendar), after more than six years in Europe.[42]

CHAPTER 18

The Counter-Revolution Against Magic

Broke yet again, Dee went straight to Richard Young's house at Stratford, east of London. Beyond their family connection, Young had political clout, as the Privy Council's chief investigator of Catholic subversion. As a Customs official who lent out the monies he collected before accounting for them to the Exchequer, he also possessed the ready cash Dee needed. The boxes and trunks of books we have already seen inventoried in Young's house in 1595 may be Dee's travelling library, deposited as security against a loan that was never redeemed.

In some respects England seemed unchanged, because while Elizabeth lived Dee could still seek her crucial patronage. Rested and restored, he gained an audience at Richmond on 9 December 1589, when he complained about the despoliation of his Mortlake library. The Privy Council appointed four commissioners to help trace his missing books and materials. He also mentioned his inability to provide for Christmas, so Elizabeth promised £100. Typically, he only received £50 and never discovered 'what is become of the other fifty'. More importantly, Elizabeth told Burghley to ask John Whitgift, now Archbishop of Canterbury, to find Dee some lucrative sinecure in the Church.

Her generosity signalled not so much her esteem for Dee as her hope that it would persuade Kelley to return. Dee no doubt implied that Kelley was on his way. On 10 December, his Court reputation somewhat restored, Dee borrowed £100 to rent his former Mortlake house from his brother-in-law Nicholas Fromoundes, since he could not repay the £400 mortgage. Five days later John and a heavily pregnant Jane returned to a devastated house, stripped of goods and furniture, the alchemical laboratories bare, and over five hundred books missing from the bookshelves.[1]

The Queen's favour encouraged others to apologise for Dee's losses. Adrian Gilbert offered unlimited compensation for the stolen goods and Dee's share in the Devonshire mines. A week later Thomas Kelley brought news that his brother Edward would return. Dee instantly borrowed £10 from Thomas. In mid-January Dee agreed compensation with Fromoundes for his purloined goods and damages. By the time their daughter Madimi, named after a young female angel, was born on 25 February 1590, John and Jane could believe that they were rebuilding some sort of normality.

This seemed established in late March when Walsingham, who believed in transmutation but not in every adept, consulted Dee about two London alchemists alleged to have made the philosopher's stone. However, tragically for Dee, 'Good Sir Francis Walsingham died' on 6 April.[2] Three days later Ambrose Dudley, Earl of Warwick, was buried. Leicester had died in September 1588. Death had transformed the political calculations of the Elizabethan Court, depriving Dee of powerful patrons at a time when war, economic crisis and the Crown's financial problems had vastly increased competition amongst courtiers and aspirants for diminishing rewards.

Dee's hopes of patronage now depended largely on the aged and over-worked Burghley, who forgot nothing, including Dee's criticisms about him uttered in Prague. Dee's hopes of advancement would also founder on the Lord Treasurer's cautious accommodation with a new order in State and Church. While Dee had been abroad a profound cultural counter-revolution, which partly aimed to suppress the occult philosophy that Dee represented, had transformed the Court. The frustrations of Dee's later career provide an object lesson in the consequences of a deliberate conservative campaign to change late Elizabethan culture.

That campaign originated in the ecclesiastical politics of Elizabethan England, whose implications for Dee's later life have never been explored. The campaign's roots stretch back to 1576, when Burghley encouraged Hatton's rise as Elizabeth's personal favourite to counterbalance Leicester. Hatton retained Elizabeth's trust because he shared her instinctive desire to enforce obedience to the Elizabethan Church established in 1559, thus stonewalling further reform. As Hatton's star rose, hopes of progressive reform of the Church sank.[3] His closeness to the Queen on Church matters increased Hatton's influence over the appointment of a new generation of bishops unsympathetic to agitation for reform, especially John Aylmer as Bishop of London in 1576. Hatton gave Aylmer Elizabeth's instructions: 'to cut off (even as her Majesty termed it) and to correct offenders on both sides which swerve from the right path of obedience.'[4] Aylmer zealously followed his orders, but his appointment foreshadowed the appearance of a far more formidable figure in the Church, whose influence would be felt for generations.

On 23 September 1583, while Dee, Kelley and Laski lay windbound on the coast of Kent, a few miles away John Whitgift was installed Archbishop of Canterbury with heraldic pomp. Bishop of Worcester since 1577 thanks to Hatton's patronage, he had administered Canterbury province following Grindal's suspension. Revolting against his former radicalism, Whitgift made his reputation by attacking the Presbyterians, partly for their reliance on spiritual inspiration that resembled Dee's belief in angelic revelations.

Criticising the Presbyterian leader Thomas Cartwright, Whitgift had stressed human learning and training against 'gifts and graces miraculously' poured into the Elect. Learning and wisdom did not come 'by inspiration only'.[5] Whitgift suspected that Presbyterian claims to divine illumination and charismatic authority merely cloaked a desire for 'popularity' with the foolish multitude, as a prelude to subversion.

Even before Whitgift became a Privy Councillor in February 1586, Elizabeth habitually backed his harder line against Presbyterians. Burghley considered Elizabeth's a 'mixed' monarchy, limited by the enduring interests of the political elite. Whitgift, however, shared Elizabeth's exalted conception of her imperial authority in Church and State matters, the basis for the powerful Ecclesiastical High Commission, which he used to suppress both real and imagined challenges to the establishment.[6]

Whitgift's influence as Archbishop of Canterbury enabled others in Elizabethan society, such as Reginald Scot, to condemn radical Protestants' desire for 'popularity' through spiritual illumination. Spiritual hysteria about further Church reform threatened social conflict. Within months of Whitgift becoming archbishop, Scot published his *Discovery of Witchcraft [and] the knavery of conjurors* (1584), dedicated to the Archdeacon of Canterbury and Dean of Rochester. Like other conformists Scot wanted to marginalise Presbyterianism from political society, by connecting Presbyterian claims to spiritual illumination with politically suspect forms of magic amongst the lower orders.

Scot argued that God revealed the future to 'the wise, the rich, the learned', not to the poor.[7] He attacked radical reformers who wanted a new Church to advance 'their magical words and curious directions'.[8] His rational attack on magical beliefs drew in Dee's occult philosophy. Miracles and prophecies had ceased with the Apostles, and all angelic revelations since Christ were impostures. The 'allegorical games' of the Kabbalah allowed 'atheists', meaning anyone Scot despised, to claim 'power over angels and devils'. Reports of seeing angels in crystals were counterfeit and popish.[9]

Scot dismissed invocations to angels such as Dee's, especially that they 'may give me a true answer of all my demands'. By publishing the seals used by adepts to trap angelic spirits in crystals, Scot hoped to debunk magic's mystique. He equated conjurors with witches and both with deluded alchemists. Thanks to Whitgift's protection, Scot could even take a concluding swipe at Leicester for protecting another deceitful conjuror in 1582, which touched Dee's own notoriety as Leicester's 'conjuror'.[10]

Many contemporaries disagreed with Scot's sweeping scepticism, but he exercised disproportionate influence over the conservative, conformist clergy grouped around Whitgift.[11] Amongst them, Aylmer tried to prosecute Dee for conjuring with the Devil in September 1584. Leicester's death freed Whitgift's protégés Richard Bancroft, Richard Cosin and

Samuel Harsnett to criticise the Presbyterians for their magical claims. They frequently cited Scot against the Presbyterian exorcist John Darrell's use of prayer and fasting to cure the demonically possessed, and they would gleefully exploit Dee's involvement with Darrell in Manchester some years later.

Books published by Dee's former pupils, John and Richard Harvey, demonstrate the increasing conservative pressure to exclude Dee's kind of prophetic politics. Both Harveys had publicised Dee's apocalyptic inter- pretations of the 1583 Great Conjunction and other cosmic signs of the end of time. Yet in early 1588 John retracted his predictions about the coming year. He defended natural magic, which he had learned from 'John Dee, a man sufficiently known for his long study, and skill in such matters'. But he now denounced angel magic as 'devilish negromantical practices', and took special pains to dismiss Trithemius on the angelic control of history, as 'erroneous reckonings, and fabulous traditions'.[12] John Harvey acknowledged Hatton as chief instigator of this work, indicating Hatton's increasing conservatism since the time when James Sandford had publicly linked his name with prophecies for 1583 and 1588.

Richard Harvey's new conservative tone reflects the same pressure. Richard had dedicated his *Astrological Discourse* on the Great Conjunction of 1583 to Bishop Aylmer of London.[13] That was foolish. He failed to appreciate how much his excited predictions of abrupt political transfor- mation conflicted with Aylmer's tough line against Presbyterian appeals to the inner spirit. Aylmer soon put him straight, denouncing Richard's predictions from England's most important pulpit at St Paul's Cathedral.[14]

By the time Dee returned to England in late 1589, Richard had aban- doned his former astrological beliefs and now condemned the Presbyterians to boot. Mixing conservative astronomy and politics, Richard predicted that if they succeeded the kingdom would descend into 'anarchy, with a moving earth ... in Copernicus guise'. Copernicans subverted the natural order of the heavens, just as Presbyterians threat- ened 'to lift fools on horseback and set kings on foot'.[15]

The late 1580s economic crisis stiffened resistance to the impover- ished Crown's rising demands for money to fight Spain. This provoked an authoritarian reaction, strengthening Whitgift's and Hatton's suspicions that religious nonconformity would generate popular revolt.[16] The dominance of their 'little faction' drove their Presbyterian opponents into desperate eschatological hopes, comparable to Dee's angelic predictions. In February 1589 Hatton opened Parliament by warning Members of Parliament against innovation, except to control 'papists or puritans'. Dee's alchemist friend Thomas Digges complained that Hatton had effectively redefined sincere Protestants as 'troublers of the state'.[17]

Days later, Bancroft, successively Hatton's and Whitgift's chaplain, proclaimed this new hard line in his *Sermon Preached at Paules Cross the 9 of February*. Robustly defending episcopacy, he smeared the Presbyterians as 'false prophets', fellows with 'Arrians, Papists, Libertines, Anabaptists and the Family of Love', who pretended inspired insights, 'despise government', and 'speak evil of them that are in dignity and authority'.

Bancroft criticised an enthusiastic manuscript prophecy 'that Elizabeth now Queen of England is ordained of God to be Queen of Jerusalem', which was uncomfortably close to Dee's belief in a restored Israel.[18] Presbyterians responded through 'Martin Marprelate, gentleman', who employed satirical street language to mock the pompous lordly bishops.[19] Whitgift enlisted Thomas Nashe to reply in kind, beginning in *An Almond for a Parrot* (1589), which echoed Whitgift's earlier attacks on popular prophetic gullibility. 'Visions are ceased', Nashe insisted, 'all extraordinary revelation ended ... wherefore broach no more heresies under colour of inspiration.' At Whitgift's bidding, Nashe later ridiculed mystical prophets, especially when Dee lost political influence in 1592.[20]

Bancroft hired John Lyly to produce popular musical playlets. Lyly lampooned astrologers using Richard Harvey's *Astrological Discourse*, attacked alchemists from Scot's *Discovery*, and created the Stage Puritan immortally satirised in Ben Jonson's *The Alchemist*, which ridiculed Dee and Kelley's magic. At some point Jonson acquired Dee's ritual magic treatise by Honorius of Thebes.[21] About the time that Bancroft preached in February 1589 appeared the cheap pamphlet *The History of the Damnable Life and Deserved Death of Doctor John Faustus*, attacking another astrologer, mathematician and conjuror who sought to perfect human knowledge by conjuring angelic revelations. It could soon be bought for fourpence. Between 1589 and 1594 a rash of plays against Devil-invoking magicians appeared on the London stage, beginning with Christopher Marlowe's *Doctor Faustus* in 1589.[22]

Whitgift's suspicions about magic are evident in his response to Elizabeth's command in December 1589 to find Dee some sinecure. He questioned Dee's activities in Poland and Bohemia, so that Burghley had to provide a testimonial 'favourably interpreting' Dee's European journeys.[23] In the coming years, wherever Dee sought preferment or to regain his rectories, Whitgift blocked him, determined to reassert episcopal authority over Church appointments and appalled by the 'evil bishops and deans' appointed through Leicester's patronage. Dee again 'made motion' for the Deanery of Gloucester in 1594.[24] Hatton had appointed Dee's replacement at Upton-upon-Severn, which illustrates the forces now ranged against him.[25]

Fortunately, Dee still had a few cards to play. After Dyer returned to England without Kelley in mid-March 1590, Dee was able to use his continuing correspondence with Kelley as leverage.[26] Kelley kept tantalising Burghley with promises to return. Burghley's reply in May studiously avoided naming alchemy but stated he believed Dyer's reports. He confirmed Elizabeth's letters of protection because 'this felicity' is 'only by you ... expected', despite criticisms around the Court, which he felt compelled to pass on, that Kelley was a fraud, a traitor, a Catholic and an impostor.[27]

Knowing Kelley's desirability nonetheless, Dee exploited their connection that early summer. News of Dee's rising Court reputation even reached distant Long Leadenham in Lincolnshire. His former curate and successor as rector there, Richard Lange, thought it politic to send him £6 in early May. On 20 May Dee took Richard Young with him to press Whitgift about restoring his rectories. As an aggressive enforcer for Whitgift's High Commission, Young's presence reminded Whitgift of Dee's family connections and his political leverage. Accordingly, he 'used me well'. The next day Dee tried to convince Aylmer of his orthodoxy by warning him about a planned bacchanalian feast at Brentford.[28]

Dee also used his alchemical learning to cultivate influential courtiers such as the explorer Richard Cavendish and Sir George Carey, Marshal of Elizabeth's household. In late May they petitioned Elizabeth and Whitgift for Dee to be made Provost of Eton College. The position seemed to be his, until a week later his rivals spread 'terrible ill news' of Kelley's 'open enmity' against Dee and consequently 'of the higher powers their ill opinions conceived of me'.[29] The provostship went elsewhere.

Dee's dependence on his correspondence with Kelley to counteract Whitgift's drive against magic reappears in July 1590. Days after receiving Kelley's latest letter, Dee went to Whitgift and 'talked with him boldly of my right to the parsonages, and of the truth of Sir Edward Kelley his Alchemy'. Two days later, Elizabeth 'disclosed her favour to me' at Court, and the day after Dee began 'my alchemical exercises'.[30]

He had resumed the angelic 'actions' in April with Bartholomew Hickman 'scrying'. These actions, of which Dee left no records, prompted him to reread the angel Uriel's promise in September 1584 that England would be spared destruction for Dee's sake. He added in the margin: 'God will give me England, that is to say, spare it from destruction for my sake.' Dee's inflated sense of his prophetic importance would certainly have reminded Whitgift of those subversives he was trying to suppress.[31]

Even worse, Dee that summer tried to exorcise his children's mentally ill nurse, Ann Frank, whom he believed was demonically possessed. He devoutly prayed for 'virtue and power' and Christ's blessing on the 'holy oil', an alchemical product with which he repeatedly anointed her, just as Catholic priests in his childhood had used consecrated oil as an exorcist's charm. Even if Dee no longer considered himself a priest, Jesuit missionaries in Catholic households were currently using similar rituals, according to a manuscript that fell into government hands in 1594. During exorcisms at Sir George Peckham's house at Denham, Whitgift learned, servant women derived devils' names from 'very strange names written upon the walls ... under the hangings'. Dee had visited Denham and had advised Peckham on American colonisation in 1583, as the Court well knew.

Ann Frank finally succeeded in killing herself in late August 1590. The coroner's inquest would have revealed Dee's exorcism, contravening

Whitgift's attempts to suppress this charismatic practice. Such association with 'devil-conjurors . . . reputed to carry about with them, their familiars in rings and glasses' would damage Dee in Whitgift's opinion.[32] Continuing public fascination with Dee's occult activities helped spread such stories. He later complained to Whitgift that 'untrue fables' about his 'studies philosophical' immediately spread over 'all the Realm'.[33]

Despite this disingenuous complaint, Dee was actually collaborating with magicians from deepest Essex who knew him by reputation, and perhaps with others. In September 1590 Edmund Hunt of Maldon, Essex, 'being long time troubled in his mind' about buried treasure at nearby Beeleigh, consulted Thomas Collyne, a 'cunning man', but also the town policeman of Maldon. Collyne told Hunt to bring earth from Beeleigh. In October, Collyne promised to take it 'to Doctor Dee, and if he should judge to be any money there', Dee 'would make suit to the Queen's Majesty to have a license to dig'.

In October 1574 Dee had petitioned Burghley for such a licence, after being approached by clients whose recurrent dreams pointed towards buried treasure. He would judge the earth by the forces of 'sympathy and antipathy'. The Witchcraft Act of 1563 had made conjuring for buried treasure a felony without royal permission, because powerful magic was required to control the demons commonly believed to guard the treasure. Collyne probably knew Dee long before he first mentions him at Mortlake on 8–9 June 1591. In 1578 Collyne had saved his neck by informing against a group of fellow conjurors, including Thomas Elkes, who knew Dee's house at Mortlake, conjured love magic, invoked spirits to reveal buried treasure, and enclosed spirits in a ring. More dangerously, they predicted that a naval gunner, Robert Mantell, who they claimed was really Edward VI, would soon reclaim his throne. Mantell was subsequently executed.[34] Dee did not request another licence for treasure, a reticence reflecting both Collyne's dubious connections and Whitgift's increasing pressure against magical practices.

Elizabeth continued to protect Dee because alchemy fascinated her. She had written to Kelley in early 1590, promising great rewards for 'the gifts that God has given' him. In May she commanded Burghley to repeat her promises to Kelley, who should 'have regard to her honour' and return to England.[35] When Dee resumed his alchemy in July, after arguing with Whitgift about the truth of Kelley's alchemy, he lent Richard Cavendish the treatise by Denis Zacaire on the philosopher's stone, a treatise he had used with Kelley in Bohemia. He imposed elaborate conditions to preserve its secrecy, knowing that Cavendish regularly discussed alchemy with Elizabeth.[36]

Meanwhile Elizabeth and Burghley had sent Dyer back to Prague to persuade Kelley to return or at least to obtain some of the philosopher's stone for the Queen to use herself. Kelley had written to Burghley in late July describing Emperor Rudolf's immense rewards. At that time he still remained Elizabeth's subject. However, in October, Dyer found Kelley sworn to Rudolf's Privy Council, having renounced his English allegiance, and therefore less inclined to give Dyer 'some medicine to have satisfied her majesty by her own blissful sight'.[37] Elizabeth and Kelley, moreover, had been carrying on their own correspondence, now unfortunately lost. Kelley pretended that Elizabeth and Burghley's refusal to make specific promises to him made Bohemia more attractive.[38] Dyer spent the winter in alchemical work with Kelley and later reported how Kelley used 'a very small quantity of medicine' to transmute 'perfect gold'.[39]

Dee's cultivation of Cavendish and frequent correspondence with Kelley paid off when Elizabeth sent for him on 27 November 1590. By then she had Dyer's and Kelley's latest letters and knew that Kelley refused to share the philosopher's stone. She and Dee may have started some alchemical experiment, since the latter noted the planetary positions for that day. Cavendish then sent Dee £32 and a hogshead of wine, but more importantly the Queen finally prodded the commissioners into action who had been supposed to restore Dee's library at Mortlake a year earlier.

Elizabeth also promised Dee another £100 to provide Christmas cheer. A few days later at Mortlake she publicly acknowledged Dee's alchemical services and actually sent Cavendish with a down payment of £50. Dee's service may have started Whitgift grumbling, for on 16 December she sent Cavendish with a verbal reassurance that Dee should 'do what I would in philosophy and alchemy, and none should check, control or molest me', though he never saw his other £50. Elizabeth no doubt expected Dee to report her patronage of him to Kelley, suggesting the far greater rewards he could expect in return.[40]

Elizabeth had built 'manifold still-houses' at Hampton Court soon after her accession and kept a distilling assistant in her Privy Chamber. Ralph Rabbards dedicated his edition of Ripley's *Compound of Alchemy ... to make the Philosophers Stone* to her the following May, equating her distillation with transmutation. Rabbards informed Elizabeth that only Ripley, Roger Bacon, Thomas Norton 'and especially Master Doctor Dee in his *Monas hieroglyphica*' knew 'the hidden art'. Applying that knowledge in the Queen's distilling houses would undoubtedly produce the philosopher's stone, which had so far eluded her distiller William Huggons. Kelley contributed verses to Rabbards's book praising the stone, and Dee, who would republish the *Monas* in Frankfurt in 1591, added clumsy verses praising Rabbards, who had been his friend since the 1550s.[41]

However, Elizabeth's offer to protect Dee proved necessary. Whitgift and Hatton had determined to marginalise magic from Church and State and made an example of Dee to emphasise the point. In meetings with Whitgift and Burghley from 21 to 24 January 1591, Dee was 'utterly put out of hope for recovering the two parsonages'.[42] Burghley felt that he could best retain influence with Elizabeth by avoiding any confrontation with Whitgift and Hatton, especially regarding their enforcement of conformity. Kelley now claimed from Prague that Hatton had inspired a whispering campaign against him and also made 'divers reproachful speeches even afore her majesty'. Hatton and Elizabeth denied the latter accusation, though the former rang true.[43]

A few months later, Dee encountered disaster. Burghley's correspondence with Kelley had naturally pretended that he merely sought alchemical remedies for his chronic ill-health.[44] But on 12 May 1591, alarmed by another reported Spanish invasion fleet, Burghley finally lost patience with Kelley and Dyer. He wrote to Dyer, denying Hatton's campaign against Kelley, but reporting increasing consensus at Court that Kelley's transmutations were fraudulent. If Dyer could not persuade Kelley to return to England, Burghley would have to accept Court opinion. Dyer could retain his credit either by bringing Kelley home or by obtaining some 'very small portion of the powder, to make a demonstration, in her majesty's own sight, of the perfection of his knowledge'. Elizabeth still believed in Kelley but needed enough powder 'to defray her charges for this summer for her navy'.[45]

Worse still for Dee, Emperor Rudolf had imprisoned Kelley the day before Burghley wrote, and had placed Dyer under house arrest. Officially, the hot-tempered Kelley had killed an imperial official in a duel. A deeper reason, Burghley intimated to Dyer, was that Kelley's transmutation made him a political prize. Catholic forces at Prague could hamstring the English war effort by throwing whatever charges might stick to prevent Kelley leaving. Hence rumours emanating from Prague mentioned many different charges against Kelley, while Rudolf placed all the English there under house arrest.[46]

Elizabeth and Burghley sent Thomas Webb, who shared in Dee's alchemy, to resolve this diplomatic catastrophe and rescue Dyer if possible. In the process they had to abandon Kelley.[47] Consequently, they wrote off Dee, who suddenly resolved to leave the Court. On 27 May he accepted Sir Thomas Jones's offer of his castle, rent free, at Newcastle Emlyn in remote Cardiganshire, and money to support his alchemy.[48] Kelley's fall seemingly ended Dee's attempt to regain his position at Court in May 1591. Yet Dee only left Mortlake in February 1596 and then for the apparently prestigious Wardenship of Christ's College, Manchester. This outcome seemed extremely unlikely in May 1591, given Whitgift and Hatton's triumph over their Presbyterian enemies and occult philosophers. Even so, Burghley's successful counter-attack against the 'little faction' would rely heavily on Dee's occult learning and soon restore him to a privileged place in Elizabeth's counsels.

CHAPTER 19

Conjuring up a Spanish Conquest

To EXPLAIN Dee's improved fortunes we must jump forward to 5 June 1604, when he published a printed petition to James I. Panicked by the draconian Bill 'Against Conjuration, Witchcraft, and dealing with evil and wicked spirits' then passing through Parliament, Dee once again denied slanders that he was 'a Conjuror . . . or Invocator of Devils'. The Act that emerged ordained death for conjuring any evil spirit.[1]

Dee's petition criticised an unnamed 'English traitor', a Catholic exile who 'in Print (Anno 1592, 7 January)' accused Dee of being 'the Conjuror belonging to' Elizabeth's Privy Council.[2] Identifying this slanderer uncovers a forgotten chapter in Dee's biography. It clarifies his connection with the notorious 'School of Night', a group of courtiers and intellectuals associated with Sir Walter Raleigh, whom Catholics stigmatised as 'atheists'. It also explains why Dee's Court career collapsed in November 1592, forcing him to write the 'Compendious Rehearsal' of his life – which despite its title was a carefully selective autobiography – to justify his appeal to Elizabeth's patronage.

It all began when Burghley's need to divert Whitgift and Hatton's increasing attacks on the Presbyterians in 1591 met Dee's need to resurrect his Court career. The Catholic exile's accusation that Dee conjured for Elizabeth's Privy Council reflects Burghley's remarkable turnaround in Church politics in the intervening few months. In late 1591 he used Dee's occult abilities to force this sea change, which led to the imprisonment, torture and execution of Catholic priests and laymen, justifying the traitor's bitter accusation about Dee's 'conjuring'.

By the time Dee was preparing to abandon the Court for Sir Thomas Jones's castle in Cardiganshire in late May 1591, Whitgift and Hatton's vendetta had brought the Presbyterians to a Star Chamber trial for seditious conspiracy. Burghley tried indirectly to slow the process. In mid-May, Elizabeth visited his country house, Theobalds. Burghley, still ignorant of Kelley's arrest, asked Dyer to send some of Kelley's philosopher's stone to defray the staggering expenses of entertaining the Queen. Burghley used pageants to draw Elizabeth's attention to his indispensability, suggesting he needed to retire from the crippling burdens of administration.[3] This indirectly signalled his displeasure at the persecution of the Presbyterians and that he was seeking to deflect their punishment.

Burghley next repeated a familiar tactic by emphasising the threat from English Catholics supporting Spain. He possibly saw how to use Dee's occult learning for this campaign, because Dee did not actually leave Mortlake. Four days after Dee had accepted Jones's offer of his castle, Bartholomew Hickman returned to 'scry' for him. On 19 June Dee noted an interview that he had had with Elizabeth. By then she knew that Kelley had been arrested and Dyer put under house arrest. Considering how Burghley would later use Dee's abilities, Dee may have predicted Spanish plans.

For in contrast to the last eighteen months, when occasional news that Kelley would not return to England had lowered Dee's Court status, his stock now rose appreciably. About 22 July the Countess of Warwick, last of the Dudleys in Elizabeth's Privy Chamber, secured for him the Queen's promise of the Mastership of St Cross Hospital at Winchester, if 'a living fit for me'. This living offered Dee even greater income than his lost rectories, and the hospital could easily house his library and alchemical laboratories.

When a chastened Dyer returned from Prague in early July, he acknowledged Dee's improving courtly reputation by sending him money via Thomas Webb. They solemnly reconciled on 28 July. That day Hickman returned to 'scry' for several sessions, and on 2 August Dee noted

'Mr William Digges his philosophical courtesy: all day', though this 'Diary' entry is too cryptic to be certain whether Dee was referring to alchemy, or casting horoscopes about the political future.[4]

In July 1590 Whitgift had assured Dee that Kelley faked his alchemical transmutations, and Whitgift and Hatton had orchestrated a whispering campaign against Kelley in early 1591. When Dyer now dined with Whitgift and described Kelley's transmutation, he received a frosty reception. Dyer claimed to have watched Kelley put base metal in a crucible, heat it, and put in 'a very small quantity of the medicine' to make 'perfect gold'. Whitgift's response took a leaf from Reginald Scot, linking such gullibility with infidelity, and he warned Dyer to 'take heed what you say'.[5]

Even worse for Burghley and Dee, Whitgift's drive against the Presbyterians provoked extreme responses in the religious underworld. On 19 July 1591, in Cheapside, London, Edmund Coppinger, a minor servant in the Queen's household, and a Yorkshire gentleman, Henry Arthington, both fervent believers in Presbyterianism, proclaimed William Hacket, an illiterate malt-maker from Northamptonshire, God's 'Prophet of Judgement' and 'King of Europe'. They believed Hacket had received 'an Angelical spirit' to remove Whitgift and Hatton, overthrow the established order, release the imprisoned Presbyterians, and usher in the millennium. Unless the 'Discipline of the Lord' was installed, they predicted, England would that year suffer grievous 'famine, pestilence and war'.

Whitgift's propagandists exploited the paper trail connecting the deluded trio with leading Presbyterians. Conformists denounced Hacket's claims to command both black and white magical powers. They compared this imposture with Presbyterian claims to an inspired ecclesiastical polity. Hacket, executed on the day Dee and Dyer reconciled, claimed to converse directly with God, to summon angels into a crystal ball and to exorcise demons through prayer.[6] The scandal gave Whitgift's cultural counter-revolution fresh impetus, by exposing the political threats in magic that closely resembled Dee's angelic practices.

In September Whitgift's protégé Richard Cosin explained how 'Anabaptistical wizards and fanatical sectaries' like Hacket did Satan's work, leading enthusiasts to the 'overthrow of states'.[7] According to Cosin, Hacket declared himself 'a Prophet of God's vengeance', though Hacket's landlord simply thought him 'a conjuror'. A mere yeoman, Hacket could be dismissed, but Coppinger had had Dudley connections and shared Dee's notions. Coppinger's belief that 'he had been very strangely and extraordinarily moved by God to go to her Majesty' and tell her 'the Lords pleasure' – that she 'reform her self, her family, the Common-wealth, and the Church' – recalls Dee's interview with Rudolph II. They both believed 'a secret mystery' would transform the world.[8]

Fortunately for Dee, he avoided Coppinger's threats against the establishment. Cosin alleged the Cheapside prophets planned to depose Elizabeth, purge Whitgift and Hatton from the Privy Council, and then establish Presbyterianism with Hacket as Emperor of Europe.[9] Only his reverent presentation of angelic revelations distinguished Dee from men depicted as subversive terrorists. Other similarities could be unsettling.

Hacket and Coppinger warned a Privy Councillor of a plot against Elizabeth revealed by occult means, just like Dee.[10] Hacket foretold the future by conjuring, including identifying foreign threats to England. Like Dee, Hacket believed that guardian angels watched over him. His revelations required diligent preparation, including the prayer and fasting that Dee used before angelic actions.[11] Like Dee, he prophesied an imminent new world that required casting out devils.[12]

These comparisons matter because Cosin emphasised that self-proclaimed prophets with their 'extraordinary callings, ravishings in spirit, carryings into Heaven' inevitably threatened the natural political order. Just at the edge of Cosin's field of vision stood the nervous figure of John Dee, no doubt relieved that whereas Hacket used 'sympathetic' magic against Elizabeth by stabbing her portrait through the heart, Dee had defended her against the impaled wax images.[13]

Nevertheless, Whitgift's campaign expanded the definition of the lunatic fringe almost to include Dee. In response, Dee laid low. From 3 August to 3 December 1591 his 'Diary' records little beyond a few weather notes. Then suddenly, at 10 a.m. on 14 December, we find him in the Lord Treasurer's secure offices at Whitehall, hearing 'a very gentle answer' from Burghley to his latest request for patronage. Six days later came another 'gentle answer', that 'the Queen would have me have something at this promotion of bishops at hand', meaning the Mastership of St Cross. What had suddenly enabled Dee to overcome Whitgift's obdurate resistance to his promotion?

Basically, Dee solved the problems facing Burghley in late 1591. Burghley was not an innovative thinker. He relied on familiar solutions to political difficulties. In 1591 he needed to prepare the realm against the anticipated Spanish invasion, defend the Presbyterians against Whitgift and Hatton, and scotch that duo's attempt at de facto toleration for English Catholics. He addressed all three problems with a Proclamation against Catholic seminary priests and Jesuits, who seduced English subjects from their obedience. He drafted it in mid-October but only published it in late November.[14] That delay had significant implications for Dee.

The Proclamation created a far more rigorous system than the existing county commissions against Catholic recusants. From late November 1591 the usually haphazard Tudor government machinery minutely enforced it, under constant badgering from Burghley. Over the next few years the imprisonment, torture and execution of Catholic priests and lay recusants reached unprecedented intensity. The Proclamation justified this persecution because Catholic missionaries advanced Philip II's ambition to dominate Christendom, especially by an Armada against England, 'greater for this year to come than ever'.[15] These 'fugitives, rebels and traitors' were recruiting a Fifth Column to support the Spanish invasion. Traitorous exiles such as Cardinal William Allen and the Jesuit Robert Parsons had organised foreign seminaries and had cited English Catholic support to encourage Philip II's invasion. Burghley announced familiar solutions in his Proclamation: diligent preaching of the Gospel to instil obedience, the strengthening of the navy and the mustering of land forces.[16]

The Proclamation included one relatively new remedy for the 'secret infection of treasons'. It ordered commissions 'in every shire, city, and port' to detect disguised priests or their supporters. Each head of household must register the origins, occupation and church attendance of residents for the previous year. Suspects had to be brought before local commissioners, and those of high rank before the Privy Council.

Anyone encountering missionary priests must inform the commissions, on pain of abetting treason. No exceptions were permitted 'for any respect of any persons, qualities or degrees'.[17] Abundant evidence from many counties confirms that parishes appointed teams of searchers who went door to door, interrogated their neighbours and reported recusants to commissions, which in turn sent quarterly reports and prisoners to the Privy Council.

Burghley in effect created a Tudor police state. He added bureaucratic instructions for effective questioning, targeting not just male but, for the first time, female recusants. A Catholic lifestyle became an offence. County commissions should arrest not just those who refused to attend church but anyone 'that probably by their behaviour and manner of life or otherwise may be suspected' to be 'Seminaries, Priests, Jesuits or Fugitives'.

Burghley issued set questions for the commissioners, which previously had been aimed at trapping hard-line traitors and missionaries, but now were to be put to all suspects. Recusants suspected of supporting the Spanish had to answer under oath a question carefully drafted to discover who had led them astray. Then followed the so-called 'bloody questions' designed to unmask disguised seminary priests and Jesuits.[18]

Burghley's motives for writing this Proclamation have been controversial ever since it appeared. Catholics denounced his allegations of invasion plots as threadbare justifications for perpetuating his power beyond Elizabeth's reign. Therefore, the Catholics alleged, the Privy Council licensed Richard Topcliffe and Richard Young to use torture to confirm the plots.[19] Topcliffe and Young certainly tortured some of the three priests and four Catholic laymen executed in early December.[20]

Catholic propagandists denounced 'the new *Cecilian Inquisition*', as the parochial teams searched house to house throughout the summer of 1592, particularly in London.[21] Topcliffe and Young relentlessly hunted down priests and laymen.[22] Commissioners obeyed the Proclamation's refusal to exempt Catholic noblemen. In late January 1592 Viscount Montague, the Catholic magnate in strategically vital Sussex, had to swear his loyalty before the Sussex recusancy commission 'if the Pope or the King of Spain' offered 'to invade this realm, for any cause'.[23]

Burghley had always been paranoid about an international Catholic conspiracy against Elizabeth. The 1591 Proclamation repeated arguments he had made in mid-1559, long before the first English overseas seminary and a generation before the first English Jesuit mission in 1580. Burghley organised events into a providential pattern that produced the same response to all later crises. By 1591 the pattern had become reality.[24]

Publicly, Robert Parsons dismissed Burghley's Proclamation as a panicky response to his own successful Valladolid seminary, founded in 1589. He scorned Burghley's hysteria about a Spanish invasion, which he said was invented to manipulate Elizabeth's fears for his own advantage.[25] Privately, William Allen conceded to Parsons that the Proclamation had indeed been inspired by Spanish invasion plans revealed 'by their secret messengers', recently captured, who 'have confessed the same'.[26]

Allen especially blamed two captured English Valladolid seminarists examined by Burghley, John Cecil alias Snowden and John Fisher or Fixer, who 'have discovered all they knew, and perhaps added somewhat of their own more than they knew'. In early January 1592 Allen confirmed to Parsons 'that they have betrayed all indeed'. Their information enabled Burghley's Proclamation to blame the predicted Spanish invasion on the traitorous subversion of Allen and Parsons.[27]

In fact, Snowden and Fixer played down Spain's ability to invade England.[28] Fixer claimed that Philip presided over a ruined economy and demoralised society.[29] Snowden assured Burghley that 'the King's forces are not to be feared for many years'.[30] Because they failed to confirm Burghley's obsession with Catholic invasion, he dismissed their 'vulgar and trivial intelligences ... to no great purpose'.[31] His conviction that the missionaries presaged an imminent Spanish invasion came from elsewhere.

Everyone knew Philip II's determination to revenge the Armada defeat of 1588. Yet effective defence required precise information about where and when the next Armada would strike. The Privy Council faced challenges that modern intelligence systems still fail – distinguishing the signal from the 'noise' of conflicting information. In August 1590 they had expected an invasion of England or Ireland in spring or summer 1591. However, without exact information, they could do little.[32] Burghley omitted threats of a Spanish invasion from a Proclamation prohibiting English merchants trading with Spain.[33] Why then did his Proclamation against Jesuits and seminaries emphasise the invasion?

It did so in part because Renaissance governments often used peace negotiations strategically, to weaken enemies while building up their own strength.[34] For several years Elizabeth's regime had been secretly negotiating with Philip's viceroy in the Netherlands, the Duke of Parma, through English Catholic exiles around Parma's Court at Brussels. Elizabeth had offered both to marry Parma's son to the Catholic Arabella Stuart, who had plausible claims to succeed her, and to allow de facto toleration of English Catholics.

If Parma took the bait he might fail to support Philip's invasion. Offered the hope of a Catholic succession, English Catholics and the Pope had less reason to support Philip. If Parma balked, leaks about the negotiations would undermine Philip's confidence in him.[35] It would also further divide some English Catholics in the Netherlands, still dreaming of reconciliation with Elizabeth's regime, from hardliners who dismissed empty promises of toleration.

By October 1591 promising discussions led the Privy Council to offer the Catholic exile Charles Paget safe conduct, to negotiate with Hatton and Whitgift about religious liberty for English Catholics. As Allen informed Parsons, Paget naively believed that Hatton and Whitgift would 'become Catholics, by which you may see what kind of practises these goodfellows ... have in hand, and with whom they deal'.[36] Radical Protestants considered Hatton a crypto-Catholic. Whitgift's suppression of Protestant dissent never undermined his Calvinist suspicion of Rome's profound errors. Hatton and Burghley differed over domestic religious policy.[37] With his ingrained suspicions about an international Catholic conspiracy, Burghley feared that the negotiations would surrender fundamental Protestant positions.

Burghley's Proclamation scuttled the peace negotiations. By hounding even politically quiescent recusants for their lifestyle, it squashed all prospect of tolerance. The Proclamation's curious publication chronology supports this motivation. Drafted in mid-October and printed by the 18th, it remained unpublished.[38] This delay indicates disagreement within the Privy Council over whether to counter Philip by deceptive negotiations or by Burghley's thoroughgoing Reformation. Hatton's death on 20 November meant Burghley won by default. Catholic informants in England certainly attributed the delay to Hatton's opposition and claimed that the Proclamation appeared the day after his death. This also explains why the Privy Council's hurried letters setting up the commissions on 23 November had to be rewritten and reissued a week later.[39]

Forcing the Proclamation through also enabled Burghley to defend the Presbyterians by diverting Whitgift's energies. By focusing the Queen's attention on the inherent political threat of Catholic recusancy because it supported a Spanish invasion, Burghley took the wind out of Whitgift's sails. Despite Whitgift's intransigent opposition, the Presbyterians gradually wriggled out of prison by the summer of 1592. By then, Burghley had busied the Ecclesiastical High Commission with persecuting Catholic recusants, further diverting Whitgift's aggressive energies from zealous Protestants.[40] But Burghley needed compelling reasons for Elizabeth to publish his Proclamation, which went against her political prejudices and Whitgift's policy.

Burghley had previously used an imminent Spanish invasion to shift Elizabeth's policy. However, an anticipated invasion in 1591 had not forced her to alter course. How did Burghley sway the Queen away from the 'peace' policy in late November? What was different now?

The answer lies in Dee's petition to James I on 5 June 1604, where he defended himself against the 'English traitor' who on 7 January 1592 slandered him as the Privy Council's conjuror. This previously elusive publication was not a book, but William Allen's letter to Robert Parsons of that date, printed in Parsons's *Apology in Defence of Ecclesiastical Subordination in England* (1601). Allen's letter also included a sensational claim that Dee concealed from James in 1604, that Burghley's

Proclamation owed much to 'Doctor Dee their conjuror or Astrologer [who] is said to have put them in more doubt, for that he hath told the Council by his calculation, that the Realm indeed shall be conquered this Summer, believe him who will'.[41]

This was not invented propaganda. Allen had reliable informants at Elizabeth's Court, and this private letter first appeared in print seven years after his death. His claim did not appear in published attacks on the Proclamation. Parsons in exile received excellent intelligence from England, so by printing Allen's letter he could use Dee's deteriorating reputation in 1601 to smear the surviving Privy Councillors from 1592.

Moreover, Burghley knew Elizabeth's deep belief in Dee's 'philosophy and alchemy' and in his astrological predictions, for Burghley accepted them himself. Dee had used magic to support Elizabeth in 1555. She had defended his alchemical *Monas hieroglyphica* in 1564.[42] Dee's 'British Empire' depended partly on alchemical research producing the philosopher's stone.[43] He had explained to her the imperial significance of the comet of November 1577. In return she had promised her protection, reiterated in December 1590, when she engaged in alchemy with Dee.[44] Burghley had accepted Dee's timetable for the new calendar for the apocalyptic 'secret matter'.[45] Therefore, Burghley could reasonably expect that Dee's astrological prediction would alarm Elizabeth into reversing course and publishing the Proclamation.

Plotting Dee's rising Court career alongside the graph of Catholic persecution also confirms Allen's accusations. The two lines run parallel, except where Whitgift could intervene against Dee. In mid-December 1591, as the Council began cranking up the persecution, Burghley gave Dee his 'gentle answers' about the Mastership of St Cross, once the existing Master, Robert Bennett, had been promoted from St Cross to a bishopric.

Bennett seemed certain to be promoted. Whitgift had introduced him to Burghley, who appointed him his chaplain before presenting him to St Cross in 1583.[46] A learned, staunch anti-Romanist, soon after his appointment he began bombarding Burghley with letters begging for further promotion.[47] However, he mysteriously failed to become a bishop in December 1591.

Politically naive, in November 1592 Dee remained mystified why Bennett, 'very worthy and sufficient to be a Bishop', had not been promoted to relieve Dee's 'incredible distress'. Bennett also missed out in another round of episcopal promotions in mid-1594.[48] That November, Bennett complained bitterly to Burghley about the humiliation of seeing even his former students promoted over his head.[49]

Whitgift kept Bennett at St Cross to deny the appointment to Dee. This became particularly necessary after May 1594, when the bishopric of Winchester fell vacant. Elizabeth could now grant Lord Cobham, a long-standing patron of Dee's mother's family, the Wildes of Gravesend, the right to appoint Dee to St Cross immediately Bennett resigned.[50] Significantly, once Dee had been sidelined as Warden of Manchester Collegiate Church, Bennett prospered. In 1596 he acquired the lucrative Deanery of Windsor, and finally resigned St Cross on becoming Bishop of Hereford in 1603.[51]

Dee's next promise of patronage in early 1592 coincided with rising anxiety about a Spanish invasion. After spies reported Spanish plans to seize an English port, the Privy Council began fortifying Plymouth.[52] In early February, London parishes prepared street barricades and troops against 'the coming in of the Spaniards'.[53] In March clearer information about threats to ports prompted Burghley to devise plans for imprisoning leading recusants.[54] Meanwhile the recusancy commissions kept up their local searches.[55] In April another Catholic pamphlet attacking the Proclamation urged a Spanish conquest, followed by Richard Verstegan's attack on the 'Cecilian Inquisition'.[56]

By then Dee's credit was drying up. His work for Burghley remained secret, so he needed some public sign of Elizabeth's 'gracious favour towards me' to restore his credit 'with all men generally'. Therefore, in March, Elizabeth granted Dee's cousin William Aubrey the rights of presentation to five absentee sinecure rectories in the diocese of St David's in Wales, where the extremely corrupt bishop had been suspended. Officially worth £75 altogether, their real income was probably double that, almost as much as Dee had been seeking for years. Aubrey exercised authority in St David's as vicar-general to Archbishop Whitgift, so he could now present Dee to all five livings.[57]

As so often for Dee, things went awry. One wonders how much Whitgift knew about those rectories. Two turned out to be already occupied. Three other men all claimed to be rector of the third. The Rector of Angle in south Pembrokeshire was Richard Meredith, bishop of the impoverished Irish see of Leighlin. Meredith, imprisoned for running foul of Burghley, cut a deal with Dee for the rectory. Sometime in 1592 he assigned his house in St Brides, London, to Dee.[58] Then the deal went sour, and on 31 December 1592 Meredith started proceedings against Dee. In February they quarrelled furiously in the Tower, both insisting they were Rector of Angle. Meredith sneered that Dee was merely a 'conjuror'. However, when Whitgift deprived Meredith of the Rectorship in 1594, he appointed another rector and subsequently resisted all Dee's claims.[59] Dee finally secured the fifth rectory, Tenby, worth £50 a year, only in March 1601.[60]

Although Elizabeth's public patronage temporarily bolstered Dee's credit, he could not keep his creditors at bay for long. Therefore, in 1592 he hired out his occult learning. Despite the 1563 Witchcraft Act he took money for work usually associated with lower-order 'cunning folk', casting horoscopes to identify robbery suspects, finding buried treasure, and exorcising the possessed. Nevertheless he had to borrow money, rent out rooms and take in pupils to continue his 'philosophy'.[61] In July 1592 he turned sixty-five, claiming 'incredible want', and still hoping that the Countess of Warwick would persuade the Queen to give him the living at St Cross.[62]

The regime's rising anxiety over the prophesied Spanish Armada helped. In late May, Elizabeth worried about foreign threats and domestic tensions. Serious Jesuit plots to assassinate her began that month.[63] In June ships from the Azores warned of a powerful Spanish Armada ready to sail, and Catholic prisoners in London buzzed with rumours of its arrival. The Privy Council, worried about invasion through Milford Haven, extended the recusancy commissions into strongly Catholic Wales.[64]

In mid-June, overwhelmed by local commissioners' success in arresting recusants, the Privy Council delegated their management to Whitgift's

High Commission, whose experience with Protestant dissent increased the persecution.[65] In late July the Privy Council began disarming all Catholics, because the exiles bragged about 'the assistance of those that are backward in religion'.[66] Whispers that predominantly Catholic Lancashire might be the invasion bridgehead raised suspicions about the local magnate, the Earl of Derby.[67]

The crisis peaked in August, the Armada season. So did Dee's hopes of patronage. On 6 August he went to 'Nonsuch to the Court', alerted by the Countess of Warwick about Elizabeth's 'gracious speeches for St Cross'. He should certainly have it, 'if it were fit for him'. Whitgift sniffed the wind, repeated Elizabeth's words to Dee, and unblinkingly confirmed that the Mastership 'is a living most fit for me'. Three days later Burghley invited Dee to a family dinner, which was repeated on the 10th. There Lord Cobham, the Wilde family patron, asked Burghley 'to help me to St Crosses, which he promised to do his best in'. Ten days later Dee spent two days with Cobham in London, pressing home his advantage.[68] With such support, what could prevent Dee obtaining the place?

Everyone seemed convinced by Dee's prediction about the invasion. Burghley discounted his own agent's intelligence denying that Philip could send an Armada that summer.[69] On 7 August the Privy Council ordered all leading recusants returned to prison.[70] Six days later they arrested lesser figures.[71] They imprisoned every prominent Catholic lawyer in London, where virulent plague exacerbated the crisis atmosphere.[72]

Elizabeth departed on Progress towards Oxford, her itinerary avoiding coastal areas vulnerable to sudden Spanish landings. As the plague increased, so did Armada sightings. Lord Admiral Howard wrote near midnight on 29 August ordering the Lord Lieutenant of Sussex to ready the militia, reporting a 'great fleet of tall Shippes discovered at Sea being Spaniards' heading for the Sussex coast.[73]

Within days, still trying to penetrate the fog of war to identify the real Spanish landing, the Privy Council obsessed over a complicated Lancashire invasion plot. This preoccupied them through mid-September, when they again harried the county commissions to arrest recusants.[74] Burghley's anxious memos in mid-October about preventing 'the general revolt of the Recusants of the realm, and particularly in Lancashire' increased the tension. Days later the Privy Council finally gave Burghley what he had sought since 1558 – they purged all Catholic justices of the peace.[75] This completed Burghley's triumph over Whitgift, marked by the release of the Presbyterian leaders and even of Henry Arthington, Hacket's disciple, in early August.

Dee's role in all this remained secret. Until he obtained public reward his cash crisis would persist. After three years at Mortlake, by autumn 1592 he owed £500 to friends, besides their gifts of food and clothing. He had pawned all his plate and Jane's jewellery and had borrowed upon bonds with promises to repay. All told he owed £833, many times the annual income he sought. Worse still, in July household suppliers cut off credit and began shaming Dee, demanding their money in public.[76] Why had Dee's public reputation, as opposed to his secret status at Court, plummeted in July?

The answer resolves a long-standing controversy. At the end of May Sir Walter Raleigh fell spectacularly from Elizabeth's favour, when enemies revealed his secret marriage to her Maid of Honour, Elizabeth Throckmorton, and the birth of their son. Devilishly handsome, extremely learned, a dashing but often brutal soldier, Raleigh seemed the complete Renaissance courtier, except for his arrogant assumption that Elizabeth had fallen for his carefully managed image. Raleigh's attempt to bluff it out infuriated the Queen almost as much as his insincere play-acting at contrition throughout June and July, when she kept him under house arrest. On 7 August, the day after Dee went to Nonsuch about St Cross, she sent the offenders to the Tower.

Since his spectacular rise to Elizabeth's favour in 1583 Raleigh had patronised Dee.[77] Contemporary opinion evidently connected the notorious pair more than Dee's 'Diary' suggests, so that Raleigh's fall dragged down Dee's political and public credit in July. Now Raleigh could defend neither himself nor his clients. His many enemies included Richard Verstegan and Robert Parsons, Catholics who were furiously attacking Burghley's Proclamation. In August 1592 Verstegan published an English summary, or *Advertisement*, for Parsons's forthcoming full-blooded Latin *Response* to Burghley's Proclamation. The *Advertisement* included perhaps the best-known libel in Elizabethan history:

> Of Sir Walter Raleigh's school of Atheism . . . and of the Conjuror that is Master thereof, and of the diligence used to get young gentlemen to this school, where in both Moses, and our Saviour; the old, and new Testaments are jested at, and the scholars taught among other things, to spell God backward.[78]

This so-called 'School of Night' was polemical slander against a leading anti-Spanish courtier, not historical fact. Yet we can now firmly identify the 'Conjuror' and trace the creation of this fiction.[79] Catholic polemics routinely branded all leading Protestant politicians as atheists, particularly Burghley. Verstegan used this commonplace in a March letter to Parsons, criticising Burghley's rumoured plan to marry his eldest grandson to Arabella Stuart, for 'The young youth is as prettily instructed in atheism as the Lady Arbella is in puresy [Puritanism], for he will not stick openly to scoff at the Bible, and will folks to spell the name of God backward'.[80]

Before the *Advertisement* was completed in August, Raleigh's fall enabled Verstegan to mount a similar attack on the fallen favourite, and thus the general mores of Elizabeth's Court. In the light of Allen's letter of 7 February 1592 describing Dee's conjuring for the Privy Council, it is now clear that amongst Catholic exiles, including Verstegan, only one man qualified as the 'Conjuror' at that Court – John Dee.[81]

Circumstances left Dee even more vulnerable to such assaults by the time Parsons published his *Response* in October. For the panic over an Armada abruptly subsided. The arrival of the autumnal Atlantic gales enabled the Privy Council to stand down the beacon watch on 23 October, later than normal.[82] An experienced observer noted three weeks later that in Court and Privy Council 'now, there is no stirring at all'. Burghley left on Elizabeth's Accession Day, 17 November, when the same observer counted the Privy Council attendance as the smallest 'I have seen on that day'.[83] The reduced Spanish threat persuaded many recusancy commissions to slacken their efforts.[84]

By early October the failure of Dee's prediction of an invasion had destroyed his political influence, enabling the 'atheism' accusations to gain traction amongst Raleigh's many Court enemies. Attacking Dee hindered Raleigh's rehabilitation. The interview Dee sought with Whitgift on 13 October dates this development precisely and indicates that the influential Archbishop was very willing to take the atheism accusations seriously. Dee tried to demonstrate his orthodoxy by showing Whitgift 'two books of blasphemy against Christ and the Holy Ghost ... desiring him to cause them to be confuted'.[85] He forgot to mention that he had owned them for years, and that in 1587 one of the blasphemous authors, Christian Francken, assured Dee that he had recanted his errors.[86]

When Parsons's *Response* appeared shortly afterwards, it further blackened Dee's reputation. Parsons promised that if Raleigh became a Privy Councillor, his education in the necromancer's school of atheism would produce a proclamation from that 'Magician', published in Elizabeth's name, abolishing divinity and the soul's immortality, and denouncing as traitors any objectors to the sweet reasonableness of libertinism.[87]

Allen's letter informing Parsons about Dee's conjuring for Burghley means we can identify Dee as Parsons's necromancer. Furthermore, Parsons's confidant in Spain, Sir Francis Englefield, once considered the author of the *Advertisement*, had investigated Dee for his magic against Queen Mary in 1555, revealed by Englefield's servant Prideaux, who had died in exile at Madrid in 1591.[88]

By early November 1592, Dee's political and financial credit seemed destroyed, shattering his hopes of advancement. Burghley had effectively used Dee against Whitgift. Having rescued the Presbyterians, derailed the negotiations with the Duke of Parma, harried the recusants, and purged Catholics from the commissions of the peace, Burghley now ruthlessly took his revenge for Dee's slanders at Prague about his niggardly patronage.

In Burghley's chamber at Hampton Court on 6 November, Dee reminded him of Elizabeth's promises about St Cross. Burghley responded with words and gestures that Dee meticulously recorded, because he knew they meant the death of his hopes. Burghley 'with his hand very earnestly smitten on his breast' told Dee 'By my faith, if her Majesty be moved in it by any other for you, I will do what I can with her Majesty to pleasure you therein.' Dee realised that if Burghley declined to take the initiative, no courtier dared challenge the triumphant Lord Treasurer. Dee rode home disconsolately, wryly concluding in his 'Compendious Rehearsal': 'And so I thanked his Honour humbly.'[89]

These events finally explain why Dee had to write his remarkable 'Compendious Rehearsal'. The sudden catastrophe compelled Dee to appeal directly to Elizabeth over Burghley's head. Even the timing of his appeal was dictated by Burghley's absence from Court. On 9 November, three days after his disastrous interview, Dee wrote a supplication to Elizabeth. The Countess of Warwick immediately showed it to her. She persuaded Elizabeth to grant Dee's request for two commissioners to assess his justifications for royal reward.

It was no coincidence that this occurred at Hampton Court while Burghley sat in the Exchequer Chamber at Whitehall. Nor was it coincidental that the commissioners, Sir John Woolley, Elizabeth's Latin Secretary, and Sir Thomas Gorge, a household official, waited until Burghley was preoccupied with the law term at Hertford north of London before riding to Mortlake on 22 November.[90]

At their suggestion, Dee had spent the intervening twelve days compiling an account of his service to Elizabeth. In his library, still missing many books, he arranged a table for the commissioners. Before it he set two 'great tables', one covered in the letters, records and testimonies accumulated during the exactly fifty years of study since he entered St John's College in November 1542. On the other he spread his manuscript and printed writings. He planned, as he read his 'Compendious Rehearsal' aloud, to support his case by handing the commissioners the relevant documents.[91]

Dee's contemporaries would have found many aspects of his 'Compendious Rehearsal' commonplace. The commissioners' advice to write it reflected their long experience with desperate Crown servants trying to squeeze rewards from their parsimonious royal mistress. By the 1590s the huge costs of the Spanish war further constrained Elizabeth's never abundant willingness to reward her servants. At the same time, competition had increased as more educated men tried to enter royal service.

Dee's presentation differed only in his elaborate stage-setting and the sheer length of his personal account, a measure of his desperation. A few weeks earlier the ex-Jesuit Christopher Parkins, about whom Dee had mistakenly warned Walsingham, had begun bombarding Burghley with requests for reward. Like Dee, he discovered that rivals snapped up promised places. His diplomatic service in Europe eventually overcame Whitgift's resistance to his promotion, securing him a pension.[92]

While Dee wrote, Robert Beale scrambled to retain his secretaryship of the Privy Council by reminding Burghley of his lengthy services.[93] Even the Queen's comptroller and Privy Councillor, Sir James Croft, felt he must ballast his appeals for patronage with detailed autobiography.[94] Similarly, after reciting almost thirty years' service to Elizabeth, Sir John Smith could tally very little beyond fair words and empty promises.[95] Sir Henry Killigrew's account of his labours also echoes Dee's detailed, complaining tone.[96]

The 'Compendious Rehearsal' particularly resembled these other autobiographies being written at the same time because it carefully selected self-serving information. Dee described his Cambridge career in considerable detail, but hurried past his time at Catholic Louvain. He spent several pages emphasising his considerable international reputation but omitted his Catholic ordination and service as Bonner's chaplain. His version of his activities in 1555 insisted he suffered imprisonment at Hampton Court alongside Elizabeth, faced treason charges in the Star Chamber, and was sent 'to the examining and custody of Bishop Bonner' with Barthlet Green.[97]

He recalled that he might have served five emperors, but omitted his expulsion from Emperor Rudolf II's lands. He listed amongst his many services his counter-magic against the wax images in 1578, though he did not mention the embarrassing collapse of that 'conspiracy'. He carefully described how his rivals had subverted Elizabeth's promises to him, through 'worldly policy, subtle practice, and rigorous advantages', since that helped his case.[98] However, other aspects of the 'Compendious Rehearsal' were unusual. Dee's vivid descriptions of Elizabeth's repeated promises to support his philosophical studies provide a remarkable insight into her passionate interest in occult philosophy, which has been consistently overlooked by her biographers.

Dee also included an idiosyncratic chapter listing thirty-six 'books' written since 1550. Like many job applications this included some padding, since two were the 'Compendious Rehearsal' itself and a one-page appendix. Others varied from a few manuscript pages to a printed dedication, up to the *Propaedeumata aphoristica* and *Monas hieroglyphica*. More impressively, he described the books, manuscripts, instruments, globes, compasses, clocks, title deeds, ancient seals, alchemical vessels and distillations that had been embezzled during his absence. He calculated £2,306 in lost rents from his rectories, his costs in returning from Europe, and his stolen books, plus his current debt of £833.[99]

He ended by petitioning for the Mastership of St Cross, to solve his financial and logistical problems. In 1574 Dee had believed Elizabeth had granted him the next vacant position there.[100] Though Burghley inserted Bennett instead, Dee still nursed dreams of transforming St Cross into a European centre for alchemical research and publication.

Within its substantial early Tudor buildings, which still survive, St Cross administered then, as it does today, two medieval charitable trusts.[101] Dee intended to convert the charities into a larger version of his 'Hospital for itinerant philosophers' at Mortlake. At St Cross he could collaborate in alchemy with many foreign scholars and their 'Mechanical servants'. Mortlake, on the popular river route between Elizabeth's palaces, could not keep 'some rarities' secret 'from vulgar Sophisters'.

As Master of St Cross, Dee's newly enhanced reputation would attract occult 'special men' from throughout Christendom, 'loath to be seen or heard of publicly in Court or City'. Landing discreetly on the south coast, they could work 'under her Majesty's inviolable protection'. Dee also planned to use St Cross to print rare 'historical and philosophical' texts with his own esoteric works. He would also copy 'philosophical' manuscripts for Elizabeth's library, as he had promised Queen Mary. Dee naturally assumed that Elizabeth would embrace the chance to enhance his European reputation, since that would also enhance her 'Monarchical diadem of fame'.[102]

To circumvent Burghley, Woolley and Gorge waited for ten days to report Dee's utter destitution. On 1 December Elizabeth immediately confirmed that Dee should have the Mastership of St Cross when she elevated Bennett to a bishopric. Meanwhile she wondered aloud about providing his desired pension of £200 from the already ransacked revenues of the vacant Bishopric of Oxford. She sent Dee £66 in loose change via Gorge. Elizabeth's close friend Lady Katherine Howard also sent her old servant Jane Dee £3.[103]

Then for six weeks Elizabeth kept Dee at arm's length. He daily attended Court, but she excluded him from the Privy Chamber, despite his wish to express his thanks personally. This shows remarkable exertion by Whitgift against the powerful influence of Mary Scudamore and the Countess of Warwick, who both had the Queen's ear, and through whom Dee applied for access. Not until 15 February 1593 could the Countess take in a short Latin note, to which Elizabeth promised to grant 'any suit meet for me'.[104]

Significantly, Elizabeth did not mention St Cross. The Queen's sudden cooling towards Dee reflects her close relationship with Whitgift. She knew that Dee would use any interview to remind her about St Cross and probably calculated that making Bennett a bishop over Whitgift's resistance was too high a price to pay.

Dee's exclusion reflected other tensions within Elizabeth's Privy Council. Burghley and Whitgift disagreed profoundly over whether radical Protestants or papists represented the greatest threat to the Elizabethan Church. The Parliament called for February 1593 would address this issue. There Whitgift shifted attention back to radical Protestants who believed in occult spiritual forces. Whitgift knew that Burghley had used Dee's prophecy of a Spanish invasion to frighten Elizabeth into publishing his Proclamation. Now Whitgift exacted his revenge. Abandoned by Burghley, Dee fell victim to Whitgift's constant reminders about the dangers in tolerating claims to spiritual illumination.

The 'Compendious Rehearsal' therefore failed to rehabilitate Dee's career. For the next two years he clawed his way back into favour by assiduously cultivating influential courtiers through occult philosophy. Eventually, Elizabeth would nominate him to a prominent place in the Church. This so alarmed Whitgift that, ironically, he would ensure that Dee became Warden of Manchester. But in November 1592 that seemed an impossible dream.

CHAPTER 20

Checkmate: Exiling the Conjuror to Manchester

Dee never again mentioned Burghley, whose opening speech to Parliament in 1593 emphasised Philip II's planned invasion through Scotland, a rumour that originated with his agents, not Dee's astrology. Parliament cracked down harder against recusants.[1] In contrast, Whitgift and his chaplain Bancroft emphasised Presbyterian subversion. Bancroft published *A Survey of the Pretended Holy Discipline* for the opening of Parliament, attacking Presbyterian 'illuminated devices' that threatened social disorder.[2]

Soon afterwards his *Dangerous positions and proceedings, published and practised within this Island of Britain* depicted William Hacket's 'rising' in the summer of 1591 as an abortive Presbyterian coup. Bancroft cited Coppinger's claim to 'an extraordinary calling' by a divine spirit that commanded him 'to bring the Queen to repentance', with 'all her Council'.[3] This closely resembled Dee's magic, as did Coppinger's desire for God's 'extraordinary graces and gifts'. He imagined, like Dee in his 'Discoveries', that he was carried into Heaven.[4]

Bancroft deliberately confused radical separatist sects with the Presbyterians, claiming that both fomented popular insurrection.[5] Using such arguments, Whitgift's clients steered through Parliament an 'Act to retain the Queen's subjects in their Obedience', the first Elizabethan statute punishing Protestant conscientious objections to the Episcopal

Church. While Parliament debated these bills in April, Richard Young interrogated Protestant separatists in the morning and Catholic recusants in the afternoon.[6]

This repressive atmosphere meant Dee could make little headway at Court. Soon after his message of thanks finally reached Elizabeth in February 1593, he had to borrow £10 from his former student and friend Thomas Digges. He had already begged Laski in vain for his pension arrears. In mid-March he dreamt that Kelley had returned to Mortlake, because Dee had returned to alchemy to solve his financial problems. Therefore, he again revived his angel magic. His 'scryer' Bartholomew Hickman began warning of cosmic changes that would occur in late September 1600.[7]

Alchemy gradually restored Dee's finances and gained him valuable connections at Court. On 17 March 1593 his alchemical colleague Thomas Webb introduced him to Sir Thomas Chaloner, who had published on alchemy. That day Francis Nichols made a £300 down payment to learn 'the conclusion of fixing and taming of silver'. They quarrelled about Dee's lessons a year later, though Nichols would follow Dee to Manchester.[8]

Further instalments from Nichols enabled Dee in late May to offer £32 for the house next door in Mortlake, which he finally purchased in September. On 18 October he also repurchased 'my cottage', previously sold for £12 in cash. In August, Dee dined several times with Sir John Puckering, Lord Keeper of the Great Seal, who controlled vast ecclesiastical patronage. Puckering spent a day at Mortlake, interrupted by Thomas Webb and an unnamed French 'philosopher'. Puckering sent a New Year's gift of £10 to Jane Dee in January 1594 and a horse to John.[9]

Dee's alchemical reputation enabled him to cultivate the highest levels of the nobility. Through Richard Cavendish he met the intellectual Margaret Clifford, Countess of Cumberland, younger sister of the Countess of Warwick and Cavendish's collaborator in alchemy. In October 1593, Dee was astonished to hear her preacher Christopher Shutt 'despising alchemical philosophers'. This did not prevent the Countess from visiting Dee to have her horoscope cast in December. That day

Peregrine Bertie, Lord Willoughby, who had visited Kelley at Prague with Dyer, supported Dee's search for the philosopher's stone with £20. Dee maintained these relationships throughout his years at Manchester.[10]

However, a few weeks later alchemy threatened to derail Dee's recovery. Thomas Webb introduced Dee to alchemical patrons, assisted with his alchemy, and kept a room in Dee's house.[11] Yet Webb's Prague mission to rescue Dyer cost him dearly. Between November 1591 and July 1592 he had borrowed at least £48 from Richard Young.[12] Webb also needed to maintain appearances at the ruinously expensive Court. To support his ambitions he took to alchemical coining and dangerous politics.

Burghley got wind of the affair and began hunting for Webb.[13] On 24 December 1593 he committed him to the Marshalsea prison. Webb and his accomplice, the young engraver Abel Fecknam, had alchemically counterfeited £2,000 worth of Elizabeth shillings.[14] They smuggled the money to Scotland, from where Burghley feared a Spanish invasion. Other men had been executed for far less.[15]

Alarmingly for Dee, on 9 January 1594 the Master of the Mint and alderman Richard Martin arrived at his house to seal up 'Mr Webb's chest, and case of boxes'. In late January, deeply engaged in alchemy, Dee yet found time to visit Webb in the Marshalsea prison.[16] This was not merely charity, because Dee could be implicated. When Webb faced a death sentence in mid-March, he panicked Dee into a 'flight of fear' by sending for him. Did Dee panic because he had helped the coining, or because he feared that Webb might save himself by branding Dee a traitor?[17]

He at least had some inkling that Webb's coining had dangerous political connections. The condemned men appealed to influential patrons, some perhaps alerted by Dee. Margaret Clifford's husband, George, Earl of Cumberland, alderman Martin and the famous painter Nicholas Hilliard all quickly intervened with Burghley's son Sir Robert Cecil for Hilliard's skilled workman Fecknam.[18] Dee could only relax when Webb's saviour turned out to be Sir Robert Cecil, suggesting Webb had been working undercover for Cecil all along, behind Burghley's back.[19] Burghley arranged Webb's pardon but commanded him into exile in the Netherlands. From there, Webb apologetically sent Dee alchemical medical recipes.[20]

Dee escaped the nasty little scandal unscathed. However, it demonstrates that little separated elite philosophical and practical alchemy from the alchemical counterfeiting usually associated with 'cunning men'.[21]

Nor would Whitgift have appreciated Dee's growing reputation as a seer following his predictions about 1592. Thomas Nashe wrote *Christ's Tears over Jerusalem* late in 1593, trying to break with Whitgift by embracing apocalyptic notions. Nashe complained about the 'superstitious' who 'under Master Dees name' spread rumours of future troubles, when 'that good reverend old man' denied 'such arrogant prescience'.[22]

Dee's reputation helped to attract alchemical enthusiasts. On 7 February 1594 he received an 'offer philosophical' from Walsingham's former client Sir Thomas Wilkes, who had beggared himself in Elizabeth's diplomatic service. Like other Court figures with no previously known interest in alchemy, Wilkes demonstrates how Dee's occult philosophy gathered support, even while it alienated Whitgift. Dee noted no request for Elizabeth's patronage for a year until February 1594, though he pressed his case by unrecorded means. For example, on the day of Wilkes's offer 'the Archbishop inclined somewhat to the request of dispensation'. This meeting represents the tip of an interesting iceberg that has completely melted away.

Dee meant dispensation for his two livings, for which he would not abandon hope until June 1594. He badly needed a steady income, because windfalls like Francis Nichols's £300 only encouraged his spending, leaving him deeper in debt when the money ran out. On 10 April 1594 he gloomily read over his 'Compendious Rehearsal' again, noting that 'to this hour' he had not seen a penny from his Welsh rectories. Having redeemed his mortgage to his brother-in-law Nicholas Fromoundes, Dee now had to remortgage his house, raising £400 to pay his most pressing debts. In June 1594 he mortgaged for £30 the neighbouring second house he had bought only the previous September.[23]

Dee's cash-flow problems made him anxious to demonstrate his spiritual gifts to the Queen. Yet that only enabled Whitgift and Bancroft to portray him as another enthusiastic prophet threatening natural authority. On 3 May 1594, again through the Countess of Warwick's influence, he 'delivered in writing the heavenly admonition' to the Queen, which she took 'thankfully'.[24]

The admonition possibly came from Kelley, whose latest letter Dee had received in late March, since Elizabeth returned one of Kelley's letters to Dee on 18 May. It certainly recalls the angelic warnings that Dee revealed to Emperor Rudolf II. Years later John Chamberlain claimed that Elizabeth died at Richmond because Dee had warned her to 'beware of Whitehall', but whether he was referring to this 'heavenly admonition' remains unclear.[25]

Exploiting Elizabeth's thankful response, on 21 May Sir John Woolley again presented Dee's suit for St Cross. As in February 1593 she would not overrule Whitgift's objections and 'granted after a sort, but referred all' to the archbishop. Dee's cousin William Aubrey, now the Queen's Master of Requests, received the same reply four days later. Recognising the stumbling block, Dee met Whitgift on 29 May, but could not move his objections. Sometime between May and November of that year an official drafted a grant enabling Lord Cobham to present Dee to St Cross when Bennett resigned the Mastership, though Elizabeth never signed it.

Dee then tried a direct assault on Elizabeth's tender feelings. On 3 June he arrayed himself, Jane and their seven children before her at Thistleworth, just west of Mortlake. She permitted Jane to kiss her hand but made no commitment when Dee requested that Whitgift should come to assess their destitution. The archbishop ignored the same request three days later.[26]

In late June Dee made the short ride to Croydon, Whitgift's country residence. The archbishop gave 'answers and discourses' that he had already agreed with Elizabeth and Burghley. They finally scotched Dee's 'hoping for anything' about his rectories. Therefore, he declared 'adieu to the Court and courting till God direct me otherwise'. He soon had another catastrophe to deal with. His son Michael fell ill with a virus on 6 July, and Dee cast his horoscope. Dee also sickened but recovered. Michael died at sunrise on 13 July, his father's melancholy sixty-seventh birthday.[27]

Somehow Dee, like his hopes for St Cross, carried on that summer. English and French alchemists worked in his laboratories. He wrote to

Edward Kelley in September complaining that he rented out rooms but still lacked wood for the coming winter. By the end of October matters had again reached crisis, and Dee asked permission from Elizabeth to declare his poverty before the Privy Council or to go abroad. Elizabeth ignored both requests, and in early December, unable to maintain Bartholomew Hickman, he sent him to Lord Willoughby's service, both as 'scryer' and alchemist.[28]

On 7 December 1594 ecclesiastical politics suddenly shifted the Court planets into alignment for Dee. In a move coordinated by Jane's old patrons, the Howards, to exploit the current round of episcopal musical chairs, Jane delivered another petition to Elizabeth in her Privy Garden at Whitehall. Lord Howard, husband of her former mistress, attended the Queen. He immediately read the petition and strongly supported it, backed up by Lord Buckhurst. Elizabeth turned to Whitgift and commanded that Dee 'should have Dr Day his place in Paul's', the chancellorship of the cathedral. Temporarily outmanoeuvred, Whitgift had to bow and pretend that he was 'willing'. But could he countenance Dee in such a prominent administrative position, in the great medieval cathedral at the heart of London, of England itself?

Whitgift's countermoves can be discerned behind the complicated politics surrounding episcopal appointments in late 1594. William Day, Chancellor of St Paul's, Dean of Windsor and Provost of Eton, enjoyed Burghley's friendship, Elizabeth's goodwill and the admiration of powerful churchmen. Yet he had been waiting for a bishopric since 1570, because courtiers expected nominees to bishoprics to show proper gratitude for their support, by allowing them to plunder their new dioceses financially.

Day had missed several promotions through bargaining for better terms. When Bishop Aylmer of London died on 5 June 1594, Burghley favoured Day to succeed him, but by October the Earl of Essex, supported by Whitgift, had secured London for Richard Fletcher, Bishop of Worcester. Essex and Whitgift wanted Day to succeed Fletcher at Worcester. Both appointments were announced in the Privy Council on 1 December. This cleared the field for Jane's successful petition six days later, and Dee's nomination as Chancellor of St Paul's.[29]

On 18 December Elizabeth granted Dee £40 to celebrate Christmas, that year a joyous celebration in the Dee household. Further demonstrating her goodwill, she nominated Fletcher as Bishop of London on 26 December, confirming his election remarkably quickly by 4 January. Dee's path to the chancellorship of St Paul's seemed open. But on 5 January 1595 after 'a friend' sent Day a survey showing his income would actually fall, Day formally withdrew his acceptance as Bishop of Worcester.[30] So Dee was left stranded again.

It may seem unlikely that Whitgift was that 'friend', who encouraged Day's withdrawal simply to prevent Dee replacing him. Day subsequently had to brave Elizabeth's anger, though within months she appointed him Bishop of Winchester without a hitch. However, despite his apparent agreement to Dee's appointment as chancellor, Whitgift first mentioned the Wardenship of Manchester Collegiate Church to Dee on 3 January, two days before Day withdrew, suggesting he already knew about Day's forthcoming decision. Manchester would be a less prominent appointment for a 'conjuror' than St Paul's.[31]

Indeed, Dee blamed Whitgift's opposition to his 'philosophical studies' for the reversal and made the only possible response. Bad news travels fast. Within hours of Day's withdrawal, through the evening of 5 January and all the next day, Dee 'very speedily' wrote a long letter to Whitgift, defending the legality and Christianity of his studies. He published it in 1599 and 1604, when his public reputation again came under fire, as *A Letter, containing a most brief Discourse Apologetical.*

The preface to Whitgift reiterated Dee's request made the previous 28 October, that, to support his 'most needful suits', he should be allowed to explain his 'studious exercises' to Elizabeth, Whitgift and other Privy Councillors. This explanation would then be published both to suppress the 'wicked reports, and fables' about his philosophy and to satisfy impartial Christian readers that his work led upwards to the celestial tabernacle. Dee obviously believed that Whitgift was the source of gossip about his magic.

Dee claimed once more that from his youth he had sought by God's favour to know His truth and by carefully weighing, numbering and measuring the world to glorify its Creator. To demonstrate his long course of studies he included in his letter the sixth chapter of his 'Compendious Rehearsal', listing all his printed and manuscript writings.[32] By 6 January Dee had abandoned any hope for the chancellorship of St Paul's, so he resurrected his scheme for St Cross. He included the 'Compendious Rehearsal' passage describing how St Cross would rescue and print ancient authors. He complained again about the despoliation of his library at Mortlake, though the conjuring slanders spreading throughout the realm grieved him more. He protested on his soul's salvation that he used only 'divinely prescribed means' to attain legitimate knowledge, advance God's glory and benefit the kingdom.

Recalling his 'cosmopolitan' allegiance, he assured Whitgift that he studied only as part of 'that holy and mystical body, Catholicly extended' over the globe, under the 'illumination' of the Holy Trinity. He prayed for Christ's imminent return, because the worldly wise scorned Dee's religion of 'Evangelical simplicity'. He concluded by asking Whitgift to defend him against slanderers, reassure charitable Christians about his orthodoxy, and warn him whenever he spoke or wrote otherwise than became a Christian.[33]

Whitgift's interference displeased Elizabeth. When Sir John Woolley asked her to sign Dee's 'bill of Manchester' on 3 February, she deferred it. The appointment entailed finding the current warden, William Chaderton, also Bishop of Chester, another bishopric. Only on 28 March did she nominate Chaderton to Lincoln, enabling her to sign Dee's bill on 18 April. Dee's patent received the Great Seal on 27 May. When the Countess of Warwick tendered Dee's thanks on 31 July, the Queen replied that she 'was sorry that it was so far from hence: but that some better thing near at hand shall be found for me'.[34]

To mark his elevation to the Wardenship, Dee had his portrait painted. It survives in the Ashmolean Museum in Oxford. He dressed formally for it, in a heavy black scholar's gown and black skullcap. His expensive, fashionably elaborate starched ruff sets off his surprisingly unlined, handsome and fresh complexion, above his carefully trimmed white drooping moustache and long, pointed beard. It is the deeply set, dark brown eyes, however, that hold the viewer, looking out cautiously, even suspiciously, on the world. As well they might, given his recent experience of Courtly machinations.

Elizabeth had never been further north than Nottingham. What to her, and perhaps Whitgift, seemed a remote exile was nothing of the kind. Manchester had excellent communications with London. A town of about two thousand people, as the regional hub for Lancashire cloth production it exported most of its cloth through London, where many local men made fortunes in trade and the law. It must, however, have stunk to high heaven in the summer. The manorial court spent most of its time ineffectually trying to prevent privies overflowing onto the streets and to ensure that people dumping their night-soil into the River Irwell did so from the middle of the bridge, not the riverbank.[35]

Partly because of the relative ease of travel, during his Wardenship Dee spent long periods at Mortlake, where he attended the Manor Court in December 1596 and observed a solar eclipse on 7 March 1598, or in London, including the entire two years from July 1598, and the summers of 1602 and 1604. He also kept up scholarly connections, sending his old friend William Camden a Roman inscription found at Manchester.[36] In September 1602 the Catholic peer Viscount Montague gave Dee a devotional work at Cowdray in Sussex.[37] In November 1604 Dee returned to London for most of that winter. He apparently left Manchester permanently sometime after the virulent outbreak of plague in early 1605.

Dee's absences from Manchester were not unusual, since like the Fellows of Manchester Collegiate Church he struggled with its long-standing religious, personal and financial squabbles. As Archbishop of Canterbury and Privy Councillor, Whitgift knew those problems well. They had bedevilled his predecessors, Archbishops Parker and Grindal.[38] By proposing Dee for the Wardenship, Whitgift not only headed him off from St Paul's but also lumbered him with Manchester's nonconforming radical Protestants, who found Dee a far less sympathetic warden than Chaderton. At the same time Whitgift repaid Dee for thwarting his anti-Presbyterian drive in 1591 with responsibility for a College that, as Dee complained to Edward Dyer in 1596, 'is almost become no College' but a 'labyrinth' of baffling financial complexity, fraud and incompetence.[39]

By 'no College' Dee meant precisely that. Northern England's largest complex of college buildings had been bought by the Earl of Derby at the dissolution in 1547 and not returned when Philip and Mary refounded the College in 1556. Lacking a physical location, the eight Fellows of that second foundation spent the 1560s and 1570s quarrelling over how to share their pillaging of the College finances.

Long leases at low rents to local gentry, which were sometimes competing leases of the same land, sapped the College's income. The final blows came in 1575 and 1577, when Elizabeth leased the grain tithes of Manchester from the College for a bargain price, initially for forty years and then for ninety-nine. A minor favourite acquired them, leaving the Fellows with only £86 a year in income from tithes.[40]

The scandal led to Elizabeth's new charter of 1578. Completely failing to remake the College into a centre for Protestant evangelisation, this document crippled Dee's last years. Fatally, it protected the existing tithe leases and failed to restore to the College its buildings, leaving the Warden and Fellows homeless, despite providing for a rent-free 'collegiate house'. Its one useful innovation stipulated that the warden and Fellows would be paid only while resident, unless the chapter authorised absence on college business. Dee's patent of appointment dispensed with this requirement, leading to quarrels with the Fellows when they refused to pay his stipend of four shillings a day during his absences.[41]

Burghley and Walsingham appointed a commission to renegotiate the College leases and raise money to repurchase the grain tithes, which completely failed.[42] Throughout Dee's Wardenship men holding leases from different foundations battled in the Westminster courts of the Duchy of Lancaster over College lands and tithes.[43] One litigant, Thomas Goodyear, visited Dee at Mortlake on 12 July 1595. He had previously sued Warden Chaderton and the Fellows over his rights to tithes.[44]

The following day Dee turned sixty-eight. Jane was a month away from giving birth to Margaret, their seventh living child. Their household in Manchester would also include Bartholomew Hickman, Francis Nichols and nine servants, including a butler, a cook and a nurse. Dee's official stipend of four shillings a day would have to support them all – if he received it. His next actions suggest Dee had already abandoned any illusions about Manchester's independence from William Stanley, sixth Earl of Derby.

In June he wrote to Derby, dined with him twice in September, and cast a horoscope for his daughter born the following 26 December. Dee persuaded Derby to rent him lodgings within the College, though despite their charter the Fellows refused to pay the rent.[45] Inevitably, now that his appointment had been settled, two days before Jane gave birth on 14 August he received a letter from Kelley inviting him back to serve Emperor Rudolf II. When in November he heard rumours of Kelley's death, he must have felt vindicated.

His appointment brought unwanted attention. The executors for his booksellers now demanded he settle his ancient debt of £63, which had been outstanding for thirteen years. At Christmas he signed a bond to pay by instalments. The bond remains, uncancelled, in the Elizabethan Chancery rolls, because Dee failed to make the payments out of his inadequate warden's stipend.[46] By then he knew more about the extent of his problems. In late October he urged the attorney general of the Duchy of Lancaster to help recover 'some land detained from the College', which suggests why he maintained Hickman to secure angelic advice.[47] Within weeks of his belated installation on 20 February 1596, Dee began campaigning to restore the College's chaotic finances. In response, lessees with competing leases from different College foundations united to defend their generous terms.

Dee also faced social tensions exacerbated by growing population pressure. Local manorial lords were converting open grazing to arable farming to profit from rising grain prices. These changes severely diminished the College income because occupiers owing tithes on open grazing land narrowly interpreted their obligations, refusing tithes once they enclosed that land for crops. Changes in agricultural methods also destroyed ancient landmarks, creating boundary disputes.

In these contests the existing long leases hamstrung the College, preventing it from exploiting changing conditions as aggressively as private landlords. The internal conflicts between the Fellows and warden, and the College's susceptibility to political pressure from the Crown and powerful courtiers also weakened its position. Above all, Dee's failure to gain redress reveals the Crown's inability to enforce justice in Lancashire through the remote Duchy Courts at Westminster, two hundred miles away.

The Collegiate Church served the vast parish of Manchester, sixty square miles containing several manors, thirty townships and seven chapelries. It took six days to perambulate the parish boundaries in May 1597. Large parts of the parish, including Manchester town itself, belonged to the manor of Manchester, while other parts owed service to the warden and Fellows as lords of the manor of Newton, which lay several miles to the north-east, bordering the manor of Failsworth, also within the parish.[48]

Soon after arriving in Manchester, Dee invited Sir John Byrom, Lord of Failsworth, to dine on 2 April 1596. Dee raised the issue of College tithes owed by Byrom's tenants, who 'promised well'. However, on 20 April Dee held his first court for the manor of Newton, where he learned that Byrom's tenants had decades earlier built houses and barns that trespassed on the open grazing of Newton Heath. Dee responded in June by arranging a commission of inquiry into the College's landholdings and tithes from the Duchy of Lancaster in London. The College's opponents furiously obstructed the inquiry, for the following January another draft commission appeared. Not until May 1598 did the Duchy finally issue a commission to inquire into 'the decay and poor estate' of the College.[49]

Byrom's tenants claimed ancient rights over Newton Heath. Dee's 'Mathematical Preface' had justified geometry as God's merciful remedy for such a social conflict. Accordingly, he employed Christopher Saxton in July 1596 to survey the boundaries of Newton manor, especially where they bordered the manors of Manchester and Failsworth. Though now known for his handsome county maps, Saxton specialised in surveying disputed boundaries, and courts often hired his skills.[50]

On 6 July he met Dee and Nicholas Mosley, Lord of Manchester, to discuss their common boundary. Saxton surveyed Manchester township, which extended far beyond the built-up area, between 10 and 13 July. He also surveyed Newton Heath and College lands in Salford. On

14 July, armed with Saxton's survey, Dee prosecuted Byrom's tenants at Manchester quarter sessions. Rebuffed, he sought advice from the legal centres of Lancaster and Chester.

In early September he tried negotiating with Byrom, who alleged that Saxton's survey of Newton Heath had illegally incorporated part of Failsworth manor. Dee had to request another commission before he left London in June 1600, to investigate the encroachments by Byrom's tenants on Newton Heath. This finally established that by enclosing common land in Failsworth, Byrom had forced his tenants to graze their cattle on Newton Heath, thereby cutting the College's income. Therefore, the encroachments still stood in November 1602, when the Duchy Court of Lancaster ordered the tenants to demolish the offending buildings and pay the fines imposed by Dee's court.[51] Byrom's tenants ignored both orders, because their landlord's enclosures meant they could not survive without grazing their animals on Newton Heath.

The poor harvests and consequent dearth of grain in 1596–7 further hampered Dee's attempts to collect the College's tithes of increasingly valuable corn. In late August he recorded 'much disquietness and controversy' about the tithe-corn in Hulme township, immediately south of Manchester. At Crumpsall township to the north he thought he had obtained the tithe-corn by consent, then the parishioners 'doubted and half-denied' and finally 'utterly denied' when the harvest failed disastrously, sending the price of corn rocketing.[52]

Dee took several tithe cases to the Chester consistory court but had to settle for partial payment when the cases dragged on into 1598.[53] Without gifts of cattle from his Radnorshire relatives and of Polish rye from his merchant friend John Pontois, Dee would have been unable to feed his household during these years of hunger and deprivation.[54] In July 1600 a commission was still vainly investigating detained tithes.[55]

Hunger increased social tensions around rights, tenures and boundaries. Those who had seized the College's lands, tithes and title deeds violently defended their gains. In October 1596 Dee sent William Nicholson to the Queen's Master of Requests, to demand justice for 'intolerable afflictions' visited on Nicholson's family by opponents of a commission of inquiry he supported. Large parts of Nicholson's houses had been pulled down and most of his goods, corn and hay 'cast out of doors'. Dee anticipated similar treatment, because London's distant authority carried little weight.[56]

In February 1597 Dee procured a Duchy Court commission to assess the calamitous state of the College. It should investigate embezzled charters and title deeds, forging of the seal, and the granting of illegally long leases. It would also scrutinise the College's spending. The commission demanded a thorough perambulation of the parish boundaries, particularly the extent of Theale Moor, where new enclosures had shifted boundary markers, enabling occupiers to claim they owed tithes in adjacent parishes. Dee undertook this perambulation over six days at Rogationtide, very precisely measuring from the 'three corner stake' dividing Manchester parish from Prestwich and Middleton. A survey of the manor of Newton in June provoked a three-day protest by several affected individuals. It was all very different from the Rogation processions of Dee's youth, which had been undertaken to drive out the Devil and the social conflict he provoked.[57]

This commission again failed to restore the College's rights. In September 1597 Dee complained to Edward Dyer that the 'very great dearth here' compounded the 'intricate, cumbersome' and lamentable affairs of this 'defamed and disordered College of Manchester'. He could hardly feed his household of eighteen on four shillings a day, and payment depended on the goodwill of the Fellows. Yet what really made him despair was that the Privy Council ignored his complaints, hence his letter to Dyer.[58]

Did Whitgift ensure that the Privy Council ignored Dee? Hard to say, but in 1598 Dee obtained yet another commission which repeated that of 1597 verbatim, right down to the perambulation of the same landmarks on Theale Moor and the interrogation of parish ancients about boundary markers.[59] It took until November 1600 for even this information to be returned to the Duchy Chamber, and interested parties managed to stall publication of the commission's findings in May 1601. The dispute remained unresolved in 1604.[60]

Given these interminable legal problems, it is hardly surprising that Dee and his family spent the two years after July 1598 'at London for the College good'.[61] In between tedious attendance at the Duchy courts, he spent this time at Mortlake, where he appeared at the Manor Court on 7 May 1600.[62] His 'Diary' ends in March 1601, but he spent the summers of 1602 and 1604 in London, and at the age of seventy-seven prepared to attend the courts again in November 1604.

Other circumstances encouraged him to avoid Manchester, despite having to cajole the Fellows into paying his stipend. The College buildings were falling apart, while the church chancel had been crumbling for twenty years. One of the College gatehouses actually collapsed under heavy rain in February 1598, taking a section of wall with it.[63] That summer, when Dee departed for London, the Earl of Derby mortgaged the 'College house at Manchester', leaving Dee without lodgings there.[64]

Dee used his lack of accommodation and the need to follow interminable court cases in London to escape his increasing confrontations with the Fellows. Their money quarrels only exacerbated a more fundamental clash of personalities, revealed in contrasting styles of religion. Seen from London, Lancashire had long appeared one of the 'dark corners of the land'. Traditional Catholicism still flourished there in the 1590s. Distant ecclesiastical supervision from Chester and York compounded the failure of many enormous, impoverished Lancashire parishes to support resident educated clergy able to preach the Protestant religion.

Closer to, Manchester appeared a bulwark against the resurgent tide of Catholicism. In south-east Lancashire, if the Bishop of Chester, who until 1595 was Warden Chaderton, wanted any sort of preaching ministry, he had to bear with nonconforming preachers, who elsewhere would have been hounded for their scruples about wearing the surplice and following the Book of Common Prayer. In the 1580s Chaderton had enforced clerical attendance at 'exercises' monitored by these radicals, including Oliver Carter of Manchester College.[65]

These meetings shaped clerical solidarity around the belief that preaching trumped external conformity. In 1590, Whitgift's protégé John

Piers, Archbishop of York, tried to enforce conformity in Manchester when he visited on his metropolitan visitation. Shocked by this new authoritarian line, eleven of Dee's future colleagues in Manchester and surrounding parishes, including Oliver Carter, 'preacher', signed a collective letter of protest to Piers.

Edmund Hopwood of Hopwood, a local justice and deputy lieutenant of the county, helped gather political support from sympathetic Privy Councillors to defeat Piers. Hopwood would consult Dee about demonic possession and prosecuting witchcraft in Manchester. Yet the letter of protest shows that Carter and other local clergy would perceive Dee, ironically, as Whitgift's stooge in imposing conformity.

The protestors reminded Piers that they refused to use the sign of the cross stipulated by the Book of Common Prayer because they lived amongst superstitious 'obstinate papists', who made 'every ceremony of our church' an idol of their church, 'but especially that of the cross'. The preachers therefore omitted the cross from ceremonies, to avoid scandalising 'zealous professors of religion' by using a symbol abused by popery.[66]

In contrast, Dee considered the sign of the cross profoundly important. Many charms and spells required its repeated use. Also, for Dee it encapsulated the Trinity, and its centre symbolised the philosopher's stone, that perfect balance of qualities, as hinted at in Theorem XX of his *Monas*. Like Elizabeth he made the sign of the cross at moments of profound religious emotion, and especially before he invoked angelic illumination.

Dee began an 'action' in April 1586, kneeling and 'making the sign of the Cross after my custom', by:

> taking my extended right hand from the forehead to the navel and from the left shoulder to the right, thus tracing two invisible lines. At the upper end of the first I speak the name of the Father, and when I almost touch the navel that of the Son; while I trace the transversal line in the middle, I speak the name of the Holy Sprit; and while I say *Amen*, I touch, or mark as it were, the point of intersection of those two lines, or the centre of the cross. (I have conceived many reasons for this my fancy).

By this he meant the philosopher's stone at the alchemical heart of the *Monas*, his memory of the great cross at St Dunstan's, with its blazing crystal at the centre, and the use of the cross in charms in the folk religion of his youth.[67] In his 'Mathematical Preface' Dee disguised this cross as a geometrical representation of mathematical proportions, whose junction represented perfect 'temperance'.[68]

This aspect of Dee's religious practice probably endeared him to many Lancashire laity. Hardline Protestants preaching against or omitting the sign of the cross found themselves reported to episcopal visitations by their churchwardens or abandoned in favour of conformist, or popish ministers.[69] Other elements of Dee's religious practice alienated Carter and other local radicals but connected him to the laity.

Dee never mentions hearing a sermon. Like Elizabeth, he emphasised the power of private prayer. When bishops visited, Dee scandalised the godly by his regular presentation as 'no preacher'. His use of set Latin prayer, especially reciting the psalms when seeking angelic guidance, would have been familiar to the local laity but papistical to the godly, who venerated extempore prayer in English. It took him four years to persuade the Fellows to accept 'upon condition' the use of organs in the church, another popish remnant for the godly.[70]

Anyway, despite the godly's loud rhetoric about the ministry of the Word, preaching at Manchester, as throughout south-east Lancashire, really was more honoured in the breach than the observance. Dee might be 'no preacher', but Oliver Carter could not live on his frequently unpaid College stipend of £24 a year. He established a second career as a solicitor, was non-resident in 1590 and 1601, and failed to preach in the latter year.[71]

Other members of the College became pluralists to make ends meet. Thomas Williamson, another preaching Fellow, held two other Lancashire livings, preaching once a year in each for ten years before Dee arranged his replacement in 1600 by 'a preacher to be gotten from Cambridge'.[72] Thomas Richardson also held two other livings, one in London.[73] In neglecting both their spiritual and their physical church, these men accurately reflected the predicament of the godly in Lancashire when Dee arrived as Warden of Manchester Collegiate Church. If anything, this made

Dee even less acceptable. The contrast between their rhetoric and their behaviour made the Fellows especially sensitive to his conservative church-manship. Also, during Dee's Wardenship local conservative gentlemen, seizing their chance now that Whitgift's drive for conformity had weak-ened the godly clergy's support at Court, coordinated prosecutions against godly ministers for nonconformity, increasing their discomfort.[74]

Dee's patent of appointment described him as a clergyman. Did the Fellows know of his Catholic ordination, Dee's only clerical qualification? Carter had graduated Bachelor of Divinity from St John's College, Cambridge, but they represented contrasting generations. Dee had been educated amongst the St John's Catholic faction that lost power at Edward VI's accession, whereas Carter's mind had been shaped by the fiery evan-gelical Protestantism which dominated the College in the 1560s.

The Fellows knew their *Acts and Monuments*, but which edition? Did they know about Dee the 'conjuror' from the earlier editions, or from Murphyn's forgeries? Had slanders about Dee's studies spread that far? Even though Carter and Williamson lived mostly out of college, could Dee keep his alchemy and angel magic secret? Carter, whose anti-papist book associated 'conjuring' with the rise of Antichrist, would have been appalled by what he did.

Dee regularly worked at Manchester with two 'scryers', his alchemical student, Francis Nichols, and Bartholomew Hickman. On 11 July 1600, soon after his return from two years in London, he recorded his 'conster-nation of mind about the discord of the two scryers about the things that they saw'. On 29 September Nichols persuaded Dee to burn all Hickman's deceitful 'revelations', because Hickman's long-predicted cosmic changes for that month had not happened. In that conflagration we lost Dee's questions to the angels, which would have revealed his responses to his Manchester 'labyrinth'.[75] The one result of Dee's 'conjuring' that might have improved relations with the godly may not have been known to them. The local Ecclesiastical Commission, dominated by conservative gentry, had never enthusiastically promoted Protestantism. The excep-tion had been the thorough anti-Catholic purges of 1592, which were ultimately inspired by Dee's prophecy of a Spanish invasion.[76]

For most of 1596, judging by the absence of quarrels from Dee's 'Diary', the Fellows seem to have accepted his attempts to restore the College finances. They could hardly object when in August he encouraged the parish leaders to find 'a preacher' for the College's evangelical mission.[77] The calm proved deceptive. On 22 January 1597 Carter announced that he would sue Dee. An acquisitive character once stabbed by an aggrieved business partner, Carter had sued both the previous wardens for unpaid wages.[78]

Ostensibly, Carter complained about Dee's failure to restore the College's finances, though he may have feared revelations about his own sharp practices.[79] By September, however, money worries had compounded Carter's objections to Dee's churchmanship. Dee recorded Carter's 'impudent and evident disobedience in the church', and though next day Carter repented, money problems destroyed the uneasy peace in November. The Fellows disagreed with Dee's interpretation of the accounts and refused the £5 for house rent specified in their charter.[80]

Something other than personality clashes was poisoning the atmosphere. Witchcraft prosecutions in Lancashire peaked in the late 1590s.[81] Much worse for Dee, from 1596 a series of books detailing sensational stories of demonic possession and exorcism held the country agog. They would make Dee even more notorious.

CHAPTER 21

Demonising the Exorcists

Dᴇᴇ's ɪɴᴠᴏʟᴠᴇᴍᴇɴᴛ with the Presbyterian minister John Darrell over the demonic possession of the 'Lancashire Seven' has never been properly explained. Dee's actions alienated the Fellows at Manchester Collegiate Church, brought him to national prominence again, exposed him to further criticism from Whitgift, and finally destroyed his hopes of escaping from his Manchester 'labyrinth' to promotion elsewhere. Darrell gained widespread notoriety during the late 1590s for apparently 'curing' the demonically possessed by group sessions of prayer and fasting. His methods had profound political implications. To his supporters they confirmed God's support for his charismatic ministry, and the Presbyterian manifesto of Church reform. To his conformist critics, notably Whitgift, Bancroft and their protégé Samuel Harsnett, Darrell used fraudulent magic designed to win Presbyterianism 'popularity', which threatened political upheaval.

On 8 December 1596 Nicholas Starkie of Cleworth near Manchester consulted Dee about the demonic possession of seven people in his household. Like most contemporaries, Starkie assumed that the learned could communicate with the spirit world. He could not know about Dee's previous attempts at exorcism, though he may have heard rumours about his angel magic. Two of Starkie's sons had shown the convulsive symp-toms of demonic possession in early 1595. After spending the huge sum of £200 without curing them, Starkie engaged Edmund Hartley, a local 'cunning man', as a household servant, who succeeded in calming them for eighteen months with 'certain popish charms and herbs'.

However, Starkie eventually suspected Hartley of bewitching three other children, a maid, and an adult family relative, the 'Lancashire Seven'. Dee's response to Starkie's plea, we should note, became a bone of contention between Presbyterians and conformists. The simplest Presbyterian version, usually repeated by historians, claimed that Dee refused to meddle in the matter and advised Starkie to consult 'some godly preachers' about 'a Public or Private fast'. That Presbyterian method of exorcism involved long, fervent extempore prayers. According to the Presbyterian story, Dee 'sharply reproved, and straightly examined' Hartley the witch, temporarily easing the symptoms. Nor, they insisted, did Dee suggest that Starkie write to Darrell, already well-known for successful exorcisms.[1]

The conformists told a different story. Of the thirteen books published about the Darrell controversy, Darrell or his supporters wrote ten. The three replies by their opponents had greater impact on Dee's reputation. Whitgift, Bancroft and Harsnett emphasised from the first Dee's involvement in the exorcisms and his knowledge of Darrell's reputation. Their tactics forced later Presbyterian accounts of the Lancashire Seven into gradually admitting that Dee played a more significant role than they had first suggested.

The conformists exploited an advantage: they had captured a manuscript, written by a Manchester preacher named Dickons, which gave a detailed account of these goings-on. Darrell claimed that Bancroft kept a copy, though it has disappeared.[2] Bancroft naturally selected from this manuscript to suit his prejudices, which included denying that Hartley was really a witch. In autumn 1598 the High Commission tried to force Darrell to admit that he had in fact instructed the Lancashire Seven how to counterfeit their symptoms of demonic possession.[3]

By emphasising Dee's involvement with Darrell, the conformists could use his established notoriety as a 'conjuror' to blacken the Presbyterians, while denouncing the witchcraft accusations and exorcisms as fraudulent. That approach helped to undercut Presbyterian claims that Darrell's power over demons confirmed their cause and further emphasised that credulity about exorcisms made the populace vulnerable to political subversion. As Bancroft and Harsnett put it, the Presbyterians 'not prevailing by the conspiracy of Hacket, nor by the libelling of Martin [Marprelate] (yet fearing to attempt the rebellion of Scotland and Geneva for their reformation) would obtain credit by working miracles in casting out Devils'.[4] The conformists repeatedly waved this red flag of religious rebellion over witchcraft and demonic possession.

Ironically, Dee's response to the accusations against Hartley sometimes seems as sceptical as Bancroft's. The local justice Edmund Hopwood prepared for Hartley's trial at Lancaster assizes by taking the depositions of Starkie's children in February 1597.[5] Darrell arrived in Lancashire on 16 March, and three days later Hopwood consulted Dee, perhaps for advice on whether he should cooperate with Darrell.

In response, Dee lent him Johann Wier's book *On the Deceits of Demons*.[6] Wier had demolished most contemporary beliefs in witchcraft and demons, supplying arguments for Scot's *Discovery of Witchcraft* that Whitgift and Bancroft had used against the Presbyterians. In April, by contrast, Dee lent Hopwood Girolamo Menghi's recent book describing elaborate Catholic exorcism rituals, which Harsnett later condemned. In August, Dee lent him the infamous witchcraft tract the *Malleus Maleficarum*, or *Hammer of the Evildoers*.[7]

Whitgift certainly saw Dee as a credulous believer in the dangerous Darrell. After speedily exorcising the Lancashire Seven, Darrell arrived in Nottingham in November 1597 for another exorcism.[8] By April 1598 he had divided Nottingham society between his godly supporters and their conservative opponents, seemingly a dress rehearsal for the religious warfare that Whitgift and Bancroft feared.[9] Unfortunately for Dee, the living of Upton-upon-Severn fell vacant again in February 1598, amidst this scandalous turmoil. If Whitgift had ever contemplated relenting, his knowledge of Dee's collaboration with Darrell, gleaned from Dickons's manuscript, sealed his fate. Though Dee immediately petitioned for Upton, within weeks he learned 'of the Lord Archbishop his hard dealing'.[10]

Worse happened after Dee departed for London in mid-summer 1598. Ostensibly, he pursued the College law suits there for the next two years. But he also hoped to save what remained of his reputation. Whitgift had imprisoned Darrell in April, while Bancroft and Harsnett constructed a High Commission show trial. They pressured three of Darrell's demoniacs into confessing their frauds, screened out witnesses who might support him, and intimidated others. In October Darrell smuggled out two accounts of his Lancashire exorcisms. One emphasised the political ramifications of Whitgift's persecution. Darrell claimed that Fulke Greville, the representative at Court of the powerful Earl of Essex while the Earl served in Ireland, had intervened with Elizabeth on his behalf.[11] The other account again justified his exorcisms, denied any claims to miraculous powers, and insisted that he only intervened when invited by Starkie and unnamed gentlemen.[12]

Darrell's manuscripts circulated in London that winter, for he later claimed that the public debated his case in both 'the streets and Taverns' and the 'Seats of Justice'.[13] What people said about Dee is lost. However, Dee's despair at Whitgift's opposition and the need to disassociate himself from Darrell explain his response in January 1599. He finally published the *Letter Apologetical* he had written to Whitgift in January 1595.

The title page depicted Dee resting on hope, humility and patience, a sheep attacked by the ravening wolf of envy and the many-headed monster of slander. Dee's fervent assertions in this pamphlet that his magic expressed orthodox Christian faith did not convince everyone. The witty, gossipy John Chamberlain, friend of Dee's critic Stephen Powle, dismissed it as 'a ridiculous babble of an old imposturing juggler'.[14]

In late May 1599, while Dee lived at Mortlake, Whitgift and Bancroft presided over Darrell's show trial in London. Harsnett prosecuted. The predictable verdict declared Darrell a counterfeit exorcist, deposed him from the ministry and committed him to prison until further punishment. However, Darrell really did enjoy support at Court and was released within two years.

Whitgift and Bancroft's contemptuous response to Dee's *Letter* appeared in November 1599, in a book begun by Bancroft and finished by

Harsnett. Both emphasised Dee's involvement to discredit Darrell. Bancroft opened by alleging that Darrell was 'sent for into Lancashire by one Master Starkie, upon the report of Master Dee his Butler, who told the said Master Starkie what Master Darrell had done' in exorcising his brother, Thomas Darling. The Presbyterian replies only gradually conceded this more detailed story, suggesting their unease about any association with Dee. Their first response merely admitted that 'Master Starkie going to Master Dee for his counsel, was advised by him, to call for some honest and godly preachers, with whom he should consult'.

More tellingly, Bancroft could add from Dickons's seized manuscript that Dee had both advised Starkie and invited Darrell to Manchester. He put Dee's letter in the worst possible light. Bancroft related how, 'Hartley the Witch, did afterwards tell Master Starkey' that 'there must be two or three at the least, with fervent and hearty prayer' to cure his children. Therefore, when Darrell arrived in response to Dee's letter he 'fulfilled the devil's words'. Dee, Bancroft pointed out, aligned himself with enthusiasts who believed Darrell 'to be such a man, as if he met with the devil, he was able to curb him'. Harsnett also criticised Dee for contributing to Darrell's personality cult.

In response, Darrell and his collaborator George More tried everything to distance themselves from Dee. More, writing in December 1599, even tried to rehabilitate Dee. He omitted Dee's letter to Darrell, reported his advice to consult godly preachers, and for the first time mentioned Dee's sharp reproof to Hartley. Later Darrell conceded that Dee had written to him but denied that he went to Lancashire 'upon Mr Dee his letter'. He emphasised that Dee's letter arrived ten weeks before his departure for Lancashire in March 1597, when he responded to letters from local justices. He needed to disassociate himself from Dee, because now Lancashire papists were also calling Darrell a 'conjuror', his prayers and fasting being merely charms against demons.[15] Under continuing pressure, however, Darrell finally divulged more details about Dee's involvement.

This enlarged account repeated the previous stories but added that Starkie 'requested Master Dee his letter unto me (though unacquainted) and obtained it, wherewith he sent his own also, which prevailed not with me'.[16] Bancroft and Harsnett had gradually forced Darrell to acknowledge that Dee had invited him to Manchester in December 1596. Bancroft and Whitgift evidently knew about that letter when Whitgift refused to countenance Dee's return to Upton in February 1598, because Dee's involvement with Darrell epitomised the subversive potential of his occult philosophy.

Dee's two years in London on College affairs did not repair his reputation amongst the Fellows back in Manchester, who while godly Protestants seem not to have been Presbyterians. After his return to Manchester in June 1600, the Fellows petitioned the Bishop of Chester to investigate Dee. They stacked the commission with local godly preachers. It would be instructive to know whether they were concerned about the College's finances or Dee's connection with Darrell, but Dee answered all their complaints verbally, and no records survive. Though in November Carter again grumbled about Dee, and unspecified 'quarrels' broke out on 18 December, the Fellows allowed Dee's house rent at the annual audit.[17]

The Earl of Essex's failed rebellion in February 1601 made it still harder for Dee to protect himself against the opprobrium the conformists heaped on magic. Whitgift and Bancroft used the rebellion to tie magic, Darrell and the Presbyterians to insurrection. Cracking down in all directions, the government ordered the Stationers' Company to burn Darrell's *True Narration*. In August 1601 the zealous John Deacon and John Walker, encouraged by Bancroft, underlined the connection between Essex and the exorcists in *Dialogical Discourses of spirits and devils*. They claimed that the Presbyterians covertly worked to advance 'some mighty Magnifico [Essex] in their secret assemblies'.

Their follow-up *Summary Answer* (1601) argued that Presbyterians used prayer and fasting like charms and enchantments. Their 'Cabalistical conceits' not only confirmed 'the wizards of the world in their wicked opinions' but like Hacket scandalised the Church and subverted the State. Following Bancroft, Deacon and Walker denied the reality of witchcraft and demonic possession. Bancroft now interfered in witchcraft cases to promote medical explanations of symptoms of possession as being simple hysteria.[18] He drafted canons in 1604 forbidding exorcism by prayer and fasting, on pain of expulsion from the ministry.[19] To the extent that conformists managed to connect magical beliefs with subversion, their cultural counter-revolution undermined Dee's remaining years.

Dee also faced problems in Manchester, where his inability to preach increasingly alienated the town's godly power brokers, led by Sir Nicholas Mosley. In November 1600 they petitioned the Privy Council for permission to remedy their chronic lack of preaching by raising funds for a lectureship. Whitgift disapproved of 'popular' lectureships, which too often encouraged tumultuous preaching. He therefore denied their proposal and made sure that the Bishop of Chester held that line.[20] The godly pressed ahead anyway, justifying Whitgift's worst fears.

In February 1603 the civic leaders repeated their petition to Sir Robert Cecil, the Queen's Secretary. Now they complained that 'Mr Dee . . . being no preacher' and only one of the Fellows bothering to reside, the College utterly failed to provide preaching. They had raised money for William Burne to lecture. Yet another graduate of St John's College, Cambridge, Burne had refused to accept Whitgift's 1583 articles prescribing liturgical practice.

If anything, this recommended Burne to the Manchester godly, who planned to replace Dee with him. They would support Burne financially until he obtained a vacant Fellowship, which Dee could not deny him if Cecil supported Burne. Beyond that, they wanted Queen Elizabeth to grant Burne the Wardenship when Dee died. They finally obtained both objectives on 30 September 1603, when the new monarch James I ordered Dee to appoint Burne to a Fellowship, and granted him the next Wardenship.[21]

By then Dee had reached the advanced age of seventy-six. Manchester's canny businessmen evidently planned for his successor because of his age, diminishing financial credit and declining social standing. The chaotic College finances meant that within a year of arriving in Manchester, in February 1597, Dee had to borrow money for ordinary housekeeping. He even pawned his daughter's christening tankard.[22] His two years attending the London courts failed to improve his cash flow, because five days before Christmas 1600 he pawned plate for £10, which was still unredeemed in May 1603. He pawned more plate for £5 in January 1601.[23] A bleak Christmas indeed, and no cheering gift from the Queen.

The fact that Dee needed collateral for such small loans indicates his declining creditworthiness amongst his shrewd neighbours. Worse still, their assessment proved correct. Although he finally secured his rector's income from Tenby in 1601, in July 1602 Dee had to obtain a protection under the Great Seal preventing his creditors taking legal action to recover their loans. That month his son Arthur consulted the psychological and spiritual healer Richard Napier about his 'discontentment for wants and griefs touching his father'.

By this time also Dee's physical and mental health seems to have been breaking down under the constant administrative and financial strain, compounded by religious and personal conflicts. In late June 1597 he experienced heavy bleeding from the anus, a symptom of some serious disease, which reappeared at intervals until his death. During the night of 19 October 1597 he experienced the first of several bouts of 'grief', perhaps an anxiety attack connected to depression, which recurred in December, January and February.[24] The fact that he stopped recording them does not mean they ceased. For the College's convoluted, expensive litigation dragged on, and Dee's depression perhaps provided a topic when he met Napier in 1604.

His own psychological problems may have given Dee new insight as a 'physician of the soul'. He again spent the autumn law term of 1602 in London. That year Darrell's latest books had appeared, which finally acknowledged that Dee had helped bring him to Manchester. Dee's role may have been greater than we know, for in early November 1602 John Chamberlain picked up rumours that 'Dr Dee hath delivered the Lady Sandes of a devil or some other strange possession'. Demonic possession was extremely topical. The notorious case of Mary Glover had fascinated the capital since the spring.[25] That month exorcism again came under official attack. Dr Thomas Holland inserted into his showcase sermon on covetousness at St Paul's Cathedral an otherwise irrelevant swipe at those who 'have gone about to show the truth of religion by casting out devils'.[26]

Dee's exorcisms only confirmed his national reputation as a magician. The severe outbreak of plague at James I's accession in March 1603 provoked speculation about its astrological causes, particularly that a planet would fall to earth. If it fell on dry land the plague would increase, but if in the sea it would cease. Some Londoners attributed this theory to the well-known astrologer Edward Gresham. Like Dee, Gresham based his astrology on accurate astronomical measurements, warded off charges of atheism, practised medicine and magic, and narrowly escaped accusations of witchcraft. Gresham knew 'that grave man and thrice great Clerk Dr Dee', an allusion to the 'thrice great' Hermes Trismegistus. Gresham reported that 'most men' considered Dee the author of the planetary theory, which 'mightily suspended the minds not of the rude multitudes only but even of the better sort'. Dee believed that momentous events would occur every ten years after the supernova in November 1572. Hearsay garbled this prophecy into a prediction of the traumatic plague.[27]

The 'better sort' possibly included James I. The intellectual King kept an open mind about spirits. His patronage of natural philosophy included occult philosophers, just as he tolerated varied religious and political beliefs to establish his regime. Dee's reputation for prophecy in 1603 may therefore be connected with his undocumented claim to have become mathematician to the King on 9 August 1603.[28] That might have consoled him for missing out again at St Cross. When Robert Bennett finally became Bishop of Hereford in April, 'divers Scots both ministers and laymen' clamoured for the Mastership, though it went to an Englishman, Arthur Lake.[29] Dee's appointment as the King's mathematician suggests that he spent part of the summer of 1603 in London, thus further encouraging the Manchester godly to replace their increasingly impoverished, absentee warden. How Dee felt about Burne waiting for him to die we do not know, but we do know how Dee felt about the last great challenge of his public career, the Witchcraft Act of 1604. He believed that it threatened his execution.

When Dee arrived in London in the summer of 1604, he learned that Parliament had for weeks been debating a new witchcraft bill, introduced into the Lords on 29 March. Bancroft sat on the Lords committee that rewrote the bill by 2 April. The Lords sent it to the Commons on 8 May, who sent it into committee on 25 May. Soon afterwards Dee learned about the committee's deliberations. He panicked, believing that the new law was aimed at him. Gossip about his 'damnable magic' had circulated in London the previous winter. His angel magic was no secret. About now another conjuror, John a Windor, copied 'out of a Book that lay in the Window' at Mortlake a traditional Latin invocation, different from Kelley's. It asked Christ to send true angels from His right hand, to be visible in a mirror to a virgin boy. Windor later used this ancient call.[30]

The Witchcraft Act of 1563 had made dealing with wicked spirits a felony only if physical harm resulted. The new bill, however, mandated death for 'any Invocation or Conjuration of any evil and wicked spirit', without qualification. Bancroft aimed to catch the Presbyterian exorcists under this general provision, but Dee took the bill personally, and he rushed into print. On 5 June the committee returned the amended bill to the Commons for its third reading. That day Dee published his printed petition to James, a copy of which still lies in the files of Sir Julius Caesar, James's Master of Requests.[31]

The petition claims that Dee presented it to James on 5 June. Whether or not this was wishful thinking, the petition summarised his fears. Describing himself as the King's servant, Dee asked to be 'tried and cleared' before James, the Privy Council or Parliament, of the perennial slanders that he was a 'Conjuror, or Caller, or Invocator of Devils'. He pointed out that the unnamed 'English traitor', actually William Allen, had used similar accusations in 1592 to slander Elizabeth's Privy Council. To clear this discredit on himself and Elizabeth's Privy Councillors who still served James, he offered his head if anyone could prove that he invoked 'Devils, or damned Spirits', or could verify the 'strange and frivolous fables' told of him by the 'many headed Multitude'. Dee then asked James to solve his financial woes and punish his enemies, who had 'so long' sought 'his utter undoing, by little and little'.[32]

There is no sign that James granted any part of Dee's petition. On 7 June the Commons passed the amended bill against 'Conjuration, Witchcraft, and dealing with wicked and evil Spirits'. The next day, Friday

8 June, Dee published a verse petition to that House. He was not just seeking to clear his name. For fifty years he had been slandered as a 'conjuror', but now he demanded a general Act against slander, with special provision 'for John Dee his case'. The Commons ignored Dee, and on Saturday sent their bill back to the Lords, who passed it immediately.[33]

Having failed to move either King or Parliament, Dee naively addressed himself to the court of public opinion. He reprinted his *Letter* of 1599, defending the 'very Christian course' of his philosophical 'exercises'. He added to it his petitions to James and the Commons.[34] Dee's last publication, the little book failed to convince anyone.

He dined with the alchemical and astrological doctor Richard Napier at the house of his friend John Pontois's employer, the great Levant merchant Richard Staper, on 26 July 1604. Napier and John Dee had much to discuss besides John's 'grief' and alchemy. For the Witchcraft Act threatened them both. Like Dee, Napier feared the name of 'conjuror', since he also used prayer, fasting and magical rituals to invoke the Archangel Gabriel.[35]

Rebuffed in London, Dee wearily returned to Manchester, where in November the Bishop of Chester's visitation duly found him 'no preacher'.[36] That month, aged seventy-seven, Dee again prepared to follow the College suits at the Duchy courts in London.[37] Then severe plague hit Manchester in late March 1605. Oliver Carter, one of its first victims, was buried on 18 March.

Tragically for John, Jane Dee caught the plague and was buried on 23 March. Dee may still have been in London at the time. They had been married for twenty-seven years. Of the seven children they brought to Manchester, Theodore had been buried 12 April 1602, aged fourteen, and Margaret on 1 February 1603, just seven-and-a-half years old. Arthur had married in 1602 and begun his own career as an alchemical and astrological doctor. By the time Jane died, she and John had two grandchildren, perhaps some small consolation to him.[38]

Dee would have found none in Manchester. As the frightening death rate from the plague accelerated, the wealthy fled, leaving behind only 'covertly rascals and slaves', who now openly criticised Sir Nicholas

Mosley, a great encloser of common land.[39] In June government and society collapsed under the strain. William Burne preached in the Collegiate Church as long as he could and finally resorted to preaching in a field 'by reason of the unruliness of infected persons'.[40] Since Dee could not preach and had no authority over Manchester town itself, after Jane's death he had no reason to stay.

Dee disappears from the written record between November 1604 and February 1606, when he suddenly reappears in London. He was not attending the Duchy courts for the College. He tried to make friends in the city the only way he knew, through his learning. On 19 February 1606 the Mercers' Company court recorded that 'Mr Doctor Dee a brother of this company presented of his free gift as a token of his good will unto this company Four Books, the first The British Monarchy alias the Petty Navy Royal, the second Propaedeumata Aphoristica, the third Monas Hieroglyphica to the Emperor Maximilian, the fourth a Letter Apologetical'.[41] At the end, Dee would need the Mercers, though one wonders what the stolid merchants made of his *Propaedeumata aphoristica* and *Monas hieroglyphica*.

More immediately, he needed angelic advice. The gap in his recorded angelic conversations does not mean that he stopped trying to contact the angels. The record abruptly starts again in London, on 20 March 1607, in his eightieth year. Bartholomew Hickman again scryed, despite Dee having burned all Hickman's 'actions' in 1600. They still began with the ritual recitation of Latin prayers asking God to send His light and truth. Dee's questions returned to his intestinal bleeding, with kidney stones adding to his misery. He planned 'a great attempt' to inform the indifferent Privy Council 'of my beggery' and to offer Sir Robert Cecil, now Earl of Salisbury, his service. He also expected help from Bancroft, now Archbishop of Canterbury. The angels offered no practical advice, only 'the hid knowledge and secrecy of God that is not as yet made known unto thee'.[42] Dee still lacked political insight. Cecil habitually supported conformists and showed little sympathy for magicians. Bancroft continued Whitgift's policy against occult explanations of the world.

Nor was Dee handling his relations with the Manchester Fellows very well. The new, uncompromisingly Protestant Fellowship, led by Burne, had finally solved the local preaching problems, but at Dee's expense. The College charter entitled him to three months' paid absence a year, but the Fellows refused to pay him beyond that, even when he was absent on College affairs. Dee remained warden to his dying day, despite claims that he resigned in 1605. In July 1607 the angels advised him to organise matters about his Wardenship 'and in all other causes of worldly affairs'. In September they urged him to content himself with 'that little that can be made of thy right in the College matters'.[43]

Needing money, from June to September he pressed for angelic help in locating stolen property for a Lancashire client, a practice that Dee evidently began in Manchester.[44] He doggedly pursued the alchemical route to riches. In July the angels promised him the Book of Dunstan, the philosopher's stone, and the 'secret wisdom of that Jewel' delivered by an angel years before. Accordingly, at Mortlake in December he began alchemical work towards finding the stone, which somehow petered out in January 1608.

More helpfully, the angels laid out the political realities. Salisbury had turned King James against Dee, describing him as one 'that doth deal with Devils and by sorcery, as you commonly term them witchcraft'. Therefore, Hickman's cruel revenge on his eighty-year-old master, for having burned all his 'actions', made some sense. Since God has hardened England against you, and you live in poverty, said the angels in September 1607, prepare to depart overseas, where God will miraculously cure you. You will not return, so abandon your library and alchemical equipment. In fact, sell your books through John Pontois. Thus the largest private library in England started to be dispersed.[45]

At this stage Dee still retained his house at Mortlake and his rectory at Tenby. Yet by July 1608 he had resigned the rectory and by August had disposed of the house. He was obeying the angelic advice of September 1607, that since God chose him alone to receive the 'wisdom only Enoch enjoyed', he must abandon his unworthy country.[46] He had exchanged letters with Landgrave Moritz of Hesse-Kassel in 1595, praising the mathematical approach to alchemy. In the summer of 1608 he again fixed his eyes on Germany, hoping to join Johannes Hartmann's scheme for an 'alchemical college' at the University of Marburg under Moritz's patronage. Like Dee, Hartmann was a mathematician turned alchemical doctor. Unlike Dee, however, Hartmann succeeded because he moulded his studies to his patron's desires. Alchemical teaching at Marburg would closely resemble Dee's mathematically precise method planned for 'Queen Elizabeth's Academy' forty years earlier, though now without Dee. He also made one last effort to secure Rudolf II's patronage, for that summer he expected money from the Emperor.[47]

Dee started yet another scheme to find buried treasure.[48] Yet by September 1608, though Pontois hoped to make money through alchemy, they were 'utterly unable to provide things necessary'.[49] Here the manuscript ends, and for all we know the angels fell silent at last. Dee still struggled on, sick, impoverished and weak, but able to record astrological phenomena. In September 1607 he had sent Thomas Harriot his observation of the spectacular comet later named for Edmond Halley.[50] Yet, whatever the travel plans for which he raised money in the summer of 1608, his last illness intervened. In a now illegible note Pontois recorded in Dee's 'Diary' some medical disaster on 15 August 1608.

Somehow, Dee braved the London winter. At the end, the intellectual of vaulting ambition, who had been instructed by God's messengers, and who had admonished emperors and princes, could only rely upon his father's people, the London merchants. On 11 January 1609 the Mercers agreed that 'Doctor Dee a brother of this Fellowship shall be gratified with 5 marks [£3 10s.] of this company's gift to help him in his sickness.'[51]

Legend has it from Richard Napier that in his last months Dee sold his books to buy food, but in fact the Jacobean world was a little kinder than that. He lived in John Pontois's house in Bishopsgate Street, a frail, white-haired figure of eighty-five, surrounded by manuscripts and books that overflowed the shelves of a large study and spilled out of numerous trunks. They included the Arabic book he called *Soyga*, which combined angel magic with alchemy and astrology, and a valuable manuscript of Paracelsus. His astrological clock survived, together with some precious mathematical instruments. His cedar chest with its hidden compartment still protected his secrets – his olive-wood rosary and cross, his angelic manuscripts, his own writings. Pontois believed implicitly in the angels, and long afterwards he kept the chest, the Holy Table and 'a certain round flat stone like Crystal'. Dee died amongst these remnants of his long life of learning at 3 a.m. on 26 March 1609. Within days a Scotsman had his Wardenship.[52]

What are we to make of the extraordinary story of John Dee? To the community of his early years, whose folk religion valued charms and spells, his magic would have seemed a natural extension of life. To some of his contemporaries, who lived through Protestant attacks on religious charms, and the Catholic response, which began the decline of magic, occult philosophy would have remained a familiar part of life and politics. To them Dee's life would have seemed, if not exactly ordinary, then at least perfectly explicable. Men, and from the Queen downwards many women, of Dee's education understood astrology, alchemy and angel magic as the common inheritance of the learned. Their practice of magic, like Dee's, shared far more with the unlearned than is sometimes acknowledged. Contemporary politicians, steeped in such learning, were comfortable using occult knowledge to advance their policies and defeat their opponents. Even those who criticised occult philosophy did so out of a deep appreciation of its hold over the imaginations of their deluded fellow men.

Only towards the end of his life, when he ran foul of cultural conservatives in the second wave of Protestant attacks on magic, can the headwinds that Dee encountered be attributed to his fervent belief in occult philosophy. The reasons for his earlier setbacks were familiar enough in Tudor England. Like many others he found it difficult to navigate the hurly-burly of mid-Tudor politics, just as his father had fallen victim to factional politics and backed the wrong side in a political crisis. John switched sides too soon in 1555 and missed the change in the political tide.

Yet his partial recovery at Elizabeth's accession actually depended on occult philosophy, and Dee's career and reputation at her Court flourished when the political planets aligned in ways that made his skills useful to influential politicians. Ultimately, he failed as political circumstances changed and the powerful no longer needed his occult talents. Sometimes he was overlooked not because of his reputation as a 'magus' but because he was outshone by more flamboyant magicians – especially John Prestall and Edward Kelley. Dee found the going hard not because he was an isolated figure, marginalised by his magic, but because he had too many rivals in magical learning and service, both in Europe and at the Court of Elizabeth I.

In the last analysis, when Dee lost political patronage he lost the power to defend the purity of his prophetic calling against enemies who smeared him as a 'conjuror'. At the end of his life such attacks smoothed the way for the conservative counter-attack on magic as the engine of subversion, which drove it to the margins of the early modern political world. To this very day the attack on magic colours our understanding of John Dee and his times.

Further Reading

Dee's Writings

Readers who are interested in reading more of Dee's writings can find his *Propaedeumata aphoristica* published in English as *John Dee on Astronomy: Propaedeumata aphoristica (1558 and 1568) Latin and English*, ed. and trans. W. Shumaker (Berkeley, Los Angeles and London, 1975); his 'Mathematical Preface', republished with an introduction by Allen G. Debus as *John Dee: The Mathematical Praeface to the Elements of Geometrie of Euclid of Megara (1570)* (New York, 1975); and his *Monas hieroglyphica* in C.H. Josten, 'A Translation of John Dee's *Monas hieroglyphica* with an Introduction and Annotations', *Ambix* 12 (1964), pp. 84–221. The text of Dee's conversations with angels from December 1581 to May 1583 in BL MS Sloane 3188, edited by Christopher Whitby as his 1981 Birmingham Ph.D. thesis, is available for free download from the British Library database EThOS (Electronic Theses Online Service). Meric Casaubon published the continuation of the conversations from 1583 as *A true & faithful relation of what passed for many yeers between Dr. John Dee . . . and some spirits* (London, 1659). This, and Dee's published writings, including *General and rare memorials pertayning to the perfect arte of navigation* (London, 1577) and *Letter Apologetical* (1599, 1604), are now widely available through the Early English Books Online database, subscribed to by many libraries.

Used with care, Joseph Peterson's edition of *John Dee's Five Books of Mystery: Original Sourcebook of Enochian Magic: From the Collected Works known as Mysteriorum libri quinque* (Boston, MA, 2003) has important material on the conversations. Even more caution is required with Donald C. Laycock, *The Complete Enochian Dictionary* (Boston, MA, York Beach, ME, 2001). Dee's crucial text in BL MS Add. 59681, 'Brytanici Imperii Limites', has been edited by Ken MacMillan with Jennifer Abeles, as *John Dee: The Limits of the British Empire* (Westport, CT, and London, 2004). There is valuable material by and about Dee at The Alchemy Website (http://www.alchemywebsite.com/) and the John Dee Publication Project (www.john-dee.org).

Major Studies on Dee

The fundamental study of Dee's collection of books and manuscripts is Julian Roberts and Andrew G. Watson, *John Dee's Library Catalogue* (London, 1990). My book also owes much to Nicholas

Clulee's deep analysis of Dee's response to contemporary natural philosophy, *John Dee's Natural Philosophy: Between Science and Religion* (London, New York, 1988), supplemented by Clulee 'The *Monas hieroglyphica* and the Alchemical Thread of John Dee's Career', *Ambix*, 52, 3 (November 2005), pp. 197–215. William H. Sherman's elegant study of Dee as an 'intelligencer' writing advice for the Court, *John Dee: The Politics of Reading and Writing in the English Renaissance* (Amherst, MA, 1995), places less emphasis on Dee's occult philosophy. Deborah Harkness has published the most detailed study of *John Dee's Conversations with Angels: Cabala, Alchemy, and the End of Nature* (Cambridge, 1999), though following Clulee she distinguishes Dee's occult philosophy from that of ordinary 'cunning men' more than I have done.

There has not been space to discuss all aspects of Dee's thought in this book. We lack a comprehensive study of his 'Mathematical Preface', but there is still much of value on his historical research, particularly about his study of Arthurian sources, in Peter J. French, *John Dee* (London, 1972). However, influenced by Frances Yates, French discussed Dee's occult philosophy mainly to demonstrate his indebtedness to Hermeticism. With that caution Yates's own study, *The Occult Philosophy in the Elizabethan Age* (London, 1979), is a useful introduction to other aspects of Dee's milieu. Much of Yates's interpretation of Dee has been corrected, and the field of Dee studies greatly expanded, in Stephen Clucas, ed., *John Dee: Interdisciplinary Studies in English Renaissance Thought* (Dordrecht, 2006), soon to be further augmented by the collection of essays in 'John Dee and the Sciences: Early Modern Networks of Knowledge', a special issue of *Studies in History and Philosophy of Science, Part A*, ed. Jennifer M. Rampling (forthcoming, 2012).

The Broader Background

On the broader background to Dee's early studies, see Mordechai Feingold, *The Mathematicians' Apprenticeship: Science, Universities and Society in England 1560–1640* (Cambridge, 1984), and Feingold, 'The Occult Tradition in the English Universities of the Renaissance: A Reassessment', in *Occult and Scientific Mentalities in the Renaissance*, ed. B. Vickers (Cambridge, 1984). Christopher I. Lehrich, *The Language of Demons and Angels: Cornelius Agrippa's Occult Philosophy* (Leiden, 2003), and the classic study by Marjorie Reeves, *The Influence of Prophecy in the Later Middle Ages: A Study in Joachimism* (Oxford, 1969), as well as her *Joachim of Fiore and the Prophetic Future* (Stroud, 1999), provide some context for Dee's developing ideas. Nicholas Crane's *Mercator: The Man who Mapped the Planet* (London, 2002) is a readable introduction to the Louvain mathematicians.

Dee and the Tudors

Apart from Rudolf II, on whom see the seminal study by R.J.W. Evans, *Rudolf II and His World* (Oxford, 1973), Dee served three Tudor monarchs. Jennifer Loach, *Edward VI*, ed. G. Bernard and P. Williams (New Haven and London, 1999), offers many new insights into the first, complementing Stephen Alford, *Kingship and Politics in the Reign of Edward VI* (Cambridge, 2002). David Loades has published numerous thoroughly researched books on Mary I and the Tudor Court generally. There are simply too many biographies of Elizabeth I to choose from, though none to my knowledge discusses her occult philosophy. The most accessible and least star-struck is Patrick Collinson's little gem, *Elizabeth I* (Oxford, 2007), published from the *Oxford Dictionary of National Biography*, which is available as an online database through subscribing libraries. The Tudor biographies amongst the fifty-seven thousand lives in the *ODNB* provide an essential introduction to many of the famous and forgotten individuals mentioned here. Each biography includes a bibliography to guide further reading.

Abbreviations

APC	*Acts of the Privy Council of England.* New series, ed. J.R. Dasent, 46 vols. (London, 1890–1964)
BL	British Library
BLO	Bodleian Library, Oxford
CPR	*Calendar of Patent Rolls*
CR	'The Compendious Rehearsal of John Dee' in *Johannis, confratris & monachi Glastoniensis, chronica sive historia de rebus Glastoniensibus.* ed. T. Hearne, 2 vols. (Oxford, 1726), ii, pp. 497–551
CSP Foreign	*Calendar of State Papers Foreign: Edward VI, Mary, Elizabeth I, 1547–1589,* ed. W.B. Turnbull et al., 25 vols. (London, 1861–1936)
CSP Spanish	*Calendar of State Papers Spain,* ed. G.A. Bergenroth et al., 19 vols. (London, 1862–1954)
CSP Spanish	*Calendar of State Papers Spain, Simancas,* ed. M.A.S. Hume, 4 vols. (London, 1892–9)
CSP Venetian	*Calendar of State Papers Venetian,* ed. R. Brown, et al., 38 vols. (London, 1864–1947)
GL	Guildhall Library, London
HEHL	Henry E. Huntington Library, San Marino, California
HMC	Historical Manuscripts Commission, *Calendars of Manuscripts*
LP	*Letters and Papers, Foreign and Domestic, of the Reign of Henry VIII,* ed. J.S. Brewer, J. Gairdner and R.H. Brodie, 22 vols. (London 1862–1932)
MH	C.H. Josten, 'A Translation of John Dee's *Monas hieroglyphica* with an Introduction and Annotations', *Ambix* 12 (1964), pp. 84–221
MP	*John Dee: The Mathematical Praeface to the Elements of Geometrie of Euclid of Megara (1570)* with an introduction by Allen G. Debus (New York, 1975)
ODNB	*Oxford Dictionary of National Biography*
PA	*John Dee on Astronomy. Propaedeumata aphoristica (1558 and 1568) Latin and English,* ed. and trans. W. Shumaker, intro. by J.L. Heilbron (Berkeley, Los Angeles and London, 1975)
R&W	J. Roberts and A.G. Watson, eds, *John Dee's Library Catalogue* (London, 1990), followed by their catalogue reference number
SP	State Papers
TNA	The National Archives, Kew

Notes

Chapter 1: A World Full of Magic

1. Eamon Duffy, *The Stripping of the Altars*, 2nd ed. (New Haven and London, 2005), pp. 280–1.
2. BLO MS Ashmole 487.
3. Duffy, *Stripping of the Altars*, pp. 266–72.
4. Ibid., pp. 73–4; *The Commonplace Book of Robert Reynes of Acle*, ed. C. Louis (New York, 1980), pp. 167, 169–70, 247–8.
5. Duffy, *Stripping of the Altars*, pp. 279, 524–63.
6. Ibid., p. 16.
7. Ibid., pp. 23–6, 136, 279.
8. Ibid., pp. 93–4, 98–100, 110, 119–20; Keith Thomas, *Religion and the Decline of Magic* (London, 1971), pp. 33–5, 44.
9. Michael Lapidge, 'Dunstan [St Dunstan] (*d.* 988)', *ODNB*, Oxford University Press, 2004; online edn, [http://www.oxforddnb.com/view/article/8288].
10. Duffy, *Stripping of the Altars*, pp. 53, 59, 112–14, 157–61; R.C.D. Baldwin, 'Thorne, Robert, the elder (*c.*1460–1519)', *ODNB*, Oxford University Press, 2004; online edn, January 2008 [http://www.oxforddnb.com/view/article/27347]; TNA E117/4/1; GL MS 4887, pp. 145, 150.
11. BL MS Cotton Charters XIII and XIV.I; Society of Antiquaries of London, MS 728/3, fos. 7v–8v; Society of Antiquaries MS 378, fo. 575, in *Miscellanea Genalogica et Heraldica*, 5th ser., 8 (1932–4), pp. 263–4; *MH*, Dedication; *LP*, xvi, no. 1391.11; TNA SP 1/229, fo. 1, in *LP* i, (I), no. 20.
12. *LP*, no. 1462.2; ibid., no. 709.51; i (II), no. 2772.32; iv (I), no. 1533.6; TNA SP 1/56, fo. 2; S.T. Bindoff, ed., *The House of Commons 1509–1558*, 3 vols. (London, 1982), ii, p. 25.
13. John Guy, 'Thomas Wolsey, Thomas Cromwell and the Reform of Henrician Government', in Diarmaid MacCulloch, ed., *The Reign of Henry VIII: Politics, Policy and Piety* (Basingstoke, 1995), pp. 53–5.
14. Centre for Kentish Studies, CKS-U908/2/5/9/2/1/4; East Sussex Record Office, SAS/PN/623; TNA PROB 11/26 fos. 49v–50r; R. Pocock, *The History of the Incorporated Towns and Parishes of Gravesend and Milton* (Gravesend, 1797), pp. 147–9; P. Lee, 'Orthodox Parish Religion and Chapels of Ease in Late Medieval England: The Case of St George's Chapel', *Archaeologia Cantiana*, CXIX (1999), pp. 55–70.

15. G.D. Ramsay, *The City of London in International Politics at the Accession of Elizabeth Tudor* (Manchester, 1975), p. 42.

16. A. Collins, *The Peerage of England*, 9 vols. (London, 1812), ii, p. 588.

17. *Two Tudor Subsidy Rolls for the City of London: 1541 and 1582*, ed. R.G. Lang (London Record Society, vol. 29, London 1993), pp. 150–1.

18. Worshipful Company of Mercers, 'Court Minutes', II, 1527–1560, fo. 112v.

19. *The Inventory of King Henry VIII*, ed. Alasdair Hawkyard (London, 1998); Günther Oestmann, 'Kratzer, Nicolaus (*b.* 1486/7, *d.* after 1550)', *ODNB*, Oxford University Press, 2004; online edn, [http://www.oxforddnb.com/view/article/15808]; BL MS Add. 70984, fo. 239v; BL MS Royal 7 C XVI, fo. 98.

20. Hugh Murray Baillie, 'Etiquette and the Planning of State Apartments in Baroque Palaces', *Archaeologia*, 101 (1967), pp. 169–99; D. Starkey, Introduction to *The English Court from the Wars of the Roses to the Civil War* (London, 1987).

21. *LP*, xi, no. 519/7; BL MS Lansdowne 110, fo. 72r; *Rotuli Parliamentorum*, III, pp. 443–4; *CPR 1405–8*, p. 3; ibid., *1413–16*, p. 152; ibid., *1436–41*, pp. 167, 188, 403, 490–1; ibid., *1461–70*, p. 70; ibid., *1476–85*, p. 103.

22. *LP*, xix (i), no. 610/7; I. Doolittle, *The Mercers Company 1579–1959* (London, 1994), p. 8.

23. TNA SP 12/254/24.

24. BL MS Lansdowne 110, fo. 113r.

25. TNA SP 1/212 fo. 179 in *LP*, xx (ii), no. 25/3.

26. Ibid., xix (i), no. 1035/87, xix; F.C. Dietz, *English Public Finance 1485–1641*, 2 vols., (2nd ed. rev., London 1964), i, pp. 153–5, 176–7; R.W. Hoyle, 'Place and Public Finance', *Transactions of the Royal Historical Society*, 6th series, 7, pp. 197–216.

27. Most Henrician Johnians listed in J.H. Venn, *Alumni Cantabrigienses* (Cambridge 1922–54), were Catholics.

28. C.H. Cooper and T. Cooper, *Athenae Cantabrigienses*, 3 vols. (Cambridge 1858), i, pp. 218–19.

29. Roger Ascham, *Works*, ed. J.A. Giles, 3 vols. (London, 1864–5), i, p. xxx; Lawrence Ryan, *Roger Ascham* (Stanford, 1963), pp. 17–18; Cooper, *Athenae*, i, p. 208; CR, p. 501.

30. Mordechai Feingold, *The Mathematicians' Apprenticeship: Science, Universities and Society in England 1560–1640* (Cambridge, 1984), pp. 35–6.

31. Ibid., pp. 35, 41; Ryan, *Ascham*, p. 223; Ascham, *Works*, ed. Giles, ii, p. 103.

32. Harold H. Joachim, ed., *Aristotle: On Coming-to-be and Passing-Away* (Oxford, 1922).

33. *Aristotelis philosophorum maximi secretum secretorum ad Alexandrum De regum regimine: De sanitatis conseruatione: de physionomia* (Bologna, 1516), and R&W, 125, 315, 1793, 1807; Feingold, 'The Occult Tradition in the English Universities of the Renaissance: A Reassessment', in *Occult and Scientific Mentalities in the Renaissance*, ed. B. Vickers (Cambridge, 1984), pp. 73–94, at 80–1.

34. *MH*, p. 137; *MP*, sig. b3v.

35. *MP*, sigs. b1r–v, b4r.

36. Ibid., sig. b4r.

37. John Bale, *Illustrium Maioris Britanniae Scriptorum* (Ipswich, 1548), fo. 114v.

38. *The Opus Majus of Roger Bacon*, ed. H. Bridges, 2 vols. (Oxford, 1897), ii, pp. 585–7.

39. Ibid., pp. 627–8.

40. BL MS Add. 36674, fos. 38r–39r.

41. Duffy, *Stripping of the Altars*, pp. 394, 400–5, 423, 439; BL MS Sloane 3188, fo. 7r–v; BL MS Add. 70984, fos. 92r–v, 257v; A.G. Watson, 'Christopher and William Carye, Collectors of Monastic Manuscripts, and "John Carye"', *The Library*, 5th ser., XX, no. 2 (June 1965), pp. 135–42.

42. John Venn (ed.), *Grace Book Delta for the years 1542–1589* (Cambridge, 1910), p. 31.

43. Duffy, *Stripping of the Altars*, pp. 436–9, 444, 449; *LP*, xxxi, (ii), p. 340.

44. Ryan, *Ascham*, p. 90, and *Original Letters Relative to the English Reformation*, ed. H. Robinson (Cambridge, 1846), pp. 150–1, 264; J. Gillow, *A Literary and Biographical History … of the English Catholics*, 5 vols. (New York, 1885–1902), i, p. 486.

45. F. Boas, *University Drama in the Tudor Age* (Oxford, 1914, 1966), pp. 16–17; G.C. Moore Smith, *College Plays Performed in the University of Cambridge* (Cambridge, 1923), pp. 51–3, 39, 21; Trinity College Archives, Senior Bursar's Accounts 1547–1563, fo. 59v; C.H. Cooper, *Annals of Cambridge*, 5 vols. (Cambridge, 1842–1908), i, p. 422; L.B. Campbell, *Scenes and Machines of the English Stage* (New York, 1923), p. 187; *MP*, sig. A1v.

46. R. Aubert et al., *The University of Louvain 1425–1975* (Leuven, 1976), pp. 117–18, 139–40, 153.

47. *CR*, pp. 506, 501; Koenraad Van Cleempoel, *A Catalogue Raisonné of Scientific Instruments from the Louvain School, 1530 to 1600* (Turnhout, 2002), illustrates many; Trinity College Archives, Senior Bursar's Accounts 1547–1563.

48. D.R. Leader, *A History of the University of Cambridge: The University to 1546* (Cambridge, 1988), pp. 324–7; J.E.A. Dawson, 'The Foundation of Christ Church Oxford and Trinity College Cambridge in 1546', *Bulletin of the Institute of Historical Research*, LVII, no. 136, November 1984, pp. 208–15.

49. W.H. Sherman, *John Dee: The Politics of Reading and Writing in the English Renaissance* (Amherst, MA, 1995).

50. GL MS 4887, p. 143.

51. *London and Middlesex Chantry Certificates, 1548*, ed. C.J. Kitching (London Record Society, 1980), pp. 13–14; H.B. Walters, *London Churches at the Reformation* (London, 1939), pp. 248–254, 638, printing part of TNA E 117/4/98.

52. *CPR Elizabeth I, vol. vii 1575–8* (London 1982), p. 339, no. 2328, more than in *Chantry Certificates, 1548*, ed. Kitching, pp. 13–14, 29.

53. GL MS 4887, p. 145; *Chantry Certificates, 1548*, ed. Kitching, p. 13.

54. *CPR Edward VI, vol. i, 1547–8*, pp. 348–9.

55. GL MS 4887, p. 148, also in Walters, *London Churches at the Reformation*, p. 246.

56. London Metropolitan Archives, Corporation of London Records, Court of Aldermen, Repertory 11, fos. 342r–343v; ibid., Repertory 20, fos. 78v, 79r. Longleat House MS TH/Box 64, pp. 35–6.

57. Longleat House MS TH/XLVIII, fos. 1, 3.

58. London Metropolitan Archives, Corporation of London Records, Court of Aldermen, Repertory 11, fos. 400 r–v, 483v, Repertory 12 (i), fos. 76v, 95v, 105v, 142v, 145v, 174r.

59. *Calendar of State Papers Domestic, Edward VI*, rev. ed., ed. C.S. Knighton (London 1992), p. 71, no. 172, SP 10/5/18; R.W. Hoyle, 'Taxation and the Mid-Tudor Crisis', *The Economic History Review*, n.s., 51, no. 4 (Nov. 1998), pp. 649–675, esp. 658, 670–1.

60. TNA E 117/4/98, printed in Walters, *London Churches*, pp. 246–7.

61. GL MS 4887, p. 150. Walters, *London Churches*, pp. 248–54.

62. Dee's annotation on the end-leaf of J. Cardan, *Libelli Quinque* (Nuremberg 1547), Royal College of Physicians, D40/2, R&W, 668.

63. GL MS 4887, p. 155.

64. Walters, *London Churches*, pp. 246–7; GL MS 4887, pp. 148–52, 155.

Chapter 2: The Rays of Celestial Virtue

1. *The Diaries of John Dee*, ed. E. Fenton (Charlbury, 1998), p. 305; *Matricule de L'Université de Louvain*, 10 vols. (Brussels 1903–80), iv, pt. 2, p. 411, no. 124, with Story at no. 142;

P. Vandermeersch, 'Some Aspects of the Intellectual Relationship Between the Southern Netherlands and England in the Sixteenth and Seventeenth Centuries', in H. De Ridder-Symoens and J.M. Fletcher, eds, *Academic Relations Between the Low Countries and the British Isles 1450–1700* (Studia Historica Gandensia, 273) (Gent, 1989), pp. 5–23; R. Aubert et al., *The University of Louvain 1425–1975* (Leuven, 1976), p. 68; *A Declaration of the lyfe and death of Iohn Story, late a Romish canonicall doctor, by profession* (London, 1571).

2. Aubert, *Louvain*, pp. 117–18, 139–40, 153.

3. H. De Vocht, *History of the Collegium trilingue … Part the Fourth. Strengthened Maturity* (Humanistica Lovaniensia, 13), pp. 318–19, 339–46; Aubert, *Louvain*, pp. 107–12.

4. Cooper, *Annals*, ii, pp. 26–35; Leader, *History of the University of Cambridge*, pp. 195–7; TNA SP 10/7/10 and 11.

5. CR, p. 503, *MP*, sig. A 1r–v, citing Aristotle, *Ethics*, and Plato, *Epinomis*.

6. CR, p. 526; Aubert, *Louvain*, pp. 112, 145; Jonathan Woolfson, *Padua and the Tudors* (Toronto, 1998), p. 43.

7. *MP*, sig. b3v–4r.

8. S. Vanden Broecke, 'Dee, Mercator, and Louvain Instrument Making: An Undescribed Astrological Disc by Gerard Mercator (1551)', *Annals of Science*, 58 (2001), pp. 219–40.

9. *MP*, sig. d2r.

10. Vanden Broecke, 'Dee, Mercator', p. 239.

11. Mercator, *Breves in Sphaeram Meditatiunculae, Includentes Methodum et Isagogen in Universam Cosmographium* (Cologne, 1563), sig. E7r–v, quoted in Vanden Broecke, 'Dee, Mercator', p. 228.

12. *MP*, sig. b4r; CR, p. 502. Elias Ashmole's partial transcript of these notes partially printed in *Diaries*, ed. Fenton, pp. 305–6.

13. N. Clulee, *John Dee's Natural Philosophy: Between Science and Religion* (London, New York, 1988), p. 39; Albohaly Alfayat (al-Khayyat), *De iudiciis nativitatem* (Nuremberg, 1546), R&W, 693, end flyleaves; Vanden Broecke, 'Dee, Mercator', p. 239, n. 20.

14. BLO MS Ashmole 423, fo. 294, MSS Ashmole 487 and 488.

15. Vanden Broecke, 'Dee, Mercator', p. 239, n. 20.

16. Ptolemy, *Four Books* (Venice, 1519), sig. B4v; Cardan, *Libelli quinque*, sig. X4v, Dee's marginal note.

17. Clulee, *Dee's Natural Philosophy*, p. 40.

18. CR, p. 501; *MP*, sig. b3r; De Vocht, *Collegium trilingue*, pp. 554–6.

19. Johannes Voerthusius, *Academiae veteris et novae ad Maximilianum Austrium II, in coronatione Francofurtensi gratulationis ergo legatio* (Frankfurt, 1563), p. 24, R&W, 552.

20. BLO MSS Ashmole 487 and 488.

21. Heilbron, Introductory Essay II, in Dee's *Propaedeumata Aphoristica*, ed. Shumaker, p. 54; Dee, *General and rare memorials pertayning to the perfect arte of navigation* (London, 1577), sig. [epsilon]3r.

22. CR, p. 503; Susan Doran, 'Pickering, Sir William (1516/17–1575)', *ODNB*, Oxford University Press, September 2004; online edn, January 2008 [http://www.oxforddnb.com/view/article/22212]; *APC*, iv, 1552–4, p. 188.

23. Cooper, *Athenae*, i, p. 326; Dee, *General and rare memorials* (London, 1577), sig. i2r; *MP*, sig. b1v; CR, pp. 503, 505, 516; *Euclid's Elements of Geometry* (London, 1661), pp. 605–8, Dee's letter to Federico Commandino, June 1563; TNA PROB 11/57, fos. 2–3; S. Adams, *Leicester and the Court* (Manchester, 2002), p. 32.

24. *MP*, sig. *2v; Ramus, *Proemium Mathematicum* (Paris, 1567), R&W, 805, and Roberts and Watson, *John Dee's Library Catalogue*, p. 93; CR, pp. 503–4, cf. Heilbron, 'Introductory Essay', pp. 5–8; Aubert, *Louvain*, p. 127; *MP*, sigs. c2r–c3v.

25. Robert J. Wilkinson, *Orientalism, Aramaic, and Kabbalah in the Catholic Reformation: The First Printing of the Syriac New Testament* (Leiden and Boston, MA, 2007), pp. 102–14, 125–9; Robert J. Wilkinson, *The Kabbalistic Scholars of the Antwerp Polyglot Bible* (Leiden and Boston, MA, 2007), pp. 57, n. 24, 85; R&W, 1619, B267.

26. CR, pp. 504–5.

27. At Paris on 17 August 1551 Dee purchased Demetrius Chalcondylas, *Erotemata, siue Institutiones grammaticae, initiandis graecae linguae studiosis* (Basle, 1546), R&W, 1661, and at Melun on 14 September he annotated Ptolemy's *Tetrabiblos*, R&W, 37.

28. J. Loach, *Edward VI*, ed. G. Bernard and P. Williams (New Haven and London, 1999), pp. 94–6; D. MacCulloch, *Thomas Cranmer: A Life* (New Haven, and London, 1996), pp. 443–4; D. Hoak, 'Rehabilitating the Duke of Northumberland', in *The Mid-Tudor Polity*, ed. J. Loach and R. Tittler (London, 1980), pp. 29–51; Hoak, 'The King's Privy Chamber, 1547–1553', in D.J. Guth and J.W. Mckenna, *Tudor Rule and Revolution* (Cambridge, 1982), p. 94; *The Chronicle and Political Papers of King Edward VI*, ed. W.K. Jordan (Ithaca, New York, 1966), p. 86; *The Life and Raigne of King Edward the Sixth. By John Hayward*, ed. B.L. Beer (Kent, OH, 1993), p. 20.

29. Trinity College, Cambridge, Senior Bursar's Accounts, 1547–1563, fos. 138r, 175r, 178v–179r, 208v–209r; ibid., Junior Bursar's Accounts, 1550–1563, fos. 31v, 63v–64r.

30. Ibid., Senior Bursar's Accounts, 1547–1563, fo. 90r; Alan Bryson, 'Cheke, Sir John (1514–1557)', *ODNB*, Oxford University Press, September 2004; online edn, October 2008 [http://www.oxforddnb.com/view/article/5211].

31. Longleat House MSS TH/I, II and III, *passim* for Cecil's frequent letters to his 'old assured friend' Thynne.

32. Trinity College, Cambridge, Senior Bursar's Accounts, 1547–1563, fos. 138r, 175r, 178v–179r, 208v–209r; ibid., Junior Bursar's Accounts, 1550–1563, fos. 31v, 63v–64r.

33. CR, p. 507.

34. *Calendar of the Carew Manuscripts preserved in the Archiepiscopal Library at Lambeth, 1575–1588*, ed. J.S. Brewer and W. Bullen (London, 1868), pp. 334–60, at p. 359; *Letters and Memorials of State, Written and collected by Sir Henry Sydney*, ed. A. Collins, 2 vols. (London, 1746), i, pp. 91, 93–5.

35. CR, p. 508; Thomas Moffet, *Nobilis or A View of the Life and Death of a Sidney*, ed. and tr. Virgil B. Heltzel and Hoyt H. Hudson (San Marino, CA, 1940), pp. 75–6; James M. Osborn, *Young Philip Sidney* (New Haven, and London, 1972), pp. 146–7.

36. *Literary Remains of King Edward VI*, ed. J.G. Nichols (London, 1857), p. 427; *MP*, sigs. *4v–a1r, a4v–b1r; Leonard Digges, *An arithmeticall militare treatise, named Stratioticos* (London, 1579), pp. 189–90.

37. *Notes and Queries*, 9th series, vol. VIII, 17 August 1901, p. 137, on Girolamo Cardano, *Libelli Quinque* (1547), endpapers, R&W, 440; G.E. Cokayne, *The Complete Peerage*, 13 vols. (London, 1910–59), vol. x, p. 408; S.M. Jack, 'Northumberland, Queen Jane and the Financing of the 1553 Coup', *Parergon*, n.s., no. 6 (1988), pp. 137–48.

38. Cokayne, *Complete Peerage*, x, p. 406; J. Strype, *Memorials of the Most Reverend Father in God, Thomas Cranmer*, 2 vols. (Oxford, 1812), ii, pp. 912–13; N.P. Sil, *William Lord Herbert of Pembroke (c.1507–1570): Politique and Patriot*, 2nd edn (Lewiston, NY 1992); Dee, notes in Cardano, *Libelli Quinque*, sig. hhh5v, R&W, 440.

39. Nicholas Crane, *Mercator: The Man who Mapped the Planet* (London, 2002), pp. 121, 208; Mark S. Monmonier, *Rhumb lines and Map Wars: A Social History of the Mercator Projection* (Chicago, 2004); R.A. Skelton, 'Mercator and English Geography in the 16th Century', *Duisburger Forschungen*, 6 (1962), pp. 158–70, at p. 164; Heilbron, 'Introductory Essay', pp. 29–31, and *PA*, p. 115 on Nuñez; *MP* sig. a4v; E.G.R. Taylor, 'The Doctrine of Nautical

Triangles Compendious', *The Journal of the Institute of Navigation*, 5, no. 1, Jan. 1953, pp. 131–40.

40. John Davis, *The Seamans Secrets* (London, 1595), sigs. R2v–R3r; Dee's fragmentary calculations from BLO MS Ashmole 242, in *Canon Gubernauticus, by John Dee (1558)*, ed. E.G.R. Taylor, Appendix A in *A Regiment for the Sea and other Writings on Navigation*, ed. Taylor, The Hakluyt Society, 2nd ser., vol. 121 (Cambridge, 1963), pp. 415–33. Dee's 1582 circumpolar chart for Sir Humphrey Gilbert survives (D.W. Waters, *The Art of Navigation in England in Elizabethan and Early Stuart Times* (London, 1958), pp. 209–12).

41. 'The astronomicall, and logisticall rules, and Canons, to calculate the Ephemerides by' in J. Dee, *A Letter, containing a most brief Discourse Apologetical* (London, 1595), sig. A4v.

42. T. Nash, *Collections for the History of Worcestershire*, 2nd edn, 2 vols. (London 1799), ii, pp. 444–8, and Appendix, p. clxvi. The *Valor Ecclesiasticus* rated Upton at £27.

43. *CPR Edward VI, iii, 1548–51*(London, 1925), pp. 71–4; *CPR Philip and Mary, 1557–8* (London, 1939), p. 125.

44. *CPR Edward VI, v, 1547–53*, p. 199.

45. 'Visitation Articles of 1551–2' in *Later Writings of Hooper*, ed. C. Nevinson (Cambridge, 1852), pp. 118–29, at p. 123; *Early Writings of Hooper*, ed. S. Carr (Cambridge, 1843), p. 508.

46. *Later Writings of Hooper*, ed. Nevinson, pp. 294, 308.

47. *APC*, iv, p. 259.

48. Hereford and Worcester Record Office, Bishop's Register (b716.093–BA.2648/9[iv]).

49. TNA C3/53/8; *The Kyre Park Charters*, ed. J. Amphlett (Oxford, 1905), and Nash, *Collections for the History of Worcestershire*, i, pp. xviii, xxvii; The Worshipful Company of Mercers, 'Court Minutes II, Acts of Court 1527–1560', fo. 264v.

50. TNA C3/53/8; Adams, *Leicester and the Court*, p. 331.

51. *LP*, xx (i) (1545), p. 379, no. 746, and see *APC*, iv, p. 162.

52. R.C. Braddock, 'The Character and Composition of the Duke of Northumberland's Army', *Albion* 6 (1974), pp. 342–55; W.J. Tighe, 'The Gentleman Pensioners, the Duke of Northumberland, and the Attempted Coup of July 1553', *Albion*, 19 (1987), pp. 1–11; R.C. Braddock, 'The Duke of Northumberland's Army Reconsidered', in ibid., pp. 13–17; Jack, 'Northumberland, Queen Jane and the Financing of the 1553 Coup', pp. 137–48, corrected in J.D. Alsop, 'A Regime at Sea; The Navy and the 1553 Succession Crisis', *Albion*, 24 (1992), pp. 577–90.

53. R.P. Cruden, *The History of the Town of Gravesend* (London, 1843), p. 169; V.T. Smith, 'The Artillery Defences at Gravesend', *Archaeologia Cantiana*, 89 (1974), pp. 141–68.

54. P. Lee, 'Orthodox Parish Religion and Chapels of Ease in Late Medieval England: The Case of St George's Chapel in Gravesend', *Archaeologia Cantiana*, 119 (1999), pp. 55–70.

55. P. Clark, *English Provincial Society from the Reformation to the Revolution: Religion, Politics and Society in Kent, 1500–1640* (Hassocks, 1977), p. 85; Pocock, *Gravesend*, p. 235.

56. D. Lloyd, *State-Worthies* (London, 1679), p. 274; *A Chronicle of England during the Reigns of the Tudors, from A.D. 1485 to 1559 by Charles Wriothesley, Windsor Herald*, ed. W.D. Hamilton, 2 vols. (Camden Society, London 1872), ii, p. 91.

57. *APC*, iv, pp. 336–7; P.L. Hughes and J.F. Larkin, *Tudor Royal Proclamations*, 3 vols. (New Haven, and London, 1964–9), ii, pp. 12–17, at p. 16; *Narratives of the Reformation*, ed. J. Nichols (Camden Society, London 1859), pp. 180–1; Richard Grafton, *A Chronicle at Large and Mere History of the Affairs of England* (London, 1569), p. 1,328.

58. Grafton, *Chronicle*, p. 1,328; Robert Horne, *Certain Homilies of Master John Calvin* (Wesel [?], 1553), sigs. A3v–A4v; *CPR Mary* i, p. 424; Hughes and Larkin, *Tudor Royal Proclamations*, ii, pp. 16–17; William Lilly, *History of His Life and Times* (London, 1715), p. 92.

59. J. Strype, *Annals of the Reformation*, 4 vols, (Oxford, 1824), II, ii, p. 559, Dee to Burghley, 3 October 1574; TNA C 66/1159/2328.

60. Strype, *Ecclesiastical Memorials*, iii, (i), p. 353; E. W. Hunt, *The Life and Times of John Hooper* (Lewiston, NY, 1992), p. 190.

61. Susan Brigden, *London and the Reformation* (Oxford, 1989), p. 529.

62. Bonner's ordination register, Guildhall Library MS 9535/1, fos. 26v–27r.

63. *The Visitation of Cheshire in the year 1580*, ed. J.P. Rylands (London, 1882), pp. 28–31, 204–5; HEHL MS EL 6191; BL MS Cotton Tiberius E. VIII, fos. 176v–177r; Tim Thornton, 'Savage family (per. c.1369–1528)', *ODNB*, Oxford University Press, Sept. 2004; online edn, May 2007 [http://www.oxforddnb.com/view/article/52794]; J. Dee, *Parallaticae Commentationis Praxeosque Nucleus quidam* (London, 1573), showing 'Gules, a lion rampant within a bordure indented Or'.

Chapter 3: Conjuring the Future

1. D.M. Loades, *The Reign of Mary Tudor: Politics, Government and Religion in England, 1553–58*, 2nd ed. (New York, 1991), p. 196; *CSP Venetian, vi (i)*, p. 107.

2. Loades, *Reign of Mary Tudor*, p. 165.

3. *CSP Venetian, vi (i)*, p. 71; *CSP Spanish, xiii, 1554–8*, p. 170.

4. TNA SP 11/5/34; *A Warning for England containing the horrible practices of the King of Spain in the kingdom of Naples* (Strasburg, 1555); *CSP Foreign*, ed. J. Stevenson (London, 1863, repr. 1966), p. lviii; Loades, *Reign of Mary Tudor*, p. 176.

5. C. Haigh, *Elizabeth I* (London, 2001), p. 26.

6. C.R. Manning, 'State Papers Relating to the Custody of the Princess Elizabeth at Woodstock, in 1554', *Norfolk Archaeology*, IV (1855), pp. 133–231, at pp. 194, 200, 202; CR, pp. 519–20.

7. *CSP Spanish, xiii, 1554–8*, p. 165, pp. 169–70; *Chapter Acts of the Cathedral Church of St Mary of Lincoln A.D. 1547–1559*, ed. R.E.G. Cole, Lincoln Record Society, 15 (Horncastle, 1920), p. 82; R. Kieckhefer, *Forbidden Rites: A Necromancer's Manual of the Fifteenth Century* (Stroud, 1997), pp. 97–107, describes divination methods.

8. Roberts and Watson, *Catalogue*, p. 88, notes to no. 395, Avicenna *De anima* (1546); *CPR Edward VI, vol. i, 1547–8*, pp. 348–9.

9. *The Loseley Manuscripts*, ed. A.J. Kempe (London, 1836), p. 20; W.R. Streitberger, *Court Revels, 1485–1559* (Toronto, 1994), pp. 193–6; R. Grafton, *Chronicle* (London, 1809), ii, pp. 526–7; S. Brigden, *London and the Reformation*, ch. viii.

10. A.J. Loomie, 'Englefield, Sir Francis (1522–1596)', *ODNB*, Oxford University Press, September 2004; online edn, January 2008 [http://www.oxforddnb.com/view/article/8811]; TNA SP 12/238, fo. 248.

11. TNA SP 12/28/38, fo. 146v, and SP 12/28/42.

12. John Field, *Ephemeris anni. 1557* (London, 1556); Thomas Churchyard, *The First Part of Churchyards Chips* (London, 1575), fo. 76r.

13. Watson, 'Christopher and William Carye', pp. 135–42; *Household Expenses of the Princess Elizabeth During her Residence at Hatfield, October 1, 1551 to September 30, 1552*, ed. Viscount Strangford, in *The Camden Miscellany, Volume the Second*, 1st ser., 55 (1853), pp. 35, 38; A. Strickland, *The Lives of the Queens of England*, 8 vols. (London, 1854), iv, pp. 110–11.

14. *APC*, v, pp. 137, 139.

15. *CSP Venetian, vi(i)*, p. 77; L. Means, 'Electionary, Lunary, Destinary, and Questionary: Toward Defining Categories of Middle English Prognostic Material', *Studies in Philology*, LXXXIX, no. 4 (Fall 1992), pp. 367–403, esp. pp. 376–85.

16. Ibid., pp. 386–94, and see J.C. Eade, *The Forgotten Sky* (Oxford, 1984), pp. 51–9.

17. BLO MS Ashmole 423, fo. 294, printed in *Diaries*, ed. Fenton, p. 306.

18. Ptolemy, *Tetrabiblos*, ed. F.E. Robbins (Cambridge, MA and London, 1940), IV, 10; S.J. Tester, *A History of Western Astrology* (Woodbridge 1987), pp. 84–5.

19. Means, 'Electionary, Lunary', p. 402; BLO MS Ashmole 337, fos. 20–57v.

20. Loades, *Reign of Mary Tudor*, p. 165.

21. TNA SP 11/5/34.

22. Louis Wiesener, *La Jeunesse de l'Elisabeth d'Angleterre* (Paris, 1878), pp. 318–19, from Noailles, *Memoires et Advis envoyez a M. de L'Aubespigne*, 1 June 1555, *Archives des Affaires Etrangeres*, t. I–II, p. 843; *APC*, v, pp. 143, 145.

23. CR, p. 520.

24. *Actes and Monuments* (London, 1563), pp. 1,253–4 (1570), p. 1,871.

25. TNA SP 11/5/34; Wiesener, *La Jeunesse de l'Elisabeth*, pp. 318–19.

26. Kieckhefer, *Forbidden Rites*, pp. 98–9; *MP*, sig. A1v–2r.

27. Ibid., sig. A3r; N. Clulee, 'At the Crossroads of Magic and Science: John Dee's *Archemastrie*', in *Occult and Scientific Mentalities in the Renaissance*, ed. B. Vickers (Cambridge, 1984), pp. 57–71.

28. G. Cardano, *De rerum varietate* (1557) R&W, 69, not found.

29. *Narratives of the Reformation*, ed. Nichols, pp. 331–3; BL MS Sloane 3188, fo. 9r–v; BL MS Sloane 3846, fo. 113v; Kieckhefer, *Forbidden Rites*, pp. 107, 244–5.

30. *Narratives of the Reformation*, ed. Nichols, pp. 229–30; *CSP Venetian, vi (i)*, p. 137.

31. W. McCaffrey, *Elizabeth I* (London, 1993, 2001), p. 23.

32. BL MS Add. 48023, fo. 354v; *APC*, v, p. 176. Dee misdates this to 19 August (CR, p. 520).

Chapter 4: A Royal Occult Institute

1. Gina Alexander, 'Bonner and the Marian Persecutions', *History*, 60 (1975), pp. 374–91 at pp. 374–7.

2. E. Bonner, *A profitable and necessarye doctryne, with certayne homelies* (London, John Cawood, 1555).

3. Ibid., preface and sig. Hh2r–v; W.H. Frere and W.M. Kennedy, *Visitation Articles and Injunctions of the Reformation period*, 3 vols. (London, 1910), ii, pp. 353, 361–2; Duffy, *Stripping of the Altars*, pp. 533, 537–43.

4. Alexander, 'Bonner', pp. 374–7.

5. Roberts and Watson, *Catalogue*, p. 4 and no. 79; *PA*, p. 117; CR, p. 526.

6. *The Trew report of the dysputacyon had and begonne in the convocaycyon hows* (Basle, A. Edmonds [i.e. Emden, J. Gheylliaert and S. Mierdman?], 1554); *The examinacion of the constant Martir of Christ, John Philpot* [Emden, E. van der Erve, 1556], fo. 108r.

7. S. Wabuda, 'Henry Bull, Miles Coverdale and the making of Foxe's Book of Martyrs'. *Studies in Church History*, 30 (1993), pp. 245–58; B. Usher, 'Backing Protestantism: The London Godly, the Exchequer and the Foxe circle', in D.M. Loades, ed., *John Foxe: An Historical Perspective* (Aldershot, 1999), pp. 105–34.

8. CR, p. 509.

9. Edmund Grindal, *The examinacion of the constaunt martir of Christ John Philpot* (London, 1559) and *Rerum in Ecclesia Gestarum Commentarii* (Basle, 1559).

10. James P. Carley, ed., *The Libraries of King Henry VIII* (London, 2000), pp. xxvii–xlvi, lxxiii–lxxvii, lxxix; George F. Warner and Julius P. Gilson, *Catalogue of Western Manuscripts in the Old Royal and King's Collection*, 4 vols. (London, 1921), i, pp. xiv–xv.

11. John Bale, *The laboryouse iourney [and] serche of Iohan Leylande, for Englandes antiquitees* (London, 1549), sigs. B8r–C1r, C3v–C4r.

12. BL MS Cotton Vitellius C. VII, fos. 310–11, in CR, pp. 490–5, and Roberts and Watson, *Catalogue*, pp. 194–5.

13. Ibid., pp. 5–6, 152–3, M91, M97, M24, M37.

14. Ibid., p. 153.

15. Ibid., pp. 153–4, R&W, CM36, M13.

16. Ibid., pp. 153–4, R&W, M107, M3, M89, M99, M157; M26.

17. Ibid., pp. 151–4.

18. G. Parry, 'Puritanism, Science and Capitalism: William Harrison and the Rejection of Hermes Trismegistus', *History of Science*, 22 (3) (1984), pp. 245–70; Lee Stavenhagen, ed. and tr., *A Testament of Alchemy* (Hanover, NH, 1974), pp. 60–4.

19. *The mirror of alchimy, composed by the thrice-famous and learned fryer, Roger Bachon* (London, 1597).

20. Clulee, *Dee's Natural Philosophy*, pp. 126–7, and notes 32–5, p. 209.

21. *MH*, p. 123.

22. Clulee, *Dee's Natural Philosophy*, pp. 126–7.

23. Ibid., p. 28; David Hockney, *Secret Knowledge: Rediscovering the Lost Techniques of the Old Masters* (New York, 2001), pp. 17, 71, 76; Roger Bacon, *Discovery of the Miracles of Art, Nature and Magick. Faithfully translated out of Dr Dees own copy, by T.M.* (London, 1659), p. 21.

24. *PA*, p. 117; CR, p. 527.

25. Hockney, *Secret Knowledge*, p. 140; R&W, B 197, B 201.

26. *PA*, pp. 103–6, 98; BLO MS Ashmole 337, fos. 20–57; see below, pp. 109–10.

27. CR, p. 507; *PA*, p. 117, CR, p. 527; Van Cleempoel, *The Louvain School*, pp. 16–18.

28. *PA*, p. 117; *MP*, sig. d1v; CR, p. 527.

29. Clulee, *Dee's Natural Philosophy*, pp. 68–9; *PA*, pp. 103, 149; CR, p. 526.

30. *PA*, p. 149.

Chapter 5: The Kabbalah of Creation

1. Patrick Collinson, 'Elizabeth I (1533–1603)', *ODNB*, Oxford University Press, 2004; online edn, May 2008 [http://www.oxforddnb.com/view/article/8636]; William Fulke, *Antiprognosticon, that is to saye, an invective against the vayne and unprofitable predictions of the astrologians as Nostrodame* (London, December 1560), sig. A8r–v; Francis Coxe, *A short treatise declaringe the detestable wickednesse of magicall sciences, as Necromancie, Coniurations of spirites, Curiouse Astrologie and such lyke* (London, 1561), sigs. A4v–A5v.

2. *APC*, vii, 1558–70, pp. 5, 7, 22; *CSP Spanish, xiv, 1558–1567*, p. 119, Aquila to the Count de Feria, 27 December 1559; Hatfield House MS CP 152/34.

3. *APC*, vii, 1558–70, p. 22. A 1559 bill against witchcraft ran out of time.

4. CR, pp. 509, 521.

5. Means, 'Electionary, Lunary', pp. 370–5, on electionary horoscopes.

6. Lincolnshire Archives Office, Leadenham Parish Register 1/1.

7. *The Examination of the Constant Martir of Christ, John Philpot* (1559), sigs. L3r–L4v. *Rerum in Ecclesia gestarum commentarii* (Basel, 1559).

8. Roberts and Watson, *Catalogue*, p. 76. Confirmed by Dee's note in R&W, 273, Giovanni Battista Ramusio, *Navigationi et Viaggi*, 3 vols. Trinity College Dublin shelfmark DD. dd. 40, 41 (Venice, 1563–5), vol. 3, fo. 148r.

9. R&W, 1596, 1571, 1604.

10. TNA SP 12/27/63.

11. R&W, 678, 897, Johannes Trithemius, *Libellus Octo questionum* (Cologne, 1534), question 3.

12. Jim Reeds, 'Solved: The Ciphers in Book III of Trithemius's *Steganographia*', *Cryptologia*, vol. 22, 4 (1998), pp. 291–317; Thomas Ernst, 'The Numerical-Astrological Ciphers in the third book of Trithemius's Steganographia', *Cryptologia*, vol. 22, 4 (1998), pp. 318–41.
13. TNA SP 12/27/63; CR, p. 507. See BL MS Sloane 2006.
14. R&W, 978, Jacques Gohory, *De usu et mysteriis notarum liber, in quo vetusta literarum et numerorum ac divinorum ex Sibylla nominum ratio explicatur* (Paris, 1550); Clulee, *Dee's Natural Philosophy*, p. 88; Paolo Rossi, *Logic and the Art of Memory*, tr. Stephen Clucas (Chicago, 2000), pp. 62–3.
15. R&W, 1846; Robert J. Wilkinson, 'Immanuel Tremellius' 1569 Edition of the Syriac New Testament', *Journal of Ecclesiastical History*, 58 (1), January 2007, pp. 9–25 at pp. 11–13.
16. CR, p. 528; *MH*, pp. 85–6, 137.
17. Ibid., pp. 127, 123.
18. Guillaume Postel, *De La République des Turcs* (Paris, 1561), title page.
19. Roberts and Watson, *Catalogue*, p. 11; Nicholas Clulee, 'John Dee and the Paracelsians', in Allen G. Debus and Michael T. Walton, eds, *Reading the Book of Nature: The Other Side of the Scientific Revolution* (St Louis, MO, 1998), pp. 111–132, at pp. 113–14; R&W, 1461–1523, 2221–2275; Walter Pagel, *Paracelsus: An Introduction to Philosophical Medicine in the Renaissance*, 2nd ed., rev. (Basel, 1986), pp. 63–4; Charles Webster, *Paracelsus: Medicine, Magic and Mission at the End of Time* (New Haven and London, 2008).
20. R&W, 1476.
21. Clulee, *Dee's Natural Philosophy*, p. 123; R&W, 1448, Gesner's alchemical *Secret Remedies* bought in 1556.
22. R&W, D2, 482, 1620, 700.
23. Dee's note in Ramusio, *Navigationi et viaggi* (Venice, 1563–5), vol. 3, fo. 148; R&W, 1419; Catholic Record Society, *Miscellanea*, vol. 7 (1911), pp. 52–3.
24. Johannes Voerthusius, *Academiae veteris et novae ad Maximilianum Austrium II, in coronatione Francofurtensi gratulationis ergo legatio* (Frankfurt, 1563), p. 24.
25. Marjorie Reeves, *The Influence of Prophecy in the Later Middle Ages: A Study in Joachimism* (Oxford, 1969), ch. VI; Marie Tanner, *The Last Descendants of Aeneas, the Habsburgs and the Mythic Image of the Emperor* (New Haven and London, 1993), *passim*.
26. Wilkinson, *Orientalism, Aramaic and Kabbalah*, p. 97, n. 11; Wilkinson, *Kabbalistic Scholars*, p. 87.
27. *MH*, pp. 117–21, 133–7, 149.
28. *MH*, pp. 119–23; Clulee, *Dee's Natural Philosophy*, pp. 77–142, and Clulee, 'The *Monas hieroglyphica* and the Alchemical Thread of John Dee's Career', *Ambix*, 52, 3 (Nov. 2005), pp. 197–215.
29. Clulee, *Dee's Natural Philosophy*, p. 84; Christopher I. Lehrich, *The Language of Demons and Angels: Cornelius Agrippa's Occult Philosophy* (Leiden, 2003), pp. 117–19; Peter Adamson, *Al-Kindi* (Oxford, 2006), p. 189.
30. Marjorie Reeves, *Joachim of Fiore and the Prophetic Future* (Stroud, 1999), pp. 6–8; *MP*, sig. *.j.v, fo. 2v.
31. Reeves, *Joachim of Fiore and the Prophetic Future*, passim, and Reeves, *Influence of Prophecy*, pp. 293–392.
32. R&W, 1271 (1531), 742 (1550), 743 (1559).
33. Agrippa, *Occult Philosophy*, ii, 19, pp. 232–4; M. Thick, *Sir Hugh Plat: The Search for Useful Knowledge in Early Modern London* (Totnes, 2010), p. 185.
34. Robert Record, *Ground of Arts* (1561), opposite sig. A1r.
35. Agrippa, *Occult Philosophy*, ii, 2, p. 171.
36. Ibid., i, p. 74; Lehrich, *Agrippa's Occult Philosophy*, pp. 134–5.

37. Agrippa, *Occult Philosophy*, i, pp. 74, 161–2.
38. Ibid., pp. 136–40.
39. Agrippa, *Occult Philosophy*, ii, 4, pp. 175–6.
40. *MH*, pp. 127, 123.
41. *MH*, pp. 133–7; Michael T. Walton, 'Robert Boyle, "The Sceptical Chymist" and Hebrew', in Gerhild Scholz Williams and Charles D. Gunnoe, eds, *Paracelsian Moments: Science, Medicine and Astrology in Early Modern Europe* (Kirksville, MO, 2002), p. 192.
42. *MH*, pp. 145–7.
43. Clulee, *Dee's Natural Philosophy*, p. 92; Leonard Digges, *A Boke named Techtonicon* (1556), sig. E4r; *MH*, pp. 121–3, 127, 133.
44. Ibid., pp. 135–7.
45. Ibid., pp. 155–9.
46. *MH*, pp. 159–61, 169; see below, pp. 151–2.
47. *MH*, pp. 165–7.
48. *MH*, pp. 169–73, 213; cf. *MP*, sig. *3v, and see below, pp. 253–4.
49. Margaret C. Jacob, *Strangers Nowhere in the World: The Rise of Cosmopolitanism in Early Modern Europe* (Philadelphia, PA, 2006), ch. 1.
50. *MH*, pp. 185–7.

Chapter 6: 'The Great Conjuror'

1. *CR*, p. 509.
2. Norman L. Jones, 'Defining Superstitions: Treasonous Catholics and the Act against Witchcraft of 1563', in Charles Carlton et al., eds, *State, Sovereigns and Society in Early Modern England: Essays in Honour of A.J. Slavin* (New York, 1998), pp. 187–203.
3. HEHL MSS EL 2652, fo. 13r, EL 2768, fo. 21v; Jones, 'Defining Superstitions', nn. 22–3.
4. Ibid., p. 194.
5. Ian Archer and Simon Adams, eds, 'A "Journal" of matters of State . . . from and before the death of king Edw. The 6th until the yere 1562', in Ian Archer et al., eds, *Religion, Politics and Society in Sixteenth-century England* (Camden Society, 5th ser., vol. 22, Cambridge, 2003), pp. 52–122, at p. 100.
6. Jones, 'Defining Superstitions', p. 191.
7. *CSP Spanish, xiv, 1558–1567*, p. 260.
8. *CPR Elizabeth I*, ii, p. 568, pardon 20 July 1563; *CPR Elizabeth I*, iii, p. 337, grant 7 December 1564; *CPR Elizabeth I*, iv, p. 210, lease replacing pension £36 p.a., 11 May 1568.
9. TNA KB 8/40, partly echoed in 'A "Journal" of matters of State', ed. Archer and Adams, p. 71 and n. 91, but contrast *CSP Spanish, xiv, 1558–1567*, p. 331.
10. BL MS Lansdowne 102, fo. 20r–v, Cecil to Smith, 13 November 1562.
11. *CSP Spanish, xiv, 1558–1567*, p. 293.
12. T.E. Hartley, *Proceedings in the Parliaments of Elizabeth I*, 3 vols. (Leicester, 1981), i, p. 71.
13. *CPR Elizabeth I*, iv, pp. 63–4; BL MS Lansdowne 102, fo. 18r, Cecil to Smith, 14 January 1563; *CSP Spanish, xiv, 1558–1567*, pp. 278–9, 285–7; Stephen Alford, *The Early Elizabethan Polity: William Cecil and the British Succession Crisis* (Cambridge, 1998), pp. 104–13.
14. TNA SP 12/27, fo. 140r.
15. 5 Eliz., c. 3.
16. *CPR Elizabeth I*, iv, pp. 63–4; BL MS Lansdowne 102/12, Cecil to Smith, 27 February 1563. Elizabeth refused to settle the succession, so Cecil and other Councillors tried in March to legislate for a prerogative council to rule in an interregnum (Alford, *Early Elizabethan Polity*, pp. 111–13).

17. BL MS Lansdowne 102, fo. 18r.
18. Ibid., fo. 20r–v.
19. Ibid., fo. 24r–v, Cecil to Smith, 27 February 1563; W. Camden, *Annals of Queen Elizabeth* (1635), p. 44.
20. Jones, 'Defining Superstitions', pp. 197–9, on 5 Eliz. I, c. 15, 16.
21. TNA KB 8/40, SP 12/31/13, Prestall to Cecil, 30 November 1563; SP 12/238/73, 76; TNA C 3/135/18.
22. *The Examination of the constant Martyr of Christ, John Philpot ... as in these particular tragedies following, it may ... most manifestly appear* (1556), fos. 67v–68r.
23. Ibid., fos. 97v–98v.
24. Winthrop S. Hudson, *The Cambridge Connection* (Cambridge, 1980); Devorah Greenberg, 'Community of the Texts: Producing the First and Second Editions of *Actes and Monuments*', *The Sixteenth-Century Journal*, xxxvi, 3 (2005), pp. 695–715.
25. W. Nicholson, ed., *Remains of Edmund Grindal* (Cambridge, 1858), pp. 226–7.
26. TNA SP 12/16/49; Hughes and Larkin, *Tudor Royal Proclamations*, ii, p. 126, Article 32 in 'Injunctions for Religion'.
27. Foxe, *Actes and Monuments* (1563), pp. 1,458–65, at p. 1,462.
28. Ibid., pp. 1,444–5.
29. 5 Eliz., c. xvi.
30. Lawrence Stone, *The Crisis of the Aristocracy* (Oxford, 1967), pp. 22–5; James A. Sharpe, *Defamation and Sexual Slander in Early Modern England: The Church Courts at York* (Borthwick papers no. 58, York, 1980), pp. 1–3; M. Lindsay Kaplan, *The Culture of Slander in Early Modern England* (Cambridge, 1997), pp. 11–25.
31. *MP*, sig. Aiv–Aiir.
32. Roberts and Watson, *Catalogue*, p. 4; Peter J. French, *John Dee* (London, 1972), pp. 4–8; Frances Yates, *The Occult Philosophy in the Elizabethan Age* (London and Boston, 1979), pp. 101–9.
33. *MP*, sig. Aiiiv.
34. BLO MS Ashmole 1789, fos. 51v–52r; *Memorials*, sig. [delta] 3r–v.
35. BLO, MS Ashmole 1789, fo. 52r, contr. *Memorials*, sig. [delta] 3v.
36. BLO, MS Ashmole 1789, fos. 51v–52v; *Memorials*, sig. [delta] 3r–v.
37. BL MS Harley 286, fo. 37r; BL MS Lansdowne 99, fos. 245r, 244v, 245v, 249r.
38. BLO, MS Ashmole 1789, fos. 51v–52r; *Memorials*, sig. [delta] 2v–3r.
39. CR, pp. 507, 519; *Memorials*, sig. e 1r–v.
40. Catholic Record Society, *Miscellanea*, 7 (1911), pp. 52–3.
41. *Tudor Subsidy Rolls*, ed. Lang, no. 151; *CSPD Edward VI*, ed. Knighton, no. 171 (S.P. 10/5/18); 'Churchwardens' Accounts of St Dunstan in the East', Guildhall Library MS 4887, pp. 145–8; TNA C 1/1221/74.
42. Guildhall Library MS 4887, pp. 150, 152, 163, 165, 166–8, 170.
43. *The Register of St Dunstan in the East*, ed. A.W.H. Clarke (Harleian Society Registers, vol. 69, London, 1939), p. 127.
44. TNA C 3/49/44, C 54/500.
45. *Stukeley Correspondence*, ii (Surtees Society, vol. 76, London, 1883), p. 319, long demolished.
46. TNA C 3/49/44, c.1565, describing Dee 'of Mortlake'; TNA SP 12/186/91; TNA E 179/185/310; TNA C 1/1221/74; BL MS Add. 70984, fo. 255r.

Chapter 7: Hunting for the Philosopher's Stone

1. Patrick Collinson, *Elizabeth I* (Oxford, 2007); Ian Archer, 'Smith, Sir Thomas (1513–1577)', *ODNB*, Oxford University Press, September 2004; online edn, January 2008 [http://www.oxforddnb.com/view/article/25906]; Mary Dewar, *Sir Thomas Smith: A Tudor Intellectual in Office* (London, 1964).

2. TNA SP 15/20/89, Nicholas Houel to Burghley, Paris, Oct. 1571; Peter Razell, ed., *The Journals of Two Travellers in Elizabethan and Early Stuart England, Thomas Platter and Horatio Busino* (London, 1995), p. 25; Jayne Archer, ' "Rudenesse itselfe she doth refine": Queen Elizabeth I as Lady Alchymia', in A. Connolly and L. Hopkins, eds, *Goddesses and Queens: The Iconography of Queen Elizabeth I* (Manchester, 2008), pp. 45–66, at p. 51; Jane A. Lawson, 'This Remembrance of the New Year: Books Given to Queen Elizabeth as New Year's Gifts', in Peter Beal and Grace Ioppolo, eds, *Elizabeth I and the Culture of Writing* (London, 2007), pp. 133–72, at pp. 151–2; TNA C66/973, C 66/970, C54/1763; HMC *Pepys*, p. 111, HMC *Salisbury* i, pp. 350–1; HEHL MS EL 6206B fo. 44r; BLO MSS Ashmole 1447, Pt. VII, p. 30, Ashmole 1402, Pt. II.

3. Hartley, *Proceedings in the Parliaments of Elizabeth I*, ii, p. 32.

4. Edmund Lodge, *Illustrations of British History*, 3 vols. (London, 1838) iii, p. 515.

5. Roy Strong, *Gloriana, the Portraits of Queen Elizabeth I* (London, 1987), pp. 79–81; Hatfield House MSS CP 88/89, CP 119/8, CP 26/96.

6. John Nichols, *The Progresses and Public Processions of Queen Elizabeth*, 3 vols. (London, 1823), i, p. 324.

7. Strong, *Gloriana*, pp. 82–3.

8. Lyndy Abraham, *A Dictionary of Alchemical Imagery* (Cambridge, 2001), pp. 133–4, 143–4.

9. TNA SP 70/146, p. 44.

10. *The Journals of Two Travellers ... Thomas Platter*, p. 35.

11. Strong, *Gloriana*, p. 82, Ernst Kantorowicz, *The King's Two Bodies* (Princeton, 1997), pp. 385–401, 413–15, 510; BLO MS Ashmole 1394, p. 75: 'De Lapide Philosophico seu de Phenice'.

12. Nichols, *Progresses of Queen Elizabeth*, i. p. 379; T.H. White, *The Bestiary: A Book of Beasts* (New York, 1960), pp. 182–4; Edward Topsell, *The Elizabethan Zoo* (Boston, 1979), pp. 108–15.

13. BLO MS Ashmole 1421, fos. 168v–169v, 171v–172r, 191r; and see below, p. 111, and Abraham, *Dictionary of Alchemical Imagery*, p. 152.

14. See below, pp. 240–1.

15. *MH*, p. 139.

16. BL MS Lansdowne 703, fos. 48r–49v; Allan Pritchard, 'Thomas Charnock's Book dedicated to Queen Elizabeth', *Ambix*, 26 (1), March 1979, pp. 56–73. Printed in Elias Ashmole, *Theatrum Chemicum Britannicum* (1652).

17. BL MS Lansdowne 703, fo. 45r; Richard Harvey, *An astrological discourse upon the great and notable coniunction of the two superiour planets, Saturne & Iupiter, which shall happen the 28 day of April, 1583* (London, 1583), sig. A3r.

18. BL MS Lansdowne 703, fo. 7v; Pritchard, 'Thomas Charnock's Book', p. 59. Others believe Dee practised 'purified' magic: Frances A. Yates, *Giordano Bruno and the Hermetic Tradition* (London, 1964), pp. 107, 80; Peter J. French, *John Dee* (London, 1972); Wayne Shumaker, *Renaissance Curiosa* (Binghamton, 1982), pp. 15–20; Clulee, *Dee's Natural Philosophy*, pp. 211–12; Deborah Harkness, *John Dee's Conversations with Angels: Cabala, Alchemy, and the End of Nature* (Cambridge, 1999), p. 40.

19. BL MS Lansdowne 703, fos. 43v–44r.

20. Ibid., 703, fos. 51r–v, 45r–47r; Pritchard, 'Thomas Charnock's Book', p. 58.

21. BL MS Lansdowne 703, fos. 3r, 21v, 16r, 24v, 37v.

22. Ibid., fos. 22r, 24v.

23. Ibid., fos. 8r, 9v, 39r.

24. Pritchard, 'Thomas Charnock's Book', p. 56, and F.S. Taylor, 'Thomas Charnock', *Ambix*, 2 (1946), pp. 148–76, at pp. 151, 172, from BLO MS Ashmole 1445, part VIII (G), fo. 38. Part VI is a treatise on the philosopher's stone dedicated to Elizabeth by Edward Cradock, Oxford Divinity Reader; BL MS Lansdowne 703, fo. 51r.

25. Ibid., title page, inscribed 'William Burleigh de B/A. Sir Robert Cicil'; Hatfield House MS CP 271/1.

26. Taylor, 'Thomas Charnock', p. 151; Pritchard, 'Thomas Charnock's Book', p. 56.

27. John de la Noy was Mercer to the Queen (*The Visitation of Surrey, 1662–8* [Harleian Society, vol. 60, London, 1910], p. 71).

28. *MH*, Theorem XXI; *CSP Foreign, 1564–5*, p. 267, Cornelius de Alneto to Cecil, from Bruges, 22 December 1564; TNA SP 12/36/12, de Lannoy to Elizabeth, 7 February 1565.

29. *CSP Foreign, 1564–5*, p. 267; *MH*, pp. 137, 161, 171–5, 189; TNA SP 12/36/13, de Lannoy to Elizabeth, 9 February 1565; Thomas Tymme, *A Light in darknesse, which illumineth for all the Monas hieroglyphica of the famous and profound Dr John Dee, Discovering natures closet and revealing the true Christian secrets of Alchimy* (London, 1610), pp. 27–8; TNA SP 15/13/23; BLO MS Ashmole 1486, Pt. IV, p. 15.

30. TNA SP 15/13/23.

31. *CSP Foreign, 1564–5*, p. 267.

32. Hatfield House MS CP 271/1; C. Kitching, 'Alchemy in the Reign of Edward VI: An Episode in the Careers of Richard Whalley and Richard Eden', *Bulletin of the Institute of Historical Research*, 44 (1971), pp. 308–15; D. Gwyn, 'Richard Eden: Cosmographer and Alchemist', *The Sixteenth-Century Journal*, 15 (1984), pp. 13–34.

33. BL MS Lansdowne 101, fos. 17r–20r.

34. BL MSS Lansdowne 121, fos. 11r–125v, Lansdowne 69, fo. 137r–v. Eden became secretary to the Vidame of Chartres, another noble alchemist (TNA SP 70/146, p. 62).

35. TNA SP 12/36/12,13; SP 12/37/3, Armigall Waad's account, 12 August 1565; Hatfield House MS CP 154/146.

36. TNA SP 12/39/39, SP 12/40/32.

37. TNA SP 12/40/32.

38. HMC *Salisbury* i, p. 330, no. 1091; Margaret Morison, 'A Narrative of the Journey of Cecilia, Princess of Sweden, to the Court of Queen Elizabeth', *Transactions of the Royal Historical Society*, n.s., 12 (1898), pp. 181–224, at pp. 213–14; HMC *Salisbury*, i, p. 325, no. 1072, p. 330. no. 1090; Hatfield House MSS CP 154/136, CP154/146.

39. HMC *Salisbury* i., pp. 332–3, no. 1104.

40. TNA SP 12/39/39, Waad to Cecil and Leicester, 7 March 1566.

41. TNA SP 12/42/70, Waad to Cecil, 8 pm 28 May 1566.

42. TNA SP 12/40/32, Waad to Cecil and Leicester, 19 July 1566, SP 12/39/88, de Lannoy to Cecil and Leicester, ? July 1566, SP 15/13/23. II, Waad's translation.

43. BL MS Lansdowne 9, fo. 191r–192v, TNA SP 12/42/30.

44. W. Murdin, *A Collection of state papers relating to affairs in the reign of Queen Elizabeth* (London, 1759), p. 763. Deborah Harkness, 'Strange Ideas and English Knowledge: Natural Science Exchange in Elizabethan London', in *Merchants & Marvels: Commerce, Science and Art in Early Modern Europe*, eds Pamela Smith and Paula Findlen (New York and London, 2002), pp. 137–60, at p. 151; Longleat House, MS DU/I, fo. 209r, petition of Barbara de Lannoy, after Feb. 1571.

45. Cecil to Norris, late July 1568, in *Cabala, sive scrinia sacra* (London, 1691), p. 139. In March 1568 Lucas de Hallye and Cornelius de Hooghe received licences to practise a 'secret science' but not multiply gold (TNA SP 12/46/60).

46. TNA SP 12/37/3, Waad to Cecil, 12 August 1565.

47. TNA C 3/135/18, transcript for Cecil in BL MS Lansdowne 87, fo. 100r–101r.

48. TNA SP 12/39/74, Pembroke to Cecil, 21 May 1566; *CPR Elizabeth I, iv, 1556–9,* p. 136, no. 880; Murdin, *Collection of state papers,* p. 763.

49. Heidelberg University Library, Cod. Pal. Germ. 598. Minor authorial changes from the 1564 text. R&W 1625 to 1634 are German dictionaries but the only one extant (#1625) Dee purchased in London in 1568.

50. *PA,* p. 128, on additions to Theorem 18.

51. Ibid., pp. 134–5, 148–9, and n. to Theorem 52, p. 224.

52. Ibid., pp. 160–1, 162–5, and n. to Theorem 77, pp. 230–1, suggesting Psalm 12:6 as an inspiration; ibid., p. 187, Theorem 109.

53. CR, pp. 518–19.

54. Ibid., p. 519. Dee noted 'our friend' Grudius's death in 1569 in Joseph Simler, *Epitome Bibliothecae Gesner* (1555) (R&W, 170), now BL 616.m.2; Grudius from Venice to Viglius in Brussels, 4 February 1570, in Wenen, Archiv des Ordens vom Goldenen Vliesze III, Burgundisch-spanisches Archiv, I. Abteilung Protokoll der Ordens Kapitel, Original vom Jahre 1540–1573, fos. 51, 4, 52, 1–3, read at www.let.leidenuniv.nl/Dutch/Latijn/GMS6.html.

Chapter 8: War Amongst the Alchemists

1. Alford, *The Early Elizabethan Polity,* pp. 182–208; Neville Williams, *Thomas Howard, Fourth Duke of Norfolk* (London, 1964).

2. Murdin, *Collection of state papers,* pp. 219, 226–7.

3. BL MS Lansdowne 11, fo. 119r; Murdin, *Collection of state papers,* p. 535.

4. Murdin, *Collection of state papers,* pp. 19, 86, 108, 121, 145, 208–9; *A Copie of a Letter lately Sent by a Gentleman, student in the Lawes of the Realme, to a frende of his concerning D. Story* (London, 1571), sig. A3r–v; W. Camden, *The History of Mary Queen of Scots* (London, 1636), sig. G7v–G8r.

5. Murdin, *Collection of state papers,* pp. 538, 219, 226–7; TNA SP 12/71/61; Camden, *History of Mary,* sig. K1r–v; Camden, *Annals,* pp. 104, 130; TNA C 3/115/18, 'the said Prestall is fugitive and meaneth to fly the realm of England'.

6. Murdin, *Collection of state papers,* p. 538; TNA SP 12/71/61. Camden, *History of Mary,* sig. K1r–v.

7. Murdin, *Collection of state papers,* pp. 71, 98, 154–5.

8. Ibid., p. 146.

9. *CSP Foreign 1569–1571,* p. 118, no. 411, Lord Scrope, Warden of the West Marches, to Cecil from Carlisle, 29 August 1569, and no. 412.

10. *A Declaration of the Lyfe and Death of John Story* (London, 1571), sig. B3r–v.

11. Murdin, *Collection of state papers,* p. 80.

12. R.M. Sargent, *The Life and Lyrics of Sir Edward Dyer* (Oxford, 1968), *passim.*

13. Murdin, *Collection of state papers,* pp. 30, 43, 46, 51.

14. *A Treatise of Treasons Against Q. Elizabeth, and the Croune of England* (London, January 1572), fos. 44r–49r, 134r, 166r, 158r.

15. *MP,* sig. A2r–v.

16. *An Epitaph, or rather a Short Discourse made upon the life and death of D. Boner, sometimes unworthy Bishop of London* (London, John Allde, 14 September 1569); *A commemoration or*

Dirige of Bastarde Edmonde Boner, alias Savage, usurped Bishoppe of London (London, 1569); Thomas Preston, *A Lamentable Tragedy, Mixed Full of Pleasant Mirth, Containing the Life of Cambises, King of Persia* (London, John Allde, 1570).

17. J. Foxe, *Actes and Monuments* (1570), p. 1,979.

18. Ibid., pp. 2,024, 1,999.

19. A fuller study of Prestall is in preparation.

20. *MP*, sigs. *4v–a1v (arithmetic), a2r–v (geometry), b1v–b3r (astronomy and cosmography), d4v–A1r (navigation), a4r–v (chorography and hydrography); sig. A1r on 1567; Roberts and Watson, *Catalogue*, pp. 42–5.

21. BL MS Lansdowne 98, fos. 1r–7r, at fos. 3r–4r.

22. BLO MS Rawlinson D. 241, *passim*; Bruce T. Moran, 'Privilege, Communication, and Chemistry: The Hermetic-Alchemical Circle of Moritz of Hessen-Kassel', *Ambix*, 32 (3), Nov. 1985, pp. 110–26, quoting Murhardsche Bibliothek, Kassel: 2 MS Chem 19, I, fo. 114r–15r.

23. CR, pp. 544–6.

24. TNA SP 12/40/49; M.G. Brennan and N.J. Kinnamon, *A Sidney Chronology* (Basingstoke and New York, 2003), p. 15.

25. CR, p. 508.

26. John Aubrey, *A Natural History of Wiltshire* (Whitefish, MT, 2004), pp. 120, 229; John Aubrey, *Brief Lives*, ed. A. Clark, 2 vols. (Oxford, 1898), ii, pp. 310–13; Thomas Moffet, *Nobilis, or a View of the Life and Death of a Sidney*, trans. and ed. Virgil B. Heltzel and Joy H. Hudson (San Marino, CA, 1940), p. 75.

27. Arthur Collins, *Letters and Memorials of State*, 2 vols. (London, 1746), i, pp. 66–7; Sargent, *Dyer*; CR, pp. 514–15; J.M. Osborn, *Young Philip Sidney*, (New Haven and London, 1972), pp. 146–7; Roberts and Watson, *Catalogue*, pp. 35, 42.

28. J.J. Goring, 'Wealden Ironmasters in the Age of Elizabeth', in E.W. Ives, R.J. Knecht, J.J. Scarisbrick, eds, *Wealth and Power in Tudor England: Essays Presented to S.T. Bindoff* (London, 1978), p. 212, and *Sidney Ironworks Accounts, 1541–1573*, ed. D.W. Crossley (Camden Society, 4 ser., vol. 15, London, 1975); M.B. Donald, *Elizabethan Copper: The History of the Company of Mines Royal 1568 to 1605* (London, 1955), pp. 71, 100.

29. Ciaran Brady, *The Chief Governors: The Rise and Fall of Reform Government in Tudor Ireland 1536–1588* (Cambridge, 1994), pp. 128–36; Brennan and Kinnamon, *Sidney Chronology*, pp. 27, 29; TNA SP 63/36/14, Mary Sidney to Burghley, 2 May 1572; TNA SP 12/86/33.

30. R&W, 1623, Postel, *Alphabetum introductio et legendi modus linguarum duodecim characteribus differentium* (Paris, 1538), with Postel's *De originibus, seu de Hebraicae linguae et gentis antiquitate* (Paris, 1538), both with many Dee annotations.

31. P.R.N. Carter, 'Powle, Sir Stephen (c.1553–1630)', *ODNB*, Oxford University Press, September 2004; online edn, January 2008 [http://www.oxforddnb.com/view/article/56051]; V.F. Stern, *Sir Stephen Powle of Court and Country* (London and Cranbury, NJ, 1992); *CPR Eliz. I, iv, 1566–9*, no. 1142 and no. 516, large grants to Powle; CR, pp. 533, 510; Longleat House MS Dud/II, fo. 111r.

32. CR, p. 544.

33. BL MS Sloane 2210, fo. 95v; BLO MS Ashmole 1486, Pt. V, p. 61.

34. Medley to Burghley, 19 April 1572, TNA SP 12/86/14, BL MS Lansdowne 19, fo. 98r; John Strype, *The Life of Sir Thomas Smith* (London, 1698), pp. 134–40, revised in Strype, *Annals of the Reformation* (1735), ii, pp. 351–3, and Appendix, pp. 79–81; Strype's dismissal of Medley as a fraud in *Smith* is followed by Mary Dewar, *Sir Thomas Smith: A Tudor Intellectual in Office* (London, 1964), pp. 149–55; Ian W. Archer, 'Smith, Sir Thomas (1513–1577)', *ODNB*, Oxford University Press, September 2004; online edn, January 2008 [http://www.oxforddnb.com/view/article/25906]; Rory Rapple, 'Gilbert, Sir Humphrey (1537–1583)', *ODNB*,

Oxford University Press, September 2004; online edn, January 2008 [http://www.oxforddnb.com/view/article/10690]; Felicity Heal and Clive Holmes, 'The Economic Patronage of William Cecil', in Pauline Croft, ed., *Patronage, Culture and Power: The Early Cecils* (New Haven and London, 2002), p. 220; Stephen Pumfrey and Frances Dawbarn, 'Science and Patronage in England, 1570–1625', *History of Science*, 42 (2004), pp. 159–60; D. Harkness, *The Jewel House: London and the Scientific Revolution* (New Haven and London, 2007).

35. 'Copper Processing', *Encyclopædia Britannica* (2006), at Encyclopædia Britannica Online, http://www.britannica.com/EBchecked/topic136794/copper-processing.

36. Medley to Burghley, 19 April 1572, TNA SP 12/86/14.

37. Medley to Robert Cecil, 3 November 1598, Hatfield House MS CP 65/42. Medley's great aunt was Lady Burghley's great-grandmother.

38. Medley to Burghley, 19 May 1572, TNA SP 12/84/14, Smith to Burghley, 16 December 1574, BL MS Lansdowne 19, fos. 97r–99r.

39. R&W, 215 (Agricola), 459 (Biringuccio, Frankfurt 1550) and 677 (Biringuccio, Venice 1540). None found.

40. Book III, ch.xiv in Lazarus Ercker, *Beschreibung allerfürnemsten mineralischen Ertzt und Berckwerksarten* (Prague, 1574), R&W, 5 (not found). Ercker's title page reproduced in Arthur Greenberg, *From Alchemy to Chemistry in Picture and Story* (Hoboken, NJ, 2007), p. 11.

41. BLO MS Rawlinson D 241, unfoliated.

42. TNA C 1/699/40, and BLO MS Ashmole 487, 10 July 1583.

43. BL MS Lansdowne 14, fos. 40r–41v, 4 December 1571.

44. TNA SP 12/188/21, HEHL MS HAD 2367.

45. TNA SP 12/86/14.

46. Mary Sidney to Burghley, 29 September 1576, BL MS Lansdowne 23, fo., 184v.

47. SP 70/146, pp. 9–10, 112–14.

48. TNA SP 15/13/122. The final patent omitted it.

49. TNA SP 70/146, pp. 33–4, 62, Smith to Richard Eden, 9 March 1572.

50. TNA SP 70/146, pp. 104–5.

51. BL MS Lansdowne 19, fo. 98r.

52. J. Ballinger, *Calendar of Wynn (of Gwydir) Papers, 1515–1690: in the National Library of Wales and elsewhere* (Aberystwyth, 1926), pp. 77–8; Walter Davies, *General View of the Agriculture and Domestic Economy of North Wales* (London, 1810), pp. 44–5, 484–5.

53. BL MSS Lansdowne 19, fo. 97r; Lansdowne 29, fo. 139r, Smith to Burghley, 8 March 1575.

54. BL MS Lansdowne 18, fo. 101r; Adams, *Leicester and the Court*, p. 332.

55. Because of the different equivalent weights of their molecules (Donald, *Elizabethan Copper*, p. 32); Humphrey to Burghley, 9 December 1574, BL MS Lansdowne 18, fo. 101r–v.

56. Ibid., fo. 103r–104r.

57. BL MS Lansdowne 19, fo. 98v.

58. *CPR Eliz. I, 1574–5*, pp. 509–10, cf. TNA SP 15/13/122.

59. BL MS Lansdowne 29, fo. 139r, Smith to Burghley, 8 March 1574, misdated 1579 in the Lansdowne *Catalogue* and Stephen Pumphrey and Frances Dawbarn, 'Science and Patronage in England: A Preliminary Study', *History of Science*, 42 (2004), pp. 137–88, at pp. 159–60. Smith died in August 1577.

60. TNA SP 12/77/64, summarised in *A Declaration of the Lyfe and Death of John Story*, sig. B3r–v, and *A Copie of a Letter lately Sent by a Gentleman*, sig. A4r–v; Hatfield House MS CP 160/111.

61. *CSP Foreign, Elizabeth, 1571–2*, p. 223, no. 690, John Lee to Burghley, 23 March 1572. Philip II practised distillation (G. Parker, *Philip II* [Boston and Toronto, 1978], p. 47).

62. *A Copie of a Letter lately Sent by a Gentleman*, sig. A4r–v; TNA SP 12/46/23.

63. *APC*, viii, pp. 264–5, 5 July 1574, and see TNA SP 12/46/23; BL MS Add. 70984, fo. 256r.

64. BL MS Lansdowne 23, fos. 184r–185r, Mary Sidney to Burghley, 29 September 1576.

65. G. Eland, *Thomas Wotton's Letter Book 1574–1586* (London, 1960), pp. 11–12.

66. TNA SP 12/152/88; Donald, *Elizabethan Copper*, pp. 214–15.

67. TNA WARD 9/221, fo. 101r, WARD 9/384, fo. 226r; Joel Hurstfield, *The Queen's Wards*, 2nd ed. (London, 1973), pp. 265–6.

68. Hatfield House MS CP 20/106.

69. Strype, *Annals* (1737), iii, p. 557; Hatfield House MSS CP 26/64, 30/100.

Chapter 9: Recovering the Lost Empire

1. 'General and rare memorials pertayning to the perfect arte of navigation', BLO MS Ashmole 1789, fos. 61–115, dictated 1–6 August 1576, printed August–September 1577, significantly changed, as *General and rare memorials pertayning to the perfect arte of navigation: annexed to the paradoxall cumpas, in playne: now first published: 24 yeres, after the first invention thereof* (London, Sept. 1577); 'Of Famous and Rich Discoveries' (BL MS Cotton Vitellius C. VII, fos. 26–269), begun 1576, mostly written 24 March–8 July 1577, now missing its first five chapters, approximately thirty folios; 'Brytanici imperii limites', begun by November 1577, continued before 4 May 1578, again expanded before 22 July 1578, BL MS Add. 59681, Dee's copy made in 1593 from a lost original. In early September 1597 Dee wrote 'Thallatokratia Brettaniki', or 'The British Sea Sovereignty' (BL MS Harley 249, fos. 95–105).

2. Sherman, *John Dee: The Politics of Reading and Writing in the English Renaissance*, pp. 148–200; David Armitage, *The Ideological Origins of the British Empire* (Cambridge, 2000), pp. 52, 80, 105–9; Christopher Hodgkins, *Reforming Empire: Protestant Colonialism and Conscience in British Literature* (Columbia, MO, and London, 2002), pp. 10–32; Frances A. Yates, *Astraea: The Imperial Theme in the Sixteenth Century* (London, 1975), pp. 29–51; French, *John Dee*, pp. 180–99; Andrew Escobedo, *Nationalism and Historical Loss in Renaissance England: Foxe, Dee, Spenser, Milton* (Ithaca, NY, 2004), pp. 20–2; Ken MacMillan with Jennifer Abeles, eds, *John Dee: The Limits of the British Empire* (Westport, CT, and London, 2004); MacMillan, 'John Dee's "Brytanici imperii limites"', *Huntington Library Quarterly*, 64 (2001), pp. 151–9; MacMillan, 'Discourse on History, Geography and Law: John Dee and the Limits of the British Empire, 1576–1580', *Canadian Journal of History*, 36 (Apr. 2001), pp. 1–25; MacMillan, 'Sovereignty "more plainly described": Early English Maps of North America, 1580–1625', *Journal of British Studies*, 42 (Oct. 2003), pp. 413–47; MacMillan, 'Disclosing a Great Error: John Dee's Answer to the Papal Bull *Inter caetera*', *Terrae Incognitae: The Journal of the Society for the History of Discoveries*, 36 (2004), pp. 12–19; Clulee, *Dee's Natural Philosophy*, pp. 180–90.

3. Robert C.D. Baldwin, 'The testing of a new academic trinity for the northern passages: the rationale and experience behind English investment in the voyages of Frobisher, Jackman, Davis and Waymouth 1576–1605', in Anna Agnarsdottir, ed., *Voyages and Exploration in the North Atlantic from the Middle Ages to the XVIIth Century: Papers Presented at the 19th International Congress of Historical Sciences Oslo 2000* (Reykjavik, 2000), pp. 61–98; W. Sherman, 'John Dee's Role in Martin Frobisher's Northwest Enterprise', in Thomas H.B. Symons, ed., *Meta Incognita: A Discourse of Discovery. Martin Frobisher's Arctic Expeditions, 2* vols. (Hull, Quebec, 1999), i, pp. 283–98.

4. *Historie Del S.D. Fernando Colombo; Nelle quali s'ha particolare, et vera relatione della vita, et de' fatti dell'Ammiraglio D. CHRISTOPHORO COLOMBO, suo padre* (Venetia, 1571), now BL shelf mark 615.d.7; W. Sherman, 'John Dee's Columbian Encounter', in S. Clucas, ed.,

John Dee: Interdisciplinary Studies in English Renaissance Thought (Dordrecht, 2006), pp. 131–40.

5. *Historie Del S.D. Fernando Colombo*, sig. M7v; Sherman, 'John Dee's Columbian Encounter', pp. 134, 136; BL MS Cotton Charters XIII and XIV.I.

6. *Historie Del S.D. Fernando Colombo*, sig. L5v; Sherman 'John Dee's Columbian Encounter', p. 136.

7. Ramusio, *Navigationi et Viaggi* (Venice, 1563–5), TCD shelf mark: DD.dd.40, 41, vol. 2, sig. D8v, and vol. 3, fo. 323v; references to the BL 615.d.7 copy of *Historie Del S.D. Fernando Colombo* in vol. 3, fos. 2r, 6r–v, 80r, 82v, 83r; on Ramusio, W. Sherman, 'Bringing the World to England: The Politics of Translation in the Age of Hakluyt', *Transactions of the Royal Historical Society*, 6th series, 14 (2004), pp. 199–207.

8. Ramusio, *Navigationi et Viaggi*, vol. 3, fo. 2r.

9. Ibid., vol. 3, fo. 7r.

10. Ibid., fo. 3, fos. 169v–170v, 82r, 183r–v, 280v, 338r, 341r, 357r, 359r, 426v; on Madoc, fos. 7r–v, 78r, 82r–83v, 398v; 39v, 169r–v, 204v; 41v, 114v; Montezuma's 'legend' of Madoc, fos. 235r, 238v.

11. Ibid., vol. 3, fos. 27r, 84v.

12. Ibid., vol. 1, fos. 374r–375r.

13. Ibid., vol. 3, fos. 417r–v, 441v, 445v, 448v, 449v–450r, 451v; MacMillan and Abeles, *John Dee: The Limits of the British Empire*, p. 38.

14. Ibid., pp. 2, 9, 13–14; MacMillan, *Sovereignty and Possession in the New World: The Legal Foundations of Empire, 1576–1640* (Cambridge, 2006), pp. 51–2; Sherman, *Dee*, and Sherman, 'Putting the British Seas on the Map: John Dee's Cartography, *Cartographia*, 35, nos. 3–4 (1998), pp. 1–10; Sherman, 'John Dee's Role in Frobisher's North-West Enterprise', *Meta Incognita*, pp. 283–97.

15. MacMillan, *Sovereignty and Possession*, pp. 31–48, 58, 61–2.

16. Ibid., pp. 56–7.

17. R. Hakluyt, *The Principall Navigations Voiages and Discoveries of the English Nation* (London, 1589), pp. 304–9, 394–7; TNA SP 15/28 Part I/54.

18. BLO MS Ashmole 487, November 1577; MacMillan and Abeles, *John Dee: The Limits of the British Empire*, p. 38.

19. Ibid., p. 12; MacMillan, *Sovereignty and Possession*, pp. 56–7, 80.

20. BLO MS Ashmole 487, November 1577; CR, p. 521; See below, pp. 111–12.

21. Heal and Holmes, 'The Economic Patronage of William Cecil', in Croft, *Patronage, Culture and Power*; Paul E.J. Hammer, 'The Uses of Scholarship: The Secretariat of Robert Devereux, Second Earl of Essex, c.1585–1601', *English Historical Review*, 109 (1994), pp. 26–51.

22. Dee, *Memorials*, p. 2; Quinn, *Voyages of Sir Humphrey Gilbert*, 2 vols. (London, 1940) i, pp. 105–17; Hakluyt, *The Principall Navigations*, pp. 394–7.

23. BL MS Cotton Charter XIII. 39; 'Memorials', BLO MS Ashmole 1789, fo. 67r–v, and *Memorials*, p. 10; CR, p. 528; William H. Sherman, 'John Dee's "Brytannicae Reipublicae Synopsis": A Reader's Guide to the Elizabethan Commonwealth', *The Journal of Medieval and Renaissance Studies*, 20, 2 (Fall 1990), pp. 293–316.

24. J. Firmicus, *Ad Mavortium Lollianum Astronomicon lib.VIII per N. Prucknerum . . . ab innumeris mendis vindicati* (Basle, 1533), University College London, shelf mark Ogden A.9, in Manilius, *Astronomica 5* (R&W, 251).

25. Dee, 'Memorials', BLO MS Ashmole 1789, fos. 61r–67v, *Memorials*, pp. 4–10.

26. TNA SP 12/110/21; BL MS Add. 59681, p. 16, printed in MacMillan and Abeles, *John Dee: The Limits of the British Empire*, p. 45.

27. TNA SP 12/113/12, items 10 and 11.

28. B. Woolley, *The Queen's Conjuror: The Science and Magic of Dr John Dee* (New York, 2001), pp. 102–4. *MP*, sig. D4v, dates the 'Paradoxal Compass' to 1559, CR, p. 527, to 1556, *Memorials*, title page, to 1553.

29. James McDermott, 'The Company of Cathay: The Financing and Organization of the Frobisher Voyages', and McDermott, '"A right heroicall heart": Sir Martin Frobisher', pp. 55–118 and 147–78 in vol. 1 of Symons, ed., *Meta Incognita*.

30. Dee, *Memorials*, p. 2; Lok, BL MS Cotton Otho E VIII, fo. 42r.

31. Ibid., fo. 44v; Sir Humphrey Gilbert, *A discourse of a discoverie for a new passage to Cataia* (H. Middleton for R. Jones, London, 1576).

32. BL MS Cotton Otho E. VIII, fo. 44v; Dee, 'Memorials', BLO MS Ashmole 1789, fo. 60r; *Memorials*, p. 2.

33. BL MS Cotton Otho E. VIII, fos. 42–47.

34. Ibid., fos. 42v, 44r–v, 47r–v. Lok spent £500 (TNA SP 12/119/29) or £1,000 (TNA SP 12/119/30) on his research library from 1552; Hakluyt, *Divers Voyages* (1582), sig. ¶2r; Hakluyt, *Principal Navigations*, 12 vols. (Glasgow, 1913), iii, pp. 197–200, v, pp. 111–15, 117, vi, p. 136; V. Stefansson, *The Three Voyages of Martin Frobisher* (London, 1938), p. 13.

35. BL MS Cotton Otho E. VIII, fo. 47v.

36. Dee, *Memorials*, p. 3; McDermott, 'Cathay and the Way Hither', in *Meta Incognita*, pp. 363–4, and nn. 32, 40; Stefansson, *The Three Voyages of Martin Frobisher*, p. xcix, Borough's Frobisher charts. Another is CPM I.69 at Hatfield House (R.A. Skelton and John Summerson, *A Description of Maps and Architectural Drawings in the Collection made by William Cecil, First Baron Burghley, now at Hatfield House* [Oxford, 1971]).

37. McDermott, 'Cathay and the Way Hither', *Meta Incognita*, p. 363.

38. HEHL MS 715, fo. 27v; TNA SP 12/110/22.

39. TNA SP 12/122/62; SP 12/119/43, 44, accepting Dee's application. Earlier investor lists omit him; BL MS Harley 167, fo. 187v.

40. James McDermott, 'The Company of Cathay', *Meta Incognita*, pp. 147–78 at p. 163; McDermott, 'Michael Lok, Mercer and Merchant Adventurer', *Meta Incognita*, pp. 119–46, at pp. 132–3.

41. TNA SP 12/129/44.I; SP 12/126/35.

42. TNA E 134/8Jas1/Hil25: Young's daughter Susan Ellis, born 1559, knew Lok 'from her Infancye'; Young was assistant in the Muscovy Company in 1569 (T.S. Willan, *The Muscovy Merchants of 1555* (Manchester, 1953), p. 75).

43. TNA E 178/2939. A full biography of Young is in preparation.

44. House of Lords Main Papers, 20 Mar 1621–4 April 1621, HL/PO/JO/10/1/16, fos. 1r, 7r.

45. HEHL MS HM 715, fo. 27v, and TNA SP 12/130/19; TNA SP 12/240/109.

46. BLO MS Ashmole 488, 20 May 1590, and see below, p. 211.

47. TNA SP 12/129/44.I, SP 12/122/62; McDermott, 'The Company of Cathay', pp. 171, 175.

48. *APC*, x, pp. 134–5, 148; TNA SP 12/122/9, p. 19.

49. Magdalene College, Cambridge, MS Pepys 2133, fo. 5r; TNA SP 12/119/46.

50. TNA E 164/35/126,127; E 164/36, accounts of William Borough, Edward Fellman and Thomas Allyn; TNA C 47/34/6.

51. TNA C 54/1055; House of Lords Main Papers, 20 Mar 1621–4 April 1621, HL/PO/JO/10/1/16, fos. 4r, 8r; BL MS Lansdowne 30, fo. 12.

Chapter 10: 'More is hid, than uttered': The Philosopher's Stone and Empire

1. Ramusio, *Navigationi et Viaggi*, vol. 3, fo. 105r; Peter Lake, 'A Tale of Two Episcopal Surveys: The Strange Fates of Edmund Grindal and Cuthbert Mayne Revisited', *Transactions of the Royal Historical Society*, 6th ser., 18 (2008), pp. 129–63, at pp. 146–7.

2. BLO MS Ashmole 1789, fo. 50r, and see *Memorials*, BL shelf mark C.21.e.12.

3. BL MS Add. 59681, p. 26, in MacMillan and Abeles, *John Dee: The Limits of the British Empire*, p. 52 (author's emphasis).

4. Sherman, *Dee*, pp. 12–19, 148–200, attacks 'The myth of the magus' and minimises the impact of Dee's occult beliefs on his imperial writings.

5. BL MS Add. 59681, pp. 72–4, printed in MacMillan and Abeles, *John Dee: The Limits of the British Empire*, pp. 97–100; *Memorials*, sig. e.*1r.

6. BL MS Add. 59681, pp. 72–4, in MacMillan and Abeles, *John Dee: The Limits of the British Empire*, pp. 97–100. Author's emphasis.

7. BL MS Add. 59681, p. 41, in MacMillan and Abeles, *John Dee: The Limits of the British Empire*, p. 67.

8. BL MS Cotton Vitellius C. VII, fo. 262r.

9. R&W, DM 70, BL MS Sloane 313; Robert Mathiesen, 'A Thirteenth-Century Ritual to Attain the Beatific Vision from the *Sworn Book of Honorius of Thebes*', in Claire Fanger, ed., *Conjuring Spirits: Texts and Traditions of Medieval Ritual Magic* (College Park, PA, 1998), pp. 143–62.

10. BL MS Sloane 3188, fo. 48r; see above, p. 50 on Trithemius, and below, pp. 147, 177 on Kelley.

11. Dee's notes in J. Trithemius, *De septem secundeis* (Frankfurt, 1545), Cambridge University Library shelf mark Dd*.4.5.11 (E); Roberts and Watson, *Catalogue*, 678, at p. 92; J. Firmicus, *Ad Mavortium Lollianum Astronomicon lib.VIII per N. Prucknerum … ab innumeris mendis vindicati* (Basle, 1533), University College London shelf mark Ogden A.9, in Manilius, *Astronomica* 5 (R&W, 251).

12. BLO MS Ashmole 1789, fo. 58v; *Memorials*, sig. e*4v.

13. Tanner, *The Last Descendants of Aeneas*, pp. 119–45; John L. Phelan, *The Millennial Kingdom of the Franciscans in the New World* (Berkeley and Los Angeles, 1970, rev. edn), pp. 5–16; John S. Mebane, *Renaissance Magic and the Return of the Golden Age: The Occult Tradition and Marlowe, Jonson, and Shakespeare* (Lincoln, NE, 1989); Alexandre Y. Haran, *Le lys et la globe: messianisme dynastique et rêve imperial en France au XVIe et XVII Siècles* (Paris, 2000).

14. BL MS Add. 59681, pp. 57–8, in MacMillan and Abeles, *John Dee: The Limits of the British Empire*, pp. 81–3; S. Anglo, *Images of Tudor Kingship* (London, 1992), pp. 45–55; and Anglo, *Spectacle, pageantry and early Tudor policy* (Oxford, 1969).

15. Edward Topsell, *Times Lamentations* (London, 1599), p. 63; *Certein Letters wherin is set forth a Discourse of the Peace that was attempted and sought to have bin put in effecte by the Lords and States of Holland and Zelande in the year of oure Lorde 1574* (London, 1576).

16. BL MS Harley 285, fos. 32r–36v, at fo. 36r, John Hastings to Burghley, Brussels, 2 December 1575.

17. *CSP Spanish*, ii, p. 523; Joseph M. Kervyn de Lettenhove, *Relations politiques des Pays-Bas et de L'Angleterre sous la regne de Philippe II*, 11 vols. (Brussels, 1882–1900), viii, p. 249; S. Adams, 'Elizabeth I and the Sovereignty of the Netherlands', *Transactions of the Royal Historical Society*, 6th ser., 14 (2004), pp. 309–19 at p. 313; *Certein letters*, sig. b7r.

18. Kervyn de Lettenhove, *Relations politiques*, viii, p. 249; *CSP Spanish*, ii, pp. 522–4.

19. Kervyn de Lettenhove, *Relations politiques*, viii, pp. 213, 222–3.

20. Sandford, 'Epistle Dedicatorie', in *Houres of Recreation, or Afterdinners, Which may aptly be called, The Garden of Pleasure* (London, 1576), sigs. A5v–A6r.

21. Jacopo Brocardo, *The Reuelation of S. Ihon reueled* (London, 1582), fo. 32v.

22. Richard Bancroft, *A Sermon Preached at Paules Crosse the 9 of Februarie, being the first Sunday in the Parleament, Anno 1588* [i.e. 1589] *by Richard Bancroft D. of Divinitie and Chaplaine to the right Honorable Sir Christopher Hatton* (London, 1588), sigs. B2r, B3r–v, B4v.

23. BL MS Harley 249, fo. 95v; Glyn Parry, 'John Dee and the Elizabethan "British Empire" in its European Context', *The Historical Journal*, 49, 3 (2006), pp. 643–75.

24. CR, p. 527; BL MS Add. 59681, pp. 72–4, in MacMillan and Abeles, *John Dee: The Limits of the British Empire*, pp. 97–100; Bart van Es, *Spenser's Forms of History* (Oxford, 2002), pp. 141–2, 147; Anthony Pagden, *Lords of all the World: Ideologies of Empire in Spain, Britain and France c.1500–c.1800* (New Haven and London, 1995), pp. 29–40.

25. BL MS Sloane 3188, fos. 6v–7r, 8r, 24r, BL MS Add. 36674, fo. 186r, and see above, pp. 31–3.

26. *MP*, sigs. d3v–d4r, A3r–v, d2v–d3r; Psellus, *De daemonibus* (Venice, 1516), R&W, 256 (Washington, D.C., Folger Shakespeare Library shelf mark BF 1501 J2 Copy 2 Cage); BL MS Add. 36674, fos. 59r–62v.

27. *MH*, p. 201.

28. 'ut Aphorismos nostros, istosque, eosdem esse (ordinis solum et phraseos excepta ratione) indicaret', 'ut in Ursonis et meis Aphorismis admirandum ullum, divinitusque immissum suspiraremur consensum' (BLO MS Ashmole 1788, iv, p. 5), referring to Trinity College, Cambridge MS O.2.50, R&W, M3, bought in 1556 from John Leland's estate.

29. 'Et tamen si vel verbatim quidem, vel (ut ita dicam) literatim integri convenirent libelli; miraculi cujusdam citius (tali in eventu)' (BLO MS Ashmole 1788, iv, p. 7).

30. Michael T. Walton and Phyllis J. Walton, 'Being up Front: The Frontispiece and the *Prisca* Tradition', *Cauda Pavonis*, n.s. 17, nos. 1 & 2 (spring and fall 1998), pp. 8–13; *Memorials*, sig. i2r, where the marginal comment 'Anno 1574, In August at Mortlake' refers to Dee's letter to Camden.

31. *Memorials*, sig. e1r–v

32. BLO MS Ashmole 1789, fos. 51v–52v; *Memorials*, sig. [delta] 3v.

33. BLO MS Ashmole 1789, fo. 97r; *Memorials*, sig. G4r, p. 55.

34. BL MS Cotton Vitellius C. VII, fo. 92v; BLO MS Ashmole 1789, fo. 114v, *Memorials*, p. 79.

35. BL MS Add. 59681, pp. 72–3, in MacMillan and Abeles, *John Dee: The Limits of the British Empire*, pp. 98–9.

36. Tanner, *Last Descendants of Aeneas*, p. 100.

37. Howard Louthan, *The Quest for Compromise: Peace-Makers in Counter-Reformation Vienna* (Cambridge, 1997), and Paula S. Fichtner, *Emperor Maximilian II* (New Haven and London, 2001). On the 1567 German translation, see above, p. 79.

38. *MH*, pp. 109, 141, 119, 135.

39. R.J.W. Evans, *Rudolf II and His World* (Oxford, 1973), p. 201; BLO MS Ashmole 1789, fo. 56r–v, *Memorials*, sig. e*1v.

40. BLO MS Ashmole 1789, fos. 51v–52r; cf. *Memorials*, sig. d2v–4r.

41. BLO MS Ashmole 1789, fo. 58v; *Memorials*, sigs. e*4v, G4r; BL MS Sloane 3846, fo. 114v.

42. BLO MS Ashmole 1789, fo. 102v; *Memorials*, p. 60.

43. Ibid., p. 54.

44. See BLO MS Ashmole 57, Dee's 1577 transcription of Thomas Norton's 'Ordinall of Alchemy'; C. Nicholl, *The Chemical Theatre* (London, 1980), pp. 18, 245 n. 88; BLO MS Ashmole 1421, fos. 167v, 172r–v. See above, pp. 84–6, on alchemy at Court and Gilbert.

45. *Memorials*, p. 62, with a manicule (pointing hand) emphasising the point. Roberts and Watson, *Catalogue*, p. 219, index under 'Khalid', refers to works read in 1551 and 1556. Khalid's treatise appeared in *The mirror of alchimy, composed by the thrice famous and learned Fryer, Roger Bachon* (London, 1597), pp. 28–53.

46. Samuel Purchas, *Hakluytus posthumus or Purchas his pilgrimes*, 5 vols. (London, 1625), i, p. 9.

47. Ibid., i, pp. 38–42.
48. *Memorials*, sigs. e4v, e.*1r; Dee to Abraham Ortelius, 16 Jan. 1577, in J.H. Hessels, ed., *Ecclesiae Londino-Batavae archivum tomus primus Abrahami Ortelii … epistolae* (Cambridge, 1887), pp. 157–60.
49. BL MS Sloane 3188, fo. 8r–v.
50. BL MS Add. 36674, fo. 176v.
51. *Memorials*, sig. H2r, not in Bodleian MS Ashmole 1789, fo. 101v; BL MS Harley 167, fos. 183–200, Jupiter symbol at fo. 183r.

Chapter 11: Rehabilitating 'The Arch-Conjuror'

1. BLO MS Ashmole 1789, fo. 60r; *Memorials*, p. 2.
2. Hammer, 'The Uses of Scholarship', pp. 26–51; G.D. Ramsay, ed., *The Politics of a Tudor Merchant Adventurer: A Letter to the Earls of East Friesland* (Manchester, 1979), pp. 12–19.
3. BL MS Cotton Charter XIII.39.
4. BLO MS Ashmole 1789, fo. 65v; *Memorials*, p. 8.
5. BLO MS Ashmole 1789, fos. 63v, 67r, 66v; *Memorials*, pp. 6, 9–10, 9.
6. BLO MS Ashmole 1789, fos. 77r, 101r; *Memorials*, pp. 21, 58.
7. 5 Elizabeth, c. 5, reviving 1 & 2 Philip and Mary, c. 5; *APC*, vii, pp. 223, 258, 260–1, 270, 303, 309, 325; and the proclamation of 6 June 1575 (TNA SP12/103/56).
8. M.F. Lloyd Prichard, ed., *Original Papers Regarding Trade in England and Abroad Drawn up by John Keymer* (New York, 1967), p. 42.
9. TNA SP 12/105/83, in Hughes and Larkin, *Tudor Royal Proclamations*, ii, pp. 395–8; A. Hassell Smith et al., eds, *The Papers of Nathaniel Bacon of Stiffkey*, 5 vols. (Norwich, 1979–2000), i, pp. 206–7, 224–31.
10. G.R. Elton, 'Piscatorial Politics in the Early Parliaments of Elizabeth I', in N. McKendrick and R.B. Outhwaite, eds, *Business Life and Public Policy* (Cambridge, 1986), pp. 1–20; Sherman, *Dee*, pp. 159–67; BLO MS Ashmole 487, 6 July 1579.
11. BLO MS Ashmole 1789, fos. 97v–98r; *Memorials*, pp. 54–5.
12. BLO MS Ashmole 1789, slip inserted between fos. 96 and 97; *Memorials*, p. 53.
13. E.H. Kossman and A.F. Mellinck, eds, *Texts Concerning the Revolt of the Netherlands* (Cambridge, 1974), pp. 126–32; Parker, *Philip II*, pp. 122–7.
14. For example, TNA SP 12/108/82, SP 12/24/70, SP 15/24/70; *Certein letters*, sig. b6r, on the Spanish 'contempt of her Majesty's honour'.
15. TNA SP 12/107/52, *CSP Foreign, Elizabeth, 1575–7*, pp. 259, 263, 269–70, 310–11; Kervyn de Lettenhove, *Relations politiques*, viii, pp. 236–7, 250, 340.
16. Ibid., pp. 316–19, printing BL MS Cotton Galba C. V, fos. 292–3; *APC*, ix, pp. 133, 155–6, reiterated on 12 August (p. 183).
17. TNA SP 12/108/23.
18. TNA SP 12/107/52; SP 12/108/67, p. 7, with Burghley's careful corrections.
19. BLO MS Ashmole 1789, fo. 61v.
20. Edward Chester in mid-July was ordered to prevent William of Orange from doubting 'that revenge for these outrages would follow' (Kervyn de Lettenhove, *Relations politiques*, viii, p. 413, in *CSP Foreign, Elizabeth, 1575–7*, pp. 352–3).
21. Kervyn de Lettenhove, *Relations politiques*, viii, pp. 340, 318–19; William Herle assured the Dutch of Burghley's 'inward affection' when the crisis erupted (*CSP Foreign, Elizabeth, 1575–7*, p. 276).
22. TNA SP 12/108/23; SP 12/108/24; SP 12/108/34; SP 12/108/38, 73.

23. TNA SP 12/45, p. 61; Murdin, *Collection of state papers*, ii, pp. 296–9; Kervyn de Lettenhove, *Relations politiques*, viii, pp. 423–8; HMC *Salisbury*, ii, p. 143; Hatfield House MS CP 9/19; *CSP Spanish*, xv, 1568–79, p. 533.

24. TNA SP 12/109/7; *APC*, ix, p. 183, 12 August 1576.

25. *CSP Foreign, Elizabeth, 1575–7*, pp. 400–1.

26. William Herle to Edward Chester, 7 August 1576, Hatfield House MS CP 9/19, in Murdin, *Collection of state papers*, ii, p. 299; Kervyn de Lettenhove, *Relations politiques*, viii, p. 427.

27. John Bossy, 'English Catholics and the French Marriage', *Recusant History*, 5 (1959), pp. 2–16; D.C. Peck, ed., *Leicester's Commonwealth: The Copy of a Letter Written by a Master of Art of Cambridge (1584) and Related Documents* (Athens, OH, and London, 1985), pp. 15–18; Thomas M. McCoog, 'The English Jesuit Mission and the French Match, 1579–81', *Catholic Historical Review*, 87, 2 (2001), pp. 185–213.

28. P. Collinson, *The Elizabethan Puritan Movement* (London, 1967), pp. 168–83, 191–6; Lake, 'Edmund Grindal and Cuthbert Mayne', pp. 132–5.

29. Collinson, *Archbishop Grindal*, chs. 14, 15; Lake, 'Edmund Grindal and Cuthbert Mayne', pp. 132–4.

30. Collinson, 'The Downfall of Archbishop Grindal and its Place in Elizabethan Political and Religious History', in his *Godly People* (London, 1983), ch. 14; W. Nicholson, ed., *The Remains of Edmund Grindal* (Cambridge, 1843), pp. 376–90.

31. Collinson, 'The Downfall of Archbishop Grindal'; Lake, 'Edmund Grindal and Cuthbert Mayne', pp. 140–1.

32. BL MS Cotton Vitellius C. VII, fo. 5r, CR, p. 511; Charles W. Foster, ed., *Lincoln Episcopal Records, in the Time of Thomas Cooper, Bishop of Lincoln 1571 to 1584* (Canterbury and York Society, London, 1913), p. 140.

33. BLO MS Ashmole 1789, fo. 52r, *Memorials*, sig. Δ 3v.

34. John Foxe, *Actes and Monuments* (1570), pp. 1,979, 1,988, 1,871, cf. *idem* (1576), pp. 1,744, 1,462, printing Foxe's personal changes in BL MS Harley 419, fo. 133r–v.

35. BLO MS Ashmole 1789, fo. 52v, cf. *Memorials*, sig. Δ 4v.

36. *Actes and Monuments* (1576), pp. 1,704, 1,711, 1,720–1.

37. Ibid., pp. 1,744–5.

38. Elizabeth Evenden, *Patents, Pictures and Patronage: John Day and the Tudor Book Trade* (Aldershot and Burlington, VT, 2008), pp. 148–51.

39. See the next chapter.

40. BLO MS Ashmole 1789, fos. 51v–52r, *Memorials* sig. Δ 2v–4r, G4r.

41. R&W, 251, Roberts and Watson, *Catalogue*, p. 85.

42. Arthur J. Slavin, 'Daniel Rogers in Copenhagen, 1588: Mission and Memory', in Malcolm R. Thorp and Arthur J. Slavin, eds, *Politics, Religion and Diplomacy in Early Modern Europe*, in *Sixteenth-Century Essays and Studies*, vol. 27 (Kirksville, MO, 1994), pp. 245–66, at pp. 256–7; Kervyn de Lettenhove, *Relations politiques*, ix, p. 243.

43. Hessels, ed., *Ortelius epistolae*, pp. 157–60. Ortelius visited Dee at Mortlake on 12 March 1577 (BLO MS Ashmole 487, 12 March 1577); Taylor, 'A Letter dated 1577 from Mercator to John Dee', p. 61.

44. BL MS Cotton Galba C. VI, fo. 45v.

45. Ibid., fos. 52r–56v, and see *CSP Foreign 1575–7*, pp. 582–5.

46. Kervyn de Lettenhove, *Relations politiques*, ix, pp. 344–5; BL MS Cotton Galba C. V, fos. 372r–375v; Kervyn de Lettenhove, *Relations politiques*, vi, pp. 764–78; *Certein letters*, sig. b7r; 'galleys and brigantines' could patrol between the Dutch islands (John Hastings to Leicester and Burghley, 26 December 1575, *CSP Foreign, Elizabeth, 1575–7*, pp. 211–12).

47. BLO MS Ashmole 487, 19 June 1577, 'Mr Thomas Besbich told me his father is one of the cooks of the Court'.

48. *Memorials*, pp. 4, 35, 37–8, cf. TNA SP 12/118/12.I, in Quinn, *Enterprises of Sir Humphrey Gilbert*, p. 174.

49. BL MS Cotton Vitellius C. VII, fo. 92v.

50. *Memorials*, pp. 43–50, sigs. F2r–G1v; BLO MS Ashmole 487, 26 May 1577.

51. Kervyn de Lettenhove, *Relations politiques*, ix, pp. 459–61; HMC, *Salisbury*, ii, pp. 156–9.

52. *APC*, ix, p. 390; Lake, 'Edmund Grindal and Cuthbert Mayne', pp. 139–41.

53. HEHL MS EL 6236; Bossy, 'English Catholics and the French Marriage', pp. 2–16.

54. BLO MS Ashmole 487, August 1577; *Memorials*, sig. e4r. The undateable SP 12/288/57 emphasised Elizabeth's genealogical claims to much of Huguenot France, the Netherlands, Castile and Leon. Wallace T. MacCaffrey, *Queen Elizabeth and the Making of Policy, 1572–1588* (Princeton, 1981), p. 209; R.B. Wernham, *The Making of English Foreign Policy, 1558–1603* (Berkeley, 1980), p. 52; F.G. Oosterhoff, *Leicester and the Netherlands, 1586–1587* (Utrecht, 1988), pp. 29–34.

55. BL MS Harley 249, fo. 95v, effectively summarising the title page illustration of *Memorials*.

56. George Gascoigne, *The princely pleasures at the courte at Kenelworth* (London, 1576), in Nichols, *The Progresses of Queen Elizabeth*, i, pp. 485–523; Van Es, *Spenser's Forms of History*, pp. 153–60; Susan Frye, *Elizabeth I: The Competition for Representation* (Oxford, 1993), pp. 56–96.

57. Roy Strong and J.A. Van Dorsten, *Leicester's Triumph* (Leiden and London, 1964), pp. 47–8, 50–9; Richard Tuck, *Philosophy and Government 1572–1651* (Cambridge, 1993), pp. 157, 261.

58. David Scott, 'William Patten and the Authorship of "Robert Laneham's letter" (1575)', *English Literary Renaissance*, 7 (1977), pp. 297–306; Jane E.A. Dawson, 'William Cecil and the British Dimension of Early Elizabethan Foreign Policy', *History*, 74 (1989), pp. 196–216; HMC, *Salisbury*, viii, no. 52.

59. *Memorials*, p. 58; BL MS Cotton Vitellius C. VII, fos. 16r–17r, 13r–v; BL MS Add. 59681, pp. 31–7, 39, in MacMillan and Abeles, *John Dee: The Limits of the British Empire*, pp. 57–64, 65.

60. BL MS Add. 59681, pp. 25–37; MacMillan and Abeles, *John Dee: The Limits of the British Empire*, p. 52; BL MS Harley 249, fo. 95v.

61. *Memorials*, p. 62 and sig. e 4v.

62. BL MS Cotton Galba C. VI, ii, fo. 247r–v, and BL MS Harley 4943, fos. 428r–429r; Geoffrey Parker, *The Grand Strategy of Philip II* (New Haven and London, 1998), pp. 102–7.

63. BL MS Cotton Galba C. V, fos. 372r–375v, on the attractions of the Protestant league.

Chapter 12: Defending Elizabeth against the Dark Arts

1. Kervyn de Lettenhove, *Relations politiques*, ix, pp. 487–91.

2. William Fleetwood to Burghley, first Sunday after Michaelmas 1577, in Thomas Wright, *Queen Elizabeth and her Times*, 2 vols (London, 1838), ii, p. 69; Edward Cheke to Davison, 19 September 1577, TNA SP 15/25/35.

3. BL MS Harley 286, fos. 31r–32r, Burghley's memorandum of 15 September 1577.

4. John Bossy, 'English Catholics and the French Marriage', pp. 2–16; *Leicester's Commonwealth*, ed. Peck, pp. 15–18; Thomas M. McCoog, 'The English Jesuit Mission and the French Match', pp. 185–213.

5. *Leicester's Commonwealth*, ed. Peck, p. 116.

6. BLO MS Ashmole 487, August 1579, the Duke's secret visit (16–26 August), February 1580, Sir Edward Stafford's return from delivering the marriage treaty to Anjou (16 February),

February 1581, the arrival of Anjou's ambassadors (23 February), July 1581, the quarrel between Leicester and the Earl of Sussex over the match (12 July), and November 1581, Anjou's removal with Elizabeth to Whitehall (16 November – *sic* for 1 November), where they exchanged rings.

7. Lake, 'Edmund Grindal and Cuthbert Mayne', pp. 140–2.

8. TNA SP 12/118/12.I, in Quinn, *Enterprises of Sir Humphrey Gilbert*, p. 174.

9. *Remains of Edmund Grindal*, ed. Nicholson, pp. 392–5.

10. BL MS Cotton Vitellius C. VII, fo. 7r, referring to 22, 24 and 28 November 1577 in BLO MS Ashmole 487, November 1577, with a sketch of the comet blazing across the top margin.

11. Henry Howard, *A defensative against the poyson of supposed prophecies* (London, 1584), sigs. E4v–F1r, V4r, sig. X1v; Thomas Twyne, *A view of certain wonderful effects, of late days come to passe* (London, 1577), sigs. B2r–v, B4v, C4r. *Of the crinitall starre, which appeareth this October and November 1580* (London, 1580).

12. CR, pp. 508, 516; TNA PROB 11/61, fos. 309v–310r; BLO MS Ashmole 487, July 1579.

13. MacMillan, 'John Dee and the Limits of the British Empire', pp. 17–18; contrast MacMillan, *Sovereignty and Possession*, pp. 63, 56–7, on Frobisher and Gilbert.

14. BLO MS Ashmole 487, 5 August 1578. Quinn, *Enterprises of Sir Humphrey Gilbert*, pp. 194–9.

15. *Historie Del S.D. Fernando Colombo*, sig. L5v; Sherman 'John Dee's Columbian Encounter', p. 136; Ramusio, *Navigationi et Viaggi*, vol. 3, fos. 27r, 84v; BL MS Add. 59681, pp. 68–72, in MacMillan and Abeles, *John Dee: The Limits of the British Empire*, pp. 93–7.

16. Ibid., p. 24; BL MS Add. 59681, pp. 31–7, 39, in MacMillan and Abeles, *John Dee: The Limits of the British Empire*, pp. 57–64, 65.

17. CR, p. 526; Leicester to Walsingham, 29 August 1578, Kervyn de Lettenhove, *Relations politiques*, x, pp. 772–3, in *CSP Foreign, 1578–9*, pp. 158–9; Elizabeth to Cobham and Walsingham, Bury St Edmunds, 9 Aug. 1578, BL MS Cotton Galba C. VI, ii, fo. 226v; Burghley to Cobham and Walsingham, same date and place, Kervyn de Lettenhove, *Relations politiques*, x, p. 710, and Wilson to Walsingham, Thetford, 9 Aug. 1578, ibid., pp. 710–11.

18. Leicester to Walsingham, 29 August 1578, Kervyn de Lettenhove, *Relations politiques*, x, pp. 772–3, and *CSP Foreign, Elizabeth, 1578–9*, p. 159; Walsingham to Leicester, Louvain, 28 August 1578, BL MS Cotton Galba C. VI, ii, fo. 93r; Burghley to Walsingham, 31 August 1578, *CSP Foreign, Elizabeth, 1578–9*, p. 164.

19. P. Collinson, 'Pulling the Strings: Religion and Politics in the Progress of 1578', in Jayne Elisabeth Archer, Elizabeth Goldring, and Sarah Knight, eds, *The Progresses, Pageants and Entertainments of Queen Elizabeth I* (Oxford, 2007), pp. 122–41, at p. 124; Lake, 'Edmund Grindal and Cuthbert Mayne', pp. 148–9.

20. Ibid., p. 149; Collinson, 'Pulling the Strings', pp. 132–3.

21. BLO MS Ashmole 487, 15 and 23 August 1578; Wilson to Walsingham, Norwich, 18 August 1578, in Kervyn de Lettenhove, *Relations politiques*, x, p. 742; Doran, *Monarchy and Matrimony* (London, 1996), pp. 150–2.

22. Wilson to Walsingham, Norwich, 18 August 1578, Kervyn de Lettenhove, *Relations politiques*, x, p. 742; ibid., pp. 772–3, Leicester to Walsingham, 29 August 1578 (*CSP Foreign, Elizabeth, 1578–9*, pp. 158–9).

23. *APC*, x, p. 309; *Calendar of Letters and State Papers (Simancas)*, ii, p. 611.

24. *APC*, x, p. 309; CR, pp. 521–2.

25. *Calendar of Letters and State Papers (Simancas)*, ii, p. 611; CR, pp. 521–2; see e.g. BL MS Sloane 3846, fos. 95r, 98r for spells defending against witchcraft.

26. *APC*, x, pp. 310–13; Collinson, 'Pulling the Strings', pp. 132–3; Lake, 'Edmund Grindal and Cuthbert Mayne', p. 149; BLO MS Ashmole 487, 22 August 1578.

27. TNA SP 15/25/113, Heneage to Walsingham, 2 September; Collinson, 'Pulling the Strings', pp. 133–5.
28. *APC*, x, p. 309.
29. TNA SP 12/140/37.
30. *APC*, x, p. 322; TNA SP 12/140/37; *Calendar of Letters and State Papers (Simancas)*, ii, p. 611; Collinson, 'Pulling the Strings', p. 141.
31. TNA SP 12/131/43; *APC*, x, pp. 322–8 ; ibid., xii, p. 162.
32. Hatfield House MSS CP 202/148, 161/57, 161/59.
33. *CR*, p. 522.
34. Ibid., p. 522; London Metropolitan Archives, Court of Aldermen, Repertory 19, 28 September and 9 October 1578.
35. Ibid., fos. 376r–378v.
36. Ibid., fos. 379r–391v.
37. BLO MS Ashmole 487, 8 and 13 October 1578.
38. TNA SP 12/126/7; Camden, *Annals*, pp. 104, 146–7.
39. TNA SP 12/126/7, Privy Council to Burghley, 12 October 1578; BL MS Lansdowne 25, fos. 146r–147r; Catholic Record Society, *Miscellanea III* (London, 1906), pp. 7–8; [R. Verstegan], *The Copy of a Letter lately written by a Spanishe gentleman to his friend in England* (Antwerp, J. Trognesius, 1589), sig. A4r–v.
40. Camden, *Annals*, p. 205; Sir Harris Nicolas, *Memoirs of the Life and Times of Sir Christopher Hatton* (London, 1847), pp. 91–4.
41. *CSP Foreign, Elizabeth, 1572–4*, p. 493, no. 1398.
42. TNA SP 12/126/40, Leicester to Burghley, 17 October 1578.
43. *APC*, x, pp. 373, 382; BL MS Harley 286, fo. 37r, Thomas Wilson to Leicester and Warwick, 13 November 1578.
44. Ibid., fo. 37r.
45. BLO MS Ashmole 487, 25 and 29 October 1578; Longleat House MS DU/II, fo. 197r.
46. BLO MS Ashmole 487, 28 October 1578, 4 November; BL MS Cotton Vitellius C. VII, fo. 7v; *CSP Foreign, Elizabeth, 1572–4*, p. 493, no. 1398; cf. BL MS Lansdowne 27, fos. 90r–91v, Dr Antonio Fenot's advice; BLO MS Ashmole 1447, Pt. VII, p. 48; Pamela H. Smith, 'Alchemy as a Language of Mediation at the Habsburg Court', *Isis*, 85, 1 (March 1994), pp. 1–25 at p. 2.
47. BLO MS Ashmole 487, 4 January 1579.
48. [Verstegan], *The Copy of a Letter*, p. 7; *Stationers' Register*, ed. E. Arber, 5 vols. (London, 1875–94), ii, pp. 339–40.
49. J. Bodin, *De la Demonomanie des sorciers* (1580), sigs. E4v, Gg1r.
50. *APC*, xi, p. 22; Kieckhefer, *Forbidden Rites*, p. 87, on the method.
51. [Verstegan], *The Copy of a Letter*, p. 7; TNA SP 12/178/74, SP 12/195/32.
52. *APC*, xi, pp. 102–3; Catholic Record Society, *Miscellanea III*, pp. 6–9; TNA SP 12/131/43; *APC*, xi, p. 212.
53. TNA SP 12/126/10; Doran, *Monarchy and Matrimony*, pp. 161–2; TNA SP 12/276/102; Bossy, 'English Catholics', pp. 2–16; McCoog, 'The English Jesuit Mission', pp. 185–213.
54. [Verstegan], *The Copy of a Letter*, p. 7; TNA SP 12/276/102, misdated 1600 in the *Calendar of State Papers Domestic* but clearly connected to 1578; Bossy, 'English Catholics', pp. 2–16, and McCoog, 'The English Jesuit Mission', pp. 185–213; TNA SP 12/186/91, 92.
55. *Holinshed's Chronicles* (London, 1587), pp. 1,314–15.
56. BLO MS Ashmole 487, 22 June 1579.

Chapter 13: 'The winking eye of Achitophel'

1. TNA SP 12/178/74, SP 12/179/62, SP 12/195/30, 32, SP 12/202/54; Catholic Record Society, *Miscellanea III*, pp. 8–27, esp. p. 27. Ironically, Leicester released Prestall in July 1588, perhaps recognising his magical powers had potential against the Armada and his malaria (TNA SP 12/195/30, 32).

2. Claire Cross, *The Puritan Earl: The Life of Henry Hastings, Third Earl of Huntingdon 1536–1595* (London, 1966), pp. 31, 34–5, 60.

3. CR, p. 517.

4. BL MS Lansdowne 31, fo. 30r–v.

5. Ibid., fo. 31r.

6. BL MS Lansdowne 99, fos. 244r–245v.

7. See above, pp. 61–2.

8. BL MS Lansdowne 99, fo. 245r.

9. Ibid., fo. 248r; BLO MS Ashmole 487, October 1580.

10. Doran, *Monarchy and Matrimony*, pp. 174–8; BL MS Cotton Vitellius C. VII, fo. 6r, CR, pp. 517–18; BL MS Lansdowne 94, fo. 120r–v; *CSP Spanish, iii, 1580–6*, p. 587.

11. BL MS Lansdowne 99, fo. 247v.

12. CR, pp. 517–18.

13. CR, pp. 517–18; BLO MS Ashmole 487, 2 November 1580.

14. BL MS Lansdowne 94, fos. 47r–51v; *A declaration of the causes mooving the Queene to give aide to the oppressed in the Lowe Countries* (London, 1585).

15. BL MS Lansdowne 94, fos. 51r, 82r.

16. TNA SP 15/31/35, Dee to Richard Young, Bremen, 20 August 1589.

17. BL MS Lansdowne 99, fo. 245r; Clifford Dobb, 'London's Prisons', *Shakespeare Survey*, 17 (1964), pp. 87–100.

18. BL MS Lansdowne 30, fos. 42r and 44r.

19. Susan Doran, *England and Europe in the Sixteenth Century* (London, 1999), pp. 73–4, 93–5; Doran, *Monarchy and Matrimony*, pp. 189–90; BL MS Harley 249, fo. 95v.

20. Doran, *Monarchy and Matrimony*, pp. 189–90; BL MS Harley 1582, fos. 38r–41r; Eva G. R. Taylor, ed., *The Troublesome Voyage of Captain Edward Fenton* (London, 1959), and Elizabeth S. Donno, *An Elizabethan in 1582: The Diary of Richard Madox, Fellow of All Souls* (London, 1976); W. Noel Sainsbury, ed., *Calendar of State Papers, Colonial Series, East Indies, China and Japan, 1513–1616* (London, 1862), pp. 67–92.

21. BLO MS Ashmole 487, July 1582.

22. James McDermott, 'Peckham, Sir George (d. 1608)', *ODNB*, Oxford University Press, September 2004; online edn, January 2008 [http://www.oxforddnb.com/view/article/21743].

23. George Peckham, *True reporte, of the late discoveries and possession* (London, 1583), sigs. D4r–E1r.

24. BLO MS Ashmole 487, June 1578, not 'King Maty' as in *Diary*, ed. Halliwell, p. 4; R. Hakluyt, *Divers Voyages touching the discoverie of America* (London, 1582), sig. ¶ 1r; R. Hakluyt, *A Particuler Discourse . . . Known as the Discourse of Western Planting* [1584], eds. D.B. Quinn and A.M. Quinn (London, 1993), pp. 72–6.

25. Hakluyt, *Principall Navigations* (1589), pp. 243–9, 485; BL MS Cotton Vitellius C. VII, fos. 264v–269v, printed in E.G.R. Taylor, 'A Letter dated 1577 from Mercator to John Dee', *Imago Mundi*, 13 (1956), pp. 56–68; MacMillan and Abeles, *John Dee: The Limits of the British Empire*, pp. 85–7.

26. T. Blundeville, *A Briefe Description of Universall Mappes and Cardes* (London, 1589), sig. C3r.

27. BLO MS Ashmole 488, 4 April 1594. Dee wrote to Abbot 'abowt my Arabike boke, Soyga'.

28. George Abbot, *A Briefe Description of the whole worlde* (London, 1605), sig. Q1r–v; Kenneth Fincham, 'Abbot, George (1562–1633)', *ODNB*, Oxford University Press, September 2004; online edn, January 2008 [http://www.oxforddnb.com/view/article/4]; Rivkah Zim, 'Sackville, Thomas, first Baron Buckhurst and first earl of Dorset (c.1536–1608)', *ODNB*, Oxford University Press, Sept. 2004; online edn, May 2008 [http://www.oxforddnb.com/view/article/24450].

29. BLO MS Ashmole 487, May 1580; BL MS Cotton Vitellius C. VII, fos. 65v, 68r; BL MS Cotton Otho VIII, fo. 30, and BL MS Lansdowne 122, fo. 30r–v, Hakluyt, *Principall Navigations* (1589), pp. 455, 459; Burghley's Ortelius atlas (B/Ortelius) at Hatfield (Skelton and Summerson, *A Description of Maps ... made by William Cecil*); Taylor, ed., *A Regiment for the Sea*, pp. 415–33.

30. BL MS Cotton Augustus I.i.1; BL MS Lansdowne 30, fo. 10r.

31. Now in the Free Library of Philadelphia; Sherman, 'Putting the British Seas on the Map', pp. 1–10.

Chapter 14: 'Misbegotten time': Reforming the Calendar

1. BLO MS Ashmole 487, June 1579, May 1581, March 1582, May 1582; BL MS Sloane 3188, fos. 9r, 10v, 12r, 51r, 102v–103r; TNA SP 81/7, fos. 140, 143–4r, SP 80/1, fo. 150v; Roberts and Watson, *Catalogue*, p. 85.

2. Robert Poole, *Time's Alteration: Calendar Reform in Early Modern England* (London, 1998), pp. 38–40.

3. BLO MS Ashmole 487, November–December 1582.

4. David Cressy, 'God's Time, Rome's Time, and the Calendar of the English Protestant Regime', *Viator: Medieval and Renaissance Studies*, 34 (2003), pp. 392–406.

5. BL MS Sloane 3188, fo. 47v; CR, p. 527; Kieckhefer, *Forbidden Rites*, pp. 75–8, gives similar examples.

6. BL MS Sloane 3188, fos. 51r–v.

7. BLO MS Ashmole 487, 24 November 1582. Halliwell, *Diary*, pp. 17–18, erroneously has 'burn my books'. BL MS Sloane 3188 records no angelic revelations from late November 1582 to 23 March 1583.

8. Probably Nicholaus Simius, *Ephemerides ab anno 1554 in annum 1568* (Venice, 1554), R&W, 637, bound with Sebastian Munster's *Horologiographia* (Basle, 1533), R&W, 636.

9. CR, pp. 501, 529–31; Dee, *Parallaticae Commentationis Praxeosque Nucleus quidam* (London, 1573), with T. Digges, *Alae seu scalae mathematicae* (London, 1573).

10. *Gnomonices, libri octo, in quibus non solum horologiorum solarium, sed aliarum quoque rerum, quae ex gnomonis umbra cognosci possunt, descriptiones Geometrice demonstrantur* (Rome, 1581), R&W, 1798. Not found. Dee also owned Clavius's *Commentary on Euclid* (Rome, 1574), R&W, 1882. Not found.

11. BLO MS Ashmole 487, 8 August 1579.

12. He quoted Paul of Middelburg, *De rectae paschae celebratione* (1513), R&W, 133; Johannes Stofler, *Calendarium Romanum* (1518), R&W, 208; Petrus Pittati, *Calendarium* (Venice, 1537), R&W, 380; Lucae Lossius, *Calendarium syllabicum* (Wittenberg, 1551), R&W, 694; Petrus Pittati, *Compendium de Romani Calendarii instauratione* (Verona, 1560), R&W, 1862; ps. Roger Bacon, 'Calendarium', Corpus Christi College, Oxford, MS 221, R&W, M158 (a), missing.

13. *Calendarium Gregorianum perpetuum* (Venice, 1582), R&W, 1205, not found. Dee also owned an undated book from Paris, *De correctione calendarii Romani propositiones xiii collectae ex*

multis disputationibus habilis per deputatos ad hoc specialiter, R&W, 1900, not found; *CSP Foreign, xvi, 1582*, p. 435, n. 441, Cobham to Walsingham 4 November 1582. Walsingham borrowed the *Calendarium* for Burghley on 18 January 1583 (BLO MS Corpus Christi College, Oxford, 254, fo. 182r).

14. BLO MS Ashmole 487, 26 February 1582; BLO MS Ashmole 1789, pp. 1–62, at p. 39. Walsingham's letter 18 January 1583 (BLO MS Corpus Christi College, Oxford [CCCO], 254, fo. 182r).

15. BLO MS Ashmole 1789, pp. 1–32, 39, 59, geocentric illustrations. Dee owned at least two copies of Copernicus's *De revolutionibus* (Nuremberg, 1543), R&W, 220, perhaps for teaching, and George Joachim Rheticus's *Narratio prima de libris revolutionum Copernici* (Basle, 1541), R&W, 768; none extant.

16. BLO MS Ashmole 1789, pp. 40–1, 61–2, 44–5.

17. Ibid., pp. 63–4.

18. Ibid., pp. 16, 50–6, 60. Dee did not necessarily conceive this religion as Protestant, despite Poole's claims (*Time's Alteration*, pp. 60, 63).

19. BLO MS Ashmole 1789, p. 49.

20. *MP*, sig. B2r–v.

21. BLO MS Ashmole 1789, p. 11.

22. Even in Stephen Alford, *Burghley: William Cecil at the Court of Elizabeth I* (New Haven and London, 2008).

23. BLO MS Don. c. 52, fo. 1r; BL MS Add. 14291, fo. 174r.

24. BLO MS Corpus Christi College, Oxford, 254, fo. 161r; BL MS Lansdowne 39, fo. 28r.

25. Margaret E. Aston, 'The Fiery Trigon Conjunction: An Elizabethan Astrological Prediction', *Isis*, 61 (1970), pp. 159–87, at pp. 160–2.

26. Leowitz, *De coniunctionibus magnis insignioribus superiorum planetarum*, Cambridge University Library shelf mark R* 5 21(E), bought 1564, and sig. L3v; Evans, *Rudolf II and his World*, p. 221; James Sandford, 'Epistle Dedicatorie', in *Houres of Recreation*, (London, 1576), sigs. A5v–A6r.

27. BL MS Add. 36674, fo. 176v; Poole, *Time's Alteration*, p. 48 and n. 15, could not explain the November deadline.

28. R. Harvey, *An astrological discourse upon the great and notable coniunction of the two superiour planets, Saturne and Jupiter* (London, 1583), STC 12909.7, pp. 5, 36, 19, 38, acknowledging Dee's tuition at sig. A3r.

29. J. Harvey, *An astrological addition or supplement to be annexed to the late discourse upon the great coniunction* (London, 1583), sigs. C5r–v, D3v, E5v. Harvey, *A discoursive probleme concerning prophecies against the terrible threatenings, and menaces, peremptorily denounced, against the kingdoms, and states of the world* (London, 1588), pp. 99–102, used Dee's recalculation of Trithemius's age of Anael.

30. BLO MS Ashmole 487, 23–24 January 1583; 'Hemisphaerii Borealis Geographica atque Hydrographica descriptio', listed in CR, p. 526.

31. TNA SP 15/28 Part I/53.

32. TNA SP 15/28 Part I/54.

33. BLO MS Ashmole 487, 11 February 1583; definition from Julius Firmicus, *Ad Mavortium Lollianum Astronomicon lib. VIII. per N. Prucknerum … ab innumeris mendis vindicati* (Basle, 1533), R&W, 251; Lucas Gauricus, *De nativitatibus* (Venice, 1551), ch. 5, R&W, 539; Girolamo Cardano, *Libelli quinque*, Bk. 5, astrological charts nos. 22, 23, 24, 28, 29, 41, R&W, 440.

34. BL MS Lansdowne 39, fo. 28r–v. Burghley's detailed notes, BL MS Lansdowne 109, fo. 65r, others Lansdowne 103, fos. 29r–37r.

35. Ibid., fo. 28r–v, Dee's petition BLO MS CCCO 254, fo. 161r.

36. Ibid., fo. 184r–v.

37. Ibid., fo. 182r; CR, p. 523.

38. BLO MS CCCO 254, fo. 182r; BL MS Sloane 3188, fo. 67v.

39. BLO MS Ashmole 487, 18 April 1583; TNA C 47/34/6, E 164/36.

40. BL MS Sloane 3188, fos. 65r, 66v, cf. TNA SP 15/28 Part I/54.

41. BL MS Sloane 3188, fo. 65r.

42. Poole, Time's Alteration, p. 53; Burghley, The Execution of Justice in England for maintenaunce of publique and Christian peace (London, 1583), sigs. C4r–v, D1r, B1r, A3v.

43. Ibid., sigs. D4v, D2v.

44. Question in Poole, Time's Alteration, pp. 54, 52.

45. Patrick Collinson, 'Elizabeth I (1533–1603)', ODNB, also published as Patrick Collinson, Elizabeth I (Oxford, 2007).

46. BL MS Add. 32092, fo. 26r, printed from BL MS Add. 14291, fo. 174r in The Gentleman's Magazine, xxxvi (1851), p. 453.

47. Poole, Time's Alteration, p. 52, dates TNA SP 12/160/28 28 April, but 'April' was the nineteenth-century Record Office speculation, as in another copy, SP 12/145, pp. 116–18.

48. BL MS Add. 32092, fo. 26r, printed from BL MS Add. 14291, fo. 174r, in The Gentleman's Magazine, p. 453.

49. Poole, Time's Alteration, p. 52, claims the proclamation countered their objections. It merely asserts their agreement and ignores their criticisms.

50. BL MS Add. 32092, fo. 26r–v, printed from BL MS Add. 14291, fo. 174r–v, in The Gentleman's Magazine, pp. 453–4.

51. BL MS Add. 32092, fo. 28r, printed from BL MS Add. 14291, fo. 176r, in The Gentleman's Magazine, p. 454.

52. Collinson, Grindal, pp. 236–46; Peter Lake, ' "The Monarchical Republic of Queen Elizabeth I" (and the Fall of Archbishop Grindal) Revisited', in John F. McDiarmid, ed., The Monarchical Republic of Early Modern England: Essays in Response to Patrick Collinson (Aldershot, 2007), pp. 129–47; Nicholson, ed., Remains of Edmund Grindal, p. 387.

53. BL MS Lansdowne 39, fo. 28r–v.

54. Thomas Cooper, Cooper's Chronicle (London, 1560, 1565).

55. Cooper, Certaine sermons vvherin is contained the defense of the gospell nowe preached (London, 1580), pp. 47, 80.

56. C.W. Foster, ed., Lincoln Episcopal Records in the Time of Thomas Cooper, S.T.P. (Canterbury and York Society, vol. 11, Lincoln, 1912), pp. 201, 140.

57. T[homas] C[ooper], An admonition to the people of England wherein are answered, not onely the slaunderous vntruethes, reprochfully vttered by Martin the libeler (London, 1589), pp. 209, 73.

58. TNA SP 12/16/49; Hughes and Larkin, Tudor Royal Proclamations, ii, p. 126, Article 32 of the 'Injunctions for Religion'; CR, p. 511.

59. CR, pp. 510–12; BLO MS Ashmole 487, 1580–1. In November 1579 he turned down Lord Clinton's offer of another Lincolnshire living for Long Leadenham (ibid.); ibid., July 1581.

60. Ibid., June 1582; Collinson, Grindal, pp. 249–50.

61. CR, pp. 511–12.

62. Foster, ed., Lincoln Episcopal Records, pp. 216, 201 n. 68.

63. CR, p. 512. He also lost Upton-upon-Severn during his time in Europe.

64. Foster, ed., Lincoln Episcopal Records, pp. 216, 201 n. 68. Lange first appears in Leadenham in 1570, and held the living until his death in March 1607 (Lincolnshire Archives Office, Leadenham Parish Register 1/1).

65. CR, p. 512.
66. Nicholson, ed., *Remains of Edmund Grindal*, pp. 226–7.
67. See above, pp. 64–6, and *The Gentleman's Magazine*, xxxvi (1851), pp. 453–4.
68. BL MS Add. 32092, fos. 29–33, printed from BL MS Add. 14291, fos. 175r–178v, in *The Gentleman's Magazine*, xxxvi (1851), pp. 456–8.
69. *Journal of the House of Lords*, ii, pp. 99–102.
70. Collinson, *Grindal*, pp. 276–8.
71. BL MS Sloane 3188, fos. 67r–v, 79v.
72. Ibid., fo. 91r, 20 April 1583.
73. 'quod defertur non aufertur', BLO MS Ashmole 487, 18 April 1583; BL MS Sloane 3188, fo. 89r.
74. Though Raleigh obtained the 'royalties' for himself, Gilbert and Davis by early 1584 (TNA SP 15/28/55).
75. See above, p. 89, on the mining lease. BLO MS Ashmole 487, 13 May 1583; BL MS Sloane 3188, fos. 90v, 106v.
76. Casaubon, *True Relation*, pp. 27–8.
77. John Foxe, *Actes and Monuments* (London, 1583), pp. 1,577–8, 1,5817.

Chapter 15: Called to a King's Office: Laski and the Second Coming

1. BLO MS Ashmole 487, 18 March 1583.
2. W.A. Bradley, ed., *The Correspondence of Sidney and Languet* (Boston, 1912), pp. 7, 13.
3. Casaubon, *True Relation*, p. 1.
4. *CSP Spain (Simancas), iii, 1580–6* (London, 1896), p. 463, Mendoza to Philip II, 22 April 1583. On the apocalypse, see above, pp. 151–2.
5. BL MS Lansdowne 35, fo. 191r; Konstanty Zantuan, 'Olbracht Laski in Elizabethan England: An Episode in the History of Culture', *The Polish Review*, 13, 4 (1968), pp. 5, 13.
6. Hatton to Burghley in Nicolas, *Memoirs of Hatton*, pp. 326–7; *CSP Foreign, January–June 1583* (London, 1913), p. 667; *CSP Foreign, July 1583–July 1584* (London, 1914), p. 7; Norman Davies, *God's Playground: A History of Poland. Vol. 1: The Origins to 1795* (Oxford, 1981), p. 425.
7. Burghley to Hatton in Nicolas, *Memoirs of Hatton*, p. 325.
8. John Ferne, *The Blazon of Gentrie: devided into two parts. The first named the Glorie of Generositie. The second, Lacyes Nobilitie* (London, 1586), sig. Aa3r; *CSP Venetian*, viii, pp. 59–60.
9. BL MS Lansdowne 35, fo. 191r; *CSP Venetian*, viii, p. 59; *Holinshed's Chronicles* (1587), pp. 1,354–5; Camden, *Annals* (1635), p. 253.
10. Thomas Birch, *Memoirs of the Reign of Queen Elizabeth I* (London, 1754), pp. 30–1.
11. BL MS Sloane 3188, fos. 103v, 107r; Zantuan, 'Olbracht Laski', p. 5.
12. Casaubon, *True Relation*, p. 1.
13. *CSP Spanish (Simancas), iii, 1580–6*, p. 463, no. 331 and n. 3.
14. *CSP Foreign, January–June 1583*, p. 341, Cobham to Walsingham, Paris, 11 May 1583.
15. *CSP Foreign, 1578*, p. 604, 1 March 1578; *CSP Spanish (Simancas), iii, 1580–6*, pp. 379–82, Mendoza to Philip, 29 June 1582; ibid., no. 275, Mendoza to Philip, 11 July 1582.
16. *CSP Spanish (Simancas), iii, 1580–6*, p. 463, no. 331 and n. 3; *CSP Foreign, January–July 1583*, p. 187, Cobham to Walsingham, 11 March 1583.
17. BLO MS Ashmole 487, 19 May 1583; BL MS Add. 15891 fo. 112r, in Nicolas, *Memoirs of Hatton*, pp. 326, 331–2.

18. *CSP Spanish (Simancas), iii, 1580–6*, p. 474, Mendoza to Juan de Idiaquez, 5 June 1583; John Bossy, *Giordano Bruno and the Embassy Affair* (New Haven and London, 1991), pp. 22–5.

19. *CSP Spanish (Simancas), iii, 1580–6*, p. 463, no. 331 and n. 3; BL MS Cotton Appendix XLVI, fo. 107v; Casaubon, *True Relation*, pp. 2–3, BL MS Cotton Vitellius C. VII, fo. 9v, and BL MS Cotton Appendix XLVI, fos. 2v–3v, angelic conversations in 'Liber sexti misteriorum (et sancti) [-] novalisque 1583', dating from the summer onwards; Casaubon, *True Relation*, p. 1; CR, p. 531.

20. Casaubon, *True Relation*, p. 4.

21. *Holinshed's Chronicles* (1587), pp. 1,354–5; Anthony Wood, *The History and Antiquities of the University of Oxford*, 2 vols. (Oxford, 1792–6), ii, pp. 215–18; BLO MS Ashmole 487, 15 June 1583; Bossy, *Embassy Affair*, pp. 22–3, 99.

22. Casaubon, *True Relation*, p. 17.

23. BL MS Cotton Appendix XLVI, fos. 12v–13r, the crown not in Casaubon, *True Relation*, p. 17.

24. Robert Parsons, *A briefe apologie, or defence of the Catholike ecclesiastical hierarchie, & subordination in England* (Antwerp, 1601), sig. +4r; Hatfield House, MS CP 140/5, fo. 51r; C. Talbot, ed., *Miscellanea: Recusant Records*, Catholic Record Society, vol. 53 (London, 1961), pp. 207–8; *Holinshed's Chronicles* (1587), pp. 1,324–5.

25. BLO MS Ashmole 487, September 1582.

26. BL MS Sloane 3188, fo. 77v; Casaubon, *True Relation*, p. 17; BLO MS Ashmole 421, fo. 191, William Lilly's 'History of his Life and Times'.

27. TNA C3/218/46.

28. Casaubon, *True Relation*, p. 21.

29. Thomas Birch, *Memoirs of Queen Elizabeth*, i, pp. 30–1; Camden, *Annals* (1635), p. 253; *CSP Venetian*, viii, pp. 59–60, 92.

30. Ferne, *The Blazon of Gentrie*, sig. A4v; CR, p. 531.

31. Davies, *God's Playground*, p. 421.

32. Casaubon, *True Relation*, p. 31. None found. The Stationers' Register ceased 15 June to 17 July 1583.

33. Ferne, *The Blazon of Gentrie*, sigs. A2v, A4v, Kk1r.

34. Casaubon, *True Relation*, pp. 22–3.

35. *CSP Spanish*, iii, p. 504.

36. Bossy, *Embassy Affair*, pp. 26–34, 101–4; Thomas Watson, dedication to Laski before 'Artificiosæ memoriæ libellus' (1583), BL MS Sloane 3731; Howard, *Defensative*, sig. E3r, and see above, p. 129.

37. Casaubon, *True Relation*, p. 26.

38. Ibid., p. 28, 2 July 1583; *CSP Foreign, July 1583–July 1584*, p. 6.

39. Casaubon, *True Relation*, pp. 28–9.

40. Ibid., p. 31.

41. BLO MS Ashmole 487, 30 July 1583. Halliwell, *Diary*, p. 21, and Fenton, *The Diaries of John Dee*, p. 100, garbled Dee's cramped entry here. It reads: 'she shaked her feres [sic] to me', which might mean a wave ('f[ing?]eres') or a fist. One hopes the former. CR, p. 512. Casaubon, *True Relation*, p. 190, on their pensions.

42. CR, p. 511; BLO MS Ashmole 487, 1 August 1583, where Halliwell, *Diary*, p. 21, and Fenton, *Diaries*, p. 100, garbled the MS 'his left hand two lesser fingers bowed in and the top of his thumb hurt'.

43. BLO MS Ashmole 487, 18 August 1583.

44. Deborah Harkness, 'Managing an Experimental Household: The Dees of Mortlake and the Practice of Natural Philosophy', *Isis*, 88 (2) (1997), pp. 247–62.

45. Casaubon, *True Relation*, p. 33; Roberts and Watson, *Catalogue*, pp. 12, 48; TNA REQ 2/77/48, REQ 2/208/41.
46. BLO MS Ashmole 487, 26 March 1591.
47. Thomas Day, *Wonderfull straunge sightes seene in the element, ouer the citie of London and other places on Munday being the seconde day of September* (London, 1583).
48. Roberts and Watson, *Catalogue*, p. 48; Casaubon, *True Relation*, p. 401.
49. Ibid., pp. 33–4; CR, p. 534.
50. BL MS Add. 36674, fos. 58–63; Roberts and Watson, *Catalogue*, pp. 49–52.
51. St. George Kieran Hyland, *A Century of Persecution Under Tudor and Stuart Sovereigns from Contemporary Records* (London, 1920), pp. 381–8, 393, 397; TNA PROB 11/61/fos. 309v–310r; Michael L. Walker, 'The Manor of Batailles and the Family of Saunder in Ewell during the 16th and 17th Centuries', *Surrey Archaeological Collections*, 54 (1955), pp. 76–100.
52. Roberts and Watson, *Catalogue*, p. 13; cf. TNA C3/218/46; Casaubon, *True Relation*, p. 50; BLO MS Ashmole 487, 19 October 1595, 1 March 1598.
53. Casaubon, *True Relation*, p. 228.
54. CR, pp. 533–4.
55. Casaubon, *True Relation*, pp. 38–40, 47, 36.
56. Ibid., pp. 40–3.
57. Ibid., pp. 47–51.
58. Ibid., pp. 59–61.
59. Ibid., pp. 62–5, 69.
60. Ibid., pp. 69–72; BL MS Sloane 3188, fos. 57r, 88r.
61. Evans, *Rudolf II and his World*, pp. 106–7, 212.
62. See http://www.uj.edu.pl/dispatch.jsp?item=uniwersytet/historia/historiatxt.jsp&lang=en.
63. Boethius, 'De consolatione philosophia', Uniwersytet Jagiellonski MS 620, Roberts and Watson, *Catalogue*, p. 117, M47.
64. Ibid., pp. 73–7.
65. Ibid., pp. 77–87; BL MS Sloane 3188, fo. 88v, spirits inadvertently called on 15 April 1583.
66. Casaubon, *True Relation*, pp. 91–2.
67. Ibid., p. 94.
68. Ibid., p. 92.
69. Ibid., p. 114.
70. Ibid., pp. 117–18; Zantuan, 'Olbracht Laski', p. 6.
71. Casaubon, *True Relation*, p. 139; *CSP Foreign, July 1583–July 1584*, pp. 557–8, Arthur de Champernon to Walsingham, Prague, 19/29 June 1584; Sir Richard Baker, *A Chronicle of the Kings of England* (London, 1643), p. 57.
72. Casaubon, *True Relation*, pp. 139–40.
73. Ibid., p. 145.
74. Ibid., p. 160; J. Harvey, *A compendious prognostication* (London, 1584), STC 455, sig. D1r–v.
75. Casaubon, *True Relation*, pp. 168–71.
76. Ibid., pp. 177–85; see above, pp. 146–7.
77. Casaubon, *True Relation*, pp. 185–90.
78. Ibid., pp. 196–212.

Chapter 16: 'Chief Governor of our Philosophical proceedings'

1. Evans, *Rudolf II and his World*, pp. 100–10.
2. BLO MS 488, 8 June 1584.
3. Evans, *Rudolf II and his World*, pp. 87–90.

4. Ibid., p. 152; Casaubon, *True Relation*, p. 225; Thadeus Hagecius, *Dialexis de nova stella* (Frankfurt, 1574), R&W, 438. Dee also owned Hajek's *Astrologica opuscula antiqua* (Prague, 1564), R&W, 431. Neither have been found.

5. Casaubon, *True Relation*, p. 212.

6. Ibid., pp. 215–17.

7. Ibid., p. 218; *MH*, pp. 181–5.

8. Casaubon, *True Relation*, pp. 221–3, 224.

9. Ibid., pp. 225, 245.

10. Ibid., pp. 229–30.

11. Ibid., p. 230.

12. Ibid., pp. 230–1; Leowitz, *De Coniunctionibus Magnis*, Dee's notes in Cambridge University Library copy R*5 21(E).

13. Casaubon, *True Relation*, pp. 231, 251.

14. Ibid., pp. 232–3, 213.

15. Ibid., p. 237, Evans, *Rudolf II and his World*, pp. 89, 223.

16. Casaubon, *True Relation*, pp. 240–9.

17. Ibid., pp. 255–6; ibid., p. 353 follows p. 256, perhaps marking this missing book, mentioned p. 354, not in BL MS Cotton Appendix XLVI; C.H. Josten, 'An Unknown Chapter in the Life of John Dee', *Journal of the Warburg and Courtauld Institutes*, 28 (1965), pp. 223–57, at p. 230.

18. Ibid., p. 230; Casaubon, *True Relation*, pp. 353–5, 390.

19. Ibid., pp. 360–1.

20. Ibid., pp. 372–3; Evans, *Rudolf II and his World*, pp. 84–5.

21. Casaubon, *True Relation*, pp. 371, 375.

22. Ibid., pp. 378–82, 389.

23. Ibid., p. 382.

24. Ibid., pp. 387–9.

25. Penny Baker, 'Lady Margaret Clifford's Alchemical Receipt Book and the John Dee Circle', *Ambix*, 52, no. 3, November 2005, pp. 271–84, at pp. 277–8.

26. BLO MS Ashmole 487, 3 February 1583; see TNA SP 12/180/23, 180/45, 180/53, 181/42, 181/60, 181/61, 181/71, 181/72, similar attacks on Burghley; BLO MS Tanner 78, fo. 100v, MS Tanner 300, fo. 47v.

27. Casaubon, *True Relation*, pp. 144, 390–3, 422; CR, pp. 523–4.

28. Casaubon, *True Relation*, pp. 387–97; Josten, 'Unknown Chapter', p. 230.

29. Casaubon, *True Relation*, p. 397, *Pymander Mercurii Trismegisti cum commento Fratris Hannibalis Rosseli. Liber primus de SS. Trinitate … Liber secundus de Spiritu S. & Angelis* (Cracow, 1585).

30. Casaubon, *True Relation*, pp. 398, 401; Josten, 'Unknown Chapter', p. 235.

31. Casaubon, *True Relation*, pp. 401–2.

32. Ibid., pp. 403–8; Josten, 'Unknown Chapter', p. 230.

33. Evans, *Rudolf II and his World*, pp. 102–4; BLO MS Ashmole 488, front-leaf note on Pucci, 12 July 1585.

34. Casaubon, *True Relation*, pp. 409–17; Evans, *Rudolf II and his World*, p. 103.

35. BLO MS Ashmole 1790, fos. 1–10, translated in Josten, 'Unknown Chapter', pp. 226–55.

36. Josten, 'Unknown Chapter', pp. 232–7; Casaubon, *True Relation*, p. 420.

37. Josten, 'Unknown Chapter', pp. 238–47.

38. BL MS Sloane 3188, MS Cotton Appendix XLVI.

39. BL MS Sloane 3191, fos. 1–13 (angelical calls), MS Sloane 3189 (Enoch's wisdom, in Kelley's handwriting), survive.

40. Josten, 'Unknown Chapter', pp. 247–54.
41. Ibid., pp. 254–5.
42. BL MS Sloane 3189 (Enoch's wisdom), BL MS Sloane 3191, fos. 1–31v (angelical calls and 'Book of the Knowledge of earthly aid and victory').
43. Casaubon, *True Relation*, pp. 418–19.
44. BL MS Cotton Appendix XLVI, printed by Casaubon as *True Relation*.
45. Evans, *Rudolf II and his World*, pp. 64–9, 140–3.
46. Ibid., p. 223, nuncio Sega's report of 29 May 1586.
47. *CSP Venetian*, viii, p. 169.
48. Casaubon, *True Relation*, pp. 420–1, misnumbered '417'.
49. Ibid., pp. 422–3.
50. Ibid., pp. 424–8, 430.

Chapter 17: The Magnificent Master Alchemist

1. *CSP Venetian*, viii, p. 169.
2. Ibid., pp. 429–34.
3. Bruce T. Moran, 'Wilhelm IV of Hesse-Kassel: Informal Communication and the Aristocratic Context of Discovery', in Thomas Nickles, ed., *Scientific Discovery: Case Studies* (London, 1980), pp. 67–96; Moran, 'German Prince-Practitioners: Aspects in the Development of Courtly Science, Technology and Procedures in the Renaissance', *Technology and Culture*, 22(2) (April, 1981), pp. 253–74. Dee owned Andreas Schoner's *Gnomonice* (Nuremberg, 1562), R&W, 261, produced under Wilhelm's patronage, and Peter Ramus's *Scholarum mathematicarum libri unus et triginta* (Basle, 1569), R&W, 331. Neither has been found.
4. Murhardsche Bibliothek, Kassel: 2 MS Chem 19, I, fos. 114r–115r, quoted in Moran, 'Privilege, communication, and chemiatry', pp. 125–6; Moran, 'Prince-Practitioning and the Direction of Medical Roles at the German Court: Maurice of Hesse-Kassel and his Physicians', in Vivian Nutton, ed., *Medicine at the Courts of Europe, 1500–1837* (London and New York, 1990), pp. 95–116.
5. Casaubon, *True Relation*, p. 434; BLO MS Tanner 309, fos. 53v–54r, Powle to Walsingham, 27 January 1587.
6. Ibid., fos. 53v–54r, 67v–68r; BLO MS Ashmole 1790, fos. 1–10, in Josten, 'Unknown Chapter', pp. 226–55; BL MS Cotton Vitellius C.7, fo. 314r.
7. *CSP Foreign, Elizabeth (1586–7)*, vol. 21 (2), pp. 123–4.
8. BLO MS Tanner 78, fo. 99r, Powle to Burghley, 10 September 1585; BL MS Cotton Vitellius C.7, fo. 318r.
9. Casaubon, *True Relation*, pp. 444–7.
10. BLO MS Ashmole 488, October–December 1586.
11. TNA SP 12/196/fo. 143; SP 15/30/30.
12. BLO MS Ashmole 488, January–March 1587.
13. Casaubon, *True Relation*, second pagination, pp. 1–3.
14. Ibid., second pagination, pp. 3–8.
15. Ibid., second pagination, pp. 8–12.
16. Ibid., second pagination, pp. 12–13, 24; cf. BL MS Cotton Appendix XLVI, fo. 100r.
17. Casaubon, *True Relation*, second pagination, pp. 16–21; BLO MS Ashmole 488, 1 May 1587.
18. Casaubon, *True Relation*, second pagination, pp. 22–3.
19. Ibid., second pagination, pp. 26–7.
20. Ibid., second pagination, pp. 28–31.
21. BLO MS Ashmole 488, 25 July 1587, 5 March 1588, 26 May and 4 July 1588.

22. Ibid., 5 July, 14 July, 13 October 1587.
23. Ibid., 9 July, 31 August 1587.
24. Ibid., 20 August, 1 September 1587, 27 August 1588.
25. Ibid., 12 December, mentioning Denis Zacaire's 'Little Book on the Philosopher's Stone', R&W, M50, Philip Rouillaschus's alchemical work published in Geneva, 1582 (R&W, 1519); neither found.
26. Ibid., 8, 12 November 1587, 28 February 1588.
27. BL MS Harley 6986, fo. 45r.
28. BLO MS Ashmole 488, 21 November, 18 December 1587.
29. Printed as George Ripley, *The Bosome-Book of Sir George Ripley* (London, 1683).
30. BLO MS Ashmole 488, 10 April 1588, 15 September 1588.
31. Ibid., 23 November 1587; BL MS Harley 6986, fo. 45r, Dee to Elizabeth from Trebon, 1/10 November 1588; CR, p. 512.
32. BLO MS Ashmole 488, 10 May, 24 August, 12–13 September, 7 December 1588.
33. Ibid., 18 December 1588.
34. Ibid., 4, 18 December 1588, *MP*, sig. Biv.
35. BLO MS Ashmole 488, 20 January 1589.
36. Ibid., 23 December 1588, and 4, 16 February 1589.
37. CR, pp. 535–6.
38. BLO MS Ashmole 488, 8/18 July 1589.
39. Ibid., 26 July/5 August; BL MS Lansdowne 61, fo. 159r–v, Dee to Walsingham, Bremen, 22 August 1589.
40. TNA SP 15/31/35.
41. BLO MS Ashmole 488, 6/16 September, 23–29 September, 4/14 October.
42. BLO MS Ashmole 488, 3/13 November, 17/27 November.

Chapter 18: The Counter-Revolution Against Magic

1. Hatfield House MS CP 29/35; BLO MS Ashmole 488, 23 November, 9, 10, 15 December; CR, pp. 512–13, 534, 540.
2. BL MS Lansdowne 64, fo. 101r; BLO MS Ashmole 487, 6 April 1590.
3. Collinson, *Grindal*, pp. 258–64.
4. Collinson, *Elizabethan Puritan Movement*, pp. 193–4, 201–2.
5. *Works of John Whitgift*, ed. J. Ayre, Parker Society, 3 vols. (Cambridge, 1851–3), iii, p. 274.
6. J. Guy, 'The 1590s: The Second Reign of Elizabeth I?', in Guy, ed., *The Reign of Elizabeth I: Court and Culture in the Last Decade* (Cambridge, 1995), pp. 1–19, at p. 11, and Guy, 'The Establishment and the Ecclesiastical Polity' in *idem*, pp. 126–49, esp. pp. 131–4.
7. Reginald Scot, *The Discoverie of Witchcraft* (London, 1584), sigs. A2v, B5r.
8. Ibid., sig. B1r.
9. Scot, *Discoverie*, pp. 156–60, 500–1, 177, 183, 199, 261, 422, 290.
10. Ibid., pp. 394–430, esp. pp. 395, 353, 467–9.
11. For example, BL MS Harley 2302, fos. 57r–105v.
12. J. Harvey, *A Discoursive Probleme concerning Prophesies* (1588), pp. 100, 102.
13. Collinson, *Elizabethan Puritan Movement*, pp. 201–5.
14. *Diary*, ed. Halliwell, pp. 33–4; T. Nashe, *Works*, ed. R.B. McKerrow, 5 vols. (Oxford, 1966), iii, pp. 82–3.
15. R. Harvey, *A Theological Discourse of the Lamb of God and his Enemies* (London, John Windet for William Ponsonby, 1590), sigs. N4v, Z4v.
16. Guy, 'The 1590s', pp. 1–2.

17. Collinson, *Elizabethan Puritan Movement*, pp. 196–7, 388, quoting T. Digges, *Humble Motives for association to retain religion established* (1601).

18. R. Bancroft, *A Sermon Preached at Paules Crosse the 9 of Februarie, being the first Sunday in the Parleament, Anno 1588* [i.e. 1589] *by Richard Bancroft ... Chaplaine to the right Honorable Sir Christopher Hatton* (London, Gregorie Seton, 1588), sigs. B2r, B3r–v, B4v; *Diary*, ed. Halliwell, p. 49, Dee's 'heavenly admonition' to Elizabeth, 3 May 1594.

19. Collinson, *Elizabethan Puritan Movement*, pp. 391–6, 403–4; D.J. McGinn, *John Penry and the Marprelate Controversy* (New Brunswick, NJ, 1966), Leland H. Carlson, *Martin Marprelate, Gentleman: Master Job Throkmorton Laid Open in his Colors* (San Marino, 1981); P. Collinson, 'Ecclesiastical Vitriol: Religious Satire in the 1590s and the Invention of Puritanism', in Guy, ed., *The Reign of Elizabeth*, pp. 150–70, at pp. 156–9.

20. T. Nashe, *An Almond for a parrat, or Cutbert Curry-knaves Almes. Fit for the knave Martin, and the rest of those impudent Beggers* (London, 1589?), STC 534, sigs. A2v–A3r, F3v, and see below, p. 241.

21. R. Warwick Bond, ed., *The Complete Works of John Lyly*, 3 vols. (Oxford, 1902), ii, pp. 420–4; Collinson, 'Ecclesiastical Vitriol', pp. 165–70; BL MS Sloane 313, Honorius of Thebes, 'Liber Huratus', R&W, DM 70.

22. BLO MS Ashmole 1487, fo. 217v; David Wootton, ed., *Christopher Marlowe, Doctor Faustus with the English Faust Book* (Indianapolis and Cambridge, 2005), pp. xi, xxiv–xxvii.

23. J. Dee, *A Letter Apologeticall*, sig. B3r.

24. Collinson, *The Religion of Protestants*, p. 9, n. 30, Whitgift's complaint 28 July 1586, and pp. 44–5, 60–1; CR, p. 509.

25. *CPR Elizabeth, viii, 1578–80*, p. 156.

26. BLO MS Ashmole 487, 14 March, 19 April 1590.

27. BLO MS Ashmole 1788, fos. 159–60; BL MS Lansdowne 103, fo. 211.

28. BLO MS Ashmole 487, 8, 20, 21 May 1590.

29. Ibid., 29, 30 May, 6 June 1590.

30. Ibid., 13, 15, 16 July 1590.

31. Ibid., 29 April, 22 July 1590; Casaubon, *True Relation*, p. 242.

32. BLO MS Ashmole 487, 22 July–29 August 1590; S. Harsnett, *A Declaration of Egregious Popish Impostures ... under the pretence of casting out devils* (London, James Roberts, 1603), sigs. Kk1v, Aa3r, Gg4v–Hh1r, C3r, Aa3v.

33. Dee, *A Letter Apologeticall*, sig. B3r.

34. Essex Record Office, D/B 3/1/8, Town Book of Maldon; BL MS Lansdowne 19, fos. 81r–82r, Lansdowne 16, fo. 17; BLO MS Ashmole 487, 8–9 June 1591; APC, x, pp. 148, 157; TNA SP 12/186/91, 92, 93.

35. BL MS Lansdowne 103, fos. 210r–211r.

36. BLO MS Ashmole 487, 31 July 1590.

37. TNA SP 81/6, fos. 56–7; SP 82/3, fo. 134, Dyer to Burghley, 31 October 1590.

38. TNA SP 81/6, fo. 76r–v.

39. *The Works of Francis Bacon*, ed. James Spedding, 8 vols. (London, 1861), vii, p. 162.

40. BLO MS Ashmole 487, 31 July, 27 November, 1, 2, 4, 16 December 1590; CR, pp. 512–13.

41. HEHL MS EL 6206B, fo. 45r–v; TNA C 66/973, 1304, C 54/1763; George Ripley, *The Compound of Alchemy ... the right and perfect meanes to make the Philosophers Stone, Aurum potabile* (London, 1591), sigs. A2r–*3v.

42. BLO MS Ashmole 487, 21–24 January 1591.

43. BL MS Cotton Titus B. II, fos. 227–8, Burghley to Kelley before 20 May 1591.

44. BL MS Lansdowne 66, fo. 164r; Lansdowne 103, fo. 208r.

45. BL MS Cotton Titus B. II, fos. 227–8.

46. BL MS Lansdowne 68, fos. 192r–195r.

47. BL MS Lansdowne 103, fo. 192r–v.

48. BLO MS Ashmole 487, 25, 27 May 1591.

Chapter 19: Conjuring up a Spanish Conquest

1. I James I, c. xii.

2. John Dee, *To the Kings most excellent Maiestie* (London, 1604), STC (2nd ed.) 6466.

3. James M. Sutton, *Materializing Space at an Early Modern Prodigy House: The Cecils at Theobalds, 1564–1607* (Aldershot and Burlington, VT, 2004), ch.3.

4. BLO MS Ashmole 487, 31 July, 3 August; BLO MS Ashmole 488, 31 July, 2 August 1591.

5. *Works of Francis Bacon*, ed. Spedding, vii, p. 162.

6. A. Walsham, ' "Frantic Hacket": Prophecy, Sorcery, Insanity, and the Elizabethan Puritan Movement', *The Historical Journal*, 41, 1 (1998), pp. 27–66; Camden, *Annals*, pp. 401–4.

7. R. Cosin, *Conspiracie for Pretended Reformation; viz. Presbyteriall Discipline. ... by William Hacket yeoman, Edmund Coppinger, and Henry Arthington Gent.* (London, 1592), sigs. b2r–v, C2v.

8. Ibid., sigs. C2v, C3v, E2v. See below, p. 242.

9. Cosin, *Conspiracie for Pretended reformation*, sigs. F3v, F4r, E2v–E3v.

10. Ibid., sigs. E4v–F1r.

11. Ibid., sigs. G4v–H1r.

12. Ibid., sig. H4r–v, sig. K3r.

13. Ibid., sigs. M4v, O1r, M4v, O3v, N3r–v, K4v, and CR, pp. 521–2.

14. *A declaration of great troubles pretended against the realme by a number of seminarie priests and Jesuits* (London, Christopher Barker, 18 October 1591), STC 7758.3, in Hughes and Larkin, *Tudor Royal Proclamations*, iii, pp. 86–95.

15. Ibid., p. 87.

16. Ibid., pp. 88–9.

17. Ibid., pp. 91–2.

18. Ibid., pp. 92–5, no. 739; M.M.C. Calthrop, *Recusant Roll No. 1, 1592–3. Exchequer Lord Treasurer's Remembrancer Pipe Office Series* (Catholic Record Society, London, 1916), p. xx.

19. Robert Southwell(?) to Richard Verstegan, London (?), early December 1591, in Anthony G. Petti, ed., *The Letters and Despatches of Richard Verstegan (c.1550–1640)* (Catholic Record Society, London, 1959), pp. 15, 8–9, 39.

20. *APC*, xxii, 1591–2, pp. 15, 39–42, 92; cf. Richard Verstegan to Robert Parsons from Antwerp, 5 March 1592, in Petti, ed., *Letters of Richard Verstegan*, pp. 39–40; TNA SP 12/240/109; *The life and Death of Edmund Genninge* (1594).

21. Richard Verstegan to Robert Parsons from Antwerp, 5 March 1592, in Petti, ed., *Letters of Richard Verstegan*, pp. 39–40; Richard Verstegan to Roger Baynes, Antwerp, 27 June 1592, in ibid., p. 50.

22. Ibid., pp. 52–8.

23. Woking, Surrey History Centre, Loseley MS 1856, p. 3, quoted in Michael Questier, 'Loyal to a Fault: Viscount Montague Explains Himself', *Historical Research*, 77, no. 196 (May 2004), pp. 225–53, at p. 252.

24. TNA SP 12/4/fo. 135r; Alford, *Early Elizabethan Polity*, pp. 54–5; TNA SP 70/39, fo. 106v, cited in Alford, *Early Elizabethan Polity*, pp. 94–5.

25. Richard Rowlands alias Verstegan, *An Advertisement written to a secretarie of my L. Treasurers of Ingland* (August 1592), sig. A5v, C1r–v, D8r; Parsons, *A Briefe Apologie*, sigs. D3v–D6r;

[Robert Parsons] *A Relation of the King of Spaines receiving in Valliodolid* (STC, 19836a), sigs. A3v, A6r, B5r.

26. Hughes and Larkin, *Tudor Proclamations*, iii, p. 89.

27. Parsons, *Apologie*, sig. F3v.

28. TNA SP 12/238/160, 21 May 1591; SP 12/238/179.

29. TNA SP 12/238/162, 163. Parsons, *Apologie*, sigs. A5r–C8r.

30. TNA SP 12/238/178, 179, 25 May 1591, and 180, 26 May 1591.

31. TNA SP 12/238/165, 166, 167, 168; SP 12/239/46; SP 12/238/180; SP 12/239/2; SP 12/239/26; SP 12/240/86.

32. BL MS Harley 703, fo. 61v, Privy Council to Lords Lieutenant of Sussex, 31 August 1590.

33. *APC*, xxii, pp. 6–11; Hughes and Larkin, *Tudor Royal Proclamations*, iii, pp. 83–6, 16 September 1591.

34. Paul C. Allen, *Philip III and the Pax Hispanica, 1598–1621: The Failure of Grand Strategy* (New Haven and London, 2000), pp. viii–ix.

35. P. Renold, ed., *Letters of William Allen and Richard Barrett 1572–1598* (Catholic Record Society, London, 1967), pp. 209–16.

36. Allen to Parsons, 26 October 1591, quoted in Parsons, *Apologie*, sigs. F2v–F3v, also in P. Ryan, ed., 'Correspondence of Cardinal Allen', *Catholic Record Society, Miscellanea VII* (Catholic Record Society, London, 1911), pp. 42–3; and *Letters of Allen*, ed. Renold, p. 211; Parsons, *Apologie*, sigs. A5r–B6v.

37. Paul E.J. Hammer, *The Polarisation of Elizabethan Politics: The Political Career of Robert Devereux, 2nd Earl of Essex, 1585–1597* (Cambridge, 1999), pp. 100–5.

38. Hughes and Larkin, *Tudor Royal Proclamations*, iii, p. 86; STC 8207, 8208; TNA SP 12/240/53, 31 October 1591.

39. *Calendar of State Papers Domestic, Elizabeth, 1591–4*, pp. 136–7; Verstegan, *Advertisement*, sigs. A7v, D6v; Robert Parsons, *Elizabethae Reginae Angliae Edictum Promulgatum Londini 29 Novemb. Anni M.D.XCI Andreae Philopatri ad Idem Edictum Responsio* (Antwerp, 1592), p. 20; *Letters of Allen*, ed. Renold, p. 230, citing TNA SP 85/1/fo. 132.

40. Collinson, *Elizabethan Puritan Movement*, pp. 428–31.

41. Parsons, *Apologie*, sig. F3r–v.

42. CR, pp. 507, 519.

43. Ibid., p. 520.

44. Ibid., p. 521.

45. See above, p. 151.

46. BL MS Lansdowne 36, fo. 66r; HMC, *Salisbury*, xiv, pp. 87–8; *CPR Elizabeth 1580–2*, p. 170.

47. BL MS Lansdowne 39, fo. 183r–v; Lansdowne 40, fo. 53r–v; Lansdowne 54, fo. 72r.

48. CR, p. 516; HMC, *Salisbury*, iv, p. 529.

49. BL MS Lansdowne 77, fo. 138r.

50. TNA SP 12/248/fo. 256r–257r.

51. TNA SP 12/256/109.

52. See, for example, TNA SP 12/241/78.

53. *Vestry Minute Books of the Parish of St Bartholomew Exchange*, ed. Freshfield, pp. 25, 29.

54. R.B. Wernham, *List and Analysis of State Papers: Foreign Series Elizabeth I*, 7 vols (London, 1964–2004), iii, p. 407, no. 723 (SP 84/44/fo. 128); TNA SP 12/241/100, 15 March 1592.

55. *Lambeth Churchwardens' Accounts*, ed. Charles Drew, 2 vols. (London, 1940–1) i, p. 182.

56. *Exemplar litterarum missarum e Germania ad D. Gulielmum Cicilium consiliarum regum* (1592); Richard Rowlands alias Verstegan, *Advertisement* (1592).

57. BLO MS Ashmole 487, 6, 9, 10, 16 March 1592; CR, pp. 513–14; W. Gwyn Thomas, 'An Episode in the Later Life of John Dee', *Welsh Historical Review*, 5 (1971), pp. 250–6.

58. BL MS Cotton Cleopatra B. II, fo. 216v.
59. Ibid., pp. 252–4; BLO MS Ashmole 487, 31 December 1592, 22 February 1593; Helen Coburn Walshe, 'Meredith, Richard (d. 1597)', *ODNB*, Oxford University Press, September 2004; online edn, January 2008 [http://www.oxforddnb.com/view/article/18578].
60. Thomas, 'The Later Life of John Dee', pp. 255–6; TNA E 331/St Davids/8.
61. BLO MS Ashmole 487, 5 April 1592; 14 April, 16 April, 15 May.
62. CR, p. 515.
63. TNA SP 12/242/25, Robert Cecil to Heneage, 25 May 1592; see TNA SP 12/247/78, 79, 91.
64. TNA HCA 13/30, 10 June 1592; SP 12/243/24, 30 September 1592. *APC*, xxii, pp. 543–4; TNA SP 12/240/97, SP 12/242/26.
65. Anthony G. Petti, *Roman Catholicism in Elizabethan and Jacobean Staffordshire* (Staffordshire Record Society, 1979), pp. 54–5.
66. *APC*, xxiii, pp. 40–2, 21 July 1592, and cf. BL MS Harley 703, fo. 67v.
67. BL MS Royal 18.D.III, fos. 82v–83r; TNA SP 12/242/116, 121, and *APC*, xxiii, pp. 163–4.
68. BLO MS Ashmole 487, 6, 9, 10, 22 August; CR, p. 515.
69. Wernham, *List and Analysis*, III, pp. 400–1; Birch, *Memoirs of Queen Elizabeth*, i, pp. 66, 76, 69–70, 80.
70. *APC*, xxiii, pp. 106–8, 110–13.
71. BL MS Harley 703, fo. 68r, Council to Sussex, and TNA SP 12/242/105, to Lord President of North, SP 12/243/76, Warwickshire response in *Minutes and Accounts of the Corporation of Stratford-upon-Avon*, ed. Edgar Fripp (Dugdale Society, 10, 1990), pp. 159–62; TNA SP 12/242/112.
72. Birch, *Memoirs of Queen Elizabeth*, i, p. 79.
73. BL MS Harley 703, fo. 68v.
74. *APC*, xxiii, pp. 163–4, 188–9, 192–3, 202–3, 227; Birch, *Memoirs*, i, p. 87; TNA SP 12/243/51.
75. TNA SP 12/243/37, dated 14 October 1592, and *APC*, xxiii, pp. 253–8, 20 October 1592; BL MS Harley 703, fo. 69r–v.
76. CR, pp. 538–41.
77. BLO MS Ashmole 487, 18 April 1583, scrying 4, 31 July 1583, 31 July, 9 October 1595.
78. Verstegan, *Advertisement*, sig. B1v.
79. M.C. Bradbrook, *The School of Night: A Study in the Literary Relationships of Sir Walter Raleigh* (Cambridge, 1936).
80. Verstegan to Parsons, Antwerp, 5 March 1592, in Petti, ed., *The Letters and Despatches of Richard Verstegan*, p. 40.
81. Ernest A. Strathmann, 'John Dee as Ralegh's "Conjuror"', *The Huntington Library Quarterly*, 10, no. 4 (1947), pp. 365–72, could not prove the connection.
82. BL MS Harley 703, fo. 69v, Council to the Lords Lieutenant of Sussex, and cf. fos. 62r, 63r for the earlier 1591 dismissal.
83. Birch, *Memoirs*, i, p. 92, Nicholas Faunt to Anthony Bacon, London, 22 November 1592.
84. *APC*, xxiii, p. 289.
85. BLO MS Ashmole 487, 13 October 1592, meaning Christian Francken, *Praecipuarum enumeratior causarum, cur Christiani cum in multis doctrinis mobiles sint et varii, in Trinitatis tamen retinuendo dogmate sint constantissimi* [Cracow, Aleksy Rodecki, 1584], R&W, D9, and Joannes Sommerus, *Refutatio scripti Petri Carolii editi Wittebergae* (Aleksy Rodecki, Cracow, 1582), R&W, D20, now in Lambeth Palace Library, shelf mark F110.
86. BLO MS Ashmole 488, 9 July 1587.
87. Parsons, *Responsio*, p. 36, sect. 43.

88. TNA SP 12/238/163. Strathmann, 'John Dee as Ralegh's "Conjuror"', pp. 356–8. Victor Houliston, 'The Lord Treasurer and the Jesuit: Robert Persons's Satirical *Responsio* to the 1591 Proclamation', *Sixteenth-Century Journal*, xxxii, 2 (2001), pp. 383–401.

89. CR, pp. 525–6.

90. CR, pp. 498–9; HMC, *Salisbury*, xiii, p. 467, no. 1250.

91. CR, p. 499.

92. HMC, *Salisbury*, iv, pp. 239, 324, 583–4; ibid., v, pp. 339, 369.

93. BL MS Lansdowne 72, fo. 197r–198v.

94. R.E. Ham, 'The Autobiography of Sir James Croft', *Bulletin of the Institute of Historical Research*, 50 (1977), pp. 48–57.

95. BL MS Lansdowne 46, fos. 69r–71v.

96. BL MS Lansdowne 106, fo. 132r–v; L. Howard, *A collection of Letters* (London, 1753), pp. 184–8.

97. CR, pp. 500–6, 519–20.

98. Ibid., pp. 505, 521–2, 509–19, 548.

99. Ibid., pp. 524–41.

100. Ibid., pp. 514–15.

101. See http://www.stcrosshospital.co.uk/

102. CR, pp. 544–9.

103. Ibid., p. 550; BLO MS Ashmole 487, 1 December 1592.

104. CR, p. 551; J. Atherton, *Ambition and Failure in Stuart England: The career of John, First Viscount Scudamore* (Manchester, 1999), p. 28.

Chapter 20: Checkmate: Exiling the Conjuror to Manchester

1. Murdin, *Collection of state papers*, ii, p. 659, Earl of Pembroke to Elizabeth, 11 February 1593; Hartley, *Proceedings*, iii, pp. 11–13, 15–19, esp. pp. 26–7, 62–3; TNA SP 12/244/91; 35 Eliz., c. 2, 'An Act against Popish Recusants'; William R. Trimble, *The Catholic Laity in Elizabethan England 1558–1603* (Cambridge, MA, 1964).

2. R. Bancroft, *A Survey of the Pretended Holy Discipline* (London, 1593), sigs. A2r, B1r.

3. R. Bancroft, *Daungerous positions and proceedings* (London, 1593), sigs. V1r–V3r.

4. Ibid., sigs. V3v–V4r.

5. Ibid., sigs. Y4v–Aa2r, Aa4v–Bb2r.

6. 35 Eliz., c. 1; HEHL, MSS EL 2101–18, 2121–3.

7. BLO MS Ashmole 487, January–March 1593, September 1600.

8. Ibid., 17 March 1593, 23 March 1594.

9. Ibid., *idem* and 20 March 1594; Beyer, 'Lady Margaret Clifford's Alchemical Receipt Book', pp. 276–7.

10. BLO MS Ashmole 487, 25 October 1593, 3 and 4 December 1593; Beyer, 'Lady Margaret Clifford's Alchemical Receipt Book', pp. 277, 283–4.

11. BLO MS Ashmole 487, 10, 11 April 1592; ibid., 12 May 1592.

12. TNA E 178/2939.

13. TNA SP 78/32, fo. 380, Sir Robert Sidney to Burghley from Dover, 23 December 1593, in R.B. Wernham, *List and Analysis, vol. V, July 1593–December 1594* (London, 1989), pp. 377–8.

14. BLO MS Ashmole 487, 24, 25, 26 December 1593.

15. Isaac H. Jeayes, *Letters of Philip Gawdy* (London, 1906), pp. 83–4; *APC*, x, p. 209.

16. BLO MS Ashmole 487, 9, 26 January 1594.

17. Ibid., 10 March 1594.

18. Hatfield House MSS CP 22/74, 26/96, 22/75.

19. HMC, *Salisbury*, v, p. 79.

20. BL MS Lansdowne 76, fo. 162r, Edward Delve to Burghley, 28 May 1594; R&W, DM 97, BLO MS Ashmole 204, part item 6, fo. 115r; *Calendar of State Papers Domestic, Elizabeth, 1591–4*, p. 524, 1 July 1594, p. 525, 4 July 1594, p. 537, 4 August 1594.

21. BLO MS Ashmole 487, December 1593, January 1594, March 1594.

22. Nashe, *Works*, ii, p. 172.

23. CR, pp. 514, 541–2; BLO MS Ashmole 487, 22 June 1594.

24. Ibid., 3 May 1594.

25. BL MS Cotton Titus C. VII, fo. 57; Nichols, *Progresses of Elizabeth* (1821), iv (i), p. 34.

26. BLO MS Ashmole 487, 21, 25, 29 May, 3, 6 June 1594.

27. Ibid., June–July 1595.

28. Ibid., December 1595.

29. HMC, *Salisbury*, v, pp. 7–8; Brett Usher, 'Day, William (1529–1596)', *ODNB*, Oxford University Press, September 2004; online edn, January 2008 [http://www.oxforddnb.com/view/article/7373].

30. HMC, *Salisbury*, v, p. 84; Joyce M. Horn, *Fasti Ecclesiae Anglicanae 1541–1857* (London, 1969), i, p. 1; Usher, 'Day, William', *ODNB*.

31. BLO MS Ashmole 487, 3 January 1595.

32. *A Letter … Apologetical*, sigs. A2r–B2v.

33. Ibid., sigs. B3r–C2r.

34. Manchester Cathedral Archives, Mancath/2/A3/1/1; TNA C66/1428/166; BLO MS Ashmole 487, 18 February, 27 May, 31 July 1595.

35. T.S. Willan, *Elizabethan Manchester* (Chetham Society 3rd ser., 27, Manchester, 1980), p. 39; Willan, 'The Trade Between England and Russia in the Second Half of the Sixteenth Century', *English Historical Review*, 63, no. 248 (July 1948), pp. 307–21, at p. 319; *The Court Leet Records of the Manor of Manchester*, ed. J.P. Earwaker, 12 vols. (Manchester, 1884–90), vols. i and ii; *Continuation of the Court Leet Records of the Manor of Manchester AD 1586–1602*, ed. J. Harland (Chetham Society, o.s., 65, Manchester, 1865).

36. BLO MS Ashmole 1788, fo. 145v; Leslie W. Hepple, 'John Dee, Harleian MS 473, and the Early Recording of Roman Inscriptions in Britain', *Britannia* 33 (2002), pp. 177–81.

37. Surrey Record Office, Kingston MS 4/2; R&W, D7 (f).

38. Manchester Cathedral Archives, MS Mancath/2/1/b.

39. BL MS Harley 249, fos. 95r–105r.

40. BL MS Lansdowne 23, fo. 106; *CPR Eliz. I, vii, 1575–8*, pp. 91–2; Manchester Cathedral Archives, Mancath/2/A/2/1/2; C. Haigh, 'Puritan Evangelism in the Reign of Elizabeth I', *The English Historical Review*, 92, no. 362 (January 1977), pp. 30–58 at pp. 41–2; TNA C54/1002.

41. *CPR Eliz. I, vii, 1575–8*, pp. 399–401; TNA C82/1580.

42. TNA SP 12/143/32; Haigh, 'Puritan Evangelism', p. 43.

43. TNA E 134/32Eliz/Trin4; TNA E 41/133; TNA E 133/6/904, 1590 Hugh Hurleston v. Thomas Goodyer.

44. BLO MS Ashmole 487, 12 July 1595; F.R. Raines, *The Fellows of the Collegiate Church of Manchester* (Chetham Society, n.s., 21, Manchester, 1891), p. 66.

45. BLO MS Ashmole 487, 11, 21 June 1595, 13, 22 September 1595, 14 November 1597.

46. TNA C54/1544.

47. BLO MS Ashmole 487, July–December 1596.

48. Arthur Redford and Ina Stafford Russell, *The History of Local Government in Manchester*, 3 vols. (London, 1939–40), i, pp. 8–9 and frontispiece.

49. BLO MS Ashmole 487, 20 April, 18 June 1596; TNA DL 44/585; Manchester Cathedral Archives, Mancath/2/A1/10, printed in H.T. Crofton, *A History of Newton Chapelry in the Ancient Parish of Manchester, Volume II, part 1* (Chetham Society, n.s., 53, Manchester, 1904), pp. 60, 64, 68, 71–4.

50. Heather Lawrence and Richard Hoyle, 'New Maps and Surveys by Christopher Saxton', *The Yorkshire Archaeological Journal*, 51 (1981), pp. 51–6.

51. Dee, 'Mathematical Praeface', sig. a2v; Lawrence and Hoyle, 'Surveys by Christopher Saxton', pp. 51–6; Stephen Bowd, 'John Dee and Christopher Saxton's Survey of Manchester (1596)', *Northern History*, 62 (2005), pp. 275–92; BLO MS Ashmole 487, April, July, September 1597; Manchester Cathedral Archives, Mancath/2/A2/2; TNA DL 4/42/9; TNA DL 4/41/20; TNA DL 1/180/C12, C12a, C12b.

52. BLO MS Ashmole 487, August 1597.

53. Cheshire and Chester Archives, Consistory Cause Papers, EDC 5/1596, nos. 32 and 31, 35–9, 41–2; BLO MS Ashmole 487, 9 February 1598; Stephen Bowd, 'In the Labyrinth: John Dee and Reformation Manchester', *Manchester Region History Review*, 19 (2008), pp. 17–43.

54. BLO MS Ashmole 487, 5 September 1596, June–July 1597.

55. BLO MS Ashmole 487, 3 July 1600; Manchester Cathedral Archives MS Mancath/2/1/d/2.

56. BL MS Lansdowne 158, fo. 16r.

57. Manchester Cathedral Archives, MS Mancath/2/1/d; BLO MS Ashmole 487, 4 May, 14–16 June 1597.

58. BL MS Harley 249, fos. 95r–105r.

59. TNA DL 44/585.

60. University of Manchester John Rylands Library Clowes Deeds CLD/551.

61. BLO MS Ashmole 487, June–July 1600.

62. *Extracts from the Court Rolls of the Manor of Wimbledon* (London, 1866), p. 171.

63. Haigh, 'Puritan Evangelism', p. 44; BLO MS Ashmole 487, 22 January 1598.

64. Barry Coward, *The Stanleys, Lords Stanley and Earls of Derby 1385–1672* (Chetham Society, 3rd ser., 30, Manchester, 1983), p. 206.

65. Christopher Haigh, *Reformation and Resistance in Tudor Lancashire* (Cambridge, 1975), pp. 299–302.

66. Lancashire Record Office, MS DDKE/acc.7840 HMC/f.103d; printed in HMC, *Kenyon MSS.*

67. Josten, 'Unknown Chapter', p. 240; *MH*, Theorem XX; Kieckhefer, *Forbidden Rites*, pp. 148, 153.

68. *MP*, sigs. a.iir–a.iiir.

69. Haigh, 'Puritan Evangelism', p. 48.

70. Ibid., p. 35; BLO MS Ashmole 487, 18 July 1600.

71. Haigh, 'Puritan Evangelism', pp. 37, 40.

72. BLO MS Ashmole 487, 18 July 1600.

73. Haigh, 'Puritan Evangelism', p. 37.

74. Ibid., p. 50.

75. BLO MS Ashmole 487, July and September 1600; Oliver Carter, *An answere ... unto certain popish questions and demaundes* (London, 1579), sigs. C4r, D5r; Bayer, 'Lady Margaret Clifford's Alchemical Receipt Book', pp. 271–84.

76. B. Coward, 'A Crisis of the Aristocracy in the 16th and early 17th Centuries? The Case of the Stanleys, Earls of Derby, 1504–1642', *Northern History*, xviii (1982), pp. 54–77, at p. 69.

77. BLO MS Ashmole 487, 1 August 1596.

78. TNA E 135/134.

79. Ibid., fos. 19v–20r.

80. BLO MS Ashmole 487, November 1597.

81. James Sharpe, 'Introduction' in Robert Poole, ed., *The Lancashire Witches: Histories and Stories* (Manchester, 2002), p. 10; Haigh, *Reformation and Resistance*, pp. 321–2.

Chapter 21: Demonising the Exorcists

1. John Darrell, *A True Narration of the Strange and Grevous Vexation by the Devil of 7 persons in Lancashire* (1600), p. 2; George More, *A true Discourse concerning the certain possession and dispossession of 7 persons in one familie in Lancashire* ([Middelburg], 1600), p. 15.

2. [John Darrell?], *The Triall of Maist[er] Dorrell, or a collection of defences against allegations* ([Middelburg, R. Schilder], 1599), sig. E 6v.

3. John Darrell, *An Apologie, or defence of the possession of William Sommers ... Cleared from the evill name of counterfeiting* (1599), sigs. D2r–D3v, F2r–F3r.

4. *Triall of Maist[er] Dorrell*, p. 80.

5. Darrell, *A True Narration*, pp. 6–7.

6. BLO MS Ashmole 487, 19 March 1597.

7. Girolamo Menghi, *Flagellum Daemonum. Exorcismos Terribiles, Potentissimus, et Efficaces*, with his *Fustus Daemonum* (Bologna, 1589); Harsnett, *Declaration*, p. 8; BLO MS Ashmole 487, April, August 1597.

8. John Darrell, *A Detection of that Sinful Shamful Lying and Ridiculous Discours, of Samuel Harshnet* (London, 1600), p. 27.

9. *Triall of Maist[er] Dorrell*, p. 44.

10. BLO MS Ashmole 487, February, March, 1598.

11. Darrell, *A breife narration of the possession, dispossession, and repossession of William Sommers* (Amsterdam, 1599), sig. A3r.

12. Darrell, *An Apologie, or defence of the possession of William Sommers ... Cleared from the evill name of counterfeiting*, fo. 18r.

13. Darrell, *A Detection of Samuel Harshnet* (London, 1600), pp. 26–9.

14. TNA SP 12/270/48, John Chamberlain, 1 February 1599.

15. Samuel Harsnett, *A Discovery of the fraudulent practises of John Darrell* (London, 1599), pp. 2, 22–3; George More, *A True Discourse concerning the certaine possession and dispossession of 7 persons in one familie in Lancashire* (1600), Darrell, *A Detection of Samuel Harshnet*, pp. 26–9, 169.

16. Darrell, *A True Narration of the Strange and Grevous Vexation by the Devil of 7 persons in Lancashire*.

17. BLO MS Ashmole 487, July, September, November–December 1600.

18. John Deacon and John Walker, *Dialogical Discourses of Spirits and Devils* (London, 1601), sig. A8v; Deacon and Walker *A Summarie Answeare* (London, 1601), 'The Epistle', sig. C4r; M. MacDonald, *Witchcraft and Hysteria in Elizabethan London* (London, 1991), pp. vii–lxiv.

19. Stuart Babbage, *Puritanism and Richard Bancroft* (London, 1962), p. 381.

20. *APC*, xxxi, pp. 44–5.

21. Hatfield House MS CP 91/125; *Calendar of State Papers Domestic, 1603–11*, pp. 41–2.

22. BLO MS Ashmole 487, February 1597.

23. Ibid., December 1600; G.J. Piccope, ed., *Lancashire and Cheshire Wills. The Third Portion* (Chetham Society, o.s. 54, Manchester, 1861), pp. 164–6.

24. TNA C 82/1676; BLO MS Ashmole 221, fo. 51v; M. MacDonald, *Mystical Bedlam: Madness, Anxiety and Healing in Seventeenth-Century England* (Cambridge, 1981), pp. 17–19; BLO MS Ashmole 487, June, October, December 1597, and January, February 1598.

25. TNA SP 12/285/48, fo. 119v, John Chamberlain to Dudley Carleton, 4 November 1602; M. MacDonald, *Witchcraft and Hysteria in Elizabethan London* (London, 1991), pp. vii–lxiv.

26. Robert Parker Sorlien, ed., *The Diary of John Manningham of the Middle Temple, 1602–1603* (Hanover, NH, 1976), p. 198.

27. BLO MS Ashmole 1807, fo. 2r–v; R&W, D20, Roberts and Watson, *Catalogue*, p. 157.

28. Dee, *A Letter, Nine Yeeres since, written and first published* (1604), title page; Dee, *To the Honourable House of Commons* (1604).

29. HEHL MSS EL 1432, 1433.

30. *Ecclesiae Londino-Bataviae Archivum Tomus Primus*, ed. Hessels, p. 788; BL MS Sloane 3846, fo. 113v.

31. *Journal of the House of Lords: volume 2: 1578–1614* (London, 1802), pp. 294–295; *Journal of the House of Commons: volume 1: 1547–1629* (London, 1802), pp. 149, 206–7, 225–6, 232; I Jac. cap. xii, *At the Parliament begun and holden at Westminster the xix of March* (London, 1604); John Dee, *To the King's Most Excellent Majesty*, (London, 1604).

32. Dee, *To the King's Most Excellent Majesty*.

33. Dee, *To the Honorable Assembly of the Commons in the present Parliament* (1604); *Commons Journal*, i, pp. 231–2, 235–6; *Lords Journal*, ii, pp. 316–17.

34. Dee, *A Letter, Nine yeeres since, first published* (London, 1604).

35. BLO MS Ashmole 221, fo. 51v; MacDonald, *Mystical Bedlam*, pp. 17–19.

36. Cheshire and Chester Record Office, Visitation Correction Book, EDV 1/13, fo. 64r.

37. BLO MS Ashmole 1788, fo. 144r.

38. *The Registers of the Cathedral Church of Manchester: Christenings, Burials and Weddings, 1573–1616* (Cambridge, 1908), pp. 336, 339, 128, 155; MacDonald, *Mystical Bedlam*, pp. 18, 29.

39. W.E.A. Axon, ed., 'Documents Relating to the Plague in Manchester in 1605', *Chetham Miscellanies, New Series Vol. III* (Chetham Society, n.s. 73, Manchester, 1915), pp. 4–5; T.S. Willan, 'Plague in Perspective: The Case of Manchester in 1605', *Transactions of the Historic Society of Lancashire and Cheshire, vol. 132* (Liverpool, 1983), pp. 29–40.

40. J. Tait, ed., *Lancashire Quarter Sessions Records. Vol. I: Quarter Sessions Rolls 1590–1606* (Chetham Society, n.s. 77, Manchester 1917), p. 171; *The Court Leet Records of the Manor of Manchester*, ed. Earwaker, ii, p. 210.

41. Mercers' Company Records, Acts of Court 1595 to 1629 (C.M. IV, fo. 69r).

42. Casaubon, *True Relation*, pp. *32–3.

43. Ibid., pp. *34–5, *41–3.

44. Ibid., pp. *36–7, 39, 42.

45. Ibid., pp. *34–5; BLO MS Ashmole 1486, Pt. IV, pp. 2–3; Roberts and Watson, *Catalogue*, p. 60.

46. Casaubon, *True Relation*, pp. *41–3; *Mortlake Parish Vestry Minute Book, 1578–1652*, ed. J.E. Anderson (Richmond, 1914), pp. 113–14.

47. Bruce T. Moran, *The Alchemical World of the German Court* (Stuttgart, 1991), pp. 51–62; Casaubon, *True Relation*, pp. *37–8.

48. Ibid., p. *43.

49. Ibid., p. *44.

50. John W. Shirley, *Thomas Harriot* (Oxford, 1983), p. 395.

51. Mercers' Company, London, Acts of Court 1595 to 1629 (C.M. IV, fo. 95r.).

52. BL MS Sloane 8 is a Latin version of 'Soyga'; Roberts and Watson, *Catalogue*, pp. 61–2, 67.

Index